T0371170

THE
DAO DE JING

THE
DAO
DE JING

LAOZI'S BOOK
OF LIFE

A NEW TRANSLATION FROM
THE ANCIENT CHINESE

with Margin Notes and Commentary by

J. H. HUANG

MARINER
CLASSICS

NEW YORK   BOSTON

THE DAO DE JING: LAOZI'S BOOK OF LIFE. Copyright © 2024 by J. H. Huang. All rights reserved. Printed in India. No part of this book may be used or reproduced in any manner whatsoever without written permission except in the case of brief quotations embodied in critical articles and reviews. For information, address HarperCollins Publishers, 195 Broadway, New York, NY 10007.

HarperCollins books may be purchased for educational, business, or sales promotional use. For information, please email the Special Markets Department at SPsales@harpercollins.com.

FIRST MARINER CLASSICS EDITION PUBLISHED 2024

Designed by Alison Bloomer

Library of Congress Cataloging-in-Publication Data has been applied for.

ISBN 978-0-06-313585-7

10 9 8 7 6 5 4 3 2 1

THIS BOOK IS DEDICATED TO MY WIFE

Carolyn Phillips

for all her love and support

Tell me, my young friend,
what in fact are we living for?

你告訴我, 老弟, 我們活著到底為了什麼?

—A QUESTION POSED TO THE AUTHOR BY
MASTER CHENG MAN-JAN 鄭曼髯大師, SPRING 1975

CONTENTS

INTRODUCTION
UNDERSTANDING THE *DAO DE JING*

Its ideas are among the most fascinating in the history of thought. . . .

After every idea has had its day with us and we have fought for it not wisely or too well, we in our turn shall tire of the battle. . . . Perhaps we shall burn every book but one behind us, and find a summary of wisdom in the *Tao-Te-Ching*.

—WILL DURANT[1]

The *Dao De Jing* is one of the most significant and popular books in the history of human thought. Written by Laozi[2]—whose work is most commonly known in the West as the *Tao Te Ching*—this ancient classic is much like the earliest parts of the Bible in that it was handed down from the Axial Age (500–300 BCE).[3] Versions unearthed in the latter part of the last century prove that the Guodian version of the *Dao De Jing* (usually referred to as the Guodian Chu bamboo slips by Western scholars)[4] was set down in written form at least 2,320 years ago.[5] Its origins were likely much more ancient than that, though, and were probably contemporaneous with Plato's most well-known work, *The Republic*, which is believed to date from 375 or 380 BCE.

Be that as it may, Laozi's thought was indisputably Chinese in origin. At first glance, this book appears to be little more than a guide for a king or lords on how to both cultivate themselves and rule their lands. But the true depth and importance of these rhythmic,[6] world-wise lines are in fact much greater, for the *Dao De Jing* was meant to guide us toward living healthy, satisfying lives that are in complete harmony with the world.

The renowned thinker Karl Jaspers (1883–1969) once described the *Dao De Jing* as "one of the most irreplaceable works of philosophy." He added, "its inner cohesion is so convincing that—despite possible interpolation and distortions [i.e., due to error-filled transcriptions and faulty translations]— one cannot doubt that it was created by a thinker of the highest rank. The man [Laozi] seems to stand before us and speak to us." As for the philosophy behind the *Dao De Jing*, Jaspers remarked, "In western terms, it deals with metaphysics, cosmogony, ethics, and politics."[7]

ABOUT THE AUTHOR[8]

Jaspers was absolutely right: The person who bestowed upon us the *Dao De Jing*—Laozi—indeed held a very high rank. A few hundred years after Laozi's lifetime, the *Shiji* (*Records of the Grand Historian*) described how Laozi was not only in charge of the Zhou court's book collections, but in his position, he would have also mastered them, making him the leading scholar of his time. This is further demonstrated by the fact that Confucius visited him to seek his advice on 禮 *lǐ* (the rites).[9] The same book also recorded that Laozi came from a place called Huxian,[10] which was initially a part of the small feudal state called Chen, located to the south of the Yellow River, but was assimilated by the much larger state of Chu in 478 BCE.[11] So, like Sunzi (the author of *Sunzi bingfa*, or *The Art of War*), Laozi was a noble descendant of the Lord of Chen's clan.

The Tang dynasty scholar Sima Zhen added a note to the *Shiji* explaining that during the Zhou dynasty (1046–256 BCE), the first Lord of Chen, E Fu, was the 陶正 *táozhèng*, an official in charge of pottery making, who served the royal court.[12] This position required such extensive scientific and technological knowledge that it—along with all incumbent cultivation and education—was handed down via dynastic succession as a way of ensuring the aristocratic clan's prosperity. That profound scientific knowledge is on full display in the *Dao De Jing.*

ABOUT THE BOOK

The names of about 330 received versions[13] of the *Dao De Jing* still exist and span the 2,000 years between the Han dynasty and the early Republic. Many of these Chinese works refer to the book by its author's name, or *Laozi*, rather than as the *Dao De Jing*, though some of the actual books are no longer extant.[14] However, as a respected modern scholar of the Daoist classics, Meng Wentong, pointed out, "When it comes to those of our country's more ancient books that are erroneous and in shambles, the worst is *Laozi*."[15]

Part of the reason for this can be ascribed to how widely this book was disseminated, as well as its extreme age. Prof. Xiong Tieji explained that due to "continual copying, reordering, and transcription and printing, alterations both large and small were made to the ancient books, and this is especially true in the ancient pre-Qin[16] book *Laozi*, which has had tremendous influence." As it was handed down, "the accuracy or inaccuracy of a line or a character, or including it or not, all had enormous impact."[17]

These errors and omissions have (at least until now) unavoidably prevented us from correctly comprehending the teachings of Laozi. To make matters worse, these misinterpretations were compounded by translations into foreign languages. We can safely say that the *Dao De Jing* is so highly regarded that "it is one of the most translated books in the world."[18] Despite this demonstrated hunger for Laozi's wisdom, many of the most popular English renderings of this book were in fact written by people who did not have the slightest acquaintance with Chinese. In a chapter pointedly titled, "Those Who Don't Know Speak: Translations of Laozi by People Who Do Not Know Chinese," scholar of the Warring States period Paul R. Goldin refers to the authors of these singularly odd works as "pseudotranslators":

[T]here are now several offerings by people who declare without embarrassment that they have no knowledge of the Chinese language, let alone the ancient idiom of the *Daode jing*. It is hard to imagine how anyone can get the idea that it is possible to translate a Chinese text without knowing Chinese. The requisite hubris is astounding. Chinese people do not attempt to translate Shakespeare without knowing English.[19]

Furthermore, as the famous *Dao De Jing* scholar Jiang Xichang once wrote, "If we do not know the veracity of an ancient book, but just read it carelessly, then what we are reading is simply a fabricated book."[20]

With this as our premise, the immense value of three recent archaeological discoveries of the *Dao De Jing* is nothing less than striking. These have provided us with the most untouched copies of the *Dao De Jing* known to exist as they appeared around the time of Christ, or only a few hundred years (per the *Shiji*) after Laozi wrote this great book. These three versions—the bamboo-slip copy of *Laozi* known as the Guodian version (which was found in a Chu tomb dating from before the Han dynasty, ca. 300 BCE), as well as two copies written on silk from the early Han dynasty (ca. 206 BCE) that were found in the Mawangdui tombs (i.e., silk versions A and B)[21]—are what I have used as the bases for this, *The Dao De Jing: Laozi's Book of Life*.

These three versions are as of this date the earliest known copies of the *Dao De Jing*, and therefore by all rights should comprise the foundation for a correct understanding of this invaluable classic. The other currently extant ancient copy of the *Dao De Jing* is from the middle period of the Western Han dynasty (ca. 73 BCE) and was also written on bamboo slips; this is part of the Peking University collection and is known as the Beida version.[22] Additional sources I have referred to while researching Laozi's teachings include *Hanfeizi*, Fu Yi's *Dao De Jing guben pian* (*The Ancient Dao De Jing*), and early annotators of the received versions, specifically Heshang Gong and Wang Bi. Added together, these sources allowed me to arrive at a reconstructed Chinese version in the main section here (for both the Book of the Dao and the Book of the De) that is to my knowledge the most reliable account possible.

When I compared these three recent archaeological findings (plus the Beida version) with the received versions, the most surprising discovery was that every one of the four ancient versions placed the Book of the De (*De Jing*) before the Book of the Dao (*Dao Jing*).[23] This is the complete opposite of what readers throughout the world—including China—have been accustomed to seeing, as reflected in its traditional title, the *Dao De Jing*. Although many scholars have suggested different reasons for this,[24] I have assumed a more conservative stance—one that relies upon the philosophical concepts in *Laozi,* specifying "the Dao is first and then the De"[25] and "the Dao encompasses the De"[26]—in order to determine that, as evinced in the received versions, the Book of the Dao ought to come before the Book of the De. My research has shown, and this translation will prove, that arranging Laozi's book in such a manner provides for a more comprehensive understanding of the *Dao De Jing*.

In addition to this flipped arrangement of the Book of the De and the Book of the Dao, other discrepancies exist between the ancient, unearthed texts and the received versions, particularly in the order of the chapters:

- THE GUODIAN VERSION was not divided up into chapters, and simply has three sections. This bamboo-slip copy of the *Dao De Jing* is not as complete as the other versions.[27] Nevertheless, the way in which its sentences are expressed shows that this version is entirely mature.

- SILK VERSIONS A AND B were each divided into 81 chapters. However, they differ from the received versions in three areas:

  » The order of chapters 40 and 41 is reversed.

  » Chapters 22, 23, and 24 in the silk versions appear in the received versions as chapters 23, 24, and 22, respectively.*

  » For obscure reasons, chapters 80 and 81 were numbered in the received versions as chapters 67 and 68, respectively.

- THE BEIDA VERSION was divided into chapters, however it remains unknown why it combined chapters 6–7, 18–19, 32–33, and 78–79.

---

* If we consider the content of these chapters, the order as displayed in the silk versions appears more reasonable, and so that is what my version of the *Dao De Jing* has followed.

METHODOLOGY

The goal of my methodology is simple: to accurately understand the meaning of the *Dao De Jing*. Based on this premise, we must first acknowledge that the *Dao De Jing* is at least 2,320 years old. It was written during China's Bronze Age, an era generally referred to in Chinese scholarship as the pre-Qin period. From this, we can safely posit that China's rules regarding language, character pronunciation, and connotations have naturally undergone radical evolutions over the past two millennia. In addition, the Chinese language is unique in that, unlike most other languages (which are alphabetical), Chinese is completely composed of glyphs that may represent either objects or abstract ideas.

While alphabetical languages constantly develop in ways that reflect current pronunciation and usage, we can still more or less read ancient Chinese because those characters directly suggest ideas, rather than pronunciation.[28] That is why it is so easy to overlook the fact that the *Dao De Jing* was written in early archaic Chinese. This is also the reason why, even though it might seem reasonable to apply modern pronunciations and definitions to each character that might comprise Laozi's words, the results are going to inevitably be twisted and misinterpreted.

Because of this, Jiang Xichang pointed out in his analytical study of the *Dao De Jing* that "the characters are remarkable in that they convey special significance. But if we do not first perform a critical interpretation of the text, we will be unable to determine its factual ancient meanings. And if we are unable to determine its factual ancient meanings, and yet still interpret it, we will be applying our own meanings."[29] In other words, virtually indecipherable misinterpretations will be inevitable.

Therefore, in order to properly study or translate the *Dao De Jing*, all of us (including native speakers of Chinese like myself) must first approach this great font of knowledge with humility. We must regard its contents as being composed of an ancient language that we have yet to understand. The problem remains—and one we freely admit is unavoidable—that a thorough comprehension of ancient Chinese writings from the pre-Qin period is extremely difficult to master. The reason for this is one that most would-be scholars or translators overlook: correct readings require a thorough grasp of the then-common practice of interchangeable or borrowed characters.[30]

If we cannot pinpoint what each of these characters means and simply try to guess their connotations from their ostensible forms, we will (no matter how hard we try) invariably end up with erroneous and twisted interpretations, as pointed out by Jiang.

To avoid this sort of blunder as we seek to fully comprehend the *Dao De Jing*, we first must attain sufficient comprehension of Chinese etymology, phonology, and semantics—which comprise the basis for the study of archaic Chinese known as 樸學 *pǔxué*—and also form the fundamental skills required to arrive at accurate determinations for each character's meaning. Another thing to always keep in mind is that the sources for a character's meaning must be derived from a contemporaneous source and/or a related book, as well as any annotations or research on them.

Second, we must not only pay attention to, but also be proficient in, the grammar of the ancient Chinese classics.[31] Even though we can refer to many reference works that specialize in this area, we have to become extremely at ease with the writings of China's pre-Qin period.

Third, a common source of misunderstanding with the ancient Chinese classics is the use of 虛字 *xūzì* (empty words).[32] These empty words are, in some ways, similar to English prepositions, as they can drastically alter connotations, depending on the sentence's structure. In fact, they are so important that they sometimes end up being responsible for conveying much of the sentence's meaning.

In addition to these three prerequisites, a precise comprehension of Laozi's teachings is possible only if the grasp of any one part is arrived at from the perspective of the *Dao De Jing* as a whole. For example, most people will hold that 無為 *wúwéi* (non-effort) is of utmost importance, when in fact Laozi also discussed in chapter 64 (lines 5–6) the significance of 有為 *yǒuwéi* (exerting effort): "Exert effort where there is not yet materialization; exercise governance where there is not yet disarray."

Even though Laozi placed the highest value on cultivating ourselves in accord with the requirements of the Dao, that does not mean that he dismissed the need to successfully position ourselves in a secular world (chapters 36 and 54, as well as chapter 20 [line 4]). And while he severely critiqued armed conflict (chapters 30, 31, and 46), he still stressed the proper cultivation of a warrior (chapter 68) and offered advice on the correct attitude one should assume when war becomes unavoidable (chapters 30, 31, and 69).

One of the most alarming of the odd beliefs surrounding Laozi's theories is that they somehow contained 愚人主義 *yúrén zhǔyì* (the principle of turning people foolish), when in fact chapter 57 (lines 12–13) clearly states: "When we [i.e., leaders] cling to stillness, then the people will settle on their own; when we desire to desire not, then the people will be with the Essential [i.e., become artless] on their own." In addition, chapter 65 (lines 5–8) points out: "So, using shrewdness in the governing of a country will be a detriment to that country, and using no shrewdness in the governing of a country will be a boon to that country." According to Laozi, what people generally manifest is, in the end, a reflection of their leaders' cultivation and governing.

For all of these reasons, those who do not consume the *Dao De Jing* as a book in its entirety, and rely instead on bits and pieces of it in an attempt to arrive at a correct understanding of Laozi's teachings, will be acting in vain. They will be deceiving themselves, and (more importantly) they will be deceiving others.

In all, the study and translation of the *Dao De Jing* are extremely difficult tasks. Just as with the works of Plato, the Bible, the Quran, the Buddhist sūtras, and all other culminations of the human spirit and civilization, this book requires significant outlays in time and energy in order to grasp the correct reading of each character in this ancient classic (including interchangeable and borrowed characters, as well as the empty words mentioned above). The Chinese language in the pre-Qin period was not as universally standardized as it is today, meaning that the ancient pronunciation of a particular character might sometimes lead to a homonym being used to represent something that, if not correctly deciphered, could create a completely erroneous reading.[33]

Therefore, my first step was the correct determination of what each character should be and how it was used during the Bronze Age before accurately rendering it into modern Chinese. To do this, I not only had to study authoritative sources on the ancient classics to determine how a character was used at a certain time, place, and context, but also depended upon my training in *pǔxué* to guide me in comprehending the *Dao De Jing*.[34]

Only when all these had been accomplished could I then progress to precisely define what each sentence and passage conveyed, under the demand that I also took into account both the progression and the entirety of the book so the attributes of Laozi's teachings were correctly echoed. Once I had achieved that step, I then worked toward analyzing and understanding each chapter not only as a stand-alone thesis, but also as one part of Laozi's book as a whole. Moreover, Laozi often relied on metaphors to illustrate his teachings, and each one of these instances had to be both identified and interpreted accordingly. Upon completing these, I began to translate each word, passage, and chapter into English. All of this is reflected in the structure of *The Dao De Jing: Laozi's Book of Life.*

In this book, the sources for interpretations can be found in the corresponding comments (starting on page 259). For the convenience of any readers who wish to delve further into this work, whenever Chinese is cited in the comments, it takes the form of the character(s), the pronunciation (in Pinyin, including tones), and its English interpretation in parentheses, such as "名 *míng* (name)." The sources for these comments can be found in the endnotes (starting on page 323); because these endnotes were designed as references, only the original Chinese sources are cited, as study at this level presupposes a strong familiarity with the ancient Chinese classics.

Lastly, each translated passage of the *Dao De Jing* was provided with English margin notes to offer what I hope is an accurate comprehension of Laozi's teachings.

To achieve all the above, I dedicated more than twenty years—and wrote four completely new drafts—until I was finally satisfied enough to lay this book in your hands.

THE SIGNIFICANCE OF THE *DAO DE JING*

Thousands of years ago, Laozi's wise teachings were the ultimate guide to the pursuit of a harmonious world and countless contented lives. The high value that was placed on Laozi's work is revealed in the number of scholars who devoted their knowledge and skills to comprehending it. Just as England's King James I sponsored a complete translation of the Christian Bible into English, China had four great emperors who, over a period of 700 years, personally penned annotations to the *Dao De Jing*: Tang Xuanzong, Song Huizong, Ming Taizu, and Qing Shizu.[35] Such an honor was never bestowed upon any other classic.

However, the importance of the *Dao De Jing* does not stop there. Rather, Laozi's work created the philosophical framework for all of China's—and much of East Asia's—way of thinking. China would not be China without Laozi's incalculable contributions. They became the basis for Daoist thought,[36] giving rise to great thinkers such as Zhuangzi and influencing China's finest poets and artists. Sometimes, however, his messages were, as some have argued, deliberately misinterpreted when they were turned into the folk religion referred to as "Daoism."[37] But, for the most part, this gentle tome has been held in the highest regard, for the *Dao De Jing* not only helped in the development of Confucian thought,[38] but also proved to be a fundamental component in the transformation of India's Buddhist religion into the various schools of Chinese Buddhism, including Chan,[39] which became known in Japan as Zen.

THE IMPORTANCE OF THE *DAO DE JING* TO THE MODERN WORLD

A correct understanding of the *Dao De Jing* is as crucial to those of us living in today's world as it was to the people of China during the Bronze Age. Its advice has proved to be both timeless and unconstrained. Because these are philosophical teachings rather than theological treatises, they can be adopted by the adherent of any religion without the fear of conflict.

All of us are now faced with a future that could easily be forever altered by radical climate change, an upended world order, fast-moving pandemics, and a noticeable decline of established moral and ethical codes. Perhaps most frightening of all, even though mankind has never lived in a world without discord, the modern arms race has given us weapons that can destroy our planet in a flash of light. Thus, as greed and ignorance have set us on the course of self-destruction, the most crucial question facing us today is, how can we reverse our actions and bring about a world where all of us can live in comfort and without fear?

The answer to this lies in the *Dao De Jing*.

道經

THE BOOK OF
THE
DAO

第一章

---

1 道可道也，

2 非恆道也。

3 名可名也，

4 非恆名也。

5 無名，萬物之始也。

6 有名，萬物之母也。

7 故恆無欲也，以觀其眇；

8 恆有欲也，以觀其所噭。

CHAPTER 1

1   A dao that can be spoken of

2   is not the eternal Dao.

The immutable and everlasting Dao transcends the constraints of language. But "from the now back to the time of yore, Its name has never vanished" (chapter 21).

3   A name that can be defined

4   is not the eternal Name.

5   That which has no name is the Origin of all things.

6   That which has a name is the Mother of all things.

The source of the birth of all things (the "Origin") and what nurtures the persistence of their lives in the world (the "Mother") are actually two stages of one Reality (chapter 52).

7   And so, it is always when there is no innate response that one observes their minuteness,

To fathom the beginning of a thing's existence, we must serenely observe its creation when it is in its most minute form, and through this we may ascertain the existence of the Origin.

8   and always when there is innate response that one observes what they pursue.

To explore how a thing endures, we have to rely on our sensory responses, through which we may ascertain the existence of the Mother.

9 兩者同出，

10 異名同謂，

11 玄之又玄，

12 眾眇之門。

9   These two have the same Source,

10   with different names for the same idea—

11   that is the transcendent within the transcendent,

12   where the Gate for the multitudes of minuteness lies.

The Origin and the Mother bring about the existence of all things, but our limited perception conceptualizes them as being different.

However, the nature of the existence of things never changes throughout their life spans.

This demonstrates that no difference fundamentally exists between the Origin and the Mother, which allows us to understand that they are rooted in the same Reality—the One that lies in the absolute unknown, in the place from which all life ceaselessly emerges.

It is here that we may begin to obtain true knowledge of the world.

第二章

---

1 天下皆知美之為美也，惡矣！

2 皆知善，此其不善矣！

---

3 有無之相生也，

4 難易之相成也，

5 長短之相刑也，

6 高下之相盈也，

7 音聲之相和也，

8 先後之相隨也。

CHAPTER 2

1   In the world, when all know that the
beautiful is beautiful, it is ugly!

2   When all know the good, this is then not
good!

*Beauty and ugliness are
emotionally polarized assessments,
while the good and the not good are
analytically polarized appraisals.*

*The notion of beauty
paradoxically requires that there
be ugliness in order to ensure
its existence, which means that
the beautiful is no longer truly
beautiful.*

*By the same measure, the
idea that some things are good
necessitates others to be not good,
thereby making the good no longer
truly good.*

3   Being and void surely beget each other,

4   difficulty and ease surely realize each other,

5   length and shortness surely form each
other,

6   height and depth surely fully embrace each
other,

7   pitches and sounds surely harmonize each
other,

8   and first and last surely succeed each other.

*The world is composed of
coexisting polarized counterparts
that to our senses separately
appear to be autonomous, when
in fact they must exist in a
mutually dependent equilibrium
and thus are indivisible.*

9　是以聖人居無為之事，

10　行不言之教。

11　萬物作而弗司也；

12　為而弗恃也；

13　成而弗居也。

14　夫唯弗居也，

15　是以弗去也。

9 Thus, sages administer affairs with non-effort

10 and issue teachings with no words.

Therefore, all of us (especially leaders) who follow the wisdom of neutrality will comprehend how crucial reality is to our lives; this in turn will cause us to abide by it.

Our behavior and views will thenceforth no longer disrupt the equilibrium of the world. (See the comment on the margin note to lines 3–8 for a more detailed understanding of this equilibrium.)

11 All things rise, but without being manipulated;

12 and exert effort, but without being confined;

13 and become realized, but without being possessed.

14 Oh, only when they are not possessed

15 will they then never leave.

All things are part of the reality of the world, and we rely on them to live.

However, they must be free of our dominion, for only then can they satisfy themselves and our needs without being ruined in the process. Otherwise, they will abandon us.

第三章

1 不上賢，

2 使民不爭。

3 不貴難得之貨，

4 使民不為盜。

5 不見可欲，

6 使民不亂。

7 是以聖人之治也：

8 虛其心，

9 實其腹，

10 弱其志，

11 強其骨—

12 恆使民無知無欲也。

13 使夫知不敢，

14 弗為而已。

15 則無不治矣。

CHAPTER 3

1   Prize not the talented

2   to make people not compete.

3   Treasure not rare valuables

4   to make people not become thieves.

5   Expose not the desirable

6   to make people not become unruly.

Our most destructive weaknesses are rooted in our insatiable cravings for fame, wealth, and self-indulgence.

Cautiously figuring out what it is that appeals to our weaknesses constitutes the initial step toward building an ideal society.

7   The governance of sages will therefore

8   empty their hearts,

9   fill their bellies,

10   soften their wills,

11   strengthen their bones—

12   and will always lead to a dearth of shrewdness and desires in their people.

When wisdom leads us to live lives grounded in our true needs, our minds will be unburdened, our physical needs satisfied, our amicability encouraged, and our bodies fortified—all of which will provide us with lives that are simple yet fulfilling.

13   Make them understand restraint

14   and to exert not, that is all.

15   No one will thereby be ungovernable.

Such wisdom will further lead us to realize how important self-discipline is if we hope to create a healthy, stable society.

第四章

---

1 道沖而用之——

2 有弗盈也。

---

3 淵兮!

4 似萬物之宗:

5 銼其銳,

6 解其紛,

7 和其光,

8 同其塵。

9 湛兮!

10 似或存。

---

11 吾不知其誰之子也——

---

12 象帝之先。

CHAPTER 4[*]

1   The Dao pulses, and thereby performs—

The Dao rhythmically surges with massive potency, and yet performs within the sphere of the world by perfectly adapting to its physical limitations.

2   yet the Realm never overflows.

3   So profound!

It is unfathomable, but the entirety of existence relies on It.
   The Dao thus ensures that all things settle within a common reality (the Essential in chapter 32). It does this by leading them to surpass their superficial differences and coalesce into an order that is both immutable and great.

4   It has dominion over all things by being their Root:

5   dulling their sharpness,

6   settling their turbulence,

7   harmonizing their light,

8   equalizing their dust.

9   So peaceful!

All things in the world thereby exist in perfect stability, and this is what sustains the world.

10   It has dominion over the existence of the Realm.

11   Whose child It is I do not know—

Everything must stem from something, and the Dao is no exception.
   However, we do not know what created the Dao.

12   It likely preceded Heavenly Providence.

Because the Dao is the sole Origin of the world, It must have existed even before what some regard as the world's supreme deity.

---

* This reading of lines 1, 2, 4, and 10 differs from the usual interpretations; see the comments on these lines on pages 264–65.

第五章

1　天地不仁，

2　以萬物為芻狗。

3　聖人不仁，

4　以百姓為芻狗。

CHAPTER 5

1   The heavens and the Earth favor no one,

2   and employ all things as straw dogs.

The examples of the heavens and the Earth show us (and especially leaders) the proper way to regard people and things.

The first lesson here uses straw to illustrate how to disconnect values from our secular concepts.

Straw is common and of very little worth, and although it can be shaped into ceremonial articles (like dogs) that possess only an ephemeral importance to suit a particular time or need (much like our Christmas trees), the value of the straw itself never changes.

This metaphor teaches us that the secular notion of value has no place in our deliberations when it comes to ultimate wisdom.

3   Sages favor no one,

4   and employ all their officials as straw dogs.

Thus, a country cannot deviate from this very practical wisdom when putting its administrators to work.

5　天地之間，

6　其猶橐籥與？

7　虛而不屈。

8　動而愈出。

9　多聞數窮——

10　不若守於中。

5   Between the heavens and the Earth,

6   is it like a bellows?

7   Empty, but never exhausted;

8   moving, and generating in abundance.

The second lesson tells us how to remain absolutely neutral while embracing all things.

It uses a bellows as a metaphor, since it has a movable top above a fixed bottom, so the air inside can be continually circulated without being manipulated.

In this world, the moving heavens lie above our still Earth. Between them, the endlessly abundant cycles of life are embraced within this neutral space.

9   Extensive knowledge hampers measures—

10   and never can equal a cleaving to harmony.

Finally, no matter how much knowledge we gain, it will never be enough to deal with every possible contingency.

We should therefore emulate the wisdom of harmony that the heavens and the Earth demonstrate.

第六章

1 谷神不死，

2 是謂玄牝。

3 玄牝之門，

4 是謂天地之根。

5 縣縣兮！

6 若存，

7 用之不勤。

CHAPTER 6

1 The Celestial Generating Spirit of the
Valley that never perishes

2 is known as the Transcendent Feminine.

*Between the heavens and the
Earth is an infinite gorge,
wherein lies the robust Source
of the infinite procreation of life
for our world. We may imagine
this as a sort of birth canal,
albeit one that far surpasses our
cognitive abilities.*

3 The Gate of the Transcendent Feminine

4 is known as the Root of the heavens and
the Earth.

*The existence of the heavens
and the Earth is nurtured at the
exact place where these new lives
emerge, thereby offering up their
sustenance. Thus, this endless
creation of new life is the reason
our world continues to endure.*

5 So ceaseless!

6 It exists in vagueness

7 while performing effortlessly.

*This source of life will never dry
up, and because It lies far beyond
our ability to truly discern It, we can
only wonder at how easily
this is realized.*

第七章

1   天長，地久。

2   天地之所以能長且久者，

3   以其不自生也，

4   故能長生。

5   是以，聖人退其身，而身先；

6   外其身，而身存。

7   不以其無私與？

8   故能成其私。

CHAPTER 7

1   The heavens endure, the Earth abides.

2   The reason why the heavens and the Earth may endure and abide

3   is because they are not themselves alive,

4   and thus may be everlasting.

5   Therefore, sages place their selves after others, and so their selves become foremost;

6   care not for their selves, and so their selves become self-sustained.

7   Is this not because they are without the self?

8   And their selves thereby become fulfilled.

Surpassing the self frees us from ineffectual isolation, thereby allowing us to enjoy the support of all. The heavens and the Earth are the best examples of this truth.

When we (and especially leaders) follow the wisdom of these examples, we will no longer compete with others, and so in turn will be able to receive their full support.

Moreover, we will no longer strive for personal gain, and in turn will be treated with great generosity by all in the world.

第八章

1 上善似水。

2 水善利萬物而有爭。

3 居眾之所惡，故幾於道矣。

4 居善地，

5 心善淵，

6 予善天，

7 言善信，

8 正善治，

9 事善能，

10 動善時。

11 夫唯不爭，故無尤。

CHAPTER 8

1   Ultimate perfection is like water.

2   Water perfectly benefits all things, and yet is magnanimous when competed with.

3   It settles where all abhor, and so is akin to the Dao.

Water is the ideal metaphor for performing without error: It allows everything to take advantage of it so that they may exist.

Water has a generous nature that gives way when obstructed. It unconditionally accepts all, even the most contaminated of environments.

Therefore, those of us who wish to comprehend the nature of the Dao simply need to observe the behavior of water.

4   Settling perfectly with the terrain,

5   centering perfectly upon the depths,

6   bestowing perfectly as does Nature,

7   expressing perfectly with certainty,

8   straightening out perfectly as a criterion,

9   working perfectly with effectiveness,

10   acting perfectly with the seasons—

The preceding description views water from the perspective of the world. These seven examples, though, consider water from the standpoint of its own nature and its spirit of absolute accommodation.

11   for it competes not, so it errs not.

Accommodation can also be understood to mean no competition, for competition is a reflection of each person's selfish motives or subjectivity, which are not in accord with reality and so prevent us from obtaining perfection.

第九章

1 揸而盈之，

2 不若其已。

3 揣而允之，

4 不可長葆也。

5 金玉盈室，

6 莫之能守也。

7 貴富而驕，

8 自遺咎也。

9 功遂身退——

10 天之道也。

CHAPTER 9

1   Conserving that there be overabundance

2   is not as ideal as ceasing this.

3   Hoarding that there be accumulation

4   cannot be maintained for long.

5   The gold and jade that fill one's chambers

6   are what can never be secured.

7   Having high status and wealth, but with arrogance,

8   will bring about one's own ruin.

9   Upon accomplishing a task, the self withdraws—

10 this is the Dao of the heavens.

This chapter deals with the concept of success.

The first four lines describe the goals of excessive or forceful efforts that always result in failure.

The accumulation of wealth is never a reliable indicator of assured success, for protecting it requires exhaustive effort, and loss remains unavoidable.

Prestige and affluence easily foster the sort of intense vanity that is the precursor to self-destruction.

When we achieve success, we should not try to possess it, but rather let it go as we move on to a new stage in life.

This is much like the seasons that the heavens regulate.

Those who follow the heavens' example will thus be able to create successful lives for themselves.

第十章

1 戴營魄抱一，

2 能毋離乎？

3 搏氣至柔，

4 能嬰兒乎？

5 脩除玄監，

6 能毋有疵乎？

7 愛民治國，

8 能毋以知乎？

9 天門啟闔，

10 能為雌乎？

11 明白四達，

12 能毋以知乎？

CHAPTER 10

1   When the yang breath and yin spirit are retained, and the One embraced,

2   can one not leave them?

The six questions in this chapter show how to achieve perfection:
By taking care of our bodies—let harmony unify the functions of the yang and the yin.

3   When breath is concentrated and turned into softness,

4   can one be as a newborn?

By strengthening our energy—always allow the Essential's vital force to flow inside us without effort.

5   When the transcendent mirror is cleansed,

6   can one have no blemish?

By attaining profound discernment—train it to transcend the perception of flaws.

7   When caring for people and ruling a country,

8   can we employ no shrewdness?

By governing—adhere to the Essential while managing public affairs.

9   When the heavens' Gate is opening and closing,

10   can we act as the female*?

By behaving correctly when there are major shifts in the world—exercise calm response rather than be subjectively active.

11   When we have clear perception and broad comprehension,

12   can we employ no knowledge?

By dealing with reality—do not rely on what is assumed to be known.

---

*   Throughout this book, Laozi uses terms such as "male" and "female" or "black" and "white" as philosophical symbols—much like "the yin" and "the yang" in *The Book of Changes* (*Yijing*)—rather than actual genders or colors.

13 生之、畜之：

14 生而弗有，

15 長而弗宰也。

16 是謂玄德。

13 Things are engendered and fostered:

14 engendered but not possessed,

15 grown but not subjugated.

16 This is the transcendent De.

With regard to all things in the world, the paramount rule is that we must not seek dominion over them, but allow them to freely obtain self-realization from the Font of the unknown.

第十一章

1 卅輻同一轂 —

2 當其無，

3 有車之用也。

4 埏埴而為器 —

5 當其無，

6 有埴器之用也。

7 鑿戶牖 —

8 當其無，

9 有室之用也。

10 故有之以為利，

11 無之以為用。

CHAPTER 11

1   Thirty spokes converge on one hub—

2   in its void

3   lies the function of the vehicle.

4   Clay is kneaded to form a vessel—

5   in its void

6   lies the function of the clay vessel.

7   Doors and windows are carved out—

8   in their voids

9   lie the function of the room.

10   Thus, it is being that provides advantage,

11   while void provides function.

Three everyday manmade utilitarian objects serve as examples to show how the principle of being and void mutually support each other so their design may be successfully developed.

The universal principle of these designs is: physical form determines the shape of the void, which in turn defines the function.

Therefore, in the design of utilitarian objects such as these, we must coordinate the proper equilibrium between being (physical form) and void, as defined in chapter 2.

第十二章

1 五色使人目盲。

2 馳騁田獵使人心發狂。

3 難得之貨使人之行妨。

4 五味使人之口爽。

5 五音使人之耳聾。

6 是以聖人之治也，

7 為腹不為目。

8 故去彼取此。

CHAPTER 12

1   The five colors make a man's eyes blind.

2   Horseracing and hunting make a man's mind irrational.

3   Rare valuables make a man's behavior deranged.

4   The five flavors make a man's mouth numbed.

5   The five musical pitches make a man's ears deaf.

If leaders (and now, by extension, we) indulge in the lavish lifestyles and fleeting excitements that wealth provides, it will impair their sense of enjoyment, disturb their peace of mind, and encourage destructive behavior.

6   That is why the cultivation of sages

7   pays attention to bellies, not eyes.

8   Therefore, forsake those and adopt this.

Therefore, if leaders (and of course, we) wish to live wisely, they must devote themselves to satisfying the practical needs that augment their lives (and ours), instead of seeking sensory enticements.

第十三章

1 寵辱，若驚。

2 貴大患，若身。

---

3 何謂 "寵辱，若驚"？

4 寵為下也。

5 得之若驚，

6 失之若驚。

7 是謂 "寵辱，若驚"。

---

8 何謂 "貴大患，若身"？

9 吾所以有患者，

10 為吾有身！

11 及吾無身，

12 有何患？

CHAPTER 13

1   Honor is mortifying and results in anxiety.

2   High positions are exceptionally harmful due to the sense of the self.

Both honor and high position may be desirable, but they entail inherent problems.

3   What is it meant by, "Honor is mortifying and results in anxiety"?

4   Honor is demeaning.

5   Gaining it results in anxiety,

6   and losing it results in anxiety.

7   This is what is meant by, "Honor is mortifying and results in anxiety."

Honor is granted to us by others, and that is demeaning because it places us in the position of supplicants.
When we have achieved it, we worry about losing it, and when we desire it, we worry about finding ways to achieve it.

8   What is meant by, "High positions are exceptionally harmful due to the sense of the self"?

9   The reason why I could be exceptionally harmed

10 would be due to my sense of the self!

11 If I were to surpass my sense of the self,

12 what could harm me?

High positions usually involve great struggles, and achieving them easily breeds feelings of arrogance and overweening pride, both of which arise out of a pronounced sense of the self.
Thus, high positions are not the problem here—a sense of the self is.

13 故貴，以身為天下，

14 若可以托天下矣。

15 愛，以身為天下，

16 若可以寄天下矣。

13   Thus, with high positions, one equates one's self with the world,

14   that one's self might thereby be commended to the world.

15   With favorable regard, one equates one's self with the world,

16   that one might thereby rely on the world.

If we happen to have a high position or are favorably regarded, as long as we free ourselves from this sense of the self, we will naturally be able to accommodate others without bias or personal objectives.

In turn, we will win the unstinting support of everyone in the world.

第十四章

1　視之而弗見，

2　名之曰微。

3　聽之而弗聞，

4　名之曰希。

5　捪之而弗得，

6　名之曰夷。

7　三者不可至計，

8　故混而為一。

9　一者，其上不攸，

10　其下不忽。

11　尋尋兮，

12　不可名也，

13　復歸於無物。

14　是謂無狀之狀，

15　無物之象——

16　是謂惚怳。

CHAPTER 14

1   That which is observed but not seen

2   is called "the concealed."

3   That which is hearkened to but not heard

4   is called "the silent."

5   That which is probed for but not felt

6   is called "the flat."

7   These three are not detectable,

8   for they are mingled into the One.

9   This One, Its crest is not bright,

10   nor is Its base dim.

11   So ever in motion,

12   It is indefinable,

13   returning back to nothingness.

14   This is "the shape of shapelessness,"

15   "the form of nothingness"—

16   this is "the Nebulous."

This discussion introduces the unusual state of the Existence— It is imperceptible to every one of our senses.

We cannot perceive this Existence in any way, so we know for certain that It must exist transcendentally as the One.

The One is full of harmonious light (see comment on this line).

It exists in the cycle of emerging and withdrawing—no one can tell what It is before It turns back to naught. This rhythmic movement is what makes It appear to us as if It were there, and then not.

17	隨而不見其後;
18	迎而不見其首。
19	執今之道，
20	以御今之有，
21	以知古始—
22	是謂道紀。

17   When followed, Its back is not visible;

18   when faced, Its front is not visible.

19   Cleave to the Dao in the now

20   to have dominion over the beings that are of the now,

21   and thereby divine the Origin from the time of yore—

22   this is "the Principle of the Dao."

Moreover, It always moves in a cycling motion by Itself, showing no beginning and no end.

We refer to this One as the Dao. Its dominion appears before us solely in the present moment as reflected in the reality of the world around us.

That is why conformity to the Dao (chapter 25) not only guides our ability to properly administer all things in this world, but also allows us to comprehend the absolute truth of the Dao, whose rule has never changed since the beginning of time.

第十五章

───────────────────────

1 　古之善為士者，

2 　微眇、玄達——

3 　深不可志。

4 　是以為之頌：

5 　豫兮、其如冬涉川；

6 　猶兮、其如畏四鄰；

7 　嚴兮、其如客；

8 　渙兮、其如凌釋；

9 　屯兮、其如樸；

10　沌兮、其如濁；

11　曠兮、其如谷。

CHAPTER 15

1   In the time of yore, they who had achieved perfection as cultivated people

Since ancient times, the greatest achievement we can aspire to is the sort of personal refinement that lies beyond secular concepts.

2   would have been enigmatically subtle, transcendentally discerning—

3   and profound beyond comprehension.

4   Therefore, they are portrayed as:

To clarify how such cultivation appears in our world, Laozi describes it as:

5   so wary, as if fording a river in winter;

proceeding prudently;

6   so circumspect, as if distrustful of nearby neighbors;

restraining personal behavior;

7   so formal, as if acting the guest;

responding with wariness;

8   so untrammeled, as if ice that is thawing;

remaining free of constraint;

9   so simple, as if the Essential;

adhering to fundamental simplicity;

10   so indistinct, as if turbid;

eschewing judgment;

11   so open, as if a valley.

and embracing all.

12　孰能濁以靜者，將徐清？

13　孰能安以動者，將徐生？

14　保此道者，不欲尚逞。

15　夫唯不逞，

16　是以能敝而不成。

12 Who can be as the turbid, that with stillness will then slowly become the clarified?

13 Who can be as the settled, that with movement will then slowly become the risen?

Furthermore, such superlatively refined people will show that they live in accord with the eternal rhythm of the waxing and waning of the world.

Here, water is used to illustrate the constant cycle in the waning (stillness) and waxing (movement) of all things.

14 They who embrace the Dao in this way will not want to favor indulgence.

15 Oh, for only when there is no indulgence,

16 may they thus have no end even though they wane.

Nature's example shows us why our conduct should never exceed the proper limits that the order of the world's constant cycle allows.

If we act accordingly, then even as waning occurs, we will be safeguarded by the natural rhythm of change, which will wax fully once again when the time comes.

第十六章

1 至虛，恆也。

2 守中，篤也。

3 萬物旁作，

4 居以須復也。

5 天道員員，

6 各復歸於其根—曰靜。

CHAPTER 16

1 Attain emptiness, and there will be constancy.

2 Cleave to harmony, and there will be regulation.

As far as the reality of the world is concerned, only two stances are correct:

One is achieved by transcending corporeality and its attendant changes.

When we transcend corporeality, we attain the "emptiness" and the surpassing of time known as "constancy."

The other stance is directed at leaders (and by extension, ourselves)—the exercise of "harmony."

Successful "regulation," according to Laozi, conforms to everyone's self-realization through non-effort, and the resulting emptiness becomes the basis for cleaving to this harmony.

3 While all things boundlessly rise,

4 settle and await their reversion.

Everything moves in constant rhythm as it flourishes and then ebbs at the end of each cycle.

Wise regulation therefore operates through stillness.

5 As the heavens direct the plenitude,

6 everything reverts to its root—there is stillness.

The rhythm of the movement of all things adheres to the cyclic motions of the heavens, which in turn conform to the Dao (chapter 25).

7 靜，是謂復命。

8 復命，常也。

9 知常，明也。

10 不知常、妄。

11 妄作、凶。

12 知常、容；

13 容乃公。

7   Stillness is a return to the Preordainment.

8   A return to the Preordainment is constancy.

Thus, the reversion of all things to stillness is what realizes the Preordainment, for stillness always dominates the end and the beginning of the cyclic motions of all things.

When It is obeyed, order is established through the dominion of stillness over movement—then all things become regulated by this order, and the world achieves constancy.

9   To grasp constancy is to be discerning.

10   To lose the grasp of constancy is a transgression.

11   And this transgression, when it occurs, is disastrous.

Constancy is a sign that the world is running normally, smoothly, and harmoniously.

Our naive interference with the world's harmony is the inevitable source of calamities, not only in the world, but also within ourselves.

12   The realization of constancy is comprehensiveness;

13   such comprehensiveness will lead to being vast.

The understanding of constancy is what will lead us to abandon personal bias toward all things, for then we will be able to accept all without partiality.

14　公乃王；

15　王乃天；

16　天乃道；

17　道乃久—

18　沒身不殆。

14 This vastness will lead to being followed by the world;

15 being followed by the world will lead to being with the heavens;

16 being with the heavens will lead to being with the Dao;

17 being with the Dao will lead to being everlasting—

18 and unto the end of one's life, one will not fail.

In this way, all the world will work in concord with us, much as the heavens act in harmony with the eternal Dao. We thereby will always be safeguarded for as long as we live in this world.

第十七章

1 　大上，下知有之。

2 　其次，親譽之。

3 　其次，畏之。

4 　其次，侮之。

5 　信不足，安有不信。

6 　猶兮！ 其貴言也。

7 　成事遂功，

8 　而百姓曰，

9 　"我自然也"。

CHAPTER 17

1 The greatest of all will have subordinates who are aware of their existence.

The quality of leaders is clearly reflected in the way their people treat them.

2 One step lower, will like and praise them.

3 One step lower, will fear them.

4 And one step lower, will ridicule them.

5 Whenever credibility is wanting, distrust will then arise.

6 So scrupulous! They weigh their words.

The underpinnings for leaders lie in having the trust of their people, because if leaders are no longer seen as trustworthy, their people will begin to lose faith. This then turns into exaggerated caution by the leaders and an unwillingness to say anything casually.

7 When an affair is achieved or a task completed,

8 their subjects but remark,

9 "We realized this ourselves."

Under the governance of great leaders, citizens will understand their duties by themselves and realize them willingly without being commanded.
In other words, leaders will let their subjects govern themselves.

第十八章

1 古大道廢，

2 安有仁義。

3 〔智慧出，

4 安有大偽。〕

5 六親不和，

6 安有孝慈。

7 邦家昏亂，

8 安有正臣。

CHAPTER 18

1   Oh, when the great Dao is disregarded,

2   then humanity and justice emerge.

3   [When shrewdness and ingenuity appear,

4   then great hypocrisy emerges.]

5   When family members are discordant,

6   then filial and parental love emerge.

7   When an entire country is corrupt and disordered,

8   then ethical officials emerge.

If a society or the world fails to follow the Dao, the opportunity to achieve perfect harmony will have been lost.

When this happens, we always attempt to heal it with the application of moral values. Although these approaches are—with the exception of the third and fourth lines—well-meaning, the results are never enough to restore peaceful consensus in society and the world.

第十九章

1 絕智棄辯，

2 民利百倍。

3 絕巧棄利，

4 盜賊無有。

5 絕偽棄慮，

6 民復季子。

7 三言以為文，不足。

8 故命之有所屬：

9 視素，保樸，

10 少私，寡欲。

CHAPTER 19

1   Forsake shrewdness, abolish distinction,

2   and the people will benefit a hundred times over.

The prohibitions in these three maxims form the path to an ideal society:
    Abandon astuteness and discrimination, for they produce conflict through bias.

3   Forsake expertise, abolish profit,

4   and thieves and bandits will disappear.

Ban cleverness and gain for personal advantage, for they encourage larceny and predation.

5   Forsake exertions, abolish reckoning,

6   and the people's ingenuousness will be revived.

Deter endeavors and scheming, for they increase competition and deviousness.

7   Those three statements are but superficial expressions and insufficient.

8   Therefore, induce them to have that which secures them:

9   a perception of the pure, an embrace of the Essential,

10 a curtailing of selfishness, and the diminishment of desires.

However, each of those admonitions realizes its goals through compulsion, which makes the results little more than superficial.
    It is therefore imperative for the behavior of everyone in a society to be cultivated in a way that causes their hearts and minds to be anchored in the fundamental perfection of their innate natures.
    This is what will allow all to achieve true contentment and happiness.

第二十章

---

1 絕學無憂。

2 唯與訶—相去幾何?

3 美與惡—相去何若?

---

4 人之所畏,亦不可以不畏人。

---

5 荒兮,其未央哉!

CHAPTER 20

1   Supreme learning is free of unease.

2   Assent or rebuke—how much is their difference?

3   Beauty or ugliness—what is their difference?

Here the dichotomy between supreme and secular knowledge is addressed.

The tensions that arise from secular perceptions of analytical appraisal and emotional assessments will incite the sort of ineffectual conflict that only provokes anxiety.

If we hope to save ourselves and the world from the unnecessary stress caused by secular knowledge, we must cling to the supreme knowledge that surpasses all division.

4   Those who are to be respected by people also cannot be those who disrespect people.

However, even when we have attained supreme knowledge, we must still live in a secular society, and thus the need to maintain mutual courtesy with all others is vital.

5   So vast, it is boundless!

This line expresses the theme of this chapter like a symphonic motif; here, it depicts the truth of supreme knowledge as being infinite.

6 　眾人熙熙，

7 　若饗於大牢，

8 　而春登臺，

9 　我泊焉未兆，

10 　若嬰兒未咳；

11 　纍兮，似無所歸。

12 　眾人皆有餘，

13 　而我獨遺——

14 　我愚人之心也？惷惷兮！

15 　俗人昭昭，

16 　我獨若昏兮！

17 　俗人察察，

18 　我獨悶悶兮！

6   The populace is so happy,

7   as if enjoying a huge banquet

8   or strolling up to a terrace in springtime,

9   while I remain so quiet and unresponsive,

10   like a newborn who has not yet smiled;

11   so listless, as if without a place to return.

These lines illustrate how the behavior of the ones with supreme knowledge appears to those who only have a secular understanding of the world. (The former are discussed in the first person, as if from their point of view.)

While secular people always pursue sensory pleasures, the interests of those who possess supreme knowledge so transcend lay comprehension that these individuals appear as unreadable as newborns—they hold no allegiances to any particular place, but rather embrace the whole world.

Therefore, secular people regard them as miserable, as if they were untethered and homeless.

12   The populace all have plenty,

13   but only I have less than enough—

14   is mine the mind of a fool? So dimwitted!

Those with secular knowledge may understand how to hoard, but the ones who possess supreme knowledge are not tethered by possessions, and so appear absurd.

15   The benighted are so brilliant,

16   while I am the one who appears befuddled!

17   The benighted are so discerning,

18   while I am the one who is so muddleheaded!

In the secular world, those who do not have even average cultivation may think of themselves as intelligent and discerning. As such, they look down on the ones who possess supreme knowledge as being not only backward, but also confused.

19 忽兮，其若晦！

20 恍兮，其若無所止！

21 眾人皆有以，

22 我獨頑以鄙！

23 吾欲獨異於人而貴食母。

19   So vague, as if it were blurry!

20   So nebulous, as if it had nowhere to tarry!

The motif is reprised here to illustrate how the nature of supreme knowledge is indistinct and wholly untethered to any confinement.

21   Everyone else has abilities,

22   while I am the one who is stupid and uncultured!

Moreover, while everyone is able to demonstrate how useful they are, those who possess supreme knowledge appear to lack any sort of special talent or breeding, for they have embraced fundamental entirety, not superficial division.

23   For, what I want differs completely from all others, through cherishing nourishment from the Mother.

Supreme knowledge does not appear to accommodate secular understanding. Rather, it nurtures the intellect of those who would learn from it through the fostering of the Dao.

第二十一章

1 孔德之容,

2 唯道是從。

3 道之物:

4 唯悦、唯惚。

5 惚兮、悦兮,

6 中有象兮。

7 悦兮、惚兮,

8 中有物兮。

9 幽兮、冥兮,

10 中有請也。

11 其請甚真,

12 其中有信—

13 自今及古,

14 其名不去,

15 以順眾父。

16 吾何以知眾父之然也?

17 以此。

CHAPTER 21

1   The manifestation of the ultimate De

2   solely obeys the Dao.

When we are able to act in perfect concordance with the De, we will conform to nothing else but the Dao.

3   The Entity of the Dao

4   is but vague, is but nebulous.

The Dao Itself is a substantive existence, but It is neither a perceptible being nor an absolute void—in other words, It is an undefinable configuration.

5   So nebulous, so vague,

6   within which lies the Form.

This configuration is formed— from the outside to the inside— out of three Elements: the Form, the Substance, and the Essence.

7   So vague, so nebulous,

8   within which lies the Substance.

9   So profound, so dim,

10 within which lies the Essence.

11 This Essence is utterly genuine,

12 and within It lies certainty.

13 From the now back to the time of yore,

14 Its name has never vanished

15 in the regulation of all tenets.

Because the Essence is incontrovertibly real, the nature of the Dao is immutable.
    And so, the Dao of the now is as It has been since the beginning of time—and is qualified to provide guidance to all of us, especially the world's rulers.

16 How can I know of the success of all tenets?

17 By dint of this.

Therefore, if we hope to understand how dominion over the world will become successful, we only need to observe how the Dao performs.

第二十二章

1　炊者不立。

2　自視者不章。

3　自見者不明。

4　自伐者無功。

5　自矜者不長。

6　其在道也曰：

7　"餘食"、"贅行"，

8　物或惡之——

9　故有欲者弗居。

CHAPTER 22*

1   Tiptoeing is not standing.

Standing is a normal behavior, but balancing on "tiptoe" here suggests that this is a personal attempt to stand out. Therefore, according to the rules of normal behavior, this person is no longer considered standing and has failed in this action.

What this means is that true success is not determined by our own ideas and efforts.

2   The self-righteous are never prominent.

3   The self-regarding are never discerning.

4   The self-glorifying are never successful.

5   The self-inflated are never revered.

What we achieve in this world is in direct correlation to the support we receive from others. However, the sort of self-determined valuation that arises out of egocentrism will inevitably thwart our goals.

6   To the Dao

7   these are called "surfeits of food" or "redundant growths,"

8   what all things surely abhor—

9   so one with aspirations will not engage with them.

The Dao conforms to "self-realization" (chapter 25). In other words, It allows all things to live freely by themselves without intervention.

Thus, an egocentric approach to life combined with forced effort will contradict conformity to the Dao. This is much like having more food than can be used or even having tumorlike growths on the body.

---

* See endnote 1 of this chapter.

第二十三章

1 曲則全。

2 枉則正。

3 洼則盈。

4 敝則新。

5 少則得；

6 多則惑。

7 是以聖人執一，

8 以為天下牧。

CHAPTER 23*

1   The curved are then the complete.

This refers to an ancient Chinese maxim (as indicated on line 15), and its spirit is exemplified by these five phenomena:

2   The crooked are then the straight.

3   The concave are then the filled.

4   The deteriorated are then the new.

In this world, all things must cycle between their polarized factors. That is why a shortcoming (as represented by the "curved," the "crooked," the "concave," and the "deteriorated") is in fact the predictable commencement of perfection.

5   The few are then the gained.

6   The many are then the confusing.

The "few" and the "many" are also a pair of polarized factors. The many come from the few, hence are only dominated by the few, and thus allow for there to be gain.

On the other hand, many may lead to confusion because of the loss of what could dominate them.

7   That is why sages cleave to the One,

8   so as to be the shepherds of the world.

Thus, if we (and especially leaders) want to achieve perfect governance, we must emulate "the One" where the harmony of the Dao resides.

---

* See endnote 1 of this chapter.

9 不自視，故章。

10 不自見，故明。

11 不自伐，故有功。

12 弗矜，故能長。

13 夫唯不爭，

14 故莫能與之爭。

15 古之所謂 "曲全" 者——

16 幾語哉?

17 誠全歸之。

9   With no self-righteousness, there then is prominence.

10   With no self-regard, there then is discernment.

11   With no self-glorification, there then is success.

12   And with no self-inflation, there then is reverence.

These four examples illustrate how to transcend egocentricity by following the spirit of being "curved" (see lines 1 and 15), for this is what allows us to achieve goals that benefit ourselves (compare with chapter 22).

13   Because they do not compete,

14   no one is able to compete with them.

Furthermore, the teaching on how to be "curved" is what allows us to become invincible.

15   In the time of yore, it was said that "the curved are complete"—

16   how could those words have been hollow?

17   For indeed, completeness follows this.

Although this saying was old even in Laozi's time, it served to convey something that is absolutely true, even today.

第二十四章

1　希言，自然。

2　飄風不終朝，

3　暴雨不終日。

4　孰為此？

5　天地而弗能久，

6　又況於人乎？

7　故從事而道者，同於道。

8　德者，同於德；

9　失者，同於失。

10　同於德者—道亦德之；

11　同於失者—道亦失之。

CHAPTER 24*

1 In silent words lies self-realization.

This chapter introduces how the Dao governs individual choices in the world.

The message that the Dao delivers is imperceptible, but the idea conveyed here is clear: All things should be allowed to freely make their own choices, unimpeded.

2 Gusty winds never last a whole morning.

3 A downpour never lasts a whole day.

4 For who wrought these?

5 Even the heavens and the Earth could never prolong them,

6 so how would it be otherwise with man?

However, the Dao does not allow anyone to violate the order of constancy in the world without suffering the consequences of their own failures.

Even "gusty winds" and a "downpour"—if viewed as willful exertions by the heavens and the Earth—could never be excepted, much less the stubborn strivings of human beings.

7 Therefore, those who realize the Dao will be in accord with the Dao.

We are thus left with two possibilities on how we proceed:

One is to cleave faithfully to the Dao through non-effort (chapter 37).

8 Those who realize gain will be in accord with gain.

9 Those who realize loss will be in accord with loss.

10 Those who are in accord with gain—the Dao will ensure that the gain is theirs.

11 Those who are in accord with loss—the Dao will ensure that the loss is theirs.

The other one is to rely upon our own efforts. Such efforts will have one of two consequences: gain or loss.

The point here is that when it comes to choices about how to proceed, the Dao will surely guarantee the consequences of our efforts.

This is yet another example of what is meant by "the Dao conforms to self-realization" (chapter 25), but it also serves as a warning that the decisions we make should be wise ones.

---

* See endnote 1 of this chapter.

第二十五章

1 有物混成，

2 先天地生。

---

3 寂！寥！

4 獨立不改，

5 可以為天下母。

---

6 未知其名，

7 字之曰道。

8 吾強為之名—曰、大。

---

9 大曰逝，

10 逝曰遠，

11 遠曰反。

CHAPTER 25

1   An Entity was mingled into realization

2   before the heavens and the Earth were born.

Eons before our world came into being, Existence Itself was formed into a coalesced state (chapter 14).

3   So soundless! So invisible!

4   It is solitary and immutable,

5   and therein acts as the Mother to the world.

This Existence transcends our perception. It is the Absolute One that embraces the quality of constancy while nurturing the lives of all things.

6   No one knew Its name

7   and referred to It as "the Dao."

8   I give It another name—that is "Greatness."

Even though we may have a vague notion of what this Entity is, we nevertheless lack the ability to provide an accurate identification.

That is why we follow the practice that can be retraced all the way back to Laozi's time by referring to It as "the Dao."

Laozi then took this a step further by describing It as "Greatness."

9   With greatness there then is departure,

10   with departure there then is remoteness,

11   and with remoteness there then is return.

The denotation of "Greatness" reveals that the Dao encompasses all things (chapter 34), and hence is not bound to a single place or time. It therefore exists in a state of constant circulation within the entire sphere of the world as described in these three lines: "departure" describes the commencement of motion, "remoteness" describes the furthest extent of that motion, and "return" describes reversion into the same stillness that existed before all motion began.

12 天大，

13 地大，

14 道大，

15 王亦大。

16 域中有四大焉，

17 王居一焉。

18 人法地，

19 地法天，

20 天法道，

21 道法自然。

12 The heavens are great,

13 the Earth is great,

14 the Dao is great,

15 and the king is also great.

16 Four are great in the Realm,

17 and the king is one of them.

In our corporeal world, the heavens lie above, the Earth below, and the Dao moves between them (chapter 4). All things in our world exist by being in accordance with these Three.

Lastly, one who is responsible for the well-being of all things in our world is considered the fourth "great one." But whoever is qualified to be on par with the significance of the heavens, the Earth, and the Dao has realized an unimaginably great honor, and so must undertake this responsibility with appropriate solemnity.

This is the grave counsel encapsulated in the last two lines here.

18 Man conforms to the Earth,

19 the Earth conforms to the heavens,

20 the heavens conform to the Dao,

21 and the Dao conforms to self-realization.

Finally, we must always keep in mind that the world is made of a fixed order, for otherwise it would collapse, which means that we have to live in accordance with what the Earth provides.

The Earth in turn exists in accordance with the seasonal movements of the heavens, while the heavens behave as dictated by the nature of the Dao—and that is always in accordance with what all things choose of their own volition.

第二十六章

1　重為輕根，

2　靜為躁君。

3　是以君子終日行，

4　不離其輜重。

5　雖有環官，

6　燕處則昭若。

7　若何萬乘之王，

8　而以身輕於天下？

9　輕則失本，

10　躁則失君。

CHAPTER 26

1   The heavy is the root of the lightweight.

Heaviness anchors lightness to provide stability. Stillness governs restlessness to provide regulation.

2   The still is the ruler of the restless.

3   That is why lords on a day's journey

4   are never far removed from their supply carts.

These two lines illustrate a way in which powerful people of high rank secure their stature through self-sufficiency, as this gives them independence, and positions them in a state of heaviness and stillness.
(Having supply carts to look after their daily needs while traveling is just an example of how this independence through self-sufficiency is always assured.)

5   Even though there are regional affairs,

6   when they abide in ease, affairs will then be in order.

As far as management of their regional affairs is concerned, no matter how powerful they are, leaders must perform with non-effort, with no words (chapter 2), and in a relaxed manner, thereby allowing self-realization to wield its powers over those affairs so that everything will run well.

7   Why would a king with ten thousand chariots

8   nonetheless allow himself to become lightweight in the world?

Leaders throughout history (especially supreme lords) have succeeded only when they were able to become the center of the world's gravity in a state of stillness, for this is what enabled them to rule the restless activities of the world.

9   Being lightweight leads to a disposal of the root.

10   Being restless leads to a disposal of the ruler.

第二十七章

1 善行者，無轍迹。

2 善言者，無瑕讁。

3 善數者，不用籌策。

4 善閉者，無關籥而不可啓也。

5 善結者，無繩約而不可解也。

6 是以，聖人恆善救人而無棄人，

7 物無棄財—

8 是謂襲明。

9 故善人，善人之師；

10 不善人，善人之資也。

CHAPTER 27

1   One who travels perfectly leaves no wheel
    tracks behind.

*Supreme achievement in any
field requires that perfection be
obtained in a way that transcends
rigid secular concepts.*

2   One who speaks perfectly has no
    blameworthy flaws.

3   One who calculates perfectly uses no tallies
    to count.

4   One who locks up perfectly needs no bolt
    on the lock, for even then it cannot be
    opened.

5   One who ties perfectly needs no knot of
    rope, for even then it cannot be untied.

6   Hence, a sage always achieves perfection in
    assisting others, that no one be abandoned,

*The spirit of supreme
achievement allows us to create
an ideal society where no one nor
their gifts will be ignored and left
behind.*

7   and in affairs, that no talent be forsaken—

8   this is known as "dual discernment."

9   Thus, good men are teachers who make
    other men good,

*Good people are essential when
building an ideal society. The
spirit of perfection is what
qualifies these people to teach or
influence anyone whose potential
for good remains untapped.*

10 and men who are not good are the material
    for the making of good men.

*This is the wisdom of non-
effort, for it lets people govern
themselves through their own
inherent goodness.*

11　不貴其師，

12　不愛其資，

13　雖知乎大迷——

14　是謂眇要。

11   When teachers are not esteemed

12   and materials are not cherished,

13   even the sagacious will become deeply confused—

14   this is called "being unclear about that which is right."

Therefore, if a society—and especially its leaders—is unable to appreciate everyone from its educators down to the people who are not yet aware of their own goodness, but instead relies solely on personal astuteness in its leadership, this society will become untenable.

第二十八章

1　知其雄，守其雌，

2　為天下谿。

3　為天下谿，

4　恆德不離。

5　恆德不離，

6　復歸於嬰兒。

7　知其白，守其辱，

8　為天下谷。

9　為天下谷，

10　恆德乃足。

11　恆德乃足，

12　復歸於樸。

CHAPTER 28

1 Understand the male and cleave to the female,

2 and so be a pool unto the world.

3 Be a pool unto the world

4 so that the eternal De never fades away.

To regain the nature of the Origin, we must journey through three stages:

The first is infancy, which signifies the nature of man's origins. To "understand" means to discern, while "cleave to" describes the way we react.

The "male" represents restlessness (through effort), while the "female" embodies stillness (through non-effort).

A "pool" is a passive receptor that accepts everything that flows into it, which is used as a metaphor for how cultivated people should embrace all that approach them without discrimination. (With regard to the De, see chapter 38.)

5 When the eternal De never fades away,

6 there will be a return to infancy.

When the De "never fades away" from us, our cultivation as human beings achieves perfection, which is referred to here as "infancy": the state where man's true nature lies.

7 Understand the clean and cleave to the unclean,

8 and so be as a valley unto the world.

9 Be as a valley unto the world

10 so that the eternal De is thereby fulfilled.

11 When the eternal De has thereby been fulfilled,

12 there will be a return to the Essential.

The second stage concerns the Essential, which represents the nature of the origin of beings.

The "clean" refers to honor, while the "unclean" means dishonor. Here, a "valley" symbolizes the source (see the comment on line 8) that benefits life, and is used as a metaphor for the cultivated people or leaders who benefit all others.

What they obtain is described here as "the De," because at this point, they would have fully embraced the Essential and, by extension, the Dao (chapter 32).

13 知其白，守其黑，

14 為天下式。

15 為天下式，

16 恆德不忒。

17 恆德不忒，

18 復歸於無極。

19 樸散則為器；

20 聖人用則為官長——

21 夫、大制無割。

13   Understand the white and cleave to the black,

14   so as to be a Standard unto the world.

15   Be a Standard unto the world,

16   so that the eternal De never errs.

17   When the eternal De never errs,

18   there will be a return to the Zenith of the Void.

The third stage refers to the origin of the world, which is described here as the "Zenith of the Void."

"Black" and "white" were used by Laozi as philosophical symbols that do not have either negative or positive attributes. Rather, the white represents the visible world, as it symbolizes what we can see in sunlight. On the other hand, the black describes what lies beyond the visible world; in other words, where the Dao abides.

"A Standard unto the world" indicates that these cultivated people or leaders have become models of decency.

"The eternal De never errs" means their guidance has become so perfect that it has reached an apex on par with the Dao.

19   The Essential disperses and thereby becomes utilitarian objects;

20   sages wield the law of constancy to be the controllers of their duties—

21   in this way, great management surpasses compartmentalization.

This coda concerns how to conduct perfect management.

Because all things stem from the Essential, they indisputably behave under Its guidance, which is never excessive nor intrusive. This is what created the law of constancy.

Therefore, cultivated people and wise leaders who clearly comprehend this will oversee human affairs in a similar manner and cleave to the Essential, rather than intervene and micromanage.

第二十九章

1 將欲取天下而為之，

2 吾見其弗得已。

3 夫天下神器也，

4 非可為者也——

5 為之者敗之，

6 執之者失之。

7 物或行、或隨、

8 或熱、或吹、

9 或強、或挫、

10 或培、或墮。

11 是以，聖人

12 去甚，

13 去泰，

14 去奢。

CHAPTER 29

1   If anyone with the aspiration to rule the world exerts efforts toward this,

No one can ever have the power to dominate the world.

    Our lives are reliant upon the world, so those who possess power must treat it with absolute reverence.

2   I perceive this will most likely be unattainable.

3   Oh, the world is a Venerated Object,

    We need to understand that all things must exist as they are without claiming dominion over them.

4   upon which no effort can be exerted—

    If we do not follow this path, everything we attempt to achieve will not only end in vain, but we might even be destroyed as a result.

5   they who exert effort upon it will fail,

6   and they who grasp at it will lose.

7   Things can be either advancing or following,

All things in the world exist in their own ways that are far beyond our control.

8   hot or cold,

9   tough or bowed,

10   waxing or waning.

11   And for this reason sages will

That is why wise people (and leaders) will always comport themselves with propriety to accommodate the world as it actually is.

12   dispense with excessiveness,

13   dispense with exaggeration,

14   dispense with extravagance.

第三十章

1 以道佐人主者，

2 不欲以兵強於天下。

3 其事好，還！

4 師之所居，

5 楚棘生之。

6 善者，果而已，

7 不以取強：

8 果而弗伐，

9 果而弗驕，

10 果而弗矜—

11 是謂果而不強。

CHAPTER 30

1   Those who serve the leaders of the people in accord with the Dao

2   will not want to use force to coerce the world.

3   When their affairs have been properly achieved, withdraw!

Stating that these officials serve their leaders in accordance with the Dao implies that their leaders have already cleaved to the Dao's principle of non-effort. These therefore are subordinates who serve them by not disturbing the world's own accord.

And so, even when they have to employ forces, they are always aware of how to do this with the utmost caution.

4   Wherever troops occupy,

5   wild bushes and thorny vines will grow.

The nature of employing forces is such that it always causes destruction, along with the devastation of lives and economic ruin.

6   Perfection is merely the achievement of fruition, that is all,

7   and has nothing to do with the use of coercion:

8   achieve fruition, but without glorification;

9   fruition, but without arrogance;

10   fruition, but without inflation—

11   this is what is meant by "fruition without coercion."

Therefore, forces must only be used to simply and appropriately accomplish a specific goal by means of absolute rationality, and nothing more.

12　物壯而老，

13　是謂不道——

14　不道，蚤已。

12   As things become excessive, they then age.

13   These are called "infringements on the Dao"—

14   infringements on the Dao perish before long.

An overriding Law of the Dao is that anyone whose actions exceed what appropriateness allows will self-destruct.

第三十一章

1　夫兵者，不祥之器也，

2　物或惡之——

3　故有欲者弗居。

———

4　君子居則貴左，

5　用兵則貴右——

6　故兵者，非君子之器也。

———

7　古曰："兵者，不祥之器也"，

8　不得已而用之。

9　銛龍為上——弗美也。

10　美之，是樂殺人。

11　夫樂殺人，

12　不可以得志於天下。

CHAPTER 31

1   Oh, armed forces are inauspicious utilitarian objects;

2   moreover, things abhor them—

3   and so, those with aspirations abide not with these.

4   Noblemen normally live with the left being esteemed,

5   while armed forces are deployed with the right being esteemed—

6   and so armed forces are not noblemen's utilitarian objects.

7   Even though it is said that "armed forces are inauspicious utilitarian objects,"

8   they are to be employed when no alternative is to be had.

9   The pursuit of peace is to be cherished— do not relish that.

10   To relish that is to revel in carnage.

11   Oh, those who revel in carnage

12   will be unable to realize their ambitions in the world.

When military means are used by leaders to achieve their objectives, they inevitably cause widespread destruction. They upset not only all the lives in their paths, but also the harmony of the world's order. Therefore, the basic principle here is that they should be avoided.

In China's system of ancient rites, the left was considered to be the side of life, which signified normality and respect in daily activities.

The right side, though, was used to suggest the sorrow caused by death (see line 14).

Thus, armed forces were considered anathema to a nobleman's nature.

Although this is how armed forces are regarded, we still cannot discount them entirely.

If necessity compels us to use forces, this can never entail the pursuit of glory, for bloodlust will do nothing but doom the world and people's lives. Therefore, when armed forces have to be used, it must be solely for specific missions that remove obstacles to harmony in the world.

Killing for killing's sake will never lead to satisfying conclusions.

13 故吉事上左，

14 喪事上右。

15 是以，偏將軍居左，

16 上將軍居右——

17 言以喪禮居之也。

18 故殺人眾，則以哀悲涖之；

19 戰勝，則以喪禮居之。

13   So, it is at celebrations that homage is paid to the left,

Even the victor on a battlefield will suffer fatalities. For this reason, a battle array in ancient China was deployed as if it were for a funeral.

14   and at funerals that homage is paid to the right.

15   That is why subordinate commanders are deployed to the left

16   and superior commanders are deployed to the right—

17   this suggests that they are being deployed as at a funeral.

18   So, when multitudes are killed, one attends to this with grief and sadness;

At the close of war, the victors must offer their heartfelt sympathy to all those who have suffered losses, and thereby appease grief on both sides.

19   when victorious in battle, one then treats this with funerary rites.

第三十二章

1 道，恆、無名、樸—

2 雖小，天地弗敢臣。

3 侯王如能守之，

4 萬物將自賓。

5 天地相合也，

6 以輸甘露。

7 民莫之命

8 而自均焉。

9 始制，有名。

10 名亦既有，

11 夫亦將知止—

12 知止所以不殆。

CHAPTER 32

1   The Dao is eternal, has no name, and is the Essential—

2   though tiny, the heavens and the Earth cannot subjugate It.

The Dao has three fundamental properties:
- *It never perishes;*
- *It is in a state that transcends identification;*
- *It is the intrinsic Element for all existence.*

When It appears in the world, It is the smallest of all, but also the greatest of all, even more than the heavens and the Earth.

3   If lords and the king cleave to It,

4   all things will turn submissive of themselves.

5   The heavens and the Earth will couple with each other

6   to let fall sweet dew.

7   And the people will need no instruction

8   on becoming equal by themselves.

Once leaders preside in harmony with the Dao, the world will be able to run naturally and with order, both of their own accord.

Because man is no longer interfering, the atmospheric cycles between the heavens and the Earth will be able to nourish all living things without impediment.

People will thereby have satisfying lives, and so treat one another kindly and fairly without being compelled.

9   The Origin divides, and there are names.

10   When these names have been had,

11   one then must know their foundation—

12   knowing their foundation is the means for avoiding failure.

Names identify things, and things come from a dispersal of the Essential.

The management of things requires an understanding of what their designations fundamentally mean.

13   俾道之在天下也,

14   猶小谷之與江海。

13 Securing the world through obeyance to the Dao

14 is much like small gulches that follow the great rivers and the sea.

Therefore, when leaders (and we) want to safeguard the corporeal world, they must first comprehend how they need to comply with the Essential of the Dao, for then they will be able to guide all things without interfering with their own accord.

第三十三章

1 知人者，知也；

2 自知者，明也。

3 勝人者，有力也；

4 自勝者，強也。

5 知足者，富也。

6 強行者，有志也。

7 不失其所者，久也。

8 死而不忘者，壽也。

CHAPTER 33

1 Those who understand others are clever;

2 those who understand themselves are discerning.

3 Those who surpass others are forceful;

4 those who surpass themselves are powerful.

5 Those who understand contentment are wealthy.

6 Those who persist in striving realize their wills.

7 Those who never lose their places are enduring.

8 Those who are dead but not forgotten are everlasting.

The following three levels of wisdom are necessary requirements for living in the secular world:

First, we must comprehend the qualities of ourselves as well as others, but grasping who we truly are is even more important.

Moreover, we may possess the ability to exceed others, but the capacity to overcome our own defects and biases is even more imperative.

Second, we must deal with life in a healthy way. This means that we have to understand how true wealth is the comprehension of contentment.

Realizing our wills depends on our own persistence, rather than competing with others in the world.

Third, a successful life requires that we never place ourselves in any situations that do not suit our true selves (see line 2).

Furthermore, we should do our best to leave behind only good, for that will give us a measure of immortality.

第三十四章

1　道汎兮!

2　其可左右也。

3　成功遂事,

4　而弗名有也。

5　萬物歸焉,

6　而弗為主。

7　則恆無欲也,

8　可名於小。

9　萬物歸焉而弗為主,

10　可名於大。

CHAPTER 34

1   Oh, the Dao is boundless!

By Its very nature, the Dao is absolutely neutral and thus is able to transcend corporeal demarcations such as the left and the right.

2   It can be to the left and to the right.

*   That is one of the reasons why the Dao is able to abide everywhere.*

3   When a task is finished, or an affair resolved,

Although the Dao has the power to exercise dominion over all, It never tries to assert possession or control over the fruition of Its performance in the world.

4   It lays no claims to these.

5   All things follow It,

Things must depend on the Dao to exist, and the Dao—due to Its neutrality—is able to perfectly accommodate and fully support them.

6   though It masters them not.

7   In always having no desires,

*   This shows us two things: the Dao is completely self-sufficient, and this self-sufficiency allows It to be an independent entity that does not need to pursue external support to exist.*

8   It may be regarded as "the little."

*   It therefore reveals Itself to us as "the little."*

9   In being followed by all things but mastering them not,

Although all things in the world depend upon the Dao to exist, the Dao exercises Its non-effort by granting them complete freedom.

10   It may be regarded as "the great."

*   This gives It the ability to be willingly followed without exception by everyone in the world, which is what led the Dao to be identified as "the great."*

11　是以，聖人之能成大也：

12　以其不為大也，

13　故能成大。

11 This is why sages are able to become great:

12 because they exert no effort toward being
    great,

13 and therefore are able to become great.

*For that reason, the power to
become great is not based on
effort, but on cleaving to the spirit
of "the little," as demonstrated
by the Dao.*

第三十五章

---

1 執大象—

2 天下往。

3 往而不害，

4 安平太。

————

5 樂與餌，

6 過客止。

————

7 故道之出言，

8 淡兮，其無味也！

————

9 視之不足見；

10 聽之不足聞—

11 而不可既也。

CHAPTER 35

1   Cleave to the great Form—

2   the world will follow.

3   In following, it remains unharmed,

4   settling in ease and peace.

5   Wherever there is music and food,

6   passersby linger.

7   However, the words uttered by the Dao

8   are so dull, they are bland!

9   When looked at, there is nothing to see;

10   when hearkened to, there is nothing to hear—

11   and yet is unconstrainable.

"The great Form" is how the Dao in the world reveals Itself to our cognition.

By cleaving to the Dao, we are encouraging the growth of healthy environments that are perfect for all things and allow them to contentedly attain self-realization without disturbance.

Music pleases our ears, and food our appetites. Wherever they are offered, they attract all, even those who drop in by chance. Nevertheless, such offerings are limited in both duration and amount, and once they are gone, so are the guests.

Therefore, these lines suggest that the attraction of sensory pleasures cannot be relied upon to bring about a permanent state of happiness in the world.

The Dao cannot compete with the corporeal satisfactions incited by music and fine food, for Its expression (as with the "silent words" in chapter 24) is utterly prosaic and dull.

However, this expression of the Dao exists in a state that transcends the ability of our senses to detect it.

In fact, its range is immeasurably great on account of the self-realization of all things.

第三十六章

1　將欲翕之，

2　必固張之。

3　將欲弱之，

4　必固強之。

5　將欲去之，

6　必固與之。

7　將欲奪之，

8　必固予之——

9　是謂微明。

10　柔弱勝強。

CHAPTER 36

1   When one wants to have something
     contract,

2   then make it expand for the time being.

3   When one wants to have something
     weakened,

4   then make it strong for the time being.

5   When one wants to have something
     removed,

6   then make it be promoted for the time
     being.

7   When one wants to have something
     deprived,

8   then make it be augmented for the time
     being—

9   this is called "shrouded achievement."

10   The soft and the weak prevail over the
     strong.

The message of this chapter has three parts:

The first one is that even though the world is safeguarded by the Dao, secular obstacles in a country or state will sometimes remain.

To resolve these, those who have power and understand the workings of the Dao will not depend on effort, but will obey the cyclic nature of things (in other words, the progression of waxing and waning) to achieve whatever they want.

Therefore, these eight lines provide us with examples of ways in which natural cycles can be accelerated toward their waning phases so the obstacles to harmony in the world are naturally and rapidly eliminated on their own.

The second part here concerns the obtainment of the power that surpasses all others. As chapter 23 says, "Because they do not compete, no one is able to compete with them." (There, "do not compete" describes the stance of "the soft and the weak.")

11　魚不可脫於淵，

12　邦之利器不可以視人。

11　A fish should never emerge from the
　　depths,

12　and means that are advantageous to a state
　　can never be revealed to men.

*The third part concerns how a
country, by necessity, must have
its secrets.*

*A fish is safe as long as it
remains deeply hidden.*

*The same is true when it
comes to a country: keep that
which is to its advantage deeply
hidden so everyone under its
governance can be safeguarded
without being disturbed by
ambitions or aspirations.*

第三十七章

1 道恆無為也。

2 侯王能守之，

3 而萬物將自化。

4 化而欲作，

5 將鎮之以無名之樸。

6 鎮之以無名之樸，

7 夫亦將知足。

8 知足以靜——

9 萬物將自定。

CHAPTER 37

1   The Dao always exerts with non-effort.

2   When lords and the king are able to cleave to It,

3   all things are then cultivated by themselves.

The Dao "conforms to self-realization" (chapter 25). Laozi's point here is that as long as leaders abide by what the Dao conforms to, all things will be able to achieve self-realization without man's disturbance.

4   Though cultivated, if desires ever arise,

5   then pacify them with the Essential that has no name.

Things do not have desires, for the Dao always nurtures them into a contented existence. Therefore, we know that this passage must refer to people.

Here, Laozi is teaching us how to put a stop to people's desires in a way that echoes the guidance in chapter 19: they must have "an embrace of the Essential," which thus transcends the discrimination that names have wrought.

6   Upon being pacified by the Essential that has no name,

7   they will then grasp contentment.

If people are able to achieve this, they will naturally settle in a state of "diminishment of desires" (chapter 19), where the Dao will offer them the possibility of bliss and freedom from longings.

8   Grasping contentment leads to stillness—

9   and all things will settle by themselves.

A world that is ruled in this way will be able to exist in constant peace and enjoy the great natural order of all things without the disruption of human desires.

德經

THE BOOK OF
THE
DE

第三十八章

---

1 上德不德，

2 是以有德。

3 下德不失德，

4 是以無德。

5 上德無為而無以為也。

6 上仁為之而無以為也。

7 上義為之而有以為也。

CHAPTER 38

1   The superior De* is free of the De

2   and so possesses the De.

3   The inferior De keeps to the De

4   and so possesses not the De.

"Keeps to" means that effort is exerted to preserve what the De should be. "Is free of," on the other hand, suggests that non-effort is being exerted, and so the true De may be acquired through self-realization.

This discussion reveals a paradoxical truth, for being free of the De allows the true De to be possessed, while keeping to the De merely allows us to intellectualize what the De might be.

5   Exalt the De by exerting non-effort that has no intention.

Societal order is based upon four ethical principles.

The first relies on the superior De of non-effort (in other words, how the Dao performs, as in chapter 37), for this conforms to self-realization. It therefore has no objectives, but its achievements will be absolute.

6   Exalt humanity by exerting efforts upon it that have no intention.

The second is humanity, which creates contentment in others through altruistic kindness, but with no objectives. (This is, in fact, the best that we can attempt to achieve through our own efforts.)

7   Exalt justice by exerting efforts upon it that have intention.

The third is justice, which attempts to build order in society by assessing what is considered fair and appropriate.

---

* In ancient times, the basic meaning of the character 德 *dé* was "obtainment" (see this chapter, endnotes 1–4).

By extension, this indicated "gain without loss" or "benefits without drawbacks," as Wang Bi's note pointed out. "The De" here is an untranslatable concept that symbolizes the state of absolute contentment (see the comment on line 1).

8 上禮為之而莫之應也，

9 則攘臂而乃之。

10 故失道而後德。

11 失德而後仁。

12 失仁而後義。

13 失義而後禮。

8   Exalt social rules by exerting efforts upon them, and if reciprocations cannot be had,

9   then with outstretched arms, pull them in.

"Social rules" are the least useful of all because our efforts will at that point do no more than barely create a superficial order through compulsory behavior. Even if we could "pull" everyone into this artificial construct, discord will nevertheless remain beneath society's surface, where it can easily develop into conflict.

10   So, when the Dao cannot be achieved, there then is the De.

"When the Dao cannot be achieved" means that non-effort has been disregarded at this point. The De here in line 10 therefore refers to the "inferior De" in line 3, which is an emulation of the De created through our exertions. Although this is not an ideal reflection of peerless achievement, it at least attempts to save the De from completely disappearing in society.

11   When the De cannot be achieved, there then is humanity.

The effect of humanity on society is in some ways akin to that of the superior De, but it is nonetheless inferior due to its inherent limitations.

12   When humanity cannot be achieved, there then is justice.

While justice helps to bring about a certain level of societal order, another problem remains: varying opinions about what is fair and appropriate. This in turn will lead to latent conflict, which is why justice is inferior to humanity.

13   When justice cannot be achieved, there then are social rules.

In last place are social rules. As pointed out above, these easily become sources of conflict, and so are the least effective of these ethical principles.

14 夫禮者忠信之薄也，

15 而亂之首也。

16 前識者，道之華也，

17 而愚之首也。

18 是以，大丈夫居其厚，

19 而不居其薄；

20 居其實，

21 而不居其華。

22 故，去彼取此。

14   Oh, social rules are the shallowness of sincerity and honesty,

15   and the harbinger of chaos.

The greatest defect of social rules is that they always give rise to hypocrisy. Therefore, even though they might suggest communal harmony, they in fact constitute only the veneer of peace.

16   Prescience is but a blossom to the Dao

17   and the harbinger of folly.

Prescience is what shapes our judgment prior to something happening. The creation of perfect order in society must conform to reality, for, as chapter 14 teaches us, we must "cleave to the Dao in the now to have dominion over the beings that are of the now."

However, those who ignore reality must rely solely on their own judgment beforehand and attempt to form societal order out of that. This is epitomized here by a metaphor—a "blossom"—that represents a flimsy mirage of the Dao with no chance of fruition.

18   Therefore, a great man abides in profundity,

19   not in shallowness;

20   abides in the fruit,

21   not in a blossom.

A great person who cleaves to the Dao, and whose influence encompasses the entire world, will thus lead it to adhere to the fundamental human qualities of sincerity and honesty, and will never be enticed by "flowery" prescience.

22   Thus, forsake that; adopt this.

If we hope to correctly create societal order, we must look to the spirit of the De, which lies in the nature of what we really are (chapters 20 and 55). It always remains here with us, unlike those constraints made out of presumed truths, like justice or social rules, which lie there.

第三十九章

1 昔之得一者：

2 天得一以清；

3 地得一以寧；

4 神得一以靈；

5 谷得一以盈；

6 侯王得一以為天下正。

7 其致之也：

8 謂天毋已清，將恐裂；

9 謂地毋已寧，將恐發；

10 謂神毋已靈，將恐歇；

11 謂谷毋已盈，將恐渴；

CHAPTER 39

1 Since the time of yore, these have obtained the One:

"The One" here represents the power of harmony through the Dao. It is what secures normal existence.

There are six fundamental factors in our world that all lives depend on. However, they must first obtain harmony within themselves before they are able to bring harmony to the world.

2 the heavens obtained the One so as to be clear;

3 the Earth obtained the One so as to be still;

4 the Celestial Generating Spirit obtained the One so as to be perfect;

5 the valleys obtained the One so as to be replete;

6 the lords and the king obtained the One so as to be the leaders of the world.

7 If the One were to be striven for:

Harmony can never be obtained through the exertion of effort, and failure to achieve harmony will lead to havoc. If this ever occurs in any of the six fundamental factors, they will be unable to function normally and cause calamities, such as strange atmospheric phenomena, earthly upheavals, the cessation of new life, drought, and the downfall of those who rule the world.

8 as when the heavens cannot achieve clarity, there would be dread of them cracking;

9 as when the Earth cannot achieve stillness, there would be dread of it erupting;

10 as when the Celestial Generating Spirit cannot achieve perfection, there would be dread of It perishing;

11 as when the valleys cannot achieve repletion, there would be dread of them drying up;

12　謂侯王毋已貴，以高，將恐蹶。

———

13　故必貴，而以賤為本；

14　必高矣，而以下為基。

15　夫是以侯王自謂孤、寡、不穀。

16　此其賤之本與？非也？

———

17　故致數與無與——

18　是故不欲祿祿若玉，

19　硌硌若石。

12   as when the lords and the king cannot
achieve esteem, due to their high stations,
there would be dread of them falling.

---

13   So, even those who are esteemed will use
humility as their foundation,

14   and even those of high station will use
lowliness as their cornerstone.

15   Oh, this is why the lords and the king refer
to themselves as "the lone," "the bereft,"
"the misfortunate."

16   Is it most likely that their foundation is
humility? Is it not?

This teaches us that leaders must seek harmony with their people by grounding their authority in the poorest of the poor, which will unite the entire country through harmonization among the highest and the lowest strata. These examples show the truth of these teachings.

---

17   That is why the conferral of many honors
has nothing to do with honor—

18   and so there will be no desire for the
grandeur of the jade

19   or the humbleness of the stone.

The honor conferred by rank is a secular perception and does not reflect the true values of the world. Therefore, leaders will dismiss this secular concept, which is symbolized here by the jade and stone pendants that constituted Chinese officials' insignia during Laozi's time.

Such a perspective will allow leaders to achieve parity with the heavens, the Earth, the Celestial Generating Spirit, and the valleys in ensuring the world's well-being.

第四十章

1 上士聞道，謹能行於其中。

2 中士聞道，若聞若亡。

3 下士聞道，大笑之；

4 弗大笑，不足以為道矣。

5 是以《建言》有之：

6 "明道如孛。

7 夷道如纇。

CHAPTER 40*

1 A superior scholar who hears of the Dao is conscientiously able to perform within It.

This chapter has six parts. The first one concerns the ability to learn the wisdom of the Dao, which has three levels:

The best initiates faithfully echo Its wisdom by cautiously practicing It without deviation.

2 An average scholar who hears of the Dao seems to hear and yet seems not.

Middling learners appear to grasp this wisdom on some levels, but are still filled with confusion.

3 An inferior scholar who hears of the Dao strongly mocks It;

4 were It not strongly mocked, It would fall short of being the Dao.

The worst of all are those who not only remain uncomprehending of the Dao, but also view Its wisdom as an absurd idea. However, the Dao is such an immense and transcendental concept that it will certainly appear absurd to those of poor intellect.

5 That is why the *Jianyan* has this:

The second part concerns the ancient teachings known as the Jianyan, *through which we may ascertain how to obtain the De by learning the wisdom of the Dao:*

6 "Enlightenment about the Dao will seem to be unclear.

A true understanding of the Dao will lead us to embrace all without discrimination, so our manner toward the world may appear unintelligible.

7 Gliding along the Dao will seem to be rough.

The path of the Dao's wisdom is plain and easy, but in practice, we must constantly beware of deviation, so the process may appear uneven.

---

* See endnote 1.

8 進道如退。

9 上德如谷。

10 大白如辱。

11 廣德如不足。

12 建德如偷。

13 質貞如渝。

| 8 | Advancement on the Dao will seem to recede. | *Our journey of learning this wisdom will progressively enable us to conform to the self-realization of all (chapter 25) through non-effort (chapter 37), which may appear to ebb due to our decreased exertion of effort.* |

| 9 | The ultimate De will seem to be as a valley. | *The third part explains how obtaining the De through the wisdom of the Dao will allow us to:* *Benefit all without differentiation (chapter 28).* |

| 10 | Great cleanliness will seem to be unclean. | *Surpass secular concepts of honor and dishonor.* |

| 11 | Comprehensive De will seem to be wanting. | *Incorporate all by cleaving to insufficiency.* |

| 12 | Established De will seem to be perfunctory. | *Perform in the world with non-effort, as if nothing were serious.* |

| 13 | Intrinsic certainty will seem to be mutable. | *Grasp the truth by accommodating the world's flux.* |

14 　大方無隅。

15 　大器曼成。

16 　大音希聲。

17 　天象無刑。

18 　道褒無名。

19 　夫唯道，善始且善成。"

14   A great square has no corners.

15   A great utilitarian object is free of completion.

16   A great pitch transcends sound.

The fourth part describes how the Law of the Dao lies in the Essential and conforms to self-realization. This gives us the ability to surpass the confinements of secular concepts, for they are defined not by actuality, but by predetermination.

This in turn will allow us to comprehend how a square need not be defined by its corners, a utilitarian object need not be defined by its eventual form, and an auditory expression need not be defined by that which can be heard.

Our minds will thus no longer be hamstrung by preconceptions, and we will be able to accept and accommodate the actuality of all in the world.

17   The great Form has no shape.

The fifth part explains how signs of the Dao can be found in Its two transcendental attributes:

It is an actual existence. However, Its configuration surpasses our perceptions.

18   The Dao is immense and has no name.

It is everywhere. However, we do not possess the ability to identify It.

19   Oh, it is only the Dao that begins in perfection and also ends in perfection."

The sixth part tells us that although the Dao is transcendental, the way It administers the world must be our sole guide to obtaining achievements without blemish.

第四十一章

1 反也者—道之動也。

2 弱也者—道之用也。

3 天下之物生於有；

4 有生於無。

CHAPTER 41*

1 Through reversal—that is how the Dao moves.

"Reversal" suggests that each of the Dao's infinite movements is cyclical, and they end and begin in stillness.

2 Through weakness—that is how the Dao performs.

We are reminded that the Dao functions through non-effort (chapter 37). Non-effort is the result of adopting self-realization in the world (chapter 25), through which It transcends competition and thereby gives the appearance of "weakness."

3 Things in the world are brought forth from Being,

4 and Being is brought forth from the Void.

"Being" can be represented by "the One," and the One is the beginning of Being. Then, through the process described as "the One brought about the Two" and "the Two brought about the Three," all things were created (chapter 42). However, the One was engendered by (or through the emergence of) the Dao (chapter 42). Thus, the Dao abides in "the Void" and appears as the Void Itself.

---

* See endnote 1.

第四十二章

1　道生一、一生二、二生三、三生萬物。

2　萬物負陰抱陽，沖氣以為和。

3　人之所惡，唯孤、寡、不穀，

4　而王公以自名也。

CHAPTER 42

1   The Dao brought about the One, the One brought about the Two, the Two brought about the Three, and the Three brought about all things.

Laozi uses a simple mathematical formula here to explain the formation and existence of things:

    "The One" was formed by the Dao's emergence from the Void. The One then created a corporeal world constructed out of an equilibrium of coexisting polarized counterpoints (chapter 2), which are referred to as "the Two" (essentially symbolized by the yin and yang).

    Finally, "the Three" was created when the Two embraced the One in the form of "the Pulsing Breath" (as implied in line 2).

2   All things bear the yin on their backs and embrace the yang, with the Pulsing Breath forming their harmony.

The existence of all things therefore lies within the state defined here as the Three, with the Two providing the physical construct, and the One in the form of the harmonizing Breath at their center.

3   What people spurn are "the lone," "the bereft," and "the misfortunate,"

4   and yet the king and lords use these to refer to themselves.

Therefore, harmony is at the essence of all existence. This is also why wise leaders must align themselves through their high positions with the most miserable of their people. They do this in part by borrowing their names as reminders to never overlook anyone. This will harmonize the highest and lowest strata, as well as secure the continuity of their country.

5   物或損之而益，益之而損。

6   故人之所教，亦議而教人。

7   故強良者，不得死。

8   我將以為學父。

5 Things are either augmented by being lessened, or lessened by being augmented.

The fundamental truth of the world is: within the scope of harmony lies the endless cycle of equilibrium between polarized factors, as exemplified in this passage.

6 And thus, that which the ancients taught shall be adapted to teach people.

7 And thus, the brutal will perish before their time.

8 I will use this as an instructive rule.

The concepts regarding harmony must be our predominant concerns in the world, and those who act in opposition to them will bring about their own destruction. This is a tenet that has been taught for thousands of years.

第四十三章

1 天下之至柔，

2 馳騁於天下之至堅。

3 無有入於無間。

4 吾是以知無為之有益也。

5 不言之教，無為之益；

6 天下希能及之也。

CHAPTER 43

1 The softest of all in the world

2 runs through the hardest of all in the world.

"The softest of all" describes the nature of water (chapter 78), which is able to penetrate the toughest of things, such as hard rock. It does this by unrelentingly wearing down any impediments. Therefore, even though water appears extremely soft, it possesses an irresistible force that allows it to overcome almost anything.

3 Non-being penetrates where there are no gaps.

By extension, that which transcends materiality is able to permeate even the most impervious of objects.

4 This is how I comprehend the advantage of non-effort.

Chapter 8 describes water as "competing not," and it is used here to illustrate the significance of non-effort.

5 Teach through no words and achieve advantages through non-effort;

6 few in the world are able to grasp this.

The exertion of non-effort (including the idea in chapter 2 that we "issue teachings with no words") is invariably beneficial, but unfortunately most people ignore this and thus rarely obtain its true advantages.

第四十四章

1　名與身—孰親？

2　身與貨—孰多？

3　得與亡—孰病？

4　甚愛必大費。

5　厚藏必多亡。

6　故知足不辱，

7　知止不殆—

8　可以長久。

CHAPTER 44

1   Reputation and the self—which is dear?

"Reputation" represents how others see us, while "the self" is who we really are.

2   The self and valuables—which is important?

"The self" refers to the existence of our physical being, while "valuables" symbolize secular values that come and go.

3   Gain and loss—which is troublesome?

While "gain" can be beneficial, it can also prove to be a burden. "Loss," on the other hand, may initially appear problematic, but it might also open new doors and be the beginning of gain. (As Laozi repeatedly teaches us, everything in the world is cyclical.)

4   Undue obsession ensures great waste.

5   Measureless hoarding ensures significant loss.

Our misfortunes often stem from the uncontrollable desire to possess more without knowing how much is enough to achieve contentment.

6   Thus, those who grasp contentment will never be shamed,

7   and those who comprehend limitations will never fail—

The wise will therefore never suffer disgrace because they know what contentment is, and they do not experience disadvantages because they know how to abide by reasonable restrictions.

8   and will endure.

第四十五章

1 大成若缺——

2 其用不敝。

3 大盈若盅——

4 其用不窮。

5 大巧若拙。

6 大成若詘。

7 大直若屈。

8 躁勝滄；

9 靜勝熱。

10 清靜為天下正。

CHAPTER 45

1 Great completion seems incomplete—

2 and its efficacy is never exhausted.

In Laozi's usage, "great" always implies the quality of being in accordance with the nature of the Dao. This is achieved by accepting all (chapter 34; in other words, through "being followed by all things but mastering them not"). "Great completion" is therefore not confined by the state of completion, but rather by ceaselessly accepting all through being "incomplete."

3 Great fullness seems empty—

4 and its efficacy is never limited.

This understanding also allows us to realize "great fullness," for its function lies in a state that is infinitely accepting of all.

5 Great skill seems clumsy.

6 Great thriving seems withered.

7 Great straightness seems crooked.

The examples in these three lines also ring true, for the character of any elementary factor that is "great" will also naturally seem to be its opposite.

8 Restlessness overcomes cold;

9 stillness overcomes heat.

Throughout their never-ending cycles, polarized factors support each other (due to the Dao, chapter 2 [comment on margin note 3–8]) at the same time that they are both surmounting and being surmounted. This passage provides two everyday examples.

10 To be serene and still is to be the leader of the world.

Therefore, even though all things in the world are constantly changing, they must be administered through serenity and stillness (chapters 16 and 26).

第四十六章

1 天下有道，

2 卻走馬以糞。

3 天下無道，

4 戎馬生於郊。

5 罪莫厚乎甚欲。

6 咎莫憯乎欲得。

7 禍莫大乎不知足。

8 知足之為足，

9 此恆足矣。

CHAPTER 46

1   When the world embraces the Dao,

2   chargers are dismissed to farm.

Horses once served as an army's main source of power. However, when the world adheres to the Dao, these animals are solely used to better people's lives, and therefore even the fastest horses are left with nothing better to do than work on farms.

3   When the world embraces not the Dao,

4   warhorses foal on the outskirts.

Conversely, a world that is not in accord with the Dao (that is, without a harmonious foundation) will have all its resources consumed by war. When that happens, even pregnant mares will be forced to ride into battle and bear their colts in the chaos near besieged city fortresses.

5   No crime is worse than obsessing over desires.

6   No sin is more harmful than gratifying these desires.

7   No calamity is greater than never knowing contentment.

That is why the source of most of the world's ills can be traced to the ambitious desires of powerful leaders who interminably pursue them at all costs.

8   When contentment is achieved through the understanding of contentment,

9   then there will always be contentment.

At most, the pursuit of our desires can only result in excitement, not contentment, for the truth is, excitement never equals contentment. If we fail to grasp this, we will never find peace in our hearts and in the world.

第四十七章

1 　不出於戶，

2 　以知天下。

3 　不闚於牖，

4 　以知天道。

5 　其出也彌遠，

6 　其知也彌少。

7 　是以，聖人弗行而知；

8 　弗見而名；

9 　弗為而成。

CHAPTER 47

1   Exit no doors,

2   and thereby understand the world.

3   Peer through no windows,

4   and thereby understand the Dao of the heavens.

5   The further we go,

6   the less we know.

7   That is why sages know, but not through looking;

8   identify, but not through seeing;

9   achieve, but not through exerting effort.

The metaphors in these four lines advise us that true cognition comes from transcending sensory contact—that reality is more than the facade the world presents to us.

The more we rely on sensory knowledge, the more this impedes our ability to comprehend reality.

Discarding a reliance on sensory knowledge permits us to truly comprehend both the nature of all things and how to obtain absolute achievement through non-effort.

第四十八章

1 為學者日益，

2 為道者日損——

3 損之或損，

4 以至無為也。

5 無為而無不為。

6 取天下，恆以無事。

7 及其有事也，

8 又不足以取天下矣。

CHAPTER 48

1   As efforts devoted to learning intensify with each passing day,

True learning is the process of jettisoning what impedes us, and thereby eventually acquiring the ability to exert the non-effort that the Dao requires.

2   efforts devoted to the Dao diminish with each passing day—

3   diminishing and diminishing,

4   until non-effort is attained.

5   With non-effort, nothing then will not be realized.

The full exercise of non-effort triggers a conformity to the Dao that accommodates self-realization in all things, and failure will thereby never be known.

6   Never employ affairs when ruling the world.

7   If affairs are employed,

8   ruling the world will thereby become impossible.

This principle of non-effort should, of course, be adopted by leaders, because their overriding obligation must be the realization of peace in the world through the elimination of affairs, not through instigating them for their own political stands or interests, as these will only disturb the world.

第四十九章

―――――――――――――――――――――――――――――――――

1 聖人恆無心，

2 以百姓之心為心。

―――――

3 善者，善之；

4 不善者，亦善之—德善也。

5 信者，信之；

6 不信者，亦信之—德信也。

―――――

7 聖人之在天下也，

8 歙歙焉，為天下渾心。

9 百姓皆屬耳目焉，

10 聖人皆孩之。

CHAPTER 49

1   Sages never possess their own minds;

2   they assume the minds of their subjects as their own.

Wise leaders always unconditionally embrace their people's way of thinking as their own.

3   Toward the good, they are good to them;

4   toward the not good, they are also good to them, so that goodness is had.

5   Toward the trusted, they are trusting to them;

6   toward the untrusted, they are also trusting to them, so that trust is had.

Therefore, they strive to achieve goodness and trust throughout society for all their people. The presumption here is that most people are good and trustworthy, while the rest will never be abandoned because they are treated fairly and without discrimination. These people may thereby have the opportunity to change for the better.

7   Sages who secure the world

8   so harmoniously will let all minds in the world have no discrimination—

9   all the people will lend them their ears and eyes,

10   and the sages will treat them all as their children.

When all of society has achieved goodness and trust, wise leaders will then guide their people to abide in a common state of ingenuousness.
This will lead people to pay close heed to their leaders on their own initiative, and the leaders will in turn carefully and kindly look after their people as if they were caring for their own offspring.

第五十章

1 出生，入死。

2 生之徒，十有三。

3 死之徒，十有三。

4 而民生生，

5 動皆之死地之十有三。

6 夫何故也？

7 以其生生也。

8 蓋聞：善執生者，

9 陵行不避兕虎，

10 入軍不被甲兵——

CHAPTER 50

1   To emerge is to live; to withdraw is to die.

"To live" and "to die" refer to the cycle of life, which encompasses two parts:

    The first is expressed by the life cycle of things, for they constantly "emerge" (as with new life in the spring) and "withdraw" (by dying back in the winter).

2   The path of life is the ten plus three.

3   The path of death is the ten plus three.

The second part refers to how calendars as timetables can only be considered accurate if they precisely tally with the actual cycle of life. This has always been represented in the Chinese lunisolar calendar by the occasional thirteenth (or leap) month—in other words, "the ten plus three."

4   Now, as people live their lives,

5   they all advance toward the place of death in the ten plus three.

If we only know to live our lives, but do not know what life is, then we are setting ourselves on the path that contravenes life without having ever actually lived our lives.

6   Oh, why is this so?

7   Because they are living their lives.

8   It has been heard that those who perfectly look after their lives

Those who accommodate themselves to the significance that life's current conveys will thereby be secured by life, even when threatened by the greatest mortal dangers.

9   shun not the rhinoceros or tiger when traversing the highlands,

10 nor equip themselves with armor and weapons when going into battle arrays—

11　兕無所椯其角，

12　虎無所措其爪，

13　兵無所容其刃。

14　夫何故也？

15　以其無死地焉！

11   there is nowhere for the rhinoceros to thrust its horn,

12   nowhere for the tiger to use its claws,

13   and nowhere for soldiers to wield their blades.

14   Ah, how could that be so?

15   Because theirs is a place with no death!

第五十一章

1 道生之，而德畜之——

2 物刑之，而器成之。

3 是以，萬物尊道而貴德。

———

4 道之尊也，

5 德之貴也，

6 夫莫之爵，而恆自然也。

———

7 道生之、畜之；

8 長之、遂之；

9 亭之、毒之；

10 養之、覆之。

CHAPTER 51

1   The Dao engenders all and the De fosters all—

2   things are formed and utilitarian objects are realized.

3   Thus, all things revere the Dao and esteem the De.

The realization of all corporeal existence comes from two fundamental powers—the Dao and the De—and everything in the world obeys them.

4   The reason why the Dao is revered,

5   and the reason why the De is esteemed—

6   these are not due to high official positions, but rather always to self-realization.

These two descriptions cannot be explained using secular concepts because they were formed by the self-realization between Them and all things.

7   The Dao engenders all, fosters all;

8   has them grown, has them matured;

9   has them halt, has them subside;

10   has them shrouded, has them revived.

The Dao and the De have "different names for the same idea" (chapter 1).

This passage's poetic description of the life of all things as brought about by the Dao follows the cycle of the seasons. Spring is the time when It "engenders" and "fosters" things. Summer sees them "growing" and "maturing." In autumn, their growth is "halted" and then "subsided." And in winter, all things are "shrouded" as they withdraw before they are "revived," and then they emerge again.

11 生而弗有也，

12 為而弗恃也，

13 長而弗宰也——

14 此之謂玄德。

11   Engenderment, but there is no possession;

12   exerted effort, but there is no restraint;

13   growth, but there is no subjugation—

14   this is known as the Transcendent De.

Although the Dao is the sole source for the obtainment of all things, It never interferes with their self-realization at any time throughout their lifespans. Because this concept lies far beyond our cognitive abilities, It is referred to as the Transcendent De.

第五十二章

1 　天下有始，以為天下母。

2 　既得其母，以知其子；

3 　既知其子，復守其母——

4 　沒身不殆。

5 　塞其兌，閉其門——終身不勤。

6 　啓其兌，濟其事——終身不救。

CHAPTER 52

1   The world had an Origin that became the
    Mother of the world.

2   When the Mother is perceived, Her
    children are recognized;

3   when Her children are recognized, there is
    a return to cleave to their Mother—

4   and until our bodies cease to be, there will
    be no failure.

5   Muzzle one's openings and shut one's
    door—and one's whole life will become
    effortless.

6   Unmuzzle one's openings and amplify
    one's affairs—and one's whole life will
    become irredeemable.

*Things in the world owe their
realization to the "Origin."
From the "Mother," they obtain
that which fosters their existence.
(As chapter 1 teaches us, the
Origin and the Mother are in
fact different names for two
manifestations of the Dao.)*

*"One observes what they pursue"
in chapter 1 is echoed in this
passage, for it not only allows us
to comprehend what the Mother
is, but also reveals that She is
fundamental to the existence of
all things in the corporeal world.
We must therefore cling to the
Mother if we hope to successfully
deal with the world.*

*These metaphors explain why we
must cleave to the Mother. The
"openings" here represent our
ears and eyes, while the "door"
represents our mouth.*
*"Affairs" in line 6 indicates
the direction of the discussion
here, which suggests that line 5 is
a description of how plans and
ideas emanate from the mouth.*
*Therefore, these two lines
teach us that we should neither
submit to our physical senses
nor pursue them, and thus not
issue words that instigate affairs,
for affairs that emanate from
our senses and our words will
inevitably cause intractable
problems and conflicts.*

7   見小曰明，

8   守柔曰強。

9   用其光，復歸其明，

10 毋遺身殃——

11 是謂襲常。

7   Perception of the small is known as discernment.

8   A cleaving to softness is known as strength.

9   Use the light, return to its illumination,

10   and leave no disasters behind for the self—

11   this is called "accordance with constancy."

One who perceives minuteness (chapter 1 [line 7]) will be able to fathom the truth of the world. "Strength," then, lies in the "softness" that surpasses rivalry. "Illumination" gives us "light," and while light exposes differentiations, illumination offers harmonization.

These metaphors show us that solely paying attention to the differences between us will lead to conflict. Illumination, though, dispels all differentiation and secures us in the world's constancy.

第五十三章

1　使我挈有知，

2　行於大道，

3　唯他是畏。

4　大道甚夷，

5　民甚好徑。

6　朝甚除，

7　田甚蕪，

8　倉甚虛。

9　服文采，

10　帶利劍，

11　猒飲食，

12　而齎財有餘——

13　是謂盜竽。

14　非道也！

CHAPTER 53

1   If I were to keep my wits

2   while traveling on a great thoroughfare,

3   my only fear would be of deviation.

4   Though the great thoroughfare is so very easy,

5   people so very much prefer shortcuts.

6   The palace is so very immaculate,

7   yet the farms are so very deserted,

8   and the granaries are so very empty.

9   Decorative silks are worn,

10   fine swords are carried,

11   food and drink are wallowed in,

12   and there is a surfeit of valuables and treasures—

13   this is called a kleptocracy,

14   which contravenes the Dao!

Laozi uses himself as the subject of this metaphor, for as a Zhou dynasty nobleman, he never walked, and so he would have demanded that his driver remain attentive to where his vehicle was being driven.

The "thoroughfare" (dào) here can be seen as a symbol for the Dao, as they share the same character and pronunciation. This passage is therefore telling us that we must circumspectly keep to the path of the Dao. Even though It appears flat, straightforward, and easy to travel on, most people still attempt to forge their own self-serving paths.

Leaders who only care about their own glory and lavish lifestyles, while abandoning their obligations to take care of their people's lives, will have achieved their wealth through theft. Their halcyon days will be short because such behavior infringes on the rule of the Dao (as indicated in chapters 30 and 55).

第五十四章

1 善建者不拔，

2 善抱者不脫，

3 子孫以其祭祀不輟。

―――

4 脩之身，其德乃貞。

5 脩之家，其德有餘。

6 脩之鄉，其德乃長。

7 脩之邦，其德乃豐。

8 脩之天下，其德乃溥。

―――

9 以身觀身。

10 以家觀家。

11 以鄉觀鄉。

12 以邦觀邦。

CHAPTER 54

1 When that which is perfectly established cannot be uprooted,

2 and that which is perfectly held cannot be removed,

3 posterity will offer up their worship without end.

Once the perfection of our achievement becomes immutable, this will result in deep gratification for generations.

4 Cultivate this in the self so that one's De becomes stabilized.

5 Cultivate this in the clan so that one's De becomes abundant.

6 Cultivate this in the community so that one's De becomes thriving.

7 Cultivate this in the state so that one's De becomes ample.

8 Cultivate this in the world so that one's De becomes all-prevailing.

To achieve such perfection, we must first focus on increasing the cultivation of the De (also known as the state of "contentment" in chapter 38 [footnote]) in ourselves, for Its influence will naturally radiate to our families, localities, and country, and eventually even the entire world.

9 Behold the self through the self.

10 Behold the clan through the clan.

11 Behold the community through the community.

12 Behold the state through the state.

The achievement of perfection requires that we ground ourselves in a pragmatic and realistic perspective toward each level influenced by this cultivation. Such a perspective will allow us to accurately comprehend how perfect our world might be.

13   以天下觀天下。

14   吾何以知天下之然哉?

15   以此。

13   Behold the world through the world.

14   How am I able to know that the world is
      thus?

15   Through this.

第五十五章

1 含德之厚者，比於赤子——

2 蜂、蠆、虺、蛇弗螫，

3 攫鳥猛獸弗搏。

4 骨弱筋柔而握固；

5 未知牝牡之合而朘怒——

6 精之至也！

7 終日號而不嚘——

8 和之至也！

9 和曰常。

10 知和曰明。

11 益生曰祥。

12 心使氣曰強。

CHAPTER 55

1   Those who embody a culmination of the De will be like newborn babies—

Newborn infants exist in a state of complete contentment with no sense of the self. Line 9 below indicates that such infants therefore live in absolute harmony with the rest of the world. Because of this, not even dangerous creatures will harm them.

2   wasps, scorpions, vipers, and snakes will not poison them,

3   nor will raptors and fierce beasts attack them.

4   Their bones are weak and their muscles soft, and yet their grip is strong;

Though their bodies are pliable, their strength is in fact robust and their life force superior.

5   they know nothing of the union between female and male, and yet they are virile—

6   what consummate essence!

7   They cry the whole day long, and yet do not hiccup—

8   what consummate harmony!

9   Harmony leads to constancy.

The above example of newborn babies shows how important "harmony" is to our lives, for this is what provides "constancy" and leads to ultimate order. Through this order, we may be able to "be discerning" (chapter 16) about the truth of the world.

10   The comprehension of constancy leads to discernment.

11   The enhancement of life leads to disaster.

12   The mind's domination over breath leads to brutality.

When we have "harmony" in our lives, this will preclude any interference stemming from our own efforts or ideas. For, our lives must be secured through harmony in order to proceed normally.

13　物壯則老，

14　是謂不道—

15　不道，蚤已。

13   Things that are excessive will then become aged

14   and are called "infringements on the Dao"—

15   infringements on the Dao perish before long.

"Enhancement," "domination," and "excessive" indicate that there is no harmony, as all these transgress against the Dao, and thus will only lead to a rapid and absolute demise.

第五十六章

1   知之者弗言；

2   言之者弗知。

3   塞其兌，

4   閉其門。

5   和其光，

6   同其塵，

7   銼其銳，

8   解其紛——

9   是謂玄同。

10   故不可得而親，

11   亦不可得而疏；

12   不可得而利，

13   亦不可得而害；

14   不可得而貴，

15   亦不可得而賤——

16   故為天下貴。

CHAPTER 56

1 Those who comprehend It do not speak of It;

2 those who speak of It do not comprehend It.

3 Muzzle the openings

4 and shut the doors.

5 Harmonize the light,

6 equalize the dust,

7 dull the sharpness,

8 and settle the turbulence—

9 this is called Transcendental Sameness.

10 It is thereby neither possible to be close,

11 nor possible to be distanced;

12 neither possible to be benefitted,

13 nor possible to be harmed;

14 neither possible to be honored,

15 nor possible to be disgraced—

16 thus they are esteemed by the world.

To "comprehend" is to clearly grasp the truth, and we may learn from the ideas conveyed in lines 3–9 that the truth under discussion here concerns the Dao. However, if we "speak," our minds become constrained by words, and these can never convey the truth that is the Dao.

The first two lines in this passage reflect our understanding of chapter 52—that those who desire to preside over the world may neither rely on their senses nor use their words to instigate affairs. Instead, as described in the rest of this passage, they must lead all things by having them transcend their superficial differences so they may settle into the order of homogeneity while the Dao performs (as shown in chapter 4 [lines 5–8]).

Those who achieve this will have a position that transcends all secular regards (as described in lines 10–15), and so will become paramount in the world.

第五十七章

1　以正之邦，

2　以奇用兵。

3　以無事取天下。

4　吾何以知其然也？

5　夫天多忌諱，而民彌畔。

6　民多利器，而邦茲昏。

7　人多智，而奇物茲起。

8　法物茲章，而盜賊多有。

CHAPTER 57

1   Employ uprightness when administering a state,

2   and employ irregularity when using forces.

3   Employ no affairs when ruling the world.

It is common knowledge that leaders must "employ uprightness" to achieve order in their countries and "irregularity" on the battlefield to defeat their foes.

What is truly unique here is the idea that leaders should also "never employ affairs when ruling the world" (which echoes the spirit of chapter 48), so the world can be stabilized in the great harmony that is the result of conforming to self-realization.

4   How do I know that it is thus?

5   Well, the more taboos rulers have, then the worse their people's disobedience will be.

6   The more schemes their people have, then the vaster the country's turmoil will be.

7   The shrewder individuals are, then the vaster the rise of aberrations will be.

8   The clearer the standards of measurement are, then the greater the number of thieves and bandits will be.

These examples help us understand why this is so:

When leaders do not ensure the cessation of all affairs under their governance, they will need to rely on prohibitions so strict that their people will turn on them.

At the very least, these affairs will lead to opportunistic intrigues among their people and a reliance on individual "shrewdness." This will then weaken societal order through "aberrations."

Finally, "standards of measurement" set out to regulate valuation, but this in turn will provide criminals with the tools they need to purloin commodities.

9 是以，聖人之言曰：

10 我無事而民自富；

11 我無為而民自化；

12 我好靜而民自正；

13 我欲不欲而民自樸。

9   That is why the words of sages declare:

10   When we have no affairs, then the people will prosper on their own;

11   when we exert non-effort, then the people will become cultivated on their own;

12   when we cling to stillness, then the people will settle on their own;

13   when we desire to desire not, then the people will be with the Essential on their own.

Perfect governance arises from the cultivation of leaders and their conformity to self-realization, for this is what will deter them from instigating affairs or exerting effort. Thus, through their serenity, these leaders will give their people peaceful lives; and by transcending desires, they will lead their people to become artless on their own.

第五十八章

1 其政悶悶，

2 其民屯屯。

3 其政察察，

4 其邦央央。

5 禍，福之所倚。

6 福，禍之所伏。

7 孰知其極？

8 其無正也，

9 正復為奇，

10 善復為妖——

11 人之迷也，

12 其日固久矣。

13 是以，方而不割，

CHAPTER 58

1   If a government is oblivious,

2   then its people will be artless.

3   If a government is surveillant,

4   then its state will be fractured.

5   Misfortune is where fortune originates.

6   Fortune is where misfortune is hidden.

7   Who knows what their ends will be?

8   These will have no certainty,

9   as the moral turn immoral

10 and the good turn evil—

11 and man's confusion will verily persist

12 for days without number.

13 Therefore, be as a square, but one that does not divide;

Leaders are here offered guidance in four areas on how to administer their countries.
   The first has to do with governance. "Oblivious" suggests that the leaders are allowing their people to achieve self-realization through non-effort and thereby pursue "artless" lives. But when leaders are "surveillant," they are distrustful and desire control, which inevitably causes great societal rifts.

The second has to do with the pursuit of fortune and the avoidance of misfortune. Because these two are always cyclical, any single-minded attempts to gamble with them will lead to unforeseen results.

The third is that things may be done for an ostensibly moral purpose or with good intentions, but—as suggested in lines 6 and 7—we are unable to control how they will ultimately turn out. (However, when viewed from a transcendental perspective, the means for perfection becomes clear.)

The fourth includes exhortations on how to properly rule a country in accordance with the Dao:
   Regulations (which are akin to the confinement of "squares") should accommodate all.

14 廉而不刺，

15 直而不肆，

16 光而不耀。

14   as a sharpness, but one that does not wound;

Constraints (which are akin to the "sharpness" of a blade) should harm no one.

15   as a straightness, but one that does not transgress;

Directness (which is akin to the "straightness" of a line) should never be excessive.

16   as a brightness, but one that does not glare.

Clarity (which is akin to the "brightness" that exposes differentiation) should never become discriminatory.

第五十九章

1　治人事天莫若嗇。

2　夫唯嗇，是以早服。

3　早服，是謂重積德。

4　重積德，則無不克。

5　無不克，則莫知其極。

6　莫知其極，可以有國。

7　有國之母，可以長久—

8　是謂深根固柢，長生久視之道也。

CHAPTER 59

1   In ruling men and cultivating the self, nothing surpasses husbandry.

"Husbandry" in this chapter refers to a parsimonious approach to governing, which gives rise to a minimalist—yet effective—control. The grasp of this concept will determine the success of a country and even a person's life.

2   Oh, it is because of husbandry that there then is obtainment beforehand.

3   Obtainment beforehand is deemed a twofold accrual of the De.

4   A twofold accrual of the De leads to omnipotence.

This suggestion that husbandry is innately parsimonious does not advocate tightfistedness, but rather sets the stage for all things to achieve self-realization.

No form of governing could be simpler than this, for it ensures that leaders will be able to obtain the De "beforehand"—that is, before actions have even begun.

"Twofold accrual of the De" means that this "obtainment" of the De will protect both the people and the leader, and in this way, they will prove unassailable.

5   Omnipotence leads to having no known limitations.

6   And in having no known limitations, one will be able to safeguard the country.

This "omnipotence" will allow the leader's influence to spread throughout the world, and in turn provide the ability to secure the country.

7   Safeguarding the country through retaining the Mother allows one to endure—

8   this is known as "the Dao of being deeply rooted and firmly established, of being the long-lived and enduring."

Husbandry is in fact achieved through non-effort, which gives the leader the wherewithal to fully cling to the Dao as "the Mother." This will then serve as a permanent safeguard from a decline in the leader's self and the country.

第六十章

---

1 治大國若烹小鮮。

2 以道立天下，其鬼不神。

3 非其鬼不神也、

4 其神不傷人也。

5 非其神不傷人也、

6 聖人亦弗傷也。

7 夫兩不相傷，

8 故德交歸焉。

CHAPTER 60

1   Administering a large country is like
cooking small fish.

*The success of governance can only
be cautiously achieved when it is in
accord with non-effort (as suggested
in line 2 [i.e., "overseen through
the Dao"] below), a concept that
applies to everything from cooking a
small fish to reigning over a country.
Therefore, this truth is universal
and can be adapted to things that
are either small and unimportant or
large and significant.*

2   When the world is overseen through the
Dao, its specters will not arise.

3   It is not just that its specters will not arise,

4   for their arising will do no one harm.

5   It is not just their arising that will do no one
harm,

6   for sages will also do no one harm.

*A world that is "overseen through
the Dao" will always conform to
self-realization (chapter 25) and
thereby achieve harmony. Because
of this, the world's "specters"—
or unforeseen disasters—will not
arise. Even if one were to appear,
it would not become disastrous
because of the harmony secured
by the Dao, as well as the leaders'
wise guidance.*

7   Since these two will harm neither,

8   the De of both will thus be conferred unto
them.

*Therefore, when a country is
administered in accordance with
the Dao, its people (expressed
here as "them") will be able
to exist in the state of peaceful
contentment provided by the De
(chapter 38, footnote).*

第六十一章

1   大邦者下流也，

2   天下之牝，天下之交也。

3   牝恆以靜勝牡—

4   為其靜也，故宜為下。

5   故大邦以下小邦，則取小邦；

6   小邦以下大邦，則取於大邦。

7   故或下以取，或下而取。

8   故大邦者，不過欲兼畜人；

9   小邦者，不過欲入事人。

CHAPTER 61

1   A large state is the downstream,

2   the world's female, the convergence of the world.

This metaphor illustrates how a major power becomes a center of gravity in the world by attracting diplomatic relationships (see lines 5–7 below), much like a river's downstream where all currents must run to, or like a female animal that attracts all nearby males.

3   Females always win over males through stillness—

4   and due to their stillness, it is thus proper that they efface themselves.

In animal courtship rituals, females employ stillness to control their suitors. This passage therefore suggests that female animals attract males much in the same way that gravity guides water downstream.

5   That is why a large state will efface itself before a small state, so as to acquire the small state;

6   and a small state will efface itself before a large state, so as to be acquired by the large state.

7   Thus, there is either self-effacement to acquire or self-effacement to be acquired.

By the same logic, when building diplomatic relationships, a major power should appear humble to win over the assent of a minor power.
Likewise, a minor power should appear humble when seeking alliance with a major one.

8   Oh, what a large state desires is to but inclusively unite with others;

9   what a small state desires is to but offer its services to others.

Diplomatic relations between major and minor powers are, at their most basic level, fashioned through the satisfaction of their respective needs, as described here.

10　夫皆得其欲，

11　則大者宜為下。

10   When they both have obtained what they desire,

11   it is proper then for the large one to efface itself.

Based on this perspective, the major power must maintain a humble manner toward the minor power in this alliance, for it is the one that will truly gain.

第六十二章

1 道者萬物之注也。

2 善人之葆也，

3 不善人之所葆也。

---

4 美言可以市，

5 尊行可以賀人。

6 人之不善，

7 何棄之有？

---

8 故立天子，置三卿，

9 雖有共之璧以先四馬，

10 不若坐而進此？

---

11 古之所以貴此者，何也？

12 不謂求以得，有罪以免與？

13 故為天下貴。

CHAPTER 62

1   The Dao is the Ruler of all things.

2   It is that which good people treasure,

3   and is that which cultivates the people who are not good.

4   Beautiful words may be used in transactions,

5   and honorable behavior may exalt people.

6   If people are not good,

7   how could they be forsaken?

8   That is why, when the emperor is enthroned or the three chief ministers are appointed,

9   even though a large jade disc is presented before four horses,

10   would it not be better to kneel and proffer this?

11   This has been valued since the time of yore. Why is that?

12   Is it not said that pleas will then be granted and offenses then pardoned?

13   And so this is what is cherished by the world.

All the world obeys the Dao. It is what good men hold as their cherished standard, and It also works to guide those who have yet to become good.

We often hold people with eloquence and lofty deeds as being exceptionally laudable. But that is not necessarily the case, for everyone is equally worthy of our care. Even those who cannot achieve our expectations of goodness should be seen as the raw material for the making of good people (chapter 27).

Hence, even at ostentatious ceremonies such as inaugurations, when symbolically precious things are offered to honor the highest-ranking officials, it would be much more beneficial to propose the greatest advice of all: that these leaders ought to guide everyone toward becoming good.

"This" refers to the advice that leaders should obey the Dao and guide their people toward becoming good. Thus, whenever individuals who lack goodness decide to become better, they should be forgiven and welcomed.

第六十三章

1 為無為。

2 事無事，

3 味無味。

4 大小。

5 多少。

6 報怨以德。

7 圖難乎其易也；

8 為大乎其細也。

9 天下之難作於易；

10 天下之大作於細。

11 是以，聖人終不為大、

12 故能成其大。

CHAPTER 63

1   Exert effort through non-effort.

Non-effort is the foundation for exerting effort, no affairs is the foundation for managing affairs, and no taste is the foundation for tasting flavors.

2   Manage affairs through no affairs.

3   Taste flavors through no taste.

4   The great come from the small.

Likewise, the small is the foundation for the great and the few for the many.

5   The many come from the few.

6   Respond to spite with kindness.

Kindness acts as the foundation for harmonizing relationships between people through the elimination of malice.

7   Deliberate over a difficulty when it is yet easy;

All difficulties start out easy, just as all great things grow from small. Thus, the key is to exert effort at the beginning when things are still malleable.

8   exert efforts toward greatness when it is yet tiny.

9   Difficulties in the world arise out of the easy;

10   greatness in the world arises out of the tiny.

11   Therefore, sages never exert efforts toward greatness,

Because of the teaching in line 10, the wise will cleave to the tiny, and the achievement of greatness will follow of its own accord.

12   and thus are able to achieve their greatness.

13　夫輕諾必寡信,

14　多易必多難。

15　是以聖人猶難之,

16　故終於無難。

13   Oh, when promises are taken lightly, one will certainly have a dearth of credibility,

Difficulties will also grow out of casual assurances and laziness, causing unnecessary problems.

14   and when there is too much ease, one will certainly have too many difficulties.

15   Therefore, sages ruminate on the difficult,

16   and thus end up with no difficulties.

That is why the wise always attempt to uncover problems at their initial stages when they are still very manageable—this is how they secure themselves and obtain success with ease.

第六十四章

1 其安也，易持也。

2 其未兆也，易謀也。

3 其臘也，易判也。

4 其幾也，易散也。

5 為之於其無有也；

6 治之於其未亂也。

---

7 合抱之木，生於毫末。

8 九成之臺，作於虆土。

9 百仞之高，始於足下。

---

10 為之者，敗之，

11 執之者，失之。

---

12 是以，聖人無為也，故無敗也；

13 無執也，故無失也。

CHAPTER 64

1   That which is stable is easily handled.

2   That which is not yet portended is easily planned.

3   That which is fragile is easily divided.

4   That which is minute is easily dispersed.

5   Exert effort where there is not yet materialization;

6   exercise governance where there is not yet disarray.

Perfect management is always exercised through effortlessness. Such management, though, must be performed while matters either have not yet come into being or are still easily manageable.

7   A tree with the span of several arms emerges like the tip of a hair.

8   A terrace with nine stories arises out of baskets of dirt.

9   A height of several hundred lengths commences from under the feet.

The great always evolve out of the small.

10   Those who exert effort will fail,

11   and those who grasp will lose.

But exerting one's will upon the self-realization of things will predictably have an adverse effect.

12   Therefore, sages exert non-effort, and so will never fail;

13   do not grasp, and so will never lose.

That is why wise leaders are constantly able to ensure their success, because they never permit their will to be exerted and thereby interfere with the self-realization of things.

14　民之從事也，

15　恆於其成而敗之。

16　〔臨事之紀：〕

17　慎終如始，

18　則無敗事矣。

19　是以，聖人欲不欲，

20　不貴難得之貨。

21　教不教，

22　復眾人之所過。

23　是以，能輔萬物之自然，

24　而弗敢為。

14   When people carry out their affairs,

15   they always fail at them when success is at hand.

16   [The canon for overseeing affairs is:]

17   Be as circumspect at the end as at the beginning,

18   and then there will be no failed affairs.

19   Therefore, sages desire to desire not

20   and value not rare goods.

21   They teach through no teaching

22   and turn all people back from their excesses.

23   And so, they are able to assist all things in their self-realization,

24   yet restrain from exerting effort on them.

Constant discretion from the very beginning to the very end is the key to avoiding failure.

Finally, wise leaders must not incite avarice in their people through their own desires and values. They should cease teaching through words or using their own concepts, and thus lead their people into revitalizing their ingenuous nature.

In the same spirit, they must encourage self-realization in all things while never wielding their own will and interfering with them.

第六十五章

1　古之為道者,

2　非以明民也,

3　將以愚之也——

4　民之難治也,以其知也。

5　故以知知邦,

6　邦之賊也;

7　以不知知邦,

8　邦之德也。

9　恆知此兩者,

10　亦稽式也。

11　恆知稽式,

12　此謂玄德。

CHAPTER 65

1   Those who exercised the Dao in the time of yore

2   did not have their people become clever,

3   but rather had them become ingenuous—

4   when people are difficult to rule, this is owing to their shrewdness.

A country's stability is determined by the stability of its people. "Shrewdness" in people will unavoidably disturb the order of constancy in the country, which becomes an impediment to the realization of its government's goals.

5   So, using shrewdness in the governing of a country

6   will be a detriment to that country,

7   and using no shrewdness in the governing of a country

8   will be a boon to that country.

When there is "shrewdness" in people, this is not caused by themselves, but by their government. Thus, a government's guidance should not be confined to merely tasking them to be of service to their country, but also working with them toward determining the country's fate.

9   A comprehensive understanding of these two

10   will then be in conformity with the Standard.

11   A comprehensive understanding of conformity with the Standard

12   is called the "Transcendent De."

In governing, a thorough grasp of the difference between having and not having shrewdness is essential. According to Laozi's teaching, those who govern should heed the spirit of understanding shrewdness while they "cleave to no shrewdness" (as inspired by chapter 28 [lines 1, 7, and 13]). This will permit their governance to be in harmony with the world's ultimate Standard, so they can obtain the "Transcendent De."

13 玄德，深矣、遠矣、

14 與物反矣—

15 乃至大順。

13 The Transcendent De is so profound and
   so far-reaching

14 that It causes things to return—

15 and thereby achieve the Great Accord.

The De is referred to as "transcendent" because It is absolutely unconstrainable, but It is nevertheless able to guide all things through their cyclic progressions back to where they began, and thus create the recurrent order of constancy in the world (chapter 16) that is known as "the Great Accord."

第六十六章

1 　江海所以能為百谷王，

2 　以其能為百谷下，

3 　是以能為百谷王。

4 　聖人之在民前也，

5 　以身後之；

6 　其在民上也，

7 　以言下之。

8 　其在民上也，

9 　民弗厚也；

10 　在民前也，

11 　民弗害也—

12 　天下樂進而弗猒。

13 　以其不爭也，

14 　故天下莫能與之爭。

CHAPTER 66

1   The reason why a great river or sea can be the king of a hundred gorges

The Chinese definition of a "king" was "one who is followed by the world."

This metaphor in lines 1–3 vividly illustrates the way in which the greatest powers are able to efface themselves in order to have all in the world follow them.

2   is because it is positioned lower than the hundred gorges,

3   and so can be the king of the hundred gorges.

4   When sages are positioned at the forefront of their people,

Leaders who learn the wisdom of the rivers and the seas will behave humbly with their people and use respectful words when addressing them.

5   they will place their selves at the hindmost;

6   and when they are above them,

7   will use words to efface themselves.

8   When they are above their people,

Thus, their people will accept them willingly, and their positions will be secured in harmony with them.

9   their people will not be burdened;

10 when at the forefront of their people,

11 their people will not feel antipathy—

12 and the world will delight in following without being enervated by them.

13 It is because they compete not

This description reveals that the true power to induce the world to follow without impediment lies in the wisdom of transcending competition.

14 that no one in the world is thereby able to compete with them.

第六十七章

1 　天下皆謂我大，

2 　大而不肖。

3 　夫唯大，故不肖。

4 　若肖，細久矣。

5 　我恆有三葆——

6 　持而葆之：

7 　一曰慈、

8 　二曰儉、

9 　三曰不敢為天下先。

10 　夫慈，故能勇，

11 　儉，故能廣，

12 　不敢為天下先，

13 　故能為成事長。

CHAPTER 67

1   All the world proclaims that mine is great,

2   great and yet as naught.

3   Because it is great, it thus is as naught.

4   If it were other than naught, it would have become trivial a long time ago.

5   I always keep to me three treasures—

6   by cleaving to them, I am then secured:

7   the first is profound love,

8   the second is frugality,

9   and the third is a restraint from leading the world.

10   It is profound love that allows for courageousness,

11   frugality that allows for all-inclusiveness,

12   and a restraint from leading the world

13   that allows one to be the sovereign over the success of affairs.

Secular knowledge is dependent upon differentiation, but according to Laozi, everything should be indiscriminately embraced.

"Mine" therefore refers to Laozi's knowledge (according to lines 5–9). Since those who cling to secular perspectives assign differences to everything, they find it easy to criticize Laozi's views.

Laozi describes what the wise use to secure themselves in the world, which consists of three principles.

These principles tell us that real courage arises out of "profound love," much like the courageous protectiveness that a mother shows for her children.

Regarding "frugality," refer to chapter 59's discussion on husbandry.

As for "restraint from leading the world," this means that we (and especially leaders) should not instigate affairs, but rather allow all things to accomplish their goals through self-realization without interference, for this will result in perfect governance.

14 今捨其慈且勇，

15 捨其儉且廣，

16 捨其後且先，

17 則必死矣。

18 夫慈，以戰則勝，

19 以守則固。

20 天將建之，

21 如以慈垣之。

14　If profound love is forsaken in favor of courage,

15　and frugality is forsaken in favor of all-inclusiveness,

16　and staying to the hindmost is forsaken in favor of being at the forefront,

17　death will be inevitable.

Ignoring these principles and striving instead for personal achievement mean that we are being dominated by egocentricity. This in turn creates an ever-widening fissure between our determination and reality, and the results will be unavoidably destructive.

18　Oh, profound love when wielded in battle will lead to victory,

19　and when wielded in defense will lead to undefeatability.

Of all these principles, profound love is the greatest, for the immense courage it provides will subdue any adversary.

20　When there is that which has been established by the heavens,

21　profound love will thereby be wielded to fortify it.

Profound love is what safeguards the existence of all in the world as provided by the heavens, and this conforms to the Dao.

第六十八章

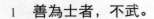

1 善為士者，不武。

2 善戰者，不怒。

3 善勝敵者，弗與。

4 善用人者，為之下。

5 是謂不爭之德；

6 是謂用人；

7 是謂配天，

8 古之極也。

CHAPTER 68

1   Those who achieve perfection as warriors surpass bravery.

2   Those who achieve perfection in battle surpass high morale.

3   Those who achieve perfection in prevailing over the enemy do not engage them.

The spirit of no competition in warfare means warriors do not depend upon bravery, battles are not determined by morale, and victory does not rely upon actual encounters.

4   Those who achieve perfection in employing their men efface themselves before them.

Wise commanders will gain their subordinates' allegiance through a respectful and considerate attitude.

5   This is called "the De of competing not";

Line 5 concludes the discussion in lines 1–3, where each is an actual means to perfectly carry out the spirit of "competing not" in accordance with the requirements of the De.

6   this is called "the employment of men";

Line 6 concludes the discussion in line 4, where the commanders are its subject.

7   this is called "concordance with the heavens"—

8   and was paramount in the time of yore.

Therefore, whoever is able to achieve the objectives in lines 5–6 will be in harmony with the heavens (and in turn conform to the Dao as described in chapter 25). This has proved to be timeless, vital advice on warfare.

第六十九章

1 用兵有言曰：

2 吾不敢為主而為客，

3 不敢進寸而退尺。

4 是謂："行無行，

5 攘無臂，

6 執無兵，

7 扔無敵矣。"

8 禍莫大於無敵，

9 無敵近亡吾葆矣。

10 故稱兵相若，

11 則哀者勝矣。

CHAPTER 69

1 A saying on the use of forces holds that:

2 I restrain myself from being the host, but rather am the guest;

3 and restrain myself from advancing an inch, but rather withdraw a foot.

In this ancient maxim on military affairs, the instigator in a conflict is referred to as "the host," while "the guest" is the responder. This tells us that we should not aggressively initiate challenges, but rather passively avoid direct clashes.

4 This is called "arraying without formations,

5 stretching without arms,

6 wielding without weapons,

7 and engaging without enemies."

Laozi then explains this using different examples that transcend the secular ways in which battles are conducted, and this echoes the teachings of chapter 68.

8 Nothing is more disastrous than taking the enemy lightly.

9 Taking the enemy lightly is tantamount to surrendering our security.

This does not mean that we may disregard the enemy even the slightest, though, for that would result in laying us open to our opponent's offensive actions.

10 When forces are raised of equal strength,

11 then the side with love will prevail.

In the end, if we match our opponents in strength, the side with love for one another will prove victorious. (This theory echoes that of chapter 67.)

第七十章

1　吾言甚易知也，

2　甚易行也，

3　而人莫之能知也，

4　而莫之能行也。

5　言有君，

6　事有宗。

7　夫唯無知也，

8　是以不我知。

9　知者希，則我貴矣。

10　是以，聖人被褐而懷玉。

CHAPTER 70

1 My words are so easily comprehended,

2 so easily put into practice,

3 yet people cannot comprehend them,

4 nor can they put them into practice.

Because Laozi's words are in accord with the Dao and conform to self-realization (chapter 25), understanding and acting upon them ought not be problematic. But when people have difficulty shuffling off their sense of the self, their comprehension will rely solely upon discrimination, and that is why they cannot fathom Laozi's words.

5 Words have their Sovereign

6 and affairs have their Provenance.

Our activities in the world consist of words (the things we say) and affairs (the things we do). Both are founded in what Laozi calls the "Sovereign" and the "Provenance," which can be understood as two names for the Dao, the sole fundament in the world.

7 It is due to ignorance

8 that they thus do not comprehend that which is mine.

Words that embody the Sovereign of the Dao will always transcend secular perceptions and surpass even the highest evaluations of others.

9 When those who comprehend are few, then that which is mine becomes precious.

10 Therefore, sages will clothe themselves in coarse garb, but underneath clasp the jade.

The appearance of those who obtain the wisdom of the Dao may thus be unremarkable, but their actual qualities have inestimable value, much like a precious piece of jade held within their unassuming robes.

The description in line 10 seems to be based on Laozi's personal experience, for it teaches us that anyone can be the equal of the sages as long as the wisdom of the Dao is obtained. Therefore, as Laozi was, we may be too.

第七十一章

1 知、不知，尚矣。

2 不知、知，病矣。

___

3 是以，聖人之不病也，

4 以其病病也，

5 是以不病。

CHAPTER 71

1 Viewing the known as the unknown is best.

Assumptions give rise to never-ending problems.

2 Viewing the unknown as the known is troublesome.

3 The reason why sages are never troubled

Awareness of this means the wise understand that they only need to attend to verifiable problems caused by assumptions, and this will make their lives easier.

4 is because they are concerned about troubles,

5 and so are never troubled.

第七十二章

1　民之不畏畏，

2　則大畏將至矣。

3　毋狎其所居，

4　毋猒其所生。

5　夫唯弗猒，

6　是以不猒。

7　是以，聖人自知，

8　而不自見也；

9　自愛，而不自貴也。

10　故去彼取此。

CHAPTER 72

1 If people do not fear that which is fearsome,

2 then that which is most feared is bound to arrive.

Dangers must be recognized for what they are so that we may exercise self-control and take steps beforehand to prevent them from worsening. Leaders, more than anyone else, must never take this lesson lightly.

3 Restrict not where they dwell

4 and constrain not their lives.

5 It is only when they are not constrained

6 that they will be not resentful.

People should be governed without being compelled so that they can find contentment both in their dwellings and in their lives. Compulsion will cause them to hate the ones who govern them, and is what will incite people to "not fear that which is fearsome."

7 For this reason, sages will have self-understanding,

8 but not be self-regarding;

9 will have self-respect, but not be self-important.

As far as the quality of leaders is concerned, they should possess such outstanding personal cultivation that they will be able to wisely efface themselves and not disturb the world through their egocentrism.

10 Thus, forsake that and adopt this.

Proper governance is therefore determined by how leaders conduct themselves within these parameters of cultivation ("this") and not by pursuing personal interests ("that").

第七十三章

1　勇於敢則殺。

2　勇於不敢則活。

3　此兩者，或利或害，

4　天之所惡。

5　孰知其故？

6　天之道，不戰而善勝；

7　不言而善應；

8　弗召而自來；

9　墠而善謀。

10　天網恢恢。

11　疏而不失。

CHAPTER 73

1   A courage that is unrestrained will lead one to be killed.

Courage has two forms: reckless and cautious. If we are brave but reckless, we will not live long. A cautiously brave person has a much better chance of surviving.

2   A courage that is restrained will lead one to survive.

Nevertheless, neither of these types of courage finds favor with the heavens. The reason for this can be found in chapter 25: "The heavens conform to the Dao, and the Dao conforms to self-realization."

3   These two are either beneficial or detrimental,

4   yet are what the heavens spurn.

Therefore, while courage is considered by mankind to be a sublime quality, it requires the effort of will, which is not in accord with the Dao of the heavens, as discussed in the next passage.

5   Who knows why this is so?

6   The Dao of the heavens does not contend, and yet has perfected prevailing;

The heavens always reflect the Dao through the implementation of self-realization without competition.

7   has no words, and yet has perfected responding;

8   is never summoned, and yet willingly arrives;

9   is lax, and yet has perfected reckoning.

10 The heavens' Net is so immense.

This metaphor suggests how sublime governance may appear to its people: the heavens embrace the world as if they were an endless net, allowing all things to enjoy their lives within an environment that may appear lenient, but is in fact exacting.

11 Though slack, It misses nothing.

第七十四章

1　若民恆且不畏死，

2　奈何以殺懼之也？

3　若民恆且畏死，

4　而為奇者，

5　吾將得而殺之。

6　夫孰敢矣？

7　若民恆且必畏死，

8　則恆有司殺者。

9　夫代司殺者殺，

10　是代大匠斲也。

11　夫代大匠斲者，

12　則希不傷其手矣。

CHAPTER 74

1   If the people are never truly frightened of death,

2   why use killing to threaten them?

3   If the people are always truly frightened of death,

4   and yet there are transgressors,

5   we shall arrest and kill them.

6   Who then will lack restraint?

7   If the people are always truly frightened of death,

8   then there will always be an executioner.

9   When taking the place of an executioner to kill,

10   this will be like taking the place of the Great Artisan to hew.

11   Those who take the place of the Grand Artisan to hew

12   will then rarely not harm their own hands.

The threat of capital punishment is useless if no one fears it. On the other hand, even if it is feared, laws will continue to be broken. According to our secular understanding, then, a government must resort to capital punishment to maintain order.

However, we must realize that no one is qualified to carry out capital punishment because this invariably requires standards that are so flawless they surpass human comprehension.

"Taking the place of the Great Artisan" refers to those who think that they may act in the Dao's stead to end a person's natural lifespan. But when we kill, we fall short of flawlessness, and this is what will doom ourselves in the end.

The Great Artisan signifies the spirit of the Dao that allows all things to achieve self-realization, and so, in the case of irredeemable transgressors, they will bring about their own punishment, even though the Dao never abandons anyone (chapters 27, 47, and 62).

第七十五章

1 人之飢也，

2 以其取食稅之多也，

3 是以飢。

4 百姓之不治也，

5 以其上之有以為也，

6 是以不治。

7 民之輕死也，

8 以求生之厚也，

9 是以輕死。

10 夫唯無以生為者，

11 是賢貴生。

CHAPTER 75

1 When men starve,

2 it is because their taxes have been levied too heavily,

3 and so they starve.

4 When subjects become ungovernable,

5 it is because their superiors are intentionally exerting effort,

6 and so they become ungovernable.

7 If people take death lightly,

8 it is because what they pursue in their lives has become too inordinate,

9 and so they take death lightly.

10 Oh, only those who do not exert effort in their lives

11 are able to perfectly treasure life.

The most important duty of all countries' leaders is to ensure that everyone is fed. Taxes therefore must be levied lightly in order that all have enough resources to live.

The basic requirement for good governance is that its subjects be allowed to live their own lives in peace. If a government continually imposes itself on them, their lives will suffer from this endless disturbance, and they will eventually become disobedient.

Moreover, leaders must understand this: People will always want to augment their lives in ways that might jeopardize their existence.

Therefore, leaders who understand how to relieve their people from the burdens inherent in living will be able to guide them toward understanding the value of their lives.

第七十六章

1 人之生也柔弱，

2 其死也橆信堅強。

3 萬物草木之生也柔脆，

4 其死也枯槁。

5 故曰：堅強，死之徒也；

6 柔弱，生之徒也。

7 是以，兵強則不勝；

8 木強則恆。

9 故強大居下，

10 柔弱居上。

CHAPTER 76

1   People when born are soft and weak,

We know from our own experiences that the life force of the newly born is tender and delicate, which is characterized here as being "soft," "weak," and "fragile." But when it reaches the end of its lifespan, it becomes "hard," "rigid," "shriveled," and "withered."

2   and at their deaths lie stretched out, hard, and rigid.

3   All things, the grasses and the trees, when born are soft and fragile,

4   and at their deaths are shriveled and withered.

5   It is therefore said that the hard and the rigid are the dead,

Thus, death is characterized by hardness and rigidity, while life is characterized by softness and weakness.

6   while the soft and the weak are the living.

7   This is why forces that are rigid will not prevail,

This natural law can therefore be applied to human behavior, for just as a tree that cannot bend will fall and die, a military operation will fail if it lacks the flexibility provided by softness.

8   and trees that are rigid will fall down.

9   Hence, the rigid and the great are positioned low,

From this, we may learn that the soft and the weak are always elevated in the natural world, while the rigid and the large are situated below them, as demonstrated by the trees around us that have tender growth at the top and thick, heavy branches at the bottom.

10   while the soft and the weak are positioned high.

第七十七章

1　天之道猶張弓者也?

2　高者抑之,

3　下者舉之——

4　有餘者損之,

5　不足者補之。

6　故天之道,

7　損有餘而補不足。

8　人之道則不然:

9　損不足而奉有餘。

10　孰能有餘而有以取奉於天者乎?

11　唯有道者乎!

CHAPTER 77

1   Is this how the heavens behave, like a drawn bow?

2   With the top pulled down

3   and the bottom raised—

4   where there is surplus, they decrease,

5   and where deficient, they supplement.

6   And so, the heavens behave

7   by decreasing surplus and supplementing deficiency.

8   How people behave, though, is otherwise:

9   they diminish where there are deficiencies and proffer this up to where there are surpluses.

10 Who is able to have surpluses, and then extract some to proffer up as the heavens do?

11 Only those who are with the Dao!

When a bow is drawn, its top and bottom move in balanced harmony to transfer their energy to the arrow.

This metaphor is meant to illustrate how the performance of the heavens conforms to the Dao (chapter 25): by decreasing where there is more and supplementing where there is less, and thereby creating a perfect state of harmony that transfers their energy to all life in the world.

Humans, on the other hand, destroy the harmony of the One by calculatedly appropriating wherever there is paucity to augment places where there is already plenty, making the less even less and the more even more.

For that reason, we must learn from the wisdom of the heavens by ensuring that the needs of all people and things are satisfied, thereby guaranteeing the healthy existence of all life in the world. Laozi's highest praise is thus reserved for "those who are with the Dao."

12 是以，聖人為而弗有，

13 成功而弗居也——

14 若此其不欲見賢也。

12 That is why sages exert effort, but not to possess,

13 and realize success, but not to control—

14 and so it follows that they never want to reveal what has been achieved.

The wise—and especially good leaders—will therefore follow these teachings to better the world through the transcendence of the sense of the self. Their achievements will thereby be perfectly realized without any personal desires, for they are allowing the world to achieve self-realization.

第七十八章

1 天下莫柔弱於水，

2 而攻，堅強者莫之能先也——

3 以其無以易之也。

4 柔之勝剛也，

5 弱之勝強也。

6 天下莫弗知也，

7 而莫之能行也。

8 故聖人之言云曰：

9 "受邦之垢，

10 是謂社稷之主。

11 受邦之不祥，

12 是謂天下之王"——

13 正言若反。

CHAPTER 78

1   Nothing in the world is softer or weaker than water,

2   and yet when struck, nothing hard or rigid can surpass it—

3   for it is that which cannot be changed.

No power is greater than that which "cannot be changed," and no quality surpasses an absolute softness and weakness that perfectly benefits all (chapter 43). Water embodies both of these characteristics.

4   The soft prevail over the hard

5   and the weak prevail over the rigid:

6   None in the world know not of these,

7   and yet none are able to behave as these.

It is amazing how water is so soft, yet it can penetrate the hardest stone, or how—though seemingly weak—it can wear away a mountain. Who among us is able to perfectly emulate this spirit?

8   Hence, the words of sages hold that:

9   "Those who have shouldered the disgrace of their states

10   are called the lords of their domains,

11   and one who has shouldered the misfortunes of the states

12   is called the king of the world"—

13   true words that seem otherwise.

When leaders adopt the spirit of water as their own, this will allow them to bear ultimate responsibility for their people, including a shouldering of their disgrace. The supreme leader of the world then must be ultimately responsible to all states to the point where the leader will be willing to suffer on their behalf.

We think of leaders as possessing positions of unimaginable power, when in fact their positions must be based on their ability to bear full responsibility for all.

第七十九章

1 和大怨，必有餘怨，

2 焉可以為善？

3 是以，聖人執左介，

4 而不以責於人。

5 故有德司介，

6 無德司徹。

7 夫天道無親——

8 恆與善人。

CHAPTER 79

1   Great animosities may be appeased, yet in the end some animosities will linger.

Deep-seated hatreds are almost impossible to erase, for scars will remain.

2   How could perfection be thereby attained?

3   This is why sages carry the left side of agreements,

4   but make no demands of others.

With an eye to avoiding this, wise leaders will treat their people as if they were entering into legal obligations with them (like the ancient custom of holding the left side of an agreement—see the comment on line 3), and thereby ensure that they have satisfied the requirements of their people, rather than requiring that their people satisfy them.

5   Thus, those who possess the De are concerned with agreements,

6   while those who do not possess the De are concerned with clarifications.

Based on this spirit, those who embrace the cultivation of the De that brings contentment to all will be concerned with whether their pacts are being harmoniously fulfilled, while those who are not of the De will be concerned with whether things are right or wrong.

7   Oh, the Dao of the heavens favors no one—

8   It is always in accord with good men.

The Dao of the heavens is impartial, but It never fails to safeguard those who possess the perfection of the De.

第八十章

1 小邦寡民，

2 使十百人之器毋用，

3 使民重死而遠徙。

4 有舟車，無所乘之。

5 有甲兵，無所陳之。

6 使民復結繩而用之。

7 甘其食，

8 美其服，

9 樂其俗，

10 安其居。

CHAPTER 80

1   A small state with few people

2   has instruments that require ten to one hundred men never be used,

3   and has its people care about their dead and not move away.

4   They have boats and carts, but no place to ride them.

5   They have armor and weapons, but no place to deploy them.

6   It has its people retrieve knotted cords and use them.

7   They take joy in their meals,

8   delight in their clothing,

9   rejoice in their customs,

10   and are happy in their dwellings.

This chapter describes Laozi's idea of a utopia. When a state is small and its population sparse, its affairs naturally become few and simple.

"Instruments that require ten to one hundred men" are never used, which means that no great projects here demand huge outlays of human labor.

This society achieves its stability by having its people be willingly tethered to their land through emotional ties to their ancestors and other deceased loved ones.

"No place to ride" boats and carts indicates that the people here do not need to travel far for any reason, even though they are well equipped. "No place to deploy" armor and weapons tells us that this state is at peace with the world, but even so they remain well prepared.

When lives reach this level of simplicity, primitive knotted cords suffice to deliver messages.

What they know in their lives is nothing but serenity and gladness.

11 鄰國相望，

12 雞狗之聲相聞，

13 民至老死，

14 不相往來。

11   Neighboring states might catch glimpses of
     each other

12   and hear the sounds of each other's
     chickens and dogs,

13   but until these people grow old and die,

14   they will never consort with each other.

Because they live such contented lives in isolation, they have no needs or interest in the outside world, to the extent that they even ignore the states that lie just beyond their borders.

第八十一章

1 信言不美；

2 美言不信。

3 知者不博；

4 博者不知。

5 善者不多；

6 多者不善。

---

7 聖人無積，

8 既以為人已愈有，

9 既以予人已愈多。

---

10 故天之道，利而不害；

11 人之道，為而弗爭。

CHAPTER 81

1 Truthful words are not beautiful,

2 and beautiful words are not truthful.

3 Wisdom then is not broad knowledge,

4 and broad knowledge then is not wisdom.

5 The perfect then are not the many,

6 and the many then are not the perfect.

7 Sages hoard naught,

8 for by devoting themselves unreservedly to others, they possess more,

9 and by giving of themselves unreservedly to others, their selves are given more.

10 Oh, the Dao of the heavens will benefit, but not harm.

11 And the Dao of man will exert effort, but without competing.

In this chapter, Laozi specifically points out that the truth is straightforward and unadorned, while flowery words should be considered suspect.

The wide-ranging knowledge mankind admires—which is actually little more than information—is not true wisdom, for Laozi teaches us that it is that which solely cleaves to the Dao.

And, while perfection lies in simplicity, complexity leads to conflict.

Moreover, the wise transcend their selves and become absolutely selfless by constantly giving, thus creating a rich environment secured through mutual kindness.

As the conclusion of this book, Laozi imparts to us the knowledge that two ultimate spirits exist in our world: "the Dao of the heavens," which supplies nothing but good to all things so they may exist in a state of bliss, and "the Dao of man" (that applies to all of us, but especially the world's leaders), which requires noncompetition to achieve perfection.

COMMENTS ON THE
TRANSLATION

LEFT COLUMN FORMAT. These numbers refer to the lines within the chapter. MN refers to a margin note on that line.

RIGHT COLUMN FORMAT. In bold type: Chinese character(s) or margin note citation, romanization (English translation as it appears in this book), followed by a colon. All Chinese characters in the discussion are accompanied by their English romanization in italics. English translations of the Chinese characters will either be in parentheses or quotes. Throughout the book, only traditional (not simplified) Chinese characters are used. The order of the entries follows that of the Chinese text.

ENDNOTE FORMAT. Parentheses will contain additional information about where the cited source is located. For example:

- V2 means Volume 2.
- Words like "jiaogu," "shigu," etc., refer to annotations and discussions in that cited book and are not italicized.
- A dictionary source will cite the character as "天1," meaning that this is the first definition for that character.
- Page numbers are listed last.
- In the endnotes, Chinese characters will not be accompanied by romanization or translations, as anyone who is interested in this level of scholarship will be expected to be fluent in written classical Chinese.
- All sources mentioned in the comments and endnotes, along with their full publishing information, are provided in the bibliography.

CHAPTER 1

1 道 **dào**: This character was first used in the Chinese text as a noun, which had many definitions in ancient Chinese. For example, it could mean a "directive canon," "method," "governance," and "teaching,"[1] or refer to "ethical guidance," "humanity," "justice," "rites," and "intellect."[2] Most important, 道 *dào* encompassed concepts such as 理 *lǐ* (axiom)[3] and 教令 *jiàolìng* (decree).[4]

　　Nearly all English translations, though, literally render this character as "the way." Yet, "the way" cannot encompass those important concepts. Moreover, Laozi describes the 道 *Dào* as being so profound and so beyond our ordinary comprehension that no words can ever precisely describe It (chapters 14 and 25). When all of these facts are taken into consideration, it becomes apparent that It should simply be referred to as "the Dao."

1 道 **dào**: The second 道 *dào* character here acted as a verb and meant 說 *shuō* (to speak [of]; to be spoken [of]).[5]

1 也 **yě** [mood word]: Here, this character meant that this sentence is a positive statement.[6]

2 恆 **héng** (eternal): This character was used as an adjective here in the earliest extant texts, but in the received versions, this was changed to the character 常 *cháng* (lit., constant), because 恆 *Héng* was the given name of the Han Wendi emperor, and so became a taboo character.

1–4 MN **The immutable and everlasting Dao transcends the constraints of language:** Chapter 25 (line 4) describes the Dao as "solitary and immutable." For "transcends the constraints of language," see chapter 14 (lines 11–12).

3 名 **míng** (defined): The second 名 *míng* character was used as a verb here. It denoted 明 *míng* (lit., to clarify),[7] and here conveyed "to indicate a fact" or "to define."[8]

5 無名 **wúmíng** (that which has no name): This signified "the Dao" (chapter 32 [line 1] and chapter 25 [lines 1–7]). 無名 *wúmíng* literally meant "has no name," but we referred to the mention of 兩者 *liǎngzhě* (these two) in line 9 to modify this interpretation as "that which has no name." 有名 *yǒumíng* in line 6 was interpreted as "that which has a name" using the same reasoning.

5 萬物之始 **wànwù zhī Shǐ** (the Origin of all things): To the ancient Chinese, 萬 *wàn* represented the extremity of numbers,[9] which is expressed here as "all." 始 *Shǐ* (the Origin) refers to the birth of things, which is still related to the Dao and therefore capitalized (chapter 51 [lines 1 and 7] and chapter 52 [line 1]).

6 有名 **yǒu míng** (that which has a name): This tells us that "the Dao" lies in the realm of things, as described in chapter 52 (line 1); see also chapter 25 (lines 1–7) and chapter 51 (lines 7–10). From chapter 20 (line 23)—"through cherishing nourishment from the Mother"—we can see that the Mother is the name of that One from whom "nourishment may be obtained" in the world.

6 萬物之母 **wànwù zhī Mǔ** (the Mother of all things): *Shijing* has the line, "Oh father who begets me. Oh mother who fosters me."[10] This reflects the Zhou dynasty (1046–256 BCE) belief that a mother is mainly responsible for nourishing and caring for her offspring. More references of this line can be found in chapter 25 (lines 1–5), chapter 52 (line 1), and chapter 51 (lines 7–10).

7   恆 *héng* (**always**): This character was used as an adverb here (refer to the comment on line 2 above).

7–8 欲 *yù* (**innate response**): In modern Chinese, this is written as 慾 *yù* (desire). A discussion in *Liji* ("*Yueji*") was used to determine the correct meaning of this character.[11]

7   其眇 *qi miǎo* (**their minuteness**): The Dao is imperceptible (chapter 14). So, we know that 其 *qí* [third person possessive] must have referred to "all things" and is therefore interpreted here as "their." As for 眇 *miǎo*, when things are initially created, they take the form of minuteness.[12]

8   噭 *jiǎo* (**pursue**): This follows the Beida version (in particular, the discussion in its endnote 3) to be read as an interchangeable character, 徼 *jiǎo*, which meant 求 *qiú* (attempt to obtain),[13] and so this is interpreted here as "to pursue."

10   謂 *wèi* (**idea**): In this instance, 謂 *wèi* was used to indicate 旨趣 *zhǐqù* (denotation; idea).[14]

11   玄 *xuán* (**transcendent**): This character was defined as either 幽遠 *yōuyuǎn* (so distant that it is indistinct)[15] or 深隱 *shēnyǐn* (profoundly hidden).[16] Wang Bi's note explains that 玄 *xuán* meant 冥 *mǐng* (obscure), as well as being 默然無有 *mòrán wúyǒu* (as silent as a nonbeing). Therefore, 玄 *xuán* is a state that lies beyond our perceptive abilities, and so "transcendent" is used as its translation.

12   眾眇之門 *zhòngmiǎo zhī Mén* (**the Gate for the multitude of minuteness**): This is the description of the birth of all things. For 眇 *miǎo*, see the third comment on line 7 above. 門 *Mén* (the Gate) acted as a metaphor for where all things emerge.[17] As chapter 51 (line 1) says: "The Dao engenders all."

9–12 MN **This demonstrates that no difference . . . the Origin and the Mother:** See chapter 52 (line 1).

9–12 MN **They are rooted in the same Reality:** The description in chapter 51 (lines 7–10) teaches us that this "Reality" is actually "the Dao." We are thereby able to further comprehend that "the Origin" and "the Mother" are names for the Dao when It performs in different ways.

9–12 MN **One that lies in the absolute unknown:** As shown, "the transcendent within the transcendent" describes "the Dao" Itself, while "the Origin" and "the Mother" of all things were used to signify the different roles of the Dao in engendering and nurturing things.

CHAPTER 2

1–2 天下皆知 . . . 不善矣 *tiānxià jiē zhī* . . . *búshàn yǐ* (**in the world . . . not good**): These two lines are concerned with the failures of man's secular concepts. Similar arguments can be found in chapter 20 (lines 2–3). 天下 *tiānxià* ([in] the world) literally meant "under the heavens" and indicated the corporeal world. However, here it was used to refer to all the people in the world, as implied by 皆知 *jiēzhī* (all know), as 皆 *jiē* indicated "all." The concept of "in the world" offered the proper context to allow this term to be understood as indicating "all people."

2   其 *qi* (**then**): This character was used here to mean 則 *zé* (then).[1]

3–8 有無 . . . 先後之相隨也 *yǒu wú* . . . *xiānhòu zhī xiāngsuí yě* (**being and void . . . first and last surely succeed each other**): Pairs of coexisting polarized counterparts are prevented from binding together by themselves due to their opposite attributes, which shows that they have to rely on the neutral power of the Dao (as inspired by chapter 34 [lines 1–2] and chapter 25 [line 21]) to unite them in equilibrium. There are six 之 *zhī* characters (lit., of) in these lines; all were used to mean 必 *bì* (surely).[2]

4 　相成 ***xiāngchéng*** (**realize each other**): As a verb, 成 *chéng* meant "to accomplish." In this line, "accomplish" was used to suggest that they "make each other be assured" (margin note on lines 1–2), and so this is interpreted as "to realize."

6 　盈 ***yíng*** (**fully embrace each other**): This character was defined as 莫不有 *mòbùyǒu* (to include without exception),[3] and is modified accordingly.

7 　音聲 ***yīnshēng*** (**pitches and sounds**): Generally, these two characters could be used interchangeably, but strictly speaking, 音 *yīn* were the five musical pitches or tunes (which in Chinese were called 宮 *gōng*, 商 *shāng*, 角 *jiǎo*, 徵 *zhǐ*, and 羽 *yǔ*), while 聲 *shēng* were the sounds made by the corresponding musical instruments.[4] These ancient concepts differ greatly from today's understanding of music.

9 　聖人 ***shèngrén*** (**sages**): Laozi always employed this term to describe those who cleave to the Dao. In his teachings, these people could be more specifically referred to as: a) wise sovereigns or leaders (as here), b) great teachers who hand down wise teachings (chapter 57 [line 9]), or c) perfectly cultivated people (chapter 70 [line 10]). The specific type of person would be determined through context.

9 　居 ***jū*** (**administer**): In this case, 居 *jū* was read as 處 *chù* (to administer).[5]

9 　無為 ***wúwéi*** (**non-effort**):[6] Wang Bi's note explains that whenever 自然 *zìrán* (self-realization)[7] is sufficient, exerted effort will fail. Non-effort therefore conforms to "self-realization."[8] "Effort" describes the attempts by people to force things into surrendering to their requirements and desires. When they do this, it invariably results in damage to their world. This is why Laozi urged us "to assist all things in their self-realization, yet restrain from exerting effort on them" (chapter 64 [lines 23–24]).

10 　不言 ***bùyán*** (**no words**): Chapter 24 (line 1) tells us that "In silent words lies self-realization." Thus, issuing "teachings with no words" is done in the same spirit as "non-effort" (see third comment above on line 9). "No words" suggested communicating through silence. We employ "words" to express our will and ideas, and so this concept of "no words" means that we are no longer exerting our will or ideas on others. (For further reference, see chapter 35 [lines 7–11].)

11–12 　萬物作 . . . 而弗恃也 ***wànwù zuò . . . ér fú shì yě*** (**all things rise . . . but without being confined**): Similar descriptions can be found in chapter 10 (lines 14–15) and chapter 51 (lines 11–13). 作 *zuò* (rise) was defined as 起 *qǐ* (to rise).[9] When the adverb 弗 *fú* (without) was used in classical Chinese, the verb's object was omitted.[10] (So, in English, the grammatical pattern here ought to have been "not . . . [object]." But because this line is translated using the passive voice, this sentence pattern is not obvious.) 恃 *shì* was read here as its interchangeable character 持 *chí* (lit., to hold); we have modified this as "to be confined" to fit the context.[11]

11–13 　萬物作而弗司也 . . . 成而弗居也 ***wànwù zuò ér fúsī yě . . . chéng ér fújū yě*** (**all things rise, but without being manipulated . . . [and] become realized, but without being possessed**): Similar descriptions can be found in chapter 10 (lines 14–15) and chapter 51 (lines 11–13). 居 *jū* (possessed) was defined as 據 *jù* (lit., to grip),[12] which has been modified to mean "to be possessed."

CHAPTER 3

1–2 不上賢, 使民不爭 *bùshàng xián, shǐ mín bùzhēng* (**prize not the talented to make people not compete**): When we treasure people's talents, we are in effect encouraging people to compete for the advantages that accompany fame.[1] That is why, when employing someone's talents, we must never laud them.[2] In ancient times, 上 *shàng* (to prize) could be read as 尚 *shàng* (to exalt; to prize).[3]

3–4 不貴難得之貨, 使民不為盜 *búguì nándé zhī huò, shǐ mín bù wéi dào* (**treasure not rare valuables to make people not become thieves**): 貨 *huò* (mod. Ch., goods) was used here to refer to 珍寶 *zhēnbǎo* (valuables),[4] while 難得 *nándé* meant "difficult to obtain," and so "rare." In ancient Chinese, 盜 *dào* (mod. Ch., to steal) was defined as 竊賄 *qièhuì* (to steal valuables; to be a thief),[5] and because this character was used here as a noun, we have interpreted it as "thieves" (see chapter 57 [endnotes 16 and 17]). If we treasure rare valuables, this will incite people to gain them by any means possible, including theft.[6] Therefore, even when we possess rare items, we must understand that they are in reality merely things, and their value is only a false impression formed by secular ideas.[7]

5–6 不見可欲, 使民不亂 *bùxiàn kěyù, shǐ mín búluàn* (**expose not the desirable to make people not become unruly**): In ancient Chinese, 見 *xiàn* (to expose) had the meaning of 顯 *xiàn* (to reveal);[8] we have modified this as "to expose." (見 has the contemporary pronunciation of *jiàn*, which means "to see.") If we expose people to the things that they desire, we are in effect encouraging them to pursue those desires at all costs. Of course, desires cannot be totally eradicated, so what we can do instead is guide (rather than compel) them to be secured by inducing "a perception of the pure, an embrace of the Essential" (chapter 19 [line 9]).

8 虛其心 *xū qí xīn* (**empty their hearts**): Wang Bi's note explains that "the heart embraces shrewdness," while chapter 57 warns us that such shrewdness will lead to "the rise of aberrations" (line 7). Through shrewdness, 心 *xīn* (the heart) will be overcome by desires. Therefore, having people "empty their hearts" will not only lead to a cessation of aberrations, but they will also be much like what the Tang Xuanzong emperor remarked: "disturbed not by the desirable."

9 實其腹 *shí qí fù* (**fill their bellies**): This meant that we should "ensure people have enough to eat."[9] By extension this means that families should lack nothing.[10]

10 弱其志 *ruò qí zhì* (**soften their wills**): This phrase suggests that "people become cultivated and courteous to each other, without unamiability."[11]

11 強其骨 *qiáng qí gǔ* (**strengthen their bones**): In ancient China, 骨 *gǔ* (bones) were considered "the substance of one's body."[12] So, this phrase meant that we should "cause people's bodies and vigor to be strong."[13]

12 恆使民無知無欲也 *héng shǐ mín wúzhī wúyù yě* (**[and] will always lead to a dearth of shrewdness and desires in their people**): See chapter 19 (lines 9–10) for a clearer understanding of this line.

13 夫 *fú* (**them**): This character was used here as 彼 *bǐ* [third person pronoun],[14] and we interpreted it as "them" to indicate "people."

13 不敢 *bùgǎn* (**restraint**): This term literally meant "to dare not" or "[to have] no audacity." But because this refers to a personal choice, we have used "restraint" to better fit the context.

14 弗為 *fúwéi* (**to exert not**): For "弗 *fú* (not) . . . [object omitted]," see chapter 2 (comment on lines 11–12). In the Chinese term, the object of 為 *wéi* (to exert) was omitted, and that has been reflected here in the English translation. This term meant to exert no efforts that exhibit shrewdness.

CHAPTER 4

1 沖[1] *chōng* (**pulses**): This was defined as 涌繇 *yǒngyáo* (to throb and churn),[2] and so is interpreted here as "to pulse."[3]

1 而 *ér* (**thereby**): This character was used to mean 乃 *nǎi* (thereby).[4]

1 用之 *yòngzhī* (**performs**): 用 *yòng* meant 施行 *shīxíng* (to perform).[5] 之 *zhī* acted as a mood word here and had no inherent meaning.[6]

2 有 *Yǒu* (**Realm**): During the pre-Qin period (prior to 221 BCE), this character could be used to mean 域 *yù* (dominion; realm).[7] Almost all other readings of this chapter took no note of the borrowed characters in these two lines, and so translated them literally as something on the order of: "The Dao is *void*, but performs without fullness [or, exhaustion]."[8]

2 盈 *yíng* (**overflow**): This character is defined as 滿 *mǎn* (full),[9] and this has been modified as "overflow"[10] to better fit the description.

3 淵 *yuān* (**profound**): This was defined as 深 *shēn* (profound).[11] In *Zhuangzi*, there is the line, "Oh, the Dao. In profoundness does It locate,"[12] which perfectly echoes Laozi's description of the Dao.

4 似萬物之宗 *sì wànwù zhī Zōng* (**[It] has dominion over all things by being their Root**): 似 *sì* was used as a borrowed character for 嗣 *sì*,[13] which in ancient Chinese could be used interchangeably with 司 *sī* (to rule).[14] It is thus rendered here as "to have dominion over." (似 *sì* was generally defined as 像 *xiàng* [seem]; however, chapter 34 [lines 1 and 5: "Oh, the Dao. . . . All things follow It"] and chapter 51 [line 7: "The Dao engenders all, fosters all"] tell us that the Dao is actually the Root of all things, and literally reading this character as "seem" would prove problematic to understanding Laozi's philosophy.) 之 *zhī* was used here to mean 為 *wéi* (to be; as),[15] while 宗 *zōng* was defined as 本 *běn* (root).[16] "The Dao . . . is the Essential" according to chapter 32 (line 1), and the Essential is the underpinning for the existence of all (see chapter 51 [lines 1–2: "The Dao engenders . . . things are formed"). As with lines 1–2, most renderings of this line did not take borrowed characters into account, and so offered translations that did not make much sense, such as "[It] *seems* the Root of all things."

5–8 These four lines describe the characteristics by which things appear to us: where "sharpness" exists at the edge of the tangible, "turbulence" lies on the surface of mass, "light" is the luminescent brink of brightness,[17] and "dust" covers the surface of the Earth. But these are only the expressions of their surfaces, not the actualities of their existences, which must lie in their fundaments.

The foundation for all fundaments in our world is the Essential of the Dao (chapter 32 [line 1]). Thus, the Dao may perform the dulling, settling, harmonizing, and equalizing through this Essential that unifies all in a constancy of order. These four lines can also be seen in chapter 56 (lines 5–8), where they are then referred to in line 9 as "Transcendental Sameness."

9　湛 *zhàn* (**peaceful**): This was defined as 安 *ān* (peaceful).[18]

10　似或存 *sì Huò cún* (**[It has] dominion over the existence of the Realm**): 似 *sì* was read as 司 *sī* (to have dominion over [see first comment on line 4 above]). 或 *huò* was the ancient form of the character 域 *yù* (see discussion in endnote 7). When the interchangeable nature of the characters 似 *sì* and 或 *huò* is ignored, as in most readings, this line is interpreted as, "[It] seems and is probably existing."

12　象帝之先 *Xiàng Dì zhī xiān* (**[It] likely preceded Heavenly Providence**): 象 *xiàng* was defined here as 似 *sì* (to seem),[19] and so "likely" is used to interpret it. 帝 *dì* represented 天帝 *Tiāndì* (Heavenly Providence),[20] and that is how it is rendered here. 天帝 *Tiāndì* could also be referred to as 上帝 *shàngdì* (endnote 18), a term that Christians have borrowed and interpreted it as "God" in modern times.

AN IN-DEPTH DISCUSSION ON THE CHARACTER 沖—
APPENDIX TO THE COMMENTS ON CHAPTER 4

Under the entry 盅 *zhōng* in *Shuowen* lies a quote from the *Dao De Jing* that reads, "道盅而用之 *Dào zhōng ér yòng zhī*."

Shuowen's definition of 盅 *zhōng* is 器虚 *qìxū* (the void inside [i.e., the concavity of] a vessel).[21] It should be noted that *Shuowen* was written in the early Eastern Han dynasty by Xu Shen (30–124 CE). Over the ensuing years, due to the high esteem in which Xu's academic authority was held, subsequent scholars believed that 盅 *zhōng* was indeed part of the *Dao De Jing*'s original text and followed this character's meaning to describe the Dao as "a void." What is interesting is that all the received versions of the *Dao De Jing* used the character 沖 *chōng*, but this was believed to have merely been an interchangeable character for 盅 *zhōng*.

However, the character 沖 *chōng* is used throughout silk version B[22] (unearthed in 1973 in the Mawangdui Tombs) and a Western Han dynasty (206 BCE–9 CE) bamboo version (collected by Peking University in 2009, and referred to as the Beida version).[23] Scholars' research[24] has shown[25] that silk version B was written about two hundred years—and the Western Han bamboo version about one hundred years—before Xu Shen wrote *Shuowen*, and so this tells us that the first instance of 盅 *zhōng* being occurred sometime during either the late Western Han or the early Eastern Han dynasty (25–220 CE). We therefore know that the original definition of this character contradicts the universally accepted belief by scholars that 沖 *chōng* was a substitute character for 盅 *zhōng*, for the opposite is true.[26] Moreover, reading this as 沖 *chōng* (pulse) means that the Dao is a tangible existence.

The proof for this can be found in Laozi's own descriptions of the Dao:

- Chapter 21 (lines 3–10) is the first place where he describes the Dao as 物 *wù* (an Entity; lit., a thing), and he then introduces us to Its configuration of the three Elements that form the Entity of the Dao.
- In chapter 25 (lines 1–4), Laozi tells us that "An Entity was mingled into realization," and he then describes how It has the capability to nurture the existence of the world. In line 7, he points out that the name of this Entity was not known, and so people "referred to It as 'the Dao.'" He goes further in chapter 32 (line 1) to declare the Dao as the 樸 *Pǔ* (Essential) that is then portrayed (line 2) as "tiny,"

while in chapter 34 he describes the Dao as being "boundless," that "It can be to the left and to the right."

All these lines prove that, according to Laozi, the Dao is by no means a void, but rather a corporeal Being, even though It lies beyond our perceptive abilities, as can be seen in chapter 14 (lines 1–8), chapter 21 (lines 3–10), and chapter 25 (lines 3–4), where It is described as a substantial solitary Existence. Based on this understanding, we may conclude that the Dao is the ultimate transcendental Being. (Prof. Wang Shumin discerningly pointed out that "the Dao is a substantial Being,"[27] which acts as a strong support for our understanding of the Dao.)

CHAPTER 5

1 不仁 *bùrén* (**favor no one**): 仁 *rén* was defined as 親 *qīn* (to be close to; to prefer),[1] and so "favor" is used to interpret it here. Therefore, 不仁 *bùrén* literally meant "without favoring," and hence is rendered here as to "favor no one."

2 以 *yǐ* (**employ**): This was used here to mean 用 *yòng* (to use; to employ).[2]

2 為 *wéi* (**as**): In this context, this character was read as 如 *rú* (like; as).[3]

2 芻狗 *chúgǒu* (**straw dogs**): Our understanding of this metaphor, as described in the margin note on this line, was derived from *Zhuangzi* ("*Tianyun*").[4] (Notes on this line by Su Che, Fan Yingyuan, Xi Tong, and so forth, all follow this.)

3 聖人 *shèngrén* (**sages**): Laozi used this term here to refer to "wise sovereigns or lords" (chapter 2 [first comment on line 9]).

4 百姓 *bǎixìng* (**all [their] officials**): This term referred to 百官 *bǎiguān* (all officials).[5] In ancient times, commoners did not have surnames, or 姓 *xìng*, as these were reserved for officials with hereditary positions.[6] In modern Chinese, this term means "all people."

6 橐籥 *tuóyuè* (**bellows**): This understanding follows Xi Tong's note, in which he referred to (Han) Gao You's note in *Huainanzi* that defined a 橐 *tuó* as "an inflated airbag" (排橐 *páituó*, which in English is sometimes described as the "lung" of a bellows), while the 籥 *yuè* was the "nozzle" through which the air is directed toward the fire.[7]

7 不屈 *bùqū* (**but never exhausted**): 屈 *qū* was defined here as 竭 *jié* (to be exhausted).[8]

8 愈出 *yùchū* (**generating in abundance**): 愈 *yù* was defined here as 益 *yì* (increasingly).[9] 出 *chū* (lit., to emerge) in this context meant 生 *shēng* (to generate).[10] We therefore modified this term as "generating in abundance."

9 聞 *wén* (**knowledge**): 聞 *wén* was defined here as 知 *zhī* (knowledge).[11]

9 數 *shù* (**measures**): This was read as 術 *shù* (measures).[12] The understanding behind this discussion on lines 7–8 was inspired by chapter 29 (lines 7–10), which we described in its margin note as, "All things in the world must exist in their own ways." Thus, no matter how broad our knowledge is, it will never be great enough to completely grasp things as they truly are.

10 中 *zhōng* (**harmony**): This character (lit., mod. Ch., middle) was defined here as 和 *hé* (harmony).[13]

CHAPTER 6[1]

1 谷神 *Gǔ Shén* (**the Celestial Generating Spirit of the Valley**): Lines 3–4 suggest that 谷 *gǔ* here represents the space between the heavens and the Earth. 神 *shén* (mod.

Ch., deity; god) was defined in *Shuowen* as "the Spirit of the heavens that brings about all things,"[2] and therefore this is interpreted here as "the Celestial Generating Spirit." (Our comprehension of this chapter and its ancient definition suggest that 神 *shén* was used by Laozi to refer to the generating energy of the 道 *Dào*.)

3   門 *Mén* (**Gate**): See chapter 1 (comment on line 12).

4   天地之根 *tiān Dì zhī Gēn* (**the Root of the heavens and the Earth**): There are two kinds of plant roots—a "taproot" that stabilizes the plant and "branch roots" that nurture it.[3] The "Root" here is therefore a metaphor that covers both meanings, for it is used to describe the place where new lives emerge (i.e., the Gate), which is also where the heavens and the Earth may obtain that which allows for their steady existence.

1–4   These four lines illustrate two facts. The first is that life in the world exists as an independent reality, while the second is that the heavens and the Earth must rely on the constant procreation of new lives to exist.

5   縣縣 *miánmián* (**ceaseless**): This term indicates that the modified condition is 不絕 *bùjué* (ceaseless).[4]

6   若存 *ruòcún* (**[It] exists in vagueness**): Wang Bi's note explains, "We may want to say that It exists, but will be unable to perceive Its likeness; we may want to say that it exists not, and yet all things rely on It to live." Literally, this term meant "[It] vaguely exists," but to provide a more fluid reading, this is interpreted as, "It exists in vagueness."

7   用之不勤 *yòng zhī bùqín* (**[while] performing effortlessly**): Wang Bi's note is followed to understand this line, with 不勤 *bùqín* used to suggest 不勞 *bùláo* (effortlessly). This comprehension agrees with "the Dao conforms to self-realization" (chapter 25 [line 21]) and "exerts with non-effort" (chapter 37 [line 1]). 之 *zhī* is a mood word that serves to smoothen the reading.[5]

CHAPTER 7

1–4   If the heavens and the Earth had had to strive to exist, they would have been in competition with all things. But because they transcended their selves, they were able to embrace the world and receive from all things that which has allowed them an everlasting existence. This, then, is the secret to how the heavens and the Earth have been able to endure since time immemorial.[1]

5–8   An analogous discussion can be found in chapter 66 (lines 4–14).

5–8 MN   **We will no longer compete . . . receive their full support:** This echoes the spirit of chapter 23 (lines 13–14).

CHAPTER 8

2   有爭 *yǒuzhēng* (**is magnanimous when competed with**):[1] 有 *yóu* was read here as 宥 *yóu* and meant 寬 *kuān* (to be magnanimous).[2] Water is described by Laozi as being both extremely soft and weak (chapter 78 [line 1]), which contravenes the usual idea of 爭 *zhēng* (defined here as 競 *jìng* [to compete]).[3]

3   幾 *jǐ* (**akin to**): This was defined as 近 *jìn* (to be akin to).[4]

5   心 *xīn* (**centering**): The character 心 *xīn* literally indicated the "heart" or the "center." Because water has no heart, this has been interpreted as referring to what it centers upon,[5] much in the way that our minds or hearts direct us.

5 淵 *yuān* (**depths**): This was defined as 深 *shēn* (depth).[6]

6 天 *Tiān* (**Nature**): In addition to having the meaning of "the heavens" in ancient Chinese, this character could also be understood to mean 自然 *Zìrán*, or "Nature."[7]

8 正善治 *zhèng shàn zhì* (**straightening out perfectly as a criterion**): 正 *zhèng* (lit., straight) was used here to describe a surface of water so still and flat that great carpenters could adapt it as their guide,[8] and so is interpreted here as "a criterion."

11 夫 *fú* (**it**): This was used here to mean 彼 *bǐ* [the third person pronoun][9] and referred here to "water."

11 唯 *wéi* (**for**): This character was used here to mean 以 *yǐ* (because; for).[10]

11 無尤 *wúyóu* (**errs not**): 尤 *yóu* meant 過 *guò* (error; to err),[11] so 無尤 *wúyóu* is interpreted here as "to err not."

CHAPTER 9

1 揶而盈之 *zhí ér yíngzhī* (**conserving that there be overabundance**): 揶 *zhí* should be understood here as 持 *chí* (to hold; to conserve);[1] 之 *zhī* [third person pronoun] acted as the object of the action. (之 *zhī* in line 3 should be read the same way.) Because "conserving" and "overabundance" implied that something was being both grasped and excessive, 之 *zhī* was omitted in the interpretation. (See chapter 4 [line 2] for a previous citation of 盈 *yíng* as meaning "to overflow," while the context here suggests that this is best interpreted as "[there] be overabundance.")

3 揣而允之 *tuán ér yǔnzhī* (**hoarding that there be accumulation**): In ancient Chinese, 揣 *tuán* could be used in the stead of 搏 *tuán* (to concentrate [something]; to hoard).[2] 允 *yǔn* was read as 羣 *qún*,[3] which meant 類聚 *lèijù* (to gather together [by category]; accumulation).[4] (The usual reading of this line is "to hammer while sharpening it," which is out of place between the descriptions that precede and follow it.)

4 葆 *bǎo* (**maintained**): This should be read here as 保 *bǎo* (lit., to protect),[5] which meant 全之 *quánzhī* (to maintain [something]).[6]

6 莫之能守也 *mò zhī néngshǒu yě* (**are what can never be secured**): This rhetorical form of the statement 莫能守之也 *mò néngshǒuzhī yě* used 之 *zhī* [third person pronoun] to indicate "gold and jade," and "what" is used to represent this.

7 而 *ér* (**but [with]**): This was defined here as 却 *què* (but),[7] and "with" was added to fit the context.

8 咎 *jiù* (**ruin**): This character was defined here as 災 *zāi* (disaster; ruin).[8]

10 天之道 *tiān zhī Dào* (**the Dao of the heavens**):[9] Chapter 25 (line 20) says: "The heavens conform to the Dao." This line therefore describes how the performance of the heavens is able to work on behalf of the Dao. (According to Laozi, the only ones that conform to the Dao are "man," "the Earth," and "the heavens" [chapter 25 (lines 18–20)]. However, the Earth remains still and inactive, while "man" and "the heavens" are able to move and be active. That is why Laozi refers to "the Dao of the heavens" and "the Dao of man," but not "the Dao of the Earth.")

CHAPTER 10

1 戴營魄 *dài yíng pò* (**[when] the yang breath and the yin spirit are retained**): 戴 *dài* in ancient times would be read here as 載 *zài* (to carry; to retain).[1] 營魄 *yíng pò* sug-

gests that this referred to the 魂魄 *húnpò* (mod. Ch., soul),[2] with 魂 *hún* in pre-Qin China defined as 陽氣 *yángqì* (yang breath or energy) and 魄 *pò* as 陰神 *yīnshén* (yin spirit).[3] When these two are combined, we have a complete person with both a body (from *pò*) and spiritual energy (from *hún*).[4]

1   抱一 ***bào Yī*** (**the One embraced**): The "One" represents the harmony formed by the yin and yang.[5]

3   搏 ***tuán*** (**concentrated**): This character would have been read here as 結聚 *jiéjù* (to concentrate; to be concentrated).[6]

4   嬰兒 ***yīngér*** (**a newborn**): See chapter 55.

5   脩除 ***xīuchú*** (**cleansed**): 脩 *xīu* was read here as 滌 *dí* (to wash).[7] 除 *chú* meant 治 *zhì* (to tidy up).[8] The object of this term is the "transcendent mirror," so "to be cleansed" was used as the verb.

5   玄監 ***xuánjiàn*** (**the transcendent mirror**): 監 *jiàn* was read here as 鑑 *jiàn* (which is to say 鏡 *jìng* [mirror]).[9] For 玄 *xuán*, see chapter 1 (comment on line 11). "Transcendent mirror" was a metaphorical expression that described the "discernment of hearts."[10]

6   疵 ***cí*** (**blemish**): In this context, 疵 *cí* would have been defined as 瑕 *xiá* (a reddish spot on pure white jade),[11] and so it is interpreted here as a "blemish."

8   毋以知 ***wú yǐzhì*** (**employ no shrewdness**): 以 *yǐ* was used in this context to mean 用 *yòng* (to use; to employ),[12] while 知 *zhì* (mod. Ch., *zhī*) would have been read here as 智 *zhì* (shrewdness).[13]

7–8   Additional guides to understanding lines 7–8 can be found in chapters 3, 19, 52 (lines 5–6), 64 (lines 19–22), and 65.

9   天門啟闔 ***tiān Mén qǐhé*** (**[when] the heavens' Gate is opening and closing**): In ancient China, people believed the heavens' Gate existed. All things emerged when It was opened, and were concealed when It closed.[14] The opening and closing of the heavens' Gate followed the seasons[15] (chapter 50 [lines 1–3]).

10   為雌 ***wéicī*** (**act as the female**): 雌 *cī* meant "the female." Chapter 61 (line 3) says: "Females always win over males through stillness." The one who remains still will not be proactive, but rather responsive, which agrees with the spirit of non-effort.

11   四達 ***sìdá*** (**broad comprehension**): 達 *dá* here meant 曉解 *xiǎojiě* (to understand; comprehension).[16] 四 *sì* (lit., four) denoted the four directions, which suggested "everywhere." Therefore, this term literally meant "comprehension about [matters that are] everywhere," and we may interpret this as "broad comprehension."

11–12   An additional discussion about the subjects here can be found in chapter 28 (lines 1–18).

13–16   生之、畜之 . . . 是謂玄德 ***shēngzhī, chùzhī . . . shìwéi xuán Dé*** (**things are engendered and fostered. . . . This is the transcendent De**): The engendering and the fostering of things come from the Dao (chapter 51 [line 7]), and "the Dao conforms to self-realization" (chapter 25 [line 21]), so the passive voice is used in the interpretation. 之 *zhī* [third person pronoun] here denoted "things." For 玄 *xuán*, see chapter 1 (comment on line 11), and for 德 *Dé*, see chapter 38 (margin note, footnote, and comment on line 1). See also chapter 51 (lines 11–14), as well as chapter 2 (lines 11–13).

CHAPTER 11

1   卅輻 *sàfú* (**thirty spokes**): 卅 *sà* meant "thirty."[1] A 輻 *fú* was a "spoke." In ancient times, a lord's vehicle was called a 路 *lù*; each of its wheels had thirty spokes, symbolizing the moon's month-long cycle of waxing and waning.[2]

2   無 *wú* (**void**): In this instance, 無 *wú* indicated the empty center of a hub. (In line 5, this character refers to the concave area of a vessel, while in line 8, this refers to the interior space in a room, as well as the openings created by a door and windows.)

4   埏埴 *yánzhí* (**clay is kneaded**): 埏 *yán* was defined as 揉 *róu* (to knead),[3] and 埴 *zhí* meant "clay."[4]

4   器 *qì* (**vessel**): As used here, this referred to a utilitarian object used to serve drink or food;[5] in other words, a "vessel."

7   鑿戶牖 *zuóhùyǒu* (**doors and windows are carved out**): This phrase described the building of houses. In ancient times, northern Chinese houses first had their walls formed out of 板築 *bǎnzhú* (rammed earth formed by wooden molds)[6] before the doors and windows were carved from this.

10–11   . . . 之 . . . 之 . . . *zhī* . . . *zhī* (. . . **while**): Both of these characters were used to connote a meaning similar to 則 *zé* (then).[7] This pattern of . . . 則 . . . 則 meant that both halves of a sentence formed with 之 *zhī* or 則 *zé* were to be given equal weight,[8] and so we used ". . . while" to express this.

10–11   Regarding these two lines, Su Che's note explains, "Without being, a void is unable to fulfill its function, and without a void, being is unable to offer up its advantages."

CHAPTER 12

1   五色 *wǔsè* (**five colors**): This term referred to 青 *qīng* (blue-green), 黃 *huáng* (ochre yellow), 赤 *chì* (cinnabar red), 白 *bái* (white), and 黑 *hēi* (black).[1] In pre-Qin China, these were considered the world's basic colors, much like the West's red, yellow, blue, white, and black. When mingled together by man, these hues can be turned into garish combinations that dazzle our eyes. But once we become used to such garishness, we risk losing the ability to enjoy the simple, genuine beauty of the world's natural colors.

1 MN   **If leaders (and now, by extension, we**): See both comments on line 6.

2   田獵 *tiánliè* (**hunting**): 田 *tián* as used here was the ancient form of 畋 *tián* (to hunt).[2] So, 田獵 *tiánliè* was a synonymous compound term.

3   妨 *fáng* (**deranged**): This was defined as 傷 *shāng* (to be deranged).[3]

4   五味 *wǔwèi* (**five flavors**): This term meant the tastes known as 甘 *gān* (sweet), 辛 *xīn* (spicy hot), 鹹 *xián* (salty), 酸 *suān* (sour), and 苦 *kǔ* (bitter).[4] When these are blended by man, they provide us with complex tastes that thrill our tongues. Jaded palates can be the result, though, as we lose the ability to enjoy the simpler, genuine flavors of food.

4   爽 *shuǎng* (**numbed**): This denoted the condition of 差失 *chāshī* (to fail),[5] and as this referred to the mouth, it is interpreted here as "numbed."

5   五音 *wǔyīn* (**five musical pitches**): The five Chinese musical pitches were called 徵 *zhǐ*, 羽 *yǔ*, 宮 *gōng*, 商 *shāng*, and 角 *jiǎo*. In the seventh century BCE, the famous

philosophical classic known as *Guanzi* borrowed the sounds of various animals to vividly describe each pitch: "徵 *zhǐ* [mod. Ch. pron., *zhēng*] is a sound akin to an alert and frightened pig being toted. 羽 *yǔ* is a sound akin to a horse whinnying in the wilderness. 宮 *gōng* is a sound akin to a cow lowing in its stall. 商 *shāng* is a sound akin to a sheep separated from its flock. 角 *jiǎo* is a sound akin to the call of a pheasant perched on a branch that is strong and clear."[6]

These five pitches can be combined into lush music, but if that is all we hear, we will easily lose the ability to truly savor the beauty of natural sounds.

6   治 ***zhì*** (cultivation): The descriptions in lines 1–5 discuss enjoyments that were, in ancient China, available only to the noble classes (although in modern times, they are obtainable by almost everyone). This then guides us to understand that 治 *zhì* here would not have had its usual interpretation of "management," but rather referred to the "cultivation" of nobles in ancient times,[7] and with us today, as well.

6   聖人 ***shèngrén*** (sages): This referred to "leaders."[8] See also the first comment on this line.

CHAPTER 13

1   寵辱 ***chóngrǔ*** (honor is mortifying): 寵 *chóng* was defined as 榮 *róng* (glory; honor).[1] The meaning of 辱 *rǔ* (humiliation; to mortify) is clearly implied in line 4.

1   若驚 ***ruòjīng*** ([and] results in anxiety): 若 *ruò* was used to mean 及 *jí* or 至 *zhì* (to reach; to result in).[2] 驚 *jīng* was another way of saying 懼懼 *jù* (fear; anxiety).[3]

2   大患 ***dàhuàn*** (exceptionally harmful): 患 *huàn* was defined as 害 *hài* (harmful; to harm).[4] 大 *dà* literally meant "great" or "greatly," but we used "exceptionally" here to better fit the context.

2   若身 ***ruò shēn*** (due to the sense of the self): As used here, 若 *ruò* would have been read as 以 *yǐ* (due to).[5]

1–2   Zhu Dezhi of the Ming dynasty suggested that these two lines were likely ancient adages.[6]

9   所以 ... 者 ***suǒyǐ ... zhě*** (the reason why): Here, 者 *zhě* [mood word] was used to emphasize that the term 所以 *suǒyǐ* (the reason why) was describing a fact,[7] and it cannot be directly translated.

9–11   吾 ***wǔ*** (my; I): The first person was used here to inspire readers to consider their own situations.

10   為 ***wèi*** (due to): This was used in this context to mean 因 *yīn* (due to).[8]

11   及 ***jí*** (if): This was used here to mean 若 *ruò* (if).[9]

8–12 MN   High positions ... feelings of arrogance and overweening pride: See chapter 9 (lines 7–8).

13   以 ... 為 ***yǐ ... wéi*** (equates ... with): In this instance, 以 *yǐ* was used to mean 使 *shǐ* (to make; to allow).[10] 為 *wéi* was to be read as 如似 *rúsì* (like; [the same] as).[11] So, this literally meant "to allow [someone] to be the same as," but we modified this as "equates ... with" to better fit the context.

14   若 ***ruò*** (thereby): This was used here to mean 則 *zé* (then; thereby).[12] This character in line 16 should be read the same way.

CHAPTER 14

2   名之曰 **míngzhī yuē** (is called): 曰 *yuē* was used here to mean 為 *wéi* (to be).[1] 之 *zhī* was a mood word with no inherent meaning.[2] The passive voice was therefore used to translate this phrase as "is called."

2   微 **wēi** (the concealed): This denoted 隱 *yǐn* (hidden; concealed).[3]

5   捪 **mín** (probed for): This was another way of saying 撫 *fǔ* (to probe for).[4]

5   得 **dé** (felt): 得 *dé* had the basic meaning of "to obtain," but because it was paired with "probed for," it is interpreted here as "felt."

6   夷 **yí** (the flat): In this context, 夷 *yí* described something as being so 平 *píng* (flat) that it could not be felt by the hands.[5]

7   三者 **sānzhě** (these three): This referred to "the concealed," "the silent," and "the flat."

7   不可至計 **bùkě zhìjì** (not detectable): 至 *zhì* was used here to mean 得 *dé* (to obtain).[6] 計 *jì* would have been read as 稽 *jì* (to detect; detection).[7] Therefore, 至計 *zhìjì* is interpreted here as "detectable."

8   故 **gù** (for): This was used here to express 原因 *yuányīn* or 緣故 *yuángù* (due to; for).[8]

8   混 **hùn** ([are] mingled): Heshang Gong's note is followed here to define this character as 合 *hé* (to combine; to mingle).

8   為一 **wéi Yī** (into the One): The Dao is an actual existence (see also the descriptions below) that lies in absolute harmony.[9] If this were not so, It would be unable to exist and thereby disperse into nonexistence.

9   攸 **yōu** (bright): The ancient reading of this character could be the same as 皦 *jiǎo* (bright),[10] and that is how it appears in the received versions.

10   忽 **hū** (dim): 忽 *hū* (mod. Ch., suddenly) would have been read here as 曶 *hū* (dim).[11]

9–10 其上 **qíshàng** (Its crest) and 其下 **qíxià** (Its base): The descriptions of the One in lines 1–6 tell us that we as humans are unable to perceive where Its crest and base might be, which therefore clearly suggests that lines 9–10 are metaphorical illustrations.[12] Through the portrayal in lines 9–10 of the One as "Its crest is not bright, nor is Its base dim," we learn that the One is full of light and in a harmonious state.

11   尋尋兮 **xúnxúnxī** (so ever in motion): In ancient Chinese, the term 尋尋 *xúnxún* could be read as 繩繩 *shéngshéng*,[13] which meant "motion without end."[14] All received versions used 繩繩 *shéngshéng* here.

12   不可名也 **bùkěmíng yě** ([it] is indefinable): Regarding 名 *míng*, see chapter 1 (comment on line 3).

14   是謂 **shìwèi** (this is): What this line describes is a fact, not an idea, so 謂 *wèi* here would have been read as 為 *wéi* (to be; is).[15] 謂 *wèi* in lines 16 and 22 should be read the same way.

16   惚恍 **Hūhuǎng** (the Nebulous): Heshang Gong's note describes the Dao's condition as being "as if It were and were not—It cannot be perceived."[16] Weighing this against the description of the Dao (in lines 14–15) as having "the shape of shapelessness" and "the form of nothingness" allows us to realize that 惚恍 *hūhuǎng* should be interpreted as "the Nebulous." (This term is used to express how we comprehend the descriptions of lines 14–15, so here, 是謂 *shìwèi* means "this is.")

17–18 而 **Ér** (It): This character was used here to mean 之 *zhī* (it)[17] and referred to the One. Because the passive voice was used in this translated prepositional phrase, the object was omitted. (In our corporeal world, when we follow a thing, we see its rear, and when we face it, we see its front. This human perspective toward physical things tells us that the "One" must exist by Itself in a state of constant, cycling motion.)

19 執 *zhí* (**cleave to**): This would have been read here as 守 *shǒu* (to cleave to).[18] Chapter 32 (line 3) and chapter 37 (line 2) both say "守之" *shǒu Zhī* (cleave to It) when referring to the Dao.

19 執今之道 *zhí jīn zhī Dào* (**cleave to the Dao in the now**): This follows silk version B; the last two characters here were damaged in version A. The reason this reading is based on silk version B is because it refers to "the Dao in the now," which is a very important metaphysical concept in keeping with Laozi's philosophy.

    His viewpoint is based on the reality of the Dao that solely lies in "the now," where the so-called "time of yore" is just the formation of countless past "nows." If we deviate from the reality in "the now" and pursue the Dao in the time of yore, this will cause us to become detached from reality even as we search for reality. Chapter 21 (lines 13–14) notes, "from the now back to the time of yore, Its [i.e., the Dao's] name has never vanished," and this can be borrowed to prove that our understanding is correct.[19]

19 MN **We refer to this One as the Dao:** See chapter 25 (lines 1–7), where line 4 says, "It is solitary and immutable." This can be considered another way of describing the "One."

20 以御今之有 *yǐ yù jīn zhī yǒu* (**to have dominion over the beings that are of the now**): The character 御 *yù* was used here to mean 治 *zhì* (to govern; to rule),[20] and so this is interpreted as "to have dominion over." 有 *yǒu* (lit., being) represented the entire corporeal world, and thus referred to all things. The performance of the Dao can fundamentally be seen in Its power over the existence of all things, as discussed in chapter 4, and that is the reason why the discussions in chapters 2 (lines 3–8 and 11–13), 10 (lines 13–16), and 51 (lines 7–14) conclude with descriptions of this dominion.

22 紀 *Jì* (**Principle**): Xi Tong's note quotes Zheng Xuan in noting that the definition of this character referred to a 總要 *zǒngyào* (comprehensive core; principle).

CHAPTER 15

1 士 *shì* (**cultivated people**): In pre-Qin China, 士 *shì* was used to denote three kinds of people: a) officials of the lowest ranking,[1] b) well-cultivated people (chapter 40),[2] and c) warriors (chapter 68). In this chapter, we follow the second definition, as this referred to people who had already achieved cultivation.[3] (If we compare the 為士 *wéi shì* of this chapter with the 為道 *wéi Dào* of chapter 65, we discover that 為士 *wéi shì* denoted personal cultivation through the Dao, while 為道 *wéi Dào* referred to governance through conforming to the Dao.)

2 微眇 *wēimiǎo* (**enigmatically subtle**): 微 *wēi* meant "concealed,"[4] and was used here to imply a state that transcends our understanding. 眇 *miǎo* should then be read here as 妙 *miào* (subtle).[5] This term was used in this context to describe the attitude of a cultivated person, so we interpreted it as "enigmatically subtle."

2 玄達 *xuándá* (**transcendentally discerning**): For 玄 *xuán*, see chapter 1 (comment on line 11). 達 *dá* here meant 曉解 *xiǎojiě* (discerning).[6]

3 志 *zhì* (**comprehension**): In ancient times, this was read as 識 *zhì* and meant 知 *zhī* (comprehension).[7]

4   頌 *sòng* (**are portrayed as**): This meant 形容 *xíngróng* (to describe; to be portrayed as).[8]

5   其如 *qírú* (**as if**): Here, 其 *qí* was used to mean 若似 *ruòsì* (as if).[9] So, 其如 *qírú* was a synonymous compound term. (This term in lines 6–11 should be read the same way.)

5–6   豫 *yù* (**wary**) and 猶 *yóu* (**circumspect**): Both characters suggested a 遲疑不決 *chíyìbùjué* (hesitant)[10] or careful attitude, but in these two lines, we defined them individually as "wary" and "circumspect."

5–11   兮 *xī* [**mood word**]: This mood word was used here to suggest that what was being described was something out of the ordinary, and therefore is interpreted as "so."

8   渙 *huàn* (**untrammeled**): This was defined here as 散 *sàn* (lit., dispersing).[11] When ice thaws into a liquid, it is no longer restrained within a hard form, and so it may accommodate any situation with ease. This character is therefore interpreted here as "untrammeled."

8   凌釋 *língshì* (**ice that is thawing**): 凌 *líng* was the same as 冰 *bīng* (ice),[12] and 釋 *shì* meant 解 *jiě* (lit., to break apart).[13] Because the subject is ice, "thaw" is used to interpret the verb.

9   屯 *tún* (**simple**): In ancient times, 屯 *tún* (to station; to stockpile) and 純 *chún* (pure; simple) could be used interchangeably.[14]

10   沌 *dūn* (**indistinct**): As an adjective, this was synonymous with 混 *hùn* (indistinct),[15] and here described someone's attitude.

10   濁 *zhuó* (**turbid**): This was defined as 水不清 *shuǐ bùqīng* (water that is unclear),[16] and so is interpreted here as "turbid."

11   曠兮、其如谷 *kuàngxī, qírú gǔ* (**so open, as if a valley**): 谷 *gǔ* (valley) was modified by "open," which conveyed a different notion from this character's usage in chapter 6 (line 1), chapter 28 (lines 8–9), and chapter 39 (line 5).

12–13   者 *zhě* [**mood word**]: This was used here as a mood word to indicate that this is a question within the statement,[17] and so 者 *zhě* is untranslatable.

12–13   將 *jiāng* (**will then**): This was used to mean 乃 *nǎi* (thus; will then).[18]

13   生 *shēng* (**risen**): This was defined as 起 *qǐ* (to rise),[19] and so we interpreted it as "risen" in this sentence.

14   保 *bǎo* (**embrace**): This meant 抱 *bào* (to embrace)[20] here.

14   不欲尚逞 *búyù shāngchěng* (**not want to favor indulgence**): 逞 *chěng*[21] was defined as 恣 *zī* (indulgence),[22] which meant that one's behavior lacked self-restraint. The teachings in chapter 29 (lines 11–14) echo the reading of this phrase.

16   成 *chéng* (**end**): 成 *chéng* was defined here as 畢 *bì* (end).[23]

15–16   The descriptions in these two lines echo the content of lines 12–13.

CHAPTER 16

1   至 *zhì* (**attain**): This was defined as 得 *dé* (to attain).[1]

1   恆 *héng* (**constancy**): Here we follow the reading made by the Guodian version's editorial board to define it as 常 *cháng* (constancy).

2   中 *zhōng* (**harmony**): The character 中 *zhōng* in this context suggested a spirit of harmony.[2]

2   篤 *dǔ* (**regulation**): In ancient times, this character could be read as 督 *dū* and had

the meaning of 理 *lǐ* (to regulate; regulation).[3] Because the stated means in this line is "cleaving to harmony," its result is interpreted as "regulation."

3 　旁作 *pángzuò* (**boundlessly rise**): 旁 *páng* was defined as 溥 *pǔ* (broad; boundless),[4] while 作 *zuò* meant 起 *qǐ* (to rise).[5]

5 　天道員員 *tiān dào yuányuán* (**as the heavens direct the plenitude**):[6] 道 *dào* here would have been read as 導 *dǎo* (to lead; to direct).[7] The term 員員 *yuányuán* was another way of saying 云云 *yúnyún*, which meant 眾盛 *zhòngshèng* (plenitude).[8] "The heavens direct the plenitude" (i.e., the state of all things that are growing) agrees with "the Earth conforms to the heavens" in chapter 25 (line 19).

6 　各 *gè* (**everything**): As "plenitude" implied "the state of all things that are growing" (comment on line 5), we know that 各 *gè* (lit., each one) denoted "everything." (Because roots must belong separately to individual things, this passage here uses 各 *gè*, not 萬物 *wànwù* [all things].)

6 　曰靜 *yuē jīng* (**[there] is stillness**): 曰 *yuē* was used here to mean 為 *wéi* (to be),[9] and so by extension "there is."

7 　命 *Mìng* (**the Preordainment**): 命 *mìng* in this context symbolized "a certain amalgamation; a predestined threshold,"[10] and so this is interpreted here as the "Preordainment."

10 　妄 *wàng* (**transgression**): This was defined as 行不正 *xíngbúzhèng* (misconduct),[11] and therefore by extension "transgression."

11 　妄作 *wàng zuò* (**[and this] transgression, [when it] occurs**): According to the comment on line 3, 作 *zuò* in this context should mean "to rise." However, "occurs" fits this context better.

12 　容 *róng* (**comprehensiveness**): This was another way of saying 包函 *bāohán* (comprehensive; comprehensiveness).[12]

13 　乃 *nǎi* (**lead to**): 乃 *nǎi* could mean 則 *zé* (lit., then), but it was used here to mean "lead to."[13] This character in lines 14–17 should be read the same way.

13 　公 *gōng* (**vast**): This would have been defined here as 廣 *guǎng* (vast).[14]

12–13 MN 　**The understanding of constancy . . . to accept all without partiality:** This is how we may wield non-effort that conforms to self-realization (chapter 25 [line 21] and chapter 37 [line 1]).

14 　王 *wáng* (**being followed by the world**): This was a very ancient definition of 王 *wáng* (lit., the king).[15] However, it is obvious that interpreting it as "being followed by the world" better illustrates Laozi's teaching here.

CHAPTER 17

1 　大上 *tàishàng* (**the greatest of all**): In ancient times, 大 *dà* (lit., big) could be read as 太 *tài*.[1] 太上 *tàishàng* might be defined as 最上 *zuìshàng* (lit., the highest)[2] and indicated those (which would have indicated "leaders" here) who excelled without peer. This is therefore expressed as "the greatest of all."

1 　下 *xià* (**subordinates**): In this instance, 下 *xià* denoted 下民 *xiàmín* (subordinates).[3]

5 　信不足 *xìnbùzú* (**credibility is wanting**): 信 *xìn* in this context meant 不疑 *bùyí* (lit., having no doubt; trusting).[4] Therefore, 不信 *búxìn* meant "distrust," and so the use of the term 信不足 *xìnbùzú* (lit., a trust that is insufficient) here clearly meant "credibility is wanting."

5   安 *ān* (**then**): 安 *ān* was used here to mean 則 *zé* (then).[5]

6   猶 *yóu* (**scrupulous**): 猶 *yóu* was defined as "hesitant,"[6] which by extension was used in this context to mean "scrupulous." (This interpretation as applied here differs from that in chapter 15 [line 6].)

8   百姓 *bǎixìng* (**subjects**): See chapter 5 (comment on line 4, and note in endnote 5).

9   自然 *zìrán* (**realized . . . ourselves**): 自 *zì* literally meant "the self." 然 *rán* should be read here as 成 *chéng* (to realize).[7]

7–9 MN   **Under the governance . . . without being commanded:** This is achieved through their leader's non-effort.

7–9 MN   **Understand their duties by themselves:** This understanding has the same spirit as that of chapter 57 (lines 10–13).

CHAPTER 18

1   古 *gǔ* (**oh**): 古 *gǔ* was to be read here as 故 *gù*,[1] which in this instance had the meaning of 夫 *fú* (oh).[2]

1   廢 *fèi* (**disregarded**): This was defined as 棄 *qì* (forsaken; disregarded).[3] It was used here to describe the world when it fails to adhere to "the great Dao."

2   安 *ān* (**then**): 安 *ān* was used to mean 則 *zé* (then).[4]

2   有 *yǒu* (**emerge**): This character literally means "to have," but we have extended this meaning to "emerge" to better fit the context. This character in lines 4, 6, and 8 is read the same way.

3–4   智慧出, 安有大偽 *zhì huì chū, ān yǒu dàwěi* (**when shrewdness and ingenuity appear, then great hypocrisy emerges**): Although these two lines do not fit the context of the rest of this chapter and have so far not been found in the earliest texts, such as the Guodian version, the idea that they posit is good, and so they are included within parentheses, with the caveat that they were probably not part of the text.

5   六親 *liùqīn* (**family members**): This term was defined as "parents and children, elder and younger siblings, and also husbands and wives."[5]

7   邦家 *bāngjiā* (**an entire country**): In the Zhou feudal system, a lord's territory was referred to as a 邦 *bāng*. (Later on, this could also be referred to as a 國 *guó* [country].) Immediately beneath a 邦 *bāng* lay the territories of the 大夫 *dàfū* (who were somewhat like Roman imperial procurators) that were known as 家 *jiā*. Together, these formed the feudal states of the time,[6] and so this term is interpreted here as "an entire country."

8   正臣 *zhèngchén* (**ethical officials**): Here, 正 *zhèng* denoted 正直 *zhèngzhí* (ethical).[7]

CHAPTER 19

1   辯 *biàn* (**distinction**): 辯 *biàn* (lit., debate) should be read here as 辨 *biàn* (distinction).[1]

3–4 MN   **Ban cleverness:** Laozi did not reject the expedience of cleverness, for all the "manmade utilitarian objects" he listed as examples in chapter 11 were created by means of cleverness. Instead, he only discouraged its use when it spurred ambition, as this would disturb the world's harmony.

5   偽 *wěi* (**exertions**): 偽 *wěi* (lit., false) should be read here as 為 *wéi* (effort; exertion),[2] which referred to man's actions in the pursuit of something.[3]

5 慮 *lǜ* (**reckoning**): In this instance, the character 慮 *lǜ* meant 計度 *jìdù* (to reckon; reckoning).[4]

6 季子 *jìzǐ* (**ingenuousness**): This term was another way of saying 稚子 *zhìzǐ* (a small child) or 嬰兒 *yīngér* (an infant).[5] Because this discussion concerned people's quality, rather than literally making them return to the state of being an infant, it is interpreted here as "ingenuousness."

7 以為 *yǐwéi* (**are but**): 以 *yǐ* was used to mean 惟 *wéi* (only; but),[6] while 為 *wéi* should be read as 是 *shì* (to be),[7] and this is interpreted accordingly.

7 文 *wén* (**superficial expressions**): This was defined here as 飾 *shì* (decorative colors),[8] and so "superficial expressions" is used to interpret it and clarify the description.

8 命 *mìng* (**induce**): This should be read as 使 *shǐ* (to make; to cause; to induce)[9] to fit Laozi's teaching. (For an understanding on how to achieve this, see chapter 57 [lines 10–13]).

8 屬 *shǔ* (**secures**): This was defined as 係 *xì*, which had the same definition as 繫 *xì* (to fasten; to anchor),[10] and so, by extension, meant "secures."

9 保 *bǎo* (**embrace**): See chapter 15 (first comment on line 14 regarding the character 保 *bǎo*).

7–10 MN These lines of Laozi's connote the same teachings as what are described in chapter 3 (lines 7–12). They tell us that neither selfishness nor desires will lead to contentment. Selfishness invariably means that others are intentionally excluded, while desires require that we compete with others for the same objectives.

CHAPTER 20

1 絕學 *juéxué* (**supreme learning**): 絕 *jué* in this context connoted 極至 *jízhì* (supreme),[1] while 學 *xué* meant learning. (Because 絕 *jué* was later recognized as 斷 *duàn* [to cut off],[2] many who study Laozi—especially in modern times—believe that his doctrine abandons "learning." However, the discussion in chapter 40[3] [lines 1–8] proves that such concepts are in fact the exact opposite of what Laozi taught.)

2–3 唯與訶 . . . 相去何若 *wéi yǔ hē . . . xiāng qù hé ruò* (**assent or rebuke . . . what is their difference**): In these lines, "assent" or "rebuke" is determined by analytical appraisal, while "beauty" and "ugliness" are emotional assessments. (Refer to chapter 2 [lines 1–2].)

4 人之所畏 *rén zhī suǒ wèi* (**those who are to be respected by people**): In this context, 畏 *wèi* (lit., fear; see chapter 72 [lines 1–2]) meant 敬 *jìng* (respect).[4] Some scholars hold that this line referred to lords.

4 亦 *yì* (**also**): This was used as 又 *yòu* (also).[5]

5 荒兮 *huāngxī* (**so vast**): Here, 荒 *huāng* acted as a borrowed character for 巟 *huāng*, which meant 廣大 *guǎngdà* (vast),[6] and "so" is used to express the mood word 兮 *xī*; see chapter 15 (comment on lines 5–11).

5 未央 *wèiyāng* (**boundless**): 未 *wèi* meant 無 *wú* (no; without),[7] while 央 *yāng* could be defined as 盡 *jìn* (end; to be bound),[8] and so "boundless" is used to interpret this phrase. (未央 *wèiyāng* was a common term in ancient China.)

6 熙熙 *xīxī* (**so happy**): This term was used to describe the state of 和樂貌 *hélèmào* (showing happiness).[9]

7 饗 *xiǎng* (**enjoying**): This would have been read here as 享 *xiǎng* (to enjoy; enjoying).[10]

7 大牢 *tàiláo* (**a huge banquet**): In ancient China, a banquet that featured at least an ox, sheep, and pig was normally called a 太牢 *tàiláo*,[11] and was considered the most extravagant form of banquet. Here, 大 *dà* was read as 太 *tài*; see chapter 17 (first comment on line 1).

8 臺 *tái* (**terrace**): In pre-Qin times, a 臺 *tái* was a huge ziggurat made of levels and constructed out of rammed earth[12] for sightseeing into the distance. As there is no exact English translation for this, "terrace" acted as an approximation.

9 泊 *bó* (**quiet**): In ancient times, this term could be read to mean something on the order of 怕 *bó*[13] (mod. Ch. pron., *pà*; lit., fear), which was defined as 靜 *jìng* (quiet).[14]

9 未兆 *wèizhào* (**unresponsive**): This was another way of saying 未作 *wèizuò* (to not yet have action).[15] We interpreted this as "unresponsive" to fit the context as described in line 10.

10 未咳 *wèikài* (**has not yet smiled**): 咳 *kài* was defined as 小兒笑 *xiǎoérxiào* (a newborn's smile).[16] In ancient China (mainly prior to 221 BCE), when a baby had lived for three months, the father would hold the right hand of his baby and caress its head; if the baby smiled, then he would give the baby a name.[17] (A person's name meant that the child had a role in society. Without it, the child could not be recognized and officially accepted by others, nor could the child be related to any place in the secular world. This is why 未咳 *wèikài* is followed by 似無所歸 *sì wùsuǒguī* [as if without a place to return] in line 11.)

11 纍兮 *léixī* (**so listless**): 纍 *léi* was defined as 羸憊貌 *léibèimào* (exhausted; listless).[18]

13 遺 *yí* (**less than enough**): This character would have been read here as 匱 *kuì* (lacking; less than enough).[19]

14 也 *yě* [**mood word**]: This was used here as 邪 *yé*,[20] which expressed the question mood.

15 俗人 *súrén* (**the benighted**): Our understanding of this term follows Xunzi's description: "[Those] who do not want to learn, have no sense of morality, and exalt wealth and profit—these are 俗人 *súrén*."[21] Therefore, "the benighted" is used to interpret this term. (This term in line 17 is read the same way.)

15 昭昭 *zhāozhāo* (**so brilliant**): 昭 *zhāo* was defined as 明 *míng* (bright; brilliant).[22]

17 察察 *cháchá* (**so discerning**): 察 *chá* was another way of saying 審 *shěn* (having clear perception about; discerning),[23] so it is interpreted here accordingly.

18 悶悶 *mènmèn* (**so muddleheaded**): Here, 悶 *mèn* should be read as 惛 *hūn*,[24] which meant 心不明 *xīnbùmíng* (mind is unclear),[25] and so this is interpreted as "[so] muddleheaded."

21 有以 *yǒuyǐ* (**has abilities**): This denoted 有所施用 *yǒusuǒshīyòng* (to have that which is useful)[26] and described a person's skills, therefore this is interpreted as "to have abilities."

22 頑以鄙 *wán yǐ bì* (**stupid and uncultured**): 頑 *wán* was defined as 愚魯 *yùlǔ* (stupid),[27] 以 *yǐ* meant 而 *ér* (and),[28] and 鄙 *bì* denoted 朴野 *pǔyě* (uncultured).[29]

23 貴食母 *guì sì Mǔ* (**[through] cherishing nourishment [from] the Mother**): 食 *sì* was used as a verb here (and therefore should not be read as *shí*) to mean "to nourish" or "to be nourished." In this description, 食母 *sì Mǔ* was meant to be read in the passive voice,[30] and so we used "through . . . from" to express this.

CHAPTER 21

1   孔德之容 *kǒng Dé zhī róng* (**the manifestation of the ultimate De**): 孔 *kǒng* was defined as 甚 *shèn* (ultimate).[1] 容 *róng* denoted 狀 *zhuàng* (appearance; manifestation).[2] (At its most elemental, the De came from the Dao. This understanding follows Wang Bi's note on chapter 38, in which he says, "How to obtain the De? Through the Dao."[3] However, some scholars believe that 孔德 *kǒng Dé* represented a cultivated man who abided by the De.)

2   唯道是從 *wéi Dào shìcóng* (**solely obeys the Dao**): 是 *shì* was used here as a positive mood word[4] to emphasize the significance of 從 *cóng* (to follow; to obey), but is untranslatable in this context. 唯 *wéi* meant "only" or "solely," as it still does in modern Chinese.

3   道之物 *Dào zhī Wù* (**the Entity of the Dao**): This was an allusion to 道之形體 *Dào zhī xíngtǐ* (the corporeal form of the Dao),[5] and so 物 *wù* is interpreted as "the Entity."

4   怳 *huǎng* (**vague**) and 惚 *hū* (**nebulous**):[6] These two characters had very similar meanings,[7] and when combined as 怳惚 *huǎnghū* or 惚怳 *hūhuǎng*, they formed synonymous compound terms that meant "vague" and "nebulous." In some received versions, 怳 *huǎng* is written as the variant character 恍 *huǎng*.

6   象 *Xiàng* (**the Form**): Though the Dao cannot clearly be seen, It is unquestionably an intact Existence that is referred to as the Entity here, so the first thing we learn about It is Its Form.

8   物 *Wù* (**the Substance**): The meaning of this 物 *wù* differed from that of line 3, for here it should be understood to mean 質 *Zhí* (Substance).[8] This Substance is what allows the Entity of the Dao to have a corporeal Existence.

9   幽 *yōu* (**profound**): This denoted 深 *shēn* (deep; profound).[9]

10 請 *Qǐng* (**the Essence**): Here, this was meant to be read as 精 *jīng* (essence).[10] The Essence is the core of the Entity of the Dao.

12 信 *xìn* (**certainty**): The use of "certainty" in this line echoed the use of 真 *zhēn* (genuine) in line 11, which described something as truly corporeal, and so this description should be understood as being tangible, rather than merely conceptual. (The meaning of 信 *xìn* here is different from the one in chapter 17 [line 5].)

14 其名不去 *Qí míng búqù* (**Its name has never vanished**): We give the Dao a "name" to identify It (as described in chapter 25 [lines 6–7]), and so what Laozi teaches us is that we as humans are witnesses to Its immutable existence.

15 以順眾父 *yǐ shùn zhòngfù* (**in the regulation of all tenets**): 順 *shùn* was defined as 理 *lǐ* (to manage; to regulate; regulation).[11] 父 *fù* (lit., father) was used here to indicate 矩 *jù* (as in Old Eng., a rod; by extension, a scepter, representing ruling authority),[12] which represented 法 *fǎ* (a tenet).[13]

11–15 MN   **The Dao of the now . . . since the beginning of time:** See chapter 14 (lines 19–22).

16 然 *rán* (**success**): Here, 然 *rán* was defined as 成 *chéng* (to realize),[14] which is modified to "success" to fit the context.

16 也 *yě* [**mood word**]: This was another way of saying 邪 *yě*,[15] which indicated that this line was a question.

CHAPTER 22[1]

1 炊 *chuī* (**tiptoeing**): 炊 *chuī* acted as a borrowed word for 企 *qǐ*,[2] and this meant 舉踵 *jǔzhǒng* (to raise one's ankle; to tiptoe).[3]

2 自視者 *zìshìzhě* (**the self-righteous**): Here, 視 *shì* would have been read as 是 *shì* (right; righteous),[4] while 自 *zì* referred to "the self." 者 *zhě* [mood word] was used here to indicate a condition, much like 的 *de* in modern Chinese.[5] All the 者 *zhě* characters in lines 2–5 should be read the same way.

2 章 *zhāng* (**prominent**): This was meant to be read here as 顯 *xiǎn* (distinguished; prominent).[6]

3 自見者 *zìjiànzhě* (**the self-regarding**): 見 *jiàn* literally meant "to see" or "seeing," so this term is modified here as "self-regarding."[7]

4 自伐者 *zìfázhě* (**the self-glorifying**): 伐 *fá* would have been defined in this context as 美 *měi* (to praise; to glorify),[8] and this term is therefore modified in our text as "self-glorifying." (In chapter 30 [line 8], this term is interpreted as "glorification" to better fit the context there.)

5 自矜者[9] *zìjīnzhě* (**the self-inflated**): 矜 *jīn* meant 自尊大 *zìzūndà* ([to feel that] one's self is superior),[10] and so we interpreted this here as "the self-inflated." (In chapter 30 [line 10], 矜 *jīn* is interpreted as "inflation" to better fit the context there.)

5 長 *zhǎng* (**revered**): This was defined here as 尊 *zūn* (revered).[11]

7 餘食 *yúshí* (**surfeits of food**) and 贅行 *zhuìxíng* (**redundant growths**): 行 *xíng* could be used interchangeably with 形 *xíng* (figure) in classical Chinese;[12] because this passage refers to "a body," this is interpreted as "growths" to better fit the context. This was combined with 贅 *zhuì*, which was defined as a 肬 *yóu* (tumor),[13] or an abnormal growth on a body. By extension, 贅行 *zhuìxíng* came to refer to "redundant growths," and this corresponds perfectly with the concept of "surfeits of food" as a description of superfluity.

8 或 *huò* (**surely**): This was used to mean 必 *bì* (surely).[14]

9 弗居 *fújū* (**not engage with them**): 居 *jū* was defined as 與 *yǔ* (to be with),[15] which we modified as "to engage with" to better clarify the description. With regard to 弗 *fú*, see chapter 2 (comment on lines 11–12).

CHAPTER 23[1]

1 This was an ancient adage (see line 15).

1 則 *zé* (**[are] then**): In modern Chinese, the character still means "then." This character in lines 2–6 is read the same way.

2–4 MN **Polarized factors:** All things in the world exist as polarized factors, as indicated in chapter 2 (lines 3–8), which discusses how these polarized factors must reside in equilibrium (as caused by the neutral power of the Dao—see chapter 2 [comment on margin note to lines 3–8]). Here, though, these polarized factors are shown to interact with each other through waning and waxing.

7 聖人 *shèngrén* (**sages**): In this context, 聖人 *shèngrén* indicated "leaders."[2]

7 執一 *zhí Yī* (**cleave to the One**): 執 *zhí* was defined as 守 *shǒu* (to cleave to),[3] and the character 一 *Yī* indicated "[the state of] harmony."[4]

7 MN **Emulate "the One" . . . the Dao resides:** See chapter 10 (endnote 5) and chapter 14 (the third comment on line 8).

9–12 Refer to chapter 22 (comments on lines 2–5).

13 夫唯 *fú wéi* **(because they):** See chapter 8 (first and second comments on line 11, as well as endnotes 9 and 10).

16 幾語哉 *jǐ yǔ zāi* **(how could these words have been hollow):** 幾 *jǐ* was used here to mean 豈 *qǐ* (how could),[5] while 語 *yǔ* meant "a saying" (or something said without proof), so "hollow" is added to clarify this concept.

CHAPTER 24[1]

1 希言，自然 *xīyán, zìrán* **(in silent words lies self-realization):** This line reads the same in all versions. Because the Chinese was written in an extremely abbreviated fashion, our reading was inspired by Su Che and Wang Bi's notes.[2] The character 言 *yán* here meant "words," and so is interpreted accordingly. Chapter 14 (lines 3–4) says, "That which is hearkened to but not heard is called 'the silent,'" and chapter 35 (lines 7 and 10) reads, "the words uttered by the Dao . . . when hearkened to, there is nothing to hear." This tells us that these "silent words" are expressions by the Dao.[3] 然 *rán* was defined as 成 *chéng* (realization),[4] and 自 *zì* referred to "self," so this term meant "self-realization."

1 MN **The message that the Dao delivers is imperceptible:** These understandings were inspired by chapter 35 (lines 7–10).

2 飄風 *piāofēng* **(gusty winds):** This was another way of saying 疾風 *jífēng* (gusty winds).[5]

5 天地而弗能久 *tiān Dì ér fúnéng jiǔ* **(even the heavens and the Earth could never prolong them):** 而 *ér* was used to mean 尚 *shāng* (even).[6] 弗 *fú* implied that the object (i.e., "them," meaning the gusty winds and downpour) of the verb 久 *jiǔ* had been omitted.[7]

2–5 MN **The order of constancy in the world:** This acts as the fundament for the order of the world; see chapter 16 (lines 5–11).

7 而 *ér* **(with):** This meant 於 *yú* (at; with).[8]

7 MN **One is to cleave faithfully to the Dao through non-effort:** Once we elect to cleave to the Dao, we will thenceforth perform through non-effort. This means that the only other option would be, of course, a reliance on our own efforts.

8 德 *dé* **(gain):** This term was defined as 得 *dé* (obtainment; gain).[9] Because this indicated a result of effort (by man), it is interpreted here as "gain" and is used in contrast to 失 *shī* (loss) in line 9.

8 **Realize:** The term 從事 *cóngshì* was omitted in both of the lines here in the Chinese text, for they were considered understood.

8–9 MN **Gain or loss:** The employment of effort signifies the pursuit of gain. Such gain cannot be as unfailingly perfect as that which is achieved through adherence to the Dao, while any consequential loss through the use of effort will be absolute.

10–11 亦 *yì* **(ensure):** This meant 必 *bì* (to be certain; to ensure).[10]

CHAPTER 25

1 有物混成 *yǒu Wù hùnchéng* (**an Entity was mingled into realization**): See chapter 14 (lines 1–8). With regard to 有物 *yǒu Wù* (an Entity), in ancient China, that which possessed semblance, form, sound, or color was considered a 物 *wù* (lit., thing).[1] Because what was being described here was "solitary and immutable" (line 4), we know that this 物 *wù* was an Entity.

3 寂 *jì* (**soundless**) and 寥 *liáo* (**invisible**): 寂 *jì* was defined as 無聲音 *wúshēngyīn* (soundless), while 寥 *liáo* meant 空無形 *kōngwúxíng* (invisible).[2]

5 可以 *kěyǐ* (**therein**): This term was used here to mean 所以 *suǒyǐ* (therefore; therein).[3]

7 字之 *zì Zhī* (**referred to It**): 字 *zì* (lit., word; name) was used here as a verb. Humans give names to whatever is considered identifiable. But when it comes to this Entity (line 1) that absolutely cannot be identified (lines 3 and 6), the most we can expect is an approximate conceptualization of what It may comprise, and so "refer" is used to interpret this. (Traditionally, there were two types of names: 名 *míng*, which were formal appellations, and 字 *zì*, which were not. This shows us how subtly Laozi weighed his words.)

8 吾強為之名 *wǔ qiǎng wèi Zhī míng* (**I give It another name**): 吾 *wǔ* (I) referred to Laozi himself, and 強 *qiǎng* was defined here as 益 *yì* (additionally).[4] This line therefore literally meant, "I additionally give It a name," which we modified for clarity as "I give It another name."

8 大 *Dà* (**Greatness**): For an explanation on why Laozi referred to It as "Greatness," see chapter 34 (lines 9–10).

9 曰 *yuē* (**[there] then [is]**): This character was used here to mean 而 *ér* (then).[5]

11 反 *fǎn* (**return**): In this context, the character 反 *fǎn* (to reverse) would have been read as being interchangeable with 返 *fǎn* (to return).[6]

9–11 MN **In a state of constant circulation:** The circulative motion of the Dao in the world as described in these three lines echoes those of chapter 15 (lines 12–13) and chapter 16 (lines 5–6).

12–17 MN **The Dao moves between them:** This is why Laozi placed the Dao after the heavens and the Earth.

18 法 *fǎ* (**conforms to**): This was denoted as 不違 *bùwéi* (to not disobey),[7] and it is modified here as to "conform to." This character in lines 19–21 should be read the same way.

21 自然 *zìrán* (**self-realization**): See chapter 24 (comment on line 1). Because the Dao is the One described as "all things follow It, though it masters them not" (chapter 34 [lines 5–6]), we know that this referred to the achievement of "self-realization" by everyone in the world, for "the Dao always exerts with non-effort" (chapter 37 [line 1]).

CHAPTER 26

3 君子 *jūnzǐ* (**lords**): This term here meant 人君 *rénjūn* (lords of the people).[1]

4 輜重 *zīzhòng* (**supply carts**): 輜重 *zīzhòng* indicated that these were "carts that carry equipment and food."[2]

5 環官 *huánguān* (**regional affairs**): In this context, 環 *huán* (lit., ring) should be read as 寰 *huán*, which referred to the lords' official regions,[3] while 官 *guān* was defined as 事 *shì* (affairs).[4]

6 燕處 *yànchù* (**abide in ease**): 燕 *yàn* would have been read here as 晏 *yàn*, which meant 安 *ān* (peace; ease).[5]

6 則昭若 *zé zhāoruò* (**[will] then be in order**): 昭 *zhāo* meant 明 *míng* (clarified),[6] and it has been modified here as "in order." 若 *ruò* was a mood word used to express a condition (just like 然 *rán*).[7] The subject of this phrase, "they," referred to affairs, and because this was considered understood, it was omitted in Laozi's narrative.

7 Only the king could have ten thousand chariots, according to the official political system of the Zhou dynasty.

8 而 *ér* (**nonetheless**): This was used to mean 乃 *nǎi* (but; nonetheless).[8]

8 以身 *yǐ shēn* (**allow himself**): 以 *yǐ* was used to mean 使 *shǐ* (to make; to let),[9] and this is modified here as "allow."

9 則 *zé* (**leads to**): See chapter 38 (endnote 14).

CHAPTER 27

1 轍迹 *chèjì* (**wheel tracks**): 轍 *chè* was the mark left by the wheel of a vehicle,[1] so 迹 *jì* (a mark; a track) simply emphasized the meaning of 轍 *chè* while providing a clearer reading. (In ancient times, any person of high rank who left home had to travel by vehicle.)[2]

2 瑕謫 *xiázhé* (**blameworthy flaws**): 瑕 *xiá* was another way of saying 疵 *cī* (blemish; flaws),[3] while 謫 *zhé* meant 責 *zé* (blame; blameworthy).[4]

3 籌策 *chóucè* (**tallies to count**): 籌 *chóu* meant 計算 *jìsuàn* (to count),[5] and 策 *cè* was another way of saying 筭 *suàn*,[6] which meant "the tallies [used in counting]."[7]

4 關籥 *guānyuè* (**bolt on the lock**): Originally, 關 *guān* referred to the bolt used to lock a gate, and 籥 *yuè* was the lock that secured the bolt.[8]

5 繆約 *mòyuē* (**knot of rope**): 繆 *mò* meant 索 *suō* (a rope),[9] while 約 *yuē* was another way of saying 束 *shù* (to tighten)[10]—in other words, a rope that has been tightened—and so, 約 *yuē* is interpreted here as a "knot."

6 救 *jiù* (**assisting**): This was another way of saying 助 *zhù* (to assist).[11]

7 物 *wù* (**affairs**): This would have been read here as 事 *shì* (affairs).[12]

7 財 *cái* (**talent**): In ancient times, 財 *cái* (lit., wealth) could be read as 材 *cái* (talent).[13]

8 襲明 *xímíng* (**dual discernment**): Here, 襲 *xí* meant 重 *chóng* (dual).[14]

10 資 *zī* (**material**): This would have been read as 材 *cái* (material).[15] This character in line 12 should be read the same.

14 眇要 *miǎoyào* (**being unclear about that which is right**): 眇 *miǎo* meant "unable to obtain clear sight,"[16] and so is interpreted here as "being unclear about." 要 *yào* was defined as 當 *dāng* (appropriate; right),[17] and so is rendered here as "that which is right."

CHAPTER 28

1 其 *qí* [**mood word**]: This character acted as a mood word to smooth the reading of this sentence.[1] The character 其 *qí* in lines 7 and 13 should be read the same way.

1 雄 *xióng* (**the male**) and 雌 *cī* (**the female**): As philosophical symbols, the male here represented "restlessness," "hardness," and "activity," while the female exemplified "stillness," "gentleness," and "passivity."[2] Chapter 26 (line 2) says, "The still is the ruler

of the restless," while chapter 36 (line 10) tells us, "The soft and the weak prevail over the strong."

1 MN   **Regain the nature of the Origin:** This pertained to the Dao, which has a simple explanation that can be found in chapter 32 (line 1).

2   谿 *xī* (**a pool**): The definition of 谿 *xī* was "a [natural] mountain channel with no outflow,"[3] so "a pool" is used to suggest this.

4   德 *Dé* (**De**): See chapter 38 (margin note on line 1).

6   嬰兒 *yīngér* (**infancy**): This term literally meant "an infant," but from the wording here, we know that this was meant to represent the state of infancy.[4]

7   白 *bái* or *bó* (**clean**) and 辱 *rǔ* (**unclean**): In this context, 白 *bái* (lit., white) represented 潔絜 *jié* (clean), while 辱 *rǔ* (lit., disgrace) meant 污 *wū* (unclean).[5]

8   谷 *gǔ* (**a valley**): This denoted "where spring water flows out and connects with a river."[6] "Water perfectly benefits all things" (chapter 8 [line 2]), and so to be "a valley unto the world" is to be someone who unfailingly benefits all.

10   足 *zú* (**fulfilled**): This character would have been read here as 成 *chéng* (complete; fulfilled).[7]

13   白 *bái* or *bó* (**the white**): The use of this character (lit., white) here differs from the way it was used in line 7, for that was in contrast with 辱 *rǔ* (unclean) and so meant "clean." In this line, though, it referred to everything discernible under the sunshine,[8] or, in other words, our visible world.

14   式 *Shì* (**a Standard**): This was defined as 模則 *mózé* (standard).[9]

18   無極 *Wú Jí* (**the Zenith of the Void**): This referred to the state of "the Origin from the time of yore" where "the Principle of the Dao" lies (chapter 14 [lines 21–22]).

19   則 *zé* (**thereby**): This was used here to mean 乃 *nǎi* (thereby).[10]

19   器 *qì* (**utilitarian objects**): In ancient times, the character 器 *qì* was not necessarily used to solely denote devices like vehicles, vessels, and rooms (as described in chapter 11). In addition, all principles or rules that could be used to produce desired results in the world were considered 器 *qì*, such as 禮 *lǐ* (rituals; etiquette) and 義 *yì* (justice).[11]

20   則 *zé* (**the law of constancy**): In this context, the character 則 *zé* was meant to refer to 常法 *chángfǎ* (the law of constancy).[12] 則 *zé* was therefore used differently here from the same character in line 19 (first comment).

20   官長 *guānzhǎng* (**the controllers of [their] duties**): 官 *guān* indicated 得事 *déshì* (in charge of affairs or duties).[13] In interpreting this term, we added "their" to modify 得事 *déshì* (duties) so as to reflect its relationship with 器 *qì* (utilitarian objects).

21   夫 *fú* (**in this way**): This was used here to mean 故 *gù* (therefore; in this way).[14]

19–21 MN   **Cleave to the Essential:** This is another way of saying "cleave to the Dao," for, as chapter 32 (line 1) says, "The Dao . . . is the Essential."

CHAPTER 29

1   將 *jiāng* (**if**): This was used here to mean 若 *ruò* (if).[1]

1   取 *qǔ* (**to rule**): In this context, 取 *qǔ* was another way of saying 治 *zhì* (to rule).[2]

2   其弗得已 *qí fúdé yǐ* (**this will most likely be unattainable**): 其 *qí* was used here to mean 殆 *dài* (most likely)[3] and to indicate that this was a prediction. 弗得 *fúdé* meant 不得之 *bùdézhī* (to not attain it [modified here as unattainable]). (之 *zhī* [the object

representing what was said in line 1 here] was always omitted in this classical Chinese sentence pattern,[4] but is included in our interpretation as "this.") 已 *yǐ* would have been used as 矣 *yǐ*[5] and simply acted as a mood word.

3   神器 ***Shénqì*** **(a Venerated Object):** 神 *shén* in this context meant 尊重 *zūnzhòng*, which referred to the reverential worship of deities or ancestors,[6] and so is interpreted here as "venerated." Ancient concepts could hold that 器 *qì*—in addition to "utilitarian objects"—could also represent things that had been shaped,[7] and so we interpreted it here as an "object."[8]

5–6 為之者敗之, 執之者失之 ***wéizhīzhě bàizhī, zhízhīzhě shīzhī*** **(they who exert effort upon it will fail . . . will lose):** This is similar to chapter 64 (lines 10–11). The first 之 *zhī* character here referred to the phrase "to rule the world" (in line 1), while the second one acted as 焉 *yān* [a mood word],[9] and we used the passive voice to interpret these two lines.

8   吹 ***chuī*** **(cold):** This would have been defined here as 寒 *hán* (cold).[10]

9   挫 ***cuò*** **(bowed):** This would have been read here as 挼 *nuò*, which meant 橈 *náo* (bent; bowed).[11] "Tough" and "bowed" were other ways of saying "strong" and "weak."

10   培 ***péi*** **(waxing)** and 墮 ***duò*** **(waning):** 培 *péi* meant 益 *yì* (to augment), while 墮 *duò* meant 落 *luò* (to fall).[12] Based on these definitions, we interpreted these two characters as "waxing" and "waning."

14   奢 ***shē*** **(extravagance):** This was defined as 充庤 *chōngchì* (overabundance),[13] but it was used to describe an attitude here, and so has been modified as "extravagance."

CHAPTER 30

1   佐 ***zuǒ*** **(to serve):** This was defined as 助 *zhù* (to assist),[1] and is modified here as "to serve."

2   強 ***qiǎng*** **(to coerce):** 強 *qiǎng* would have been read here as 凌暴 *língbào* (to bully; to coerce).[2]

3   其事好, 還[3] ***qíshì hǎo, huán*** **([when] their affairs have been properly achieved, withdraw):** 其事 *qíshì* (their affairs) here referred to a mission that employed troops. Because 好 *hǎo* would have been defined under these circumstances as 宜 *yí* (appropriate),[4] "properly achieved" is used to interpret it to fit the context. 還 *huán* indicated "to withdraw [forces]."

4–5 師之所居, 楚棘生之 ***shī zhī suǒjū, chǔji shēngzhī*** **(wherever troops occupy, wild bushes and thorny vines will grow):** The Guodian text does not include these two lines. However, in this instance, we follow the silk versions and all other editions not only because this passage speaks with such authority, but also because it fits the use of forces exceptionally well.

6   果 ***guǒ*** **(fruition):** Wang Bi's note indicates that 果 *guǒ* (lit., fruit) here should be understood to mean 濟 *jì* (fulfillment). "Fruition" therefore turned out to be an oddly perfect equivalent.

7   以 ***yǐ*** **(to do with):** This was used here to mean 連及 *liánjí* (to be involved with; to do with).[5]

8   而 ***ér*** **(but):** This was used here to mean 然 *rán* (but).[6] 而 *ér* in lines 9–11 should be read the same way.

8&10 伐 *fá* (**glorification**) and 矜 *jīn* (**inflation**): See chapter 22 (comments on lines 4–5), but these have been modified as nouns to fit the context here.

12 壯 *zhuàng* (**excessive**): See chapter 55 (comment on line 13).

12 而 *ér* (**then**): This was used differently in line 8, as here it meant 則 *zé* (then).[7]

12 老 *lǎo* (**age**): As employed here, this character implied becoming rigid or stiff (per Heshang Gong's note), and therefore suggested a state of decline.

14 蚤已 *zǎoyǐ* (**perish before long**): 蚤 *zǎo* indicated 速 *sù* (soon),[8] which is modified here as "before long." 已 *yǐ* meant 止 *zhǐ* (ceased) or 棄 *qì* (forsaken),[9] and so is interpreted here as "perish."

12–14 Chapter 55 (lines 13–15) offers similar admonitions, which concern a person's unruly behavior, while in this chapter, they are directed at the use of military force to coerce the world.

CHAPTER 31

1 兵者 *bīngzhě* (**armed forces**): 兵 *bīng* was usually understood to mean "weapons" or "soldiers," but from the context of this chapter (especially lines 5–16), this clearly referred to "armed forces."

1 不祥 *bùxiáng* (**inauspicious**): 祥 *xiáng* meant 吉 *jí* (auspicious),[1] so 不祥 *bùxiáng* (lit., not auspicious) is interpreted accordingly. (This description was based on the nature of armed forces; with regard to 不祥 *bùxiáng*, see also chapter 78 [second comment on line 11].)

1 器 *qì* (**utilitarian objects**): "Armed forces" were employed to achieve their assigned missions, and so were considered here as "utilitarian objects." The guide to a clearer understanding of line 1 may be found in lines 7–17.

2 物或惡之 *wù huò èzhī* (**moreover, things abhor them**): 物 *wù* (things) represented all corporeal existence. 或 *huò* was used here to mean 又 *yòu* (also; moreover).[2]

3 弗 *fú* (**not . . . these**): See chapter 2 (comment on lines 11–12).

4 居 *jū* (**normally live**): This reading follows Fan Yingyuan's jizhu note, which explains this term as 常居 *chángjū* (to normally live).

5 用兵則貴右 *yòngbīng zé guì yòu* (**while armed forces are deployed with the right being esteemed**): In other words, this meant a field commander's troops would have been deployed as the right flank in battle. This concept is echoed in line 16.

4–5 則 . . . 則 *zé . . . zé* (**while**): This pattern describes the two connected parts as comparatives,[3] so we used "while" (in line 5) to interpret it here.

7 古曰 *gǔ yuē* (**even though it is said**): 古 *gǔ* was read here as 故 *gù*[4] and meant 雖 *suī* (even though).[5]

9 銛龍[6] 為上—弗美也 *tiǎnlóng wéi shàng—fú měi yě* (**the pursuit of peace is to be cherished—do not relish that**): This passage echoes the spirit of chapter 30 (lines 6–11). 銛 *tiǎn* (mod. Ch. pron., *xiān* [sharp]) in this context denoted 挑取 *tiāoqǔ* (to take [after selecting]),[7] and so we have modified it as "pursuit" to interpret this. 龍 *lóng* (lit., dragon) had the ancient meaning of 和同 *hétóng* (harmony; peace).[8] Thus, in this context, we rendered the term 銛龍 *tiǎnlóng* as "the pursuit of peace." 上 *shàng* (preferred) would have been read here as 尚 *shàng*,[9] which meant 貴 *guì* (to regard highly; to cherish).[10] As for 弗 *fú* (do not . . . [that]), see chapter 2 (comment on lines 11–12); "that" in this case referred to armed forces.

14 　上右 *shàng yòu* (**homage is paid to the right**): Ancient tradition held that when in mourning, one should use the right side to express homage. An example of this is that when Confucius's elder sister passed away, he stood with his right hand folded over his left.[11]

17 　言 *yán* (**suggests**): This literally means "to express an opinion or an idea," so we modified this as "to suggest" to clarify the description.

18 　隶 *lì* (**attends**): This was defined as 臨 *lín* (to attend).[12]

19 　居 *jū* (**treats**): This was another way of saying 處 *chù* (to administer; to manage), [13] and we modified this as "to treat" to fit the context.

CHAPTER 32

1 　樸 *Pǔ* (**the Essential**): This character literally indicated 質 *zhí* (essence; the Essential).[1]

2 　小 *xiǎo* (**tiny**): Although tiny is similar in meaning to little, the English descriptor "tiny" is used here to describe the actual state of the Dao. This differs from how 小 *xiǎo* (little) was used in chapter 34 (lines 7–8), where this character helped to describe Its expression as "having no desires" (and therefore led us to understand that the Dao resides within Itself, which is why in line 8 It is regarded as "the little.").

2 　弗敢 *fúgǎn* (**cannot . . . It**): 敢 *gǎn* was used here to mean 能 *néng* (can).[2] 弗 *fú* represented "not . . . It" (chapter 2 [comment on lines 11–12]), with "It" being the Dao.

4 　賓 *bīn* (**turn submissive**): This was another way of saying 服 *fú* (to obey; to become or to turn submissive).[3]

6 　以輸甘露 *yǐshū gānlù* (**to let fall sweet dew**): 輸 *shū* was defined as 墮 *duò* (to let fall).[4] "Sweet dew" suggested the commencement of infinite abundance.[5]

7 　民莫之命 *mín mòzhīmìng* (**and the people will need no instruction**): This phrasing turned 民莫命之 *mín mòmìng zhī* into a rhetorical statement, which literally meant "[as for] the people, [their lord] will not instruct them," and so is modified accordingly.

3–8 MN　**In harmony with the Dao:** In other words, only non-effort would then be performed in the world.

3–8 MN　**Treat one another . . . without being compelled:** This ideal result was predicated on two things: one is that the people adhered to their innate nature (chapter 19 [line 10 and the margin note on lines 7–10]), and the other is that their livelihoods were made secure through equal access to natural resources (as implied in lines 5–6), which would eliminate the need to struggle for survival.

9 　始制, 有名 *Shǐ zhì, yǒu míng* (**the Origin divides, and there are names**): 制 *zhì* was defined as 裁 *cái* (to cut; to divide).[6] The Origin is attributed to the Dao,[7] which can be more correctly understood here to mean the Essential.[8] When the Essential is split apart, this gives rise to utilitarian objects[9] (including, by extension, things). Even though the Essential Itself has no name, each utilitarian object (or thing) that arises out of It can be identified, and thereby a name will be given.

10 　亦 *yì* [**mood word**]: This character in this context had no inherent meaning[10] and was used here to emphasize the idea of 既 *jì* (to have been) and express the mood of past tense.

11 　夫亦將知止 *fú yì jiāngzhī zhǐ* (**one then must know their foundation**): 夫 *fú* was

used here to mean 彼 *bǐ* [the third person pronoun],[11] which is rendered as the "one" who possesses the power to manage everything that had been named. In this context, 亦 *yì* meant 則 *zé* (then),[12] while 將 *jiāng* was employed as a way of saying 必 *bì* (must).[13] Finally, 止 *zhǐ* ([their] foundation) had the definition of 下基 *xiàjī* (foundation).[14] As we already have names (line 10)—representing corporeal facts—this term referred to the Essential, which, according to Laozi's teachings, acted as the foundation of those corporeal facts. This understanding of the foundation echoes the description of the Dao in line 13.

12 不殆 *búdài* (**avoiding failure**): 殆 *dài* meant 敗 *bài* (fail; failure),[15] and 不 *bú* (lit., no) is modified here as "to avoid" to better fit the description.

13 俾道 *bǐ Dào* (**obeyance to the Dao**): 俾 *bǐ* meant 從 *cóng* (to follow; to obey; obeyance).[16]

13 在 *zài* (**securing**): This would have been read here as 存 *cún* (to preserve; to secure).[17]

14 與 *yǔ* (**follow**): 與 *yǔ* was used here to mean 從 *cóng* (to follow).[18]

CHAPTER 33

1 知也 *zhìyě* (**clever**): In ancient times, 知 *zhī* was often used interchangeably with 智 *zhì* (clever).[1] Its correct reading was determined by context.

1–2 MN **Wisdom . . . in the secular world:** As we read this chapter, we must keep in mind that although Laozi is guiding us toward the transcendence of secular concepts, this does not mean that the importance of our secular lives is being disregarded, for he noted in chapter 20 (line 4) that "Those who are to be respected by people also cannot be those who disrespect people," in addition to the descriptions in chapter 22 (lines 2–5) and chapter 23 (lines 9–12).

3 有力 *yǒulì* (**forceful**): Literally, this denoted "having force," so we used "forceful" to interpret it.

6 有志 *yǒuzhì* (**realize their wills**): 有 *yǒu* (lit., to have) was used here to mean 得 *dé* (to attain; to realize),[2] with "their" added in English to clarify the subject of this clause.

CHAPTER 34

1 汎 *fàn* (**boundless**): This denoted 不係 *búxì* (unbound),[1] and we have modified it accordingly.

1–2 MN **By Its very nature, the Dao is absolutely neutral:** If the Dao did not possess such a nature, then the statements in lines 5–6 would have proven themselves to be unsubstantiated (and the Dao therefore could not have been described as "having no desires" in line 7).[2] But because the nature of the Dao is neutral, It is able "to conform to self-realization" (chapter 25 [line 21]) through non-effort, and this is what can cause the world's polarized factors to join as one (chapter 2 [lines 3–8] and chapter 23 [lines 1–4]).

4 "It" refers to "the Dao," and is not specifically named here. However, in ancient Chinese, words could be omitted whenever they were considered understood and therefore redundant.

3–4 MN **It never tries . . . Its performance in the world:** This echoes the spirit described in chapter 25 (line 21) and chapter 9 (lines 9–10), as well as chapter 2 (lines 11–13) and chapter 51 (lines 11–14).

5   歸焉 *guī Yān* (**follow It**): 歸 *guī* was defined as 就 *jiù* (to turn to; to follow).[3] 焉 *yān* [mood word] was used here to indicate 之 *zhī* (It)[4] and denoted the Dao.

8   於 *yú* (**as**): This was used to mean 為 *wéi* (to be; as).[5]

8   小 *xiǎo* (**the little**): Compare this with chapter 32 (first comment on line 2).

5–8 MN   **Accommodate and fully support them:** This echoes the spirit of the Dao described as "non-effort" (chapter 37 [line 1]) and "conforms to self-realization" (chapter 25 [line 21]).

5–8 MN   **Self-sufficiency:** This understanding was inspired by the notion of "having no desires," for it logically follows that if the Dao were to master things, It would need to satisfy Its desires by having dominion over them, and thereby could not be considered self-sufficient. Without the independence that is achieved through self-sufficiency, no one can be neutral toward the world. See also chapter 26 (margin note on lines 3–4).

9–10 大 *dà* (**the great**): From the descriptions of these lines, we can see that "the great" can be comprehended as comprising both descriptions of the Dao[6] and ubiquity.

9–10 MN **Granting them complete freedom:** See chapter 25 (line 21).

9–10 MN **To be willingly followed . . . what led the Dao to be identified as "the great":** This gives us a deeper understanding of how "the great" signifies all-pervasive influence. (If the Dao had been concerned with being "the master" of all things, It would have become confined by this and therefore unable to embrace all. Such limitations would have meant that It never could have become "the Great.")

CHAPTER 35

1   執 *zhí* (**cleave to**): This would have been read here as 守 *shǒu* (to hold to; to cleave to).[1]

1   大象 *dà Xiàng* (**the great Form**): 大象 *dà Xiàng* symbolized the Dao.[2]

2   往 *wǎng* (**follow**): This would have been understood in this context to mean 歸往 *guīwǎng* (to follow).[3]

3   **It:** This English word was added to this line (but not line 4) to clarify that the subject is 天下 *tiānxià* (the world). The subject "it" was omitted in lines 3–4 of the Chinese text, as this was understood from the implication in line 2.

4   安平太 *ānpíngtài* (**settling in ease and peace**): 安 *ān* was another way of saying 定 *dìng* (to settle).[4] 平 *píng* would have been defined here as 安舒 *ānshū* (ease).[5] 太 *tài* could be read as 泰 *tài*, which in ancient times meant 安 *ān* (peace).[6]

1–4 MN   **By cleaving to the Dao . . . to contentedly attain self-realization without disturbance:** See chapter 25 (line 21).

5   餌 *ěr* (**food**): The character 餌 *ěr* was in ancient times defined as 食 *shí* (food).[7]

5–6 MN   **Once they [i.e., music and food] are gone, so are the guests:** This understanding follows Su Che's note.

7   故 *gù* (**however**): In ancient times, 故 *gù* (lit., therefore) could be used interchangeably with 顧 *gù* (however).[8]

7   道之出言 *Dào zhī chūyán* (**the words uttered by the Dao**): This echoes chapter 24 (line 1), as inspired by Wang Bi's note on that line.

8 無味 *wúwèi* (**bland**): Music and fine food attract people who desire to savor what is offered. At the other end of the spectrum, "words uttered by the Dao" transcend our perceptive abilities, and so appear unable to entice our senses.

7–8 MN **Its expression . . . and dull:** See chapter 24 (line 1), as well as chapter 14 (lines 3–4).

9–10 不足 *bùzú* (**there is nothing**): This term was another way of saying 不能 *bùnéng* (to be unable to),[9] which is modified here to match the context.

11 不可既 *bùkějì* (**unconstrainable**): This term meant the same thing as 不可盡 *bùkějìn* (cannot be limited),[10] and so is interpreted accordingly.

CHAPTER 36

1 將 *jiāng* (**when**): This could be defined as "if"; see chapter 29 (first comment on line 1), although it is modified here as "when" to better fit the description. The character 將 *jiāng* in lines 3, 5, and 7 should be read the same way.

1 翕 *xì* (**contract**): This was defined as 斂 *liàn* (to contract).[1]

1 之 *zhī* (**something/it**): 之 *zhī* normally, as here, represented the third person. When used as the subject of lines 1, 3, 5, and 7, it was rendered as "something." However, 之 *zhī* was used as the object in lines 2, 4, 6, and 8, and so was interpreted as "it."

2 必 *bì* (**then**): 必 *bì* was used here to connote the meaning of 則 *zé* (then).[2] This character in lines 4, 6, and 8 should be read the same way.

2 固 *gù* (**for the time being**): This was another way of saying 姑 *gū*, which is defined as 且 *qiě* (for the time being).[3] The character 固 *gù* in lines 4, 6, and 8 should be read the same way.

6 與 *yǔ* (**promoted**): In this context, 與 *yǔ* was to be read as 舉 *jǔ* (to lift; to promote).[4]

8 予 *yù* (**augmented**): 予 *yù* was literally defined as "to give," but we have modified this here to clarify the concept being discussed and to fit the context.

9 微明 *wēimíng* (**shrouded achievement**): 微 *wēi* meant 幽隱 *yōuyǐn* (hidden; shrouded),[5] and 明 *míng* was defined here as 成 *chéng* (to achieve; achievement).[6]

12 邦之利器 *bāng zhī lìqì* (**means that are advantageous to a state**):[7] This deals with how governance is conducted, and does not particularly concern extensive military power (chapter 30 [line 2]: "not want to use force to coerce the world"). 利 *lì* meant 利益 *lìyì* (to be advantageous).[8] 器 *qì* here denoted 用 *yòng* (usage)[9] or 手段 *shǒuduàn* (means),[10] and so this term is interpreted accordingly. (Previous annotations on 利器 *lìqì* are extremely varied and perplexing. Our understanding of this term, though, follows Laozi's own teaching—"using no shrewdness in the governing of a country will be a boon to that country" (chapter 65 [lines 7–8])—as can be seen in the margin note on this line.)

12 視 *shì* (**revealed to**): This should be read here as 示 *shì* (to show; to reveal).[11]

CHAPTER 37

1 無為 *wúwéi* (**non-effort**): Wang Bi's extremely important note says that "non-effort" means "[to act] in accordance with self-realization."[1]

1 MN **The Dao "conforms to self-realization":** This follows Wang Bi's note; see the first comment above on this line.

3 而 *ér* (**then**): 而 *ér* was used here to mean 則 *zé* (then).[2]

3   化 *huà* (**cultivated**): 化 *huà* here meant 遷善 *qiānshàn* (to improve),[3] so "cultivated" is used to interpret it in this context.

4   而 *ér* (**if**): This 而 *ér* was used here to mean 如 *rú* (if)[4] and is used differently from the same character in line 3.

5   將 *jiāng* (**then**): This character was used here to mean 則 *zé* (then).[5] Such a reading follows the Guodian version. As a continuation of line 2, the subject (i.e., lords or the king) was considered understood and therefore omitted. However, all other versions added the character 吾 *wǔ* (I; we) before 將 *jiāng*, turning this into the term 吾將 *wǔ jiāng* (I [or we] will), which obfuscated the subject under discussion.[6] This character in line 7 should be read the same way.

5   鎮之 *zhènzhī* (**pacify them**): 鎮 *zhèn* was defined as 安 *ān* (to appease; to pacify).[7] 之 *zhī* (them) here represented "the people," which is where desires lie (see the margin note on this line). It is understood that the one who would "pacify them" was a lord or king.

5   無名之樸 *wúmíng zhī Pǔ* (**the Essential that has no name**): Chapter 32 (line 1) says that "the Dao . . . has no name, and is the Essential." So, this term was specifically used to indicate the property of the Dao that is able to pacify our desires. (Refer to chapter 19 [lines 9–10].)

4–5 MN   **The Dao always nurtures them into a contented existence:** See chapter 1 (line 6), chapter 25 (lines 1–5), chapter 51 (lines 7–10), and chapter 52 (line 1).

7   夫亦 *fú yì* (**they will then**): 夫 *fú* was used here to mean 彼 *bǐ* (they [i.e., the people]),[8] while 亦 *yì* in this instance meant 則 *zé* (then).[9]

8   知足 *zhīzú* (**grasping contentment**): This term in the Beida version was read as 不辱 *bùrǔ* (not shamed). However, 知足 *zhīzú* in chapter 44 (line 6) is the cause ("grasp contentment") for 不辱 *bùrǔ* ("will never be shamed"). In the received versions, this term was written as 不欲 *búyù* (abandon desires), but if we already grasp contentment, then we will certainly have no need for desires.

8   以靜 *yǐjìng* (**leads to stillness**): 以 *yǐ* was used here to mean 使 *shǐ* (to cause).[10] This meaning is extended here as "to lead to" in order to better fit the context.

CHAPTER 38

1   德 *Dé* (**the De**): Obtainment of the De comes from the Dao.[1] In ancient times, this character had the basic definition of 得 *dé* (obtainment),[2] and its later meanings evolved out of this. That is why, when we see 德 *dé* in classical writings, we must first clearly and precisely identify the connotation of "obtainment" that 德 *dé* is representing in that context.[3] Therefore, because 德 *dé* could have many different meanings, we cannot interpret it with a single word, and so it is rendered simply as the De.[4]

1–2 上德不德, 是以有德 *shàng Dé bù Dé, shìyǐ yǒu Dé* (**the superior De is free of the De and so possesses the De**): When we obey the principle of the Dao (chapter 37) and thereby are able to perform with non-effort,[5] we no longer need to be concerned about the 德 *Dé*, for It will always be with us. Therefore, 不德 *bù Dé* is interpreted as "free of the De."[6] 有 *yǒu* literally meant "to have," but this has been modified here as "to possess" to better fit the context.

1–2 An understanding of how the teaching conveyed by these two lines may be put into practice can be found in chapter 2 (lines 9–15).

5 上 **shàng (exalt):** This character would have been read here as 尚 *shàng* (to prize; to exalt).[7] This also applies to the 上 *shàng* characters in lines 6–8.

5 無以為 **wúyǐwèi ([has] no intention):** 以為 *yǐwèi* here was another way of saying 所為 *suǒwèi* (intention).[8] This also applies to the use of 以為 *yǐwèi* in lines 6–7.

8 上禮為之而莫之應也 **shàng lǐ wéizhī ér mòzhīyīng yě (exalt social rules by exerting efforts upon them, and if reciprocations cannot be had):** 禮 *lǐ* could mean either "ritual" or "social rules"; the context indicated that it would have been the latter. 而 *ér* was used here to mean 如 *rú* (if).[9] Moreover, 莫之應也 *mòzhīyīng yě* was another way of saying 莫能當之 *mònéng dāngzhī* (lit., it cannot have a proper response).[10]

9 攘臂 **rǎngbì ([with] outstretched arms):** 攘 *rǎng* was defined as 推 *tuī* (to push; to stretch out),[11] which we have modified here as "outstretched" to provide a smoother reading.

9 乃 **nǎi (pull [them in]):** In ancient Chinese, this could have been read as if it were 扔 *rèng*,[12] which meant 引 *yǐn* (to pull).[13] (We have added "them in" to clarify the meaning here.)

9 This metaphor described the use of coercion to constrain rudeness.

12 MN **While justice . . . will lead to latent conflict:** Wang Bi's note indicates that "justice leads to conflict."[14]

14–15 These two lines act as a critical conclusion to the preceding passage. The subjects under discussion are the four ethical values that are always pursued with effort. "The [inferior] De" is based on man's comprehension of what the Dao must be (see margin note on line 10), while "humanity" is more concerned with the needs of others; neither of these, therefore, has anything to do with prescience (line 16). The other two values are "justice" and "social rules," which are formed by predetermined standards derived from prescience, and these values are then applied to judge situations as they occur.

16 前識者 **qiánshízhě (prescience):** 識 *shí* would have been read here as 知 *zhī* (knowledge),[15] and because 前 *qián* was defined as "in advance" or "ahead," 前識 *qiánshí* therefore meant "foreknowledge" or "prescience." 者 *zhě* was a mood word that emphasized the subject here and cannot be translated.[16]

18 大丈夫 **dàzhàngfū (a great man):** This referred to "one [usually a leader] who comprehends the Dao."[17]

18 厚 **hòu (profundity):**[18] According to line 14, this term would have suggested "sincerity and honesty."

20 實 **shí (fruit):** By referring to line 16, we may understand that this metaphorical description referred to "cleaving to the Dao."

22 MN **We must look to the spirit of the De . . . what we really are:** Regarding the achievement of this, see chapter 28 (lines 1–6) and chapter 19 (lines 9–10).

22 MN **Justice or social rules, which lie there:** This rendering is based on the meanings in lines 7–9 and 12–15. (The Qing Shizu emperor's note can also be used here as a reference.)[19]

CHAPTER 39

1 昔 **xī ([since] the time of yore):** The discussion here used the perspective of "from the now back to the time of yore" (chapter 21), so "since" has been added for clarification.

1 得一 **dé Yī (obtained the One):** As used here, 得 *dé* (obtainment; to obtain) implied

realization of "the De,"[1] and 一 *Yī* ("the One") represented a harmonious state.[2] The term 得一 *dé Yī* in lines 2–6 should also be interpreted this way.

4 神 *Shén* (**the Celestial Generating Spirit**): See chapter 6 (comment on line 1).

4 靈 *líng* (**perfect**): This was defined as 善 *shàn* (good; perfect),[3] which meant that "the Celestial Generating Spirit" creates all things without defect.

5 谷 *gǔ* (**valleys**): See chapter 28 (comment on line 8).

6 天下正 *tiānxià zhèng* (**leaders of the world**): 正 *zhèng* should be defined here as 君 *jūn* (ruler; leader).[4]

6 The description in this line echoes that of chapter 23 (lines 7–8).

7 其致之也 *qí zhì Zhī yě* (**if the One were to be striven for**): 其 *qí* was used here to mean 若 *ruò* (if),[5] and 之 *zhī* [third person pronoun] represented "the One" as discussed above. The reason for this assertion is that 得一 *dé Yī* ([have] obtained the One), as described in lines 2–6, must be achieved through "non-effort,"[6] while striving for It will certainly fail, as described below.

8 謂 *wèi* (**as [when]**): This was used here to suggest 譬 *pì* (for instance; as [when]).[7] All instances of 謂 *wèi* in lines 9–12 are interpreted the same way.

8 毋已 *wúyǐ* (**cannot**): 毋 *wú* was read here as 無 *wú* [negative mood word],[8] while 已 *yǐ* could be read as 以 *yǐ*,[9] which meant 能 *néng* (can),[10] so "cannot" is used. The term 毋已 *wúyǐ* in lines 9–12 are all interpreted this way.

8 將 *jiāng* (**would be**): This was used in this instance to mean 則 *zé* (then; would be).[11] This character as it appears in lines 9–12 all have the same reading.

8 天 . . . 裂 *tiān . . . liè* (**the heavens . . . cracking**): In ancient times, it was believed that whenever a calamity was imminent, the heavens would portend this with strange colors, unusual phenomena, and omens that were then referred to as 天裂 *tiān liè* (the heavens crack).[12]

9 地 . . . 發 *dì . . . fā* (**the Earth . . . erupting**): 發 *fā* should be read here as 興 *xīng* (to rise; to erupt).[13] The Earth in its normal state is still. On the other hand, movements via eruptions on the Earth's surface—such as earthquakes, volcanic disruptions, and the like—are both unusual and destructive.[14]

10 神 . . . 歇 *Shén . . . xiē* (**the Celestial Generating Spirit . . . perishing**): 歇 *xiē* was defined as 息 *xī* (to cease; to perish).[15] 神 *Shén* is that which brings about all things (chapter 6 [line 1]), and so if Its performance diminishes, all things in the world will be extinguished.

11 谷 . . . 渴 *gǔ . . . kě* (**the valleys . . . drying up**): 渴 *kě* here meant 水盡 *shuǐjìn* (water dries up).[16] Rivers come from 谷 *gǔ* (valleys), and so when water no longer flows in them, this can destroy a country (see endnote 14).

12 侯王 . . . 蹶 *hóu wáng . . . jué* (**the lords and the king . . . falling**): 蹶 *jué* was defined as 顛覆 *diānfù* (to fall).[17]

12 以 *yǐ* (**due to**): In this context, this meant 因 *yīn* (due to).[18]

13 必 *bì* (**even**) and 而 *ér* (**will**): 必 *bì* was used here to mean 雖 *suī* (though; even),[19] while 而 *ér* meant 必 *bì* (must; will).[20] The readings of these two characters in line 14 are the same.

15 夫 *fú* (**oh**): This mood word had the function of beginning a discussion, but it had no inherent meaning here,[21] so we rendered this as "oh."

15 孤、寡、不穀 *gū, guǎ, bùgū* ("the lone," "the bereft," "the misfortunate"): Here, 孤 *gū* meant 單獨 *dāndú* (the isolated; the lone).[22] 寡 *guǎ* was defined as 無妻、無夫 *wúqī, wúfū* (a widow, a widower),[23] and so this has been interpreted here as "bereft." 不穀 *bùgū* was another way of saying 不祿 *búlù* (the misfortunate).[24] These were the names by which lords or the kings nominatively referred to themselves during the pre-Qin period.[25]

16 此其賤之本與 *cǐ qí jiàn zhībĕn yú* (is it not most likely that their foundation is humility): 其 *qí* was used here to mean 殆 *dài* (probable; most likely), which gave this line a questioning mood with an assertive note,[26] while 之 *zhī* should be read as 為 *wéi* (to be; is).[27] 與 *yú* had the same meaning here as 歟 *yú* [a mood word], which served to provide a questioning tone.[28]

16 非也 *fēiyě* (is it not): 也 *yě* was used here to mean 邪 *yē* [a mood word], which indicated a question.[29]

17 致數與無與 *zhì shuòyù wúyù* (the conferral of many honors has nothing to do with honor): 致 *zhì* meant 送詣 *sòngyì* (to proffer; to confer),[30] but in this case the passive voice was used,[31] and so has been modified accordingly. 數 *shuò* was another way of saying 數數 *shuòshuò*,[32] which meant 汲汲 *jíjí* (constant; many).[33] 與 *yù* should be read here as 譽 *yù* (honors), as these two characters were interchangeable in ancient times.[34] 無 *wú* was to be read as 勿 *wù* [a negative marker in formal speech],[35] and so 無與 *wúyù* literally meant "should not be honored," but to provide a smoother reading, we interpreted this as "has nothing to do with honor." (In pre-Qin China, true honor was recognized via public announcement and accompanied by promotion and gifts.)[36]

18–19 祿祿 *lùlù* (the grandeur) and 硌硌 *luòluò* (the humbleness): When used as modifiers in ancient Chinese, 祿 *lù* might be written as 琭 *lù* or even 碌 *lù*, while 硌 *luò* sometimes had the form of 落 *luò*. The term 祿祿 *lùlù* (or 琭琭 *lùlù*) described the appearance of jade, which, of all precious stones, was held in the highest esteem, and so it is interpreted here as "the grandeur." 硌硌 *luòluò* (or 落落 *luòluò*) referred to stone, which was regarded as inferior and considered commonplace with a humble appearance, and so this has been interpreted here as "the humbleness."[37]

18–19 MN **The jade and stone pendants that constituted Chinese officials' insignia:** In ancient times, a king's supreme position was indicated by the five perfect pieces of jade he wore. Each rank beneath him would be signified by fewer jades and more stones with the lowest rank having only "one jade and four stones."[38]

CHAPTER 40[1]

1 士 *shì* (scholar): In pre-Qin times, this character was used to refer to three categories (see chapter 15 [comment on line 1 and endnote 2]). In this chapter, the descriptions in lines 1–4 show that its definition as 學士 *xuéshì* (scholars) should be applied here.

6 孛 *bèi* (unclear): In this context, the character 孛 *bèi* would have been read as 昧 *mèi*, which meant 不明 *bùmíng* (unclear).[2]

6 MN **Embrace all . . . may appear unintelligible:** Refer to the descriptions in chapter 20.

7　夷 *yí* (**gliding along**): As used here, this character had the same meaning as the obsolete character that combined 夷 *yí* with the 彳 *chì* (short steps) radical (彳 + 夷)[3] and connoted "walking [or moving] smoothly,"[4] or, in other words, "gliding along."

7　纇 *lèi* (**rough**): This character referred to something that was 不平 *bùpíng* (not smooth; rough).[5]

7 MN　**Beware of deviation:** See chapter 53 (lines 1–3). With regard to the attitude of awareness, see chapter 15 (lines 1–7).

9　如谷 *rú gǔ* (**as a valley**): The significance of 谷 *gǔ* (valley) as used here can be found in chapter 28 (comment on line 8), and our understanding is as described in that line's margin note.

9 MN　**Obtaining the De through the wisdom of the Dao:** This follows Wang Bi's note on chapter 38, in which he says, "How to obtain the De? Through the Dao."

10　大 *dà* (**great**): This denoted that what was being modified had the properties of the Dao (see chapter 34 [first comment on lines 9–10]). 大 *dà* in lines 14–16 should be read with the same understanding.

10　An explanation of this line can be found in chapter 28 (line 7).

11 MN **Cleaving to insufficiency:** See chapter 45 (lines 1, 3, and 5–7).

12　偷 *tōu* (**perfunctory**): As used here, this character would have been defined as 苟且 *gǒuqiě* (perfunctory).[6]

13　質貞 *zhízhēn* (**intrinsic certainty**): 質 *zhí* indicated 性 *xìng* (nature; intrinsic quality), while 貞 *zhēn*—which the Guodian editorial board read as 真 *zhēn* (lit., truth)—meant 不變 *búbiàn* (immutability; certainty).[7]

13　渝 *yú* (**mutable**): This was defined as 變 *biàn* (changeable; mutable).[8]

13 MN **Grasp the truth by accommodating the world's flux:** See chapter 29 (lines 7–14), as well as chapter 25 (line 21).

14 MN **The Law of the Dao lies in the Essential and conforms to self-realization:** See chapter 32 (line 1), as well as chapter 25 (line 21).

15　曼成 *mànchéng* (**free of completion**): 曼 *màn* here meant 無 *wú* (without; free of).[9]

16　大音希聲 *dàyīn xīshēng* (**a great pitch transcends sound**): Regarding 音 *yīn* and 聲 *shēng*, see chapter 2 (comment on line 7) and chapter 12 (comment on line 5). And per the description in chapter 14 (lines 3–4), 希 *xī* indicated a sound that could not be heard, so "transcends" is used here as its interpretation.

17　天象 *tiān Xiàng* (**the great Form**): In ancient times, 天 *tiān* would be understood to mean 大 *dà* (great).[10] 大象 *dà Xiàng* is how the Dao expresses Itself in the world.[11]

17　無刑 *wúxíng* (**has no shape**): 刑 *xíng* (mod. Ch., penalty; sentence) in ancient times could be read as if it were 形 *xíng* (shape).[12]

17　With regard to the term "no shape," see chapter 14 (lines 1–16).

18　襃 *bǎo* (**immense**): This was defined as 盛大 *shèngdà* (boundless; immense).[13]

CHAPTER 41[1]

1　In chapter 14 (lines 17–18), the movement of the Dao is described as, "When followed, Its back is not visible; when faced, Its front is not visible." This tells us that the Dao always performs within a self-contained cyclical movement, and thus any increase in Its reverse actions is directly balanced by a decrease in motion. Complete balance between these two forces results in an equilibrium that appears to us as stillness, and that is where a new cyclical movement begins.

(In the *Dao De Jing*, the Dao's movements are described in three ways: The first is as noted above. Second, as in chapter 14 [lines 11–16], the Dao is also portrayed as existing in a never-ending cycle of emerging and withdrawing.[2] Finally, chapter 25 [lines 9–11] shows us how the Dao moves within the sphere of the world, in a process of "departure," "remoteness," and "return." What all these have in common is that they are implemented through reverse movement.)

2   Chapter 37 (line 1) relates that "the Dao always exerts with non-effort."[3] Moreover, chapter 25 (line 21) points out that "the Dao conforms to self-realization." Comparing these two statements allows us to conclude that no gap exists between exerting "non-effort" and conforming to "self-realization," and so we may visualize how the Dao's performance must invariably be through "weakness."

(Chapter 43 [lines 1–4] says, "The softest of all [至柔 *zhìróu*] in the world runs through the hardest of all. . . . This is how I comprehend the advantage of non-effort." In Chinese, 柔 *róu* [soft] may act as a synonym for 弱 *ruò* (weak),[4] thus underlining the direct relationship between "[the exertion of] non-effort" and "[the performance of] weakness.")

CHAPTER 42

1   道生一 ***Dào shēng Yī*** (**the Dao brought about the One**): Sima Guang's note indicates that this meant "[the Dao] came into Being from the Void."[1]

1   三生萬物 ***sān shēng wànwù*** (**the Three brought about all things**): Line 2 describes how all things are structured, that they "bear the yin on their backs" as they "embrace the yang," while the "Pulsing Breath" forms harmony between these factors. Chapter 4 (line 1) tells us that the Pulsing Breath is in fact how the Dao performs. Many have written annotations on this line, but only those by the Tang Xuanzong emperor and Wu Cheng suggest the same understanding as ours. (It should be noted that they considered the yin and the yang as being two types of breath, or 氣 *qì*. However, such an interpretation cannot accommodate the two verbs Laozi used here: 負 *fù* [bear] and 抱 *bào* [embrace]. These verbs thus turned the yin and the yang into little more than symbols, and in this respect cannot be followed; see endnote 2.)

1 MN **Laozi uses a simple mathematical formula . . . existence of all things:** This mathematical description of how all things are generated gives rise to the suggestion that these might possibly suggest something on the order of the "Fibonacci sequence," in which each number is the sum of the two preceding ones, such as 0, 1, 1, 2, 3, and so on.

2   陰 ***yīn*** (**yin**) and 陽 ***yáng*** (**yang**): 陰 *yīn* signified 靜 *jìng* (stillness), while 陽 *yáng* represented 動 *dòng* (movement).[2]

3–4 See chapter 39 (line 15).

6   故人 ***gùrén*** (**the ancients**): 故 *gù* here was a borrowed character for 古 *gǔ* (ancient).[3]

6   亦 ***yì*** (**shall be**): This was used here to mean 將 *jiāng* (shall be [i.e., future tense]).[4]

6   議 ***yì*** (**adapted**): This character suggested 定事宜 *dìng shìyí* (determining the appropriateness of an affair),[5] which is extended here to "adapted."

6   而 *ér* (**to**): This character was used here to mean 以 *yǐ* (in order to; to).[6]

8   學父 *xuéfù* (**[an] instructive rule**): In this context, 學 *xué* (lit., learning) would have been read as 教 *jiào* (to instruct; instructive).[7] 父 *fù* (lit., father) here meant 矩 *jù* (rule).[8]

CHAPTER 43

1–2 MN   **The nature of water . . . to penetrate . . . such as hard rock**: This understanding follows Lin Xiyi's note (in *Laozi yi*).

3   無有 *wúyǒu* (**non-being**): This indicated an existence that has no corporeal form.

4 MN   **"Competing not" . . . non-effort**: From the preceding descriptions, we are able to comprehend the ways in which nonresistance behaves (by competing not), thus allowing success to be achieved without impediment.

CHAPTER 44

1   親 *qīn* (**dear**): The meaning of this term was the opposite of 疏 *shū* (disregarded; marginalized),[1] and so is interpreted here as "dear."

2   貨 *huò* (**valuables**): See chapter 3 (comment on lines 3–4).

2   多 *duō* (**important**): This meant 重 *zhòng* (valuable)[2] here, which has been modified as "important."

4   愛 *ài* (**obsession**): As used here, this character denoted 慕 *mù* (admiration; obsession).[3]

5   厚 *hòu* (**measureless**): 厚 *hòu* was used in this context to mean 多 *duō* (much more; incalculable; measureless).[4]

7   殆 *dài* (**fail**): See chapter 32 (second comment on line 12).

8   可以 *kěyǐ* (**thus**): In this context, this term would have been read as 所以 *suǒyǐ* (thus), which meant that 可 *kě* (lit., may) was used to denote 所 *suǒ* (lit., what).[5]

CHAPTER 45

1   若 *ruò* (**seems**): This character may be interpreted as "to seem," and should be read the same way in lines 3 and 5–7.

2   用 *yòng* (**efficacy**): 用 *yòng* literally meant "usage," but we modified that definition here as "efficacy" to better fit the context. 用 *yòng* in line 4 should be read the same way.

2   敝 *bì* (**exhausted**): This character would have been defined here as 盡 *jìn* (to deplete; to exhaust).[1]

3   盅 *zhōng* (**empty**): Here, the character 盅 *zhōng* would have meant 空虛 *kōngxū* (emptiness; empty).[2]

6   成 *chéng* (**thriving**): In this context, 成 *chéng* would have been read as 盛 *shèng* (prospering; thriving); these two characters could be used interchangeably in ancient times.[3]

6   詘 *qū* (**withered**): This was defined as 絕止 *juézhǐ* (to cease; to expire).[4] Because it was used in contrast to "thriving," we modified it here as "withered."

8   滄 *cāng* (**cold**): This character was used to mean 寒 *hán* (cold).[5]

CHAPTER 46

1   有道 *yǒu Dào* (**embraces the Dao**): 有 *yǒu* literally meant "to have; to convey" and this meaning is modified here as "to embrace" to clarify the context.

2   卻走馬以糞 *què zǒumǎ yǐ fèn* (**chargers are dismissed to farm**): 卻 *què* would

have been read here as 除 *chú* (to be rid of; to dismiss).[1] 走 *zǒu* meant 疾趨 *jíqū* (to run fast),[2] so 走馬 *zǒumǎ* was a fast horse or charger. 糞 *fèn* was defined here as 田 *tián* (to farm).[3]

5   皐 *zuì* (**crime**): This was the ancient form of 罪 *zuì* (crime).[4]

5   厚乎 *hòuhū* (**worse than**): Here, 厚 *hòu* was defined as 重 *zhòng* (great; greater),[5] and we have modified it here as "worse" to fit the context. 乎 *hū* was employed in this context to mean 於 *yú* (than).[6] 乎 *hū* in lines 6–7 should be interpreted the same way.

5   甚欲 *dānyù* (**obsessing over desires**): 甚 (mod. Ch. pron., *shèn*)[7] was the original form of 媅 *dān*[8] and had the same meaning as 耽 *dān* (to obsess).[9]

6   憯乎 *cǎnhū* (**harmful than**): In ancient times, 憯 *cǎn* was interchangeable with 惨 *cǎn*[10] and meant 害 *hài* (harm; harmful).[11] With regard to 乎 *hū*, see the second comment on line 5 above.

5–7   The descriptions in these three lines teach us that when we are ensnared by our desires, we undergo three stages: 1) our thoughts and emotions become obsessed; 2) after an initial taste of success, we begin to pursue those desires irrationally and incessantly; and finally 3) we become befuddled by those desires as we attempt to both amass more and protect what we have attained, and so never realize and enjoy the contentment that a peaceful life unfettered by those desires can offer. (Our reading of these three lines follows the Guodian version. Lines 6–7 are, for no apparent reason, reversed in both silk versions, as well as in the Beida version. If the Guodian version had remained hidden in a tomb, we would have never been able to logically decode this magnificent teaching.)

CHAPTER 47

2   以 *yǐ* (**thereby**): This was used here to mean 遂 *suì* (thus; thereby).[1] 以 *yǐ* was employed in a similar fashion in line 4.

3   闚 *kuī* (**peer**): This referred to 自內觀外 *zìnèi guānwài* (looking at the outside from inside),[2] and so is interpreted here as to "peer."

3   牖 *yǒu* (**windows**): This referred to the sort of wood-framed windows that were set into walls. (The modern word for window is 窗 *chuāng*, but in ancient times, this character referred solely to a framed opening in a room.)[3]

5–6   彌遠 . . . 彌少 *míyuǎn . . . míshǎo* (**further . . . less**): These two terms were used as adverbs here. 彌 *mí* had the basic meaning of 益 *yì* (increase; more),[4] but when it is used as an amplifier, as in lines 5–6 for 遠 *yuǎn* (far) and 少 *shǎo* (few), it turns them into the terms "further" and "less."

7   行 *xíng* (**looking**): This would have been read here as 視 *shì* (to look).[5]

CHAPTER 48

1   益 *yì* (**intensify**): 益 *yì* literally meant "increasing," but is interpreted here as "intensify" to better describe the exertion of "increased" effort toward learning.

1–2   . . . 者 . . . 者 . . . *zhě . . . zhě* (**as . . .**): Both characters were used here to mean 則 *zé* (then).[1] In this sentence pattern, the first half points to the cause, while the second part describes its effect.[2] We therefore used "as . . ." to give this a better reading. (The descriptions in lines 1–4 echo what is described in chapter 40 [line 8]: "Advancement on the Dao will seem to recede.")[3]

5 　而 *ér* (**then**): This was used to mean 則 *zé* (then).[4]

5 　無不為 *wúbùwéi* (**nothing . . . will not be realized**): In this instance, 為 *wéi* meant 成 *chéng* (to be realized).[5]

5 　Chapter 47 (line 9) says, "Achieve, but not through exerting effort," which echoes the significance of this line.

6 　In silk version B, this reads, 取天下, 恆無事 *qǔ tiānxià, héng wúshì.* (This section of silk version A was damaged. However, after referring to chapter 57 [line 3], as well as all the other versions, we can confidently add 以 *yǐ* [through] before 無事 *wúshì* [no affairs] to create a smoother reading. The meaning of this line echoes that of chapter 57 [line 3].)

6 　取 *qǔ* (**ruling**): Heshang Gong's note indicates that 取 *qǔ* meant 治 *zhì* (to rule).

7 　及 *jí* (**if**): This was to be read here as 若 *ruò* (if).[6]

8 　又 *yòu* (**thereby**): This character was used here to mean 乃 *nǎi* (thereby).[7]

CHAPTER 49

2 　以 *yǐ* (**assume**): This character was used to mean 用 *yòng* (to use),[1] and this is adapted here as "assume" to better fit the context.

4 　德 *dé* (**is had**): This would have been read here as 得 *dé* (to obtain; to be had).[2] The character 德 *dé* in line 6 had the same reading.

7 　聖人之在天下也 *shèngrén zhī zài tiānxià yě* (**sages who secure the world**): 之 *zhī* [usually a mood word signifying possession] was used here to turn this whole phrase into a noun.[3] Therefore, 聖人之在天下 *shèngrén zhī zài tiānxià* is a noun phrase in archaic Chinese, with 在 *zài* meaning 存 *cún* (to secure),[4] while 也 *yě* was a mood word that indicated a pause in the narration.[5]

8 　歙歙焉 *xīxīyān* (**so harmoniously**): 歙 *xī* was read here as 合 *hé* (lit., to combine)[6] and meant 和 *hé* (congruous; harmoniously).[7] Repeating this character and then adding the character 焉 *yān* [a mood word] served to emphasize what was being said.[8] (The spirit of the term 歙歙焉 *xīxīyān* echoes the descriptions in lines 3–6.)

9 　屬 *shǔ* (**lend**): This was read here as 注 *zhù*,[9] which was defined as 傾注 *qīngzhù* (to lean toward).[10] Per the context, we interpreted it as "lend."

9 　焉 *yān* [**mood word**]: This mood word (see line 8 above) indicated the end of a statement.[11]

7–10 MN **Wise leaders will then guide their people . . . ingenuousness:** This mutually resonates with the spirit of chapter 19 (lines 7–10).

CHAPTER 50[1]

2 　徒 *tú* (**path**): The character 徒 *tú* (mod. Ch., disciple; follower) would have been read here as 塗 *tú* (path).[2] This character in line 3 had the same interpretation.

2–3 MN **This has always been represented in the Chinese lunisolar calendar by the occasional thirteenth (or leap) month:** Such understanding was derived from the definition of 閏 *rùn* (leap [month]).[3]

4 　而 *ér* (**now**): This character was used here as a mood word that meant 今 *jīn* (now).[4]

5 　之死地 *zhī sǐdì* (**advance toward the place of death**): 之 *zhī* [mood word usually signifying possession] would have been defined here as 往 *wǎng* (to go; to advance toward).[5]

4–7 MN **If we only know to live our lives . . . without having ever actually lived our lives:** This understanding was inspired by a discussion in *Lülan* that grew out of lines 4–7 here: "No one does not live the life that he has, yet no one knows the reason for living the life that he has."[6] Therefore, only when we have the wisdom to know why it is that we live, will we be able to truly live our lives.

8 蓋聞 *gài wén* **(it has been heard):** 蓋 *gài* was used in this context to mean 曾 *céng* (once; to have been).[7]

8 執生 *zhíshēng* **(look after [their] lives):** In this context, 執 *zhí* meant 守 *shǒu* (to guard),[8] which is modified here as "to look after."

9 陵 *líng* **(highlands):** This referred to a 土山 *tǔshān* (mountain composed of earth) that was both high and wide,[9] and so is interpreted here using the closest approximation.

9 兕 *sì* **(rhinoceros):** This meant the same thing as 犀 *xī* (rhinoceros).[10]

10 軍 *jūn* **(battle arrays):** From the context in line 13, we understand that 軍 *jūn* (lit., army; military) actually referred here to 軍陣 *jūnzhèn* (battle arrays).[11]

10 被 *bèi* **(equip):** This would have been read here as 披 *pī* (or *pēi*; lit., to garb oneself with).[12] In the ancient Chinese classics, whenever a verb was used in a compound term (as in this line with 甲兵 *jiǎbīng* [armor and weapons]), it was simply adapted to fit the definition of the first character (much as 被 *bèi* was understood in this instance to describe how the armor was being used). This meaning has therefore been modified here as "equip."

11 揣 *duǒ* **(thrust):** This was defined as 剟 *duó* (to hit; to thrust).[13]

12 措 *cuò* **(use):** In this context, the character 措 *cuò* meant 用 *yòng* (to use).[14]

13 容 *róng* **(wield):** This would have been read as 用 *yòng* (to use; to wield).[15]

CHAPTER 51

1 道生之 *Dào shēng zhī* **(the Dao engenders all):** From the context, it is clear that what is being engendered is everything in the world, so 之 *zhī* (which denoted the object of the verb here) is to be interpreted in this context as "all."[1] (The 之 *zhī* character in lines 7–10 would also have been read the same way.)

2 物刑之 *wù xíngzhī* **(things are formed):** 之 *zhī* here acted as a mood word and had no specific meaning.[2] (The next 之 *zhī* character would also have been understood this way.)

2 器成之 *qì chéngzhī* **(utilitarian objects are realized):** This meant that the realization of all utilitarian objects must obey the Dao.[3]

4 道之尊也 *Dào zhī zūn yě* **(the reason why the Dao is revered):** 之 *zhī* was used here to mean 所以 *suǒyǐ* (the reason why).[4] 也 *yě* was employed to emphasize the subject under discussion and introduce the ensuing passage.[5]

6 夫 *fú* **(these):** This character was used here to mean 此 *cǐ* (this; these),[6] which referred to "the reason why" in lines 4–5.

6 之 *zhī* **(owing to):** This was another way of saying 以 *yǐ*, which would have been interpreted as 因 *yīn* (due to).[7] We then modified this as "owing to" here.

6 爵 *jué* **(high official positions):** In ancient times, this character referred to the ranks of the feudal nobles.[8] We therefore modified that meaning here as "high official positions."

6 恆自然 *héng zìrán* (**always [to] self-realization**): The context of the first half of this line shows that a more logical way of stating this would have been 恆之 [i.e., 以] 自然[9] *héng zhī* [i.e., *yǐ*] *zìrán*. However, this phrase does in fact follow the rhetorical rules of classical Chinese, for when 之 *zhī* (or 以 *yǐ* [due to; owing to]) was understood, it could then be omitted. In English, however, we have to add it here (simplified as "to") to clarify the description.

8 遂 *suì* (**matures**): This would have been defined as 成 *chéng* (to fulfill; fulfilled),[10] which is modified here as "matures."

9 亭 *tíng* (**halts**): This character meant 定 *dìng* (to halt).[11]

9 毒 *dú* (**subsides**): In this context, 毒 *dú* would have been read as 安 *ān* (to settle; to subside).[12]

10 養 *yǎng* (**shrouds**): This character was another way of saying 隱 *yǐn* (to shroud).[13]

10 覆 *fù* (**revives**): The character 覆 *fù* ought to have meant the same as 復 *fù* (to recover; to revive).[14]

7–10 MN **This passage's poetic description of the life of all things . . . follows the cycle of the seasons:** Our understanding of these four lines follows Fan Yingyuan's note.

14 之 *zhī* [**mood word**]: This character was used here as a mood word and had no inherent meaning.[15]

14 謂 *wèi* (**known as**): Literally, 謂 *wèi* meant "called," and this is modified as "known as."

11–14 Similar descriptions can be seen in chapter 2 (lines 11–13) and chapter 10 (lines 13–16).

CHAPTER 52

1 With regard to our understanding of this line, in addition to its margin note, see chapter 51 (lines 1 and 7).

2 既 *jì* (**when**): In ancient Chinese, 既 *jì* could be read as 及 *jí* (until; as soon as).[1] We have modified this as "when" to smooth the reading here. This character in line 3 should be read the same way.

2 得 *dé* (**perceived**): This character was defined here as 知 *zhī* (to perceive).[2]

5 兌 *duì* (**openings**): 兌 *duì* in ancient Chinese literally meant 穴 *xuè* (cave; hole; opening).[3] Here it was used in a metaphorical sense to refer to our sensory organs, such as the ears, eyes, nose, and mouth,[4] and so our margin note describes these as "sensory abilities."

5 門 *mén* (**door**): This was a symbol for the "mouth."[5]

5 This description can also be found in chapter 56 (lines 3–4).

7 曰 *yuē* (**[is] known as**): This character literally meant to "call," and has been modified as "known" to better fit the context. 曰 *yuē* in line 8 was read the same way.

9 用其光, 復歸其明 *yòng qí guāng, fùguī qí míng* (**use the light, return to its illumination**): This line showed how 光 *guāng* (light) comes from 明 *míng* (illumination).[6] The nature of light is that it shines on things and thereby allows us to perceive differences. Illumination, on the other hand, is the source of that light. It thus remains within the harmony of its brightness and exists without outside influence. The spirit of this line

agrees with the concepts in chapter 28 (lines 1, 7, and 13). The first 其 *qí* (the) vaguely suggested the idea of "that,"[7] and so this has been interpreted here as "the." The second 其 *qí* (its) was used to express 明 *míng* (illumination), which is associated with 光 *guāng* (light).

11   襲 *xí* (**accordance with**): This was defined here as 合 *hé* (to agree; accordance with).[8]

CHAPTER 53

1   挈有知 *qiè yǒu zhì* (**to keep [my] wits**): Here, 挈 *qiè* meant 持 *chí* (to keep);[1] 知 *zhì* was to be read the same as 智 *zhì* and meant 聰明 *cōngmíng* (wits).[2] The meaning of 有 *yǒu* (to have) was contained within the use of "to keep" here.

2   大道 *dàdào* (**a great thoroughfare**): In this context, 道 *dào* referred to a long road that led directly to a destination.[3]

3   他 *tā* (**deviation**): This would have been read here as 迆 *yí* (deviation).[4]

1–3 MN   **As a Zhou dynasty nobleman, he never walked . . . his vehicle was being driven:** Our understanding was derived from a passage in *Lunyu* where Confucius says that because he was a procurator (大夫 *dàifū*), he could never walk, and must always be driven everywhere.[5]

4   夷 *yí* (**easy**): This character could be defined as 易 *yì* (easy).[6]

5   徑 *jìng* (**shortcuts**): In this context, 徑 *jìng* (lit., path; trail) meant 捷徑 *jiéjìng* (shortcuts).[7]

6   除 *chú* (**immaculate**): This was defined as 潔好 *jiéhǎo* (immaculate).[8]

9   文采 *wéncǎi* (**decorative silks**): In ancient times, patterned silk was referred to as 文 *wén*, while those with colors were known as 采 *cǎi*,[9] and so we used "decorative silks" as its interpretation.

11   猒 *yàn* (**wallowed in**): In this context, 猒 *yàn* was defined as 足 *zú* (to gratify; to wallow in).[10]

12   齎財 *jīcái* (**valuables and treasures**): This term referred to "gold and jade," or, in other words, "valuables and treasures."[11]

13   盜竽 *dàoyú* (**a kleptocracy**): This term was actually a clever metaphor. A 竽 *yú* was a bamboo instrument that would always be played first in ancient concerts to lead the other instruments. Therefore, 竽 *yú* represented leadership here. The other character, 盜 *dào*, meant "thief" or "theft," so leadership that operated through graft or theft would be nothing other than a "kleptocracy." When a leader is the key kleptocrat, minor thieves will inevitably follow in his wake.[12]

CHAPTER 54

1–3 MN   The way to achieve this can be found in lines 4–8.

3   以 *yǐ* (**offer up**): This character here would have meant 用 *yòng* (to employ).[1] Because it referred to "worship," its meaning is extended to "offer up."

4   之 *zhī* (**in**): In this context, the character 之 *zhī* had the meaning of 於 *yú* (at; in).[2] 之 *zhī* in lines 5–8 should be read the same way.

4   乃 *nǎi* (**becomes**): This was used here to mean 於是 *yúshì* (henceforth; will be),[3] which we modified as "becomes" to better clarify the description.

4   貞 *zhēn* (**stabilized**): This meant 定 *dìng* (to be stabilized).[4]

5 餘 *yú* (**abundant**): The definition of 餘 *yú* was 饒 *ráo* (plenty; abundant).[5]

6 長 *cháng* (**thriving**): 長 *cháng* here denoted 盛 *shèng* (to thrive).[6]

7 豐 *fēng* (**ample**): This meant 盈足 *yíngzú* (to be adequate; ample).[7]

8 溥 *pǔ* (**all-prevailing**): This had the definition of 遍 *piàn* (to be [all] prevailing);[8] 溥 *pǔ* therefore suggested that one's De may influence all in the world, and so "all-prevailing" is used here.

9–15 It is highly possible that this theory inspired the late Confucian school sometime during the late Warring States period and led to the vital doctrine contained in 大學 *Dàxué* (*The Great Learning*).

9–15 MN **We ground ourselves in a pragmatic and realistic perspective:** In other words, we have to surpass our sense of egocentricity.[9]

14 然 *rán* (**thus**): In this context, 然 *rán* was read as 如此 *rúcǐ* (thus).[10]

15 以此 *yǐ cǐ* (**through this**): "Through this" referred to the account in line 13.

CHAPTER 55

1 含德之厚 *hán Dé zhī hòu* (**embody a culmination of the De**): 含 *hán* meant 懷 *huái* (to embrace; to embody),[1] while 厚 *hòu* was defined as 至 *zhì* (culmination).[2]

1 赤子 *chìzǐ* (**newborn babies**): A 赤子 *chìzǐ* literally meant a "red child," or a newborn that was still red from its mother's womb.[3]

2 螫 *zhē* (**poison**): This referred to 蟲行毒 *chóngxíngdú* (lit., an insect that inflicts poison),[4] and so it is interpreted here as to "poison."[5]

5 朘怒 *zuīnù* (**they are virile**): A male newborn's genitalia were called 朘 *zuī*.[6] The character 怒 *nù* (lit., rage) was defined in this context as 作 *zuò* (to become aroused),[7] which we translated using a more genteel equivalent.

7 嚘 *yóu* (**hiccup**): This was defined as 氣逆 *qìnì* (to hiccup).[8]

9 曰 *yuē* (**leads to**): 曰 *yuē* was used here to connote the meaning of 則 *zé* (then; to lead to).[9] This character in lines 10–12 should be read the same way.

11 祥 *xiáng* (**disaster**): In this context, 祥 *xiáng* (lit., fortune) meant 眚 *shěng* (disaster).[10]

12 強 *qiáng* (**brutality**): 強 *qiáng* was used here to convey the meaning of 暴 *bào* (violence; brutality).[11]

13 壯 *zhuàng* (**excessive**): This character suggested the idea of being 極 *jí* (excessive).[12]

15 蚤已 *záoyǐ* (**perish before long**): See chapter 30 (comment on line 14).

13–15 These lines can also be seen in chapter 30 (lines 12–14). The difference is that the narration in this chapter concerns the correct care of our lives, while chapter 30 is about using forces. Regardless of these differences on how we live or how forces are used, the same rule applies.

CHAPTER 56

1–2 之 *Zhī* (**It**): As explained in the margin note on these two lines, "It" represented "the Dao." (This follows the Guodian version, whereas the silk, Beida, and all received versions do not include this 之 *zhī* character. Such reading, though, could easily lead us to mistake 知 *zhī* [to comprehend] as 智 *zhì* [clever; wise].[1] If that were to happen, we would then lose all logical connection with the succeeding text in lines 3–8.)

1–2 弗 *fú* (**not . . . It**): See chapter 2 (comment on lines 11–12).

3-8 其 *qí* [mood word]: This character was used in these eight lines as a mood word.[2]

3-9 MN **Nor use their words to instigate affairs:** This echoes the spirit of chapter 2 (line 10).

10 得 *dé* (**possible**): This was used to mean 能 *néng* (can; possible).[3] The character 得 *dé* in lines 11–15 should be interpreted this way as well.

CHAPTER 57

1 以 *yǐ* (**employ**): The character 以 *yǐ* here meant 用 *yòng* (to use; to employ).[1] This character in lines 2–3 had the same reading.

1 之 *zhī* (**administering**): In this context, the character 之 *zhī* would have been read as 治 *zhì* (to administer).[2]

3 取天下 *qǔ tiānxià* (**ruling the world**): See chapter 29 (second comment on line 1).

4 然 *rán* (**thus**): 然 *rán* meant 如此 *rúcǐ* (thus) here. See chapter 54 (comment on line 14).

4 也 *yě* [mood word]: In this context, the character 也 *yě* would have been read as 邪 *yē* [mood word used to indicate a question].[3]

5 夫 *fú* (**well**): This character was used here as a mood word to begin a discussion,[4] and we have used "well" to express this.

5 天 *tiān* (**rulers**): In this context, 天 *tiān* would have been understood to mean 君 *jūn* (lords; rulers).[5]

5 而 *ér* (**then**): This was used here to mean 則 *zé* (then).[6] This character as it appears in lines 6–8 and 10–13 would have been read the same way.

5 彌畔 *mípàn* (**worse . . . disobedience**): Here, 彌 *mí* would have been read as the amplifier 益 *yì* (increase; more);[7] we have interpreted this as "worse" to fit the context. 畔 *pàn* was defined here as 叛 *pàn* (lit., to betray; betrayal),[8] which could mean 違 *wěi* (to disobey; disobedience).[9]

6 利器 *lìqì* (**schemes**): In this context, the term 利器 *lìqì* meant 權謀 *quánmóu* (a scheme).[10]

6 茲 *zī* (**vaster**): In ancient Chinese, this character could have the same meaning as 滋 *zī*, which was defined as 益 *yì* (increase; more).[11] This has been modified as "vaster" to better describe the situation in this line. The character 茲 *zī* in lines 7–8 would have been read the same way.

7 奇物 *qíwù* (**aberrations**): Here, this referred to 邪事 *xiéshì* (aberrations).[12]

8 法物 *fǎwù* (**the standards of measurement**): In the past, many have attempted to explain this term in various ways. However, our understanding has been inspired by the following two Chinese classics:

- *Yìjing* (*The Book of Changes*) says: "That which is created and used is called a 法 *fǎ* [rule; standard]." Kong Yingda noted under this line that "法 *fǎ* meant sages created these things, then employed them and handed them down as standards, hence they were referred to as 法 *fǎ*."[13]
- *Guanzi* introduces twelve types of measurement, such as rulers, weights, and volumes, all of which were referred to as 法 *fǎ*.[14]

Based on these, we know that 法物 *fǎwù* indicated "standards of measurement."

8 茲章 *zīzhāng* (**clearer**): For 茲 *zī*, see the second comment on line 6 above. 章 *zhāng* would have been read here as 明 *míng* (clear),[15] and so this term has been interpreted as "clearer."

8 盜賊 *dàozéi* (**thieves and bandits**): In ancient times, a 盜 *dào* was "one who steals valuables,"[16] and so is interpreted here as "a thief." 賊 *zéi* meant "one who robs and kills,"[17] or, in other words, "a bandit." (In modern Chinese, the meanings of these two terms have been reversed.)

12 正 *zhèng* (**settle**): In this context, the character 正 *zhèng* would have been read as 定 *dìng* (to settle).[18]

13 Compare this with chapter 64 (lines 19–20), which says, "Sages desire to desire not, and value not rare goods."

CHAPTER 58

1 其 *qí* (**if**): This was used here to mean 若 *ruò* (if).[1] This character in line 3 should be read the same way.

1 悶悶 *mènmèn* (**oblivious**): 悶悶 *mènmèn* was defined as 不覺貌 *bùjuémào* (unaware; oblivious).[2]

1 The spirit of this line mutually echoes that of chapter 17 (line 1).

1 MN **"Oblivious" suggests . . . non-effort:** The Tang Xuanzong emperor's note points out that 悶悶 *mènmèn* meant 無為寬大 *wúwéi kuāndà* (to exert non-effort and be magnanimous).

2 其 *qí* (**then**): In this instance, 其 *qí* was used to mean 則 *zé* (then).[3] This character in line 4 should be read the same way.

2 屯屯 *túntún* (**artless**): 屯屯 *túntún* was read as 純純 *chúnchún* (artless).[4]

3 察察 *cháchá* (**surveillant**): This described the action of 檢姦偽 *jiǎnjiānwéi* (vigilant for illicit behavior and fraud),[5] and so is interpreted here as "surveillant."

4 夬夬 *guàiguài* (**fractured**): 夬 *guài* was defined as 分決 *fēnjué* (to split; to fracture).[6] Because this term was used here as an adjective, it has been translated accordingly.

3–4 This entire description echoes the idea conveyed in chapter 57 (lines 5 and 8).

5 倚 *yǐ* (**originates**): The character 倚 *yǐ* here was defined as 因 *yīn* (to cause; to originate).[7]

6 伏 *fú* (**hidden**): In this context, 伏 *fú* meant 匿藏 *nìcáng* (to hide; hidden).[8]

7 極 *jí* (**end**): This character was defined here as 終 *zhōng* (end).[9]

8 其無正也 *qí wúzhèng yě* (**these will have no certainty**): 正 *zhèng* would have been defined here as 定 *dìng* (certain; certainty).[10] (This line was used to introduce a different discussion in lines 9–10. In the past, most commentators read this as the conclusion to lines 5–7. Such reading was problematic, though, as that passage was concluded in line 7.)

9 正 *zhèng* (**moral**) and 奇 *jī* (**immoral**): The Qing Shizu emperor's note points out that 奇 *jī* meant 邪 *xié* (eccentric; immoral), so 正 *zhèng* could be understood here to mean "moral."

13 方而不割 *fāng ér bùgē* (**[be as] a square, but one that does not divide**): 割 *gē* in this context meant 裂 *liè* (to divide).[11] 而 *ér* was used here to mean 乃 *nǎi* (but);[12] this character in lines 14–16 should be read the same way. The meaning of this line echoes the spirit of chapter 40 (line 14).[13]

14 廉而不刺 *lián ér búcì* (**[as] a sharpness, but one that does not wound**): In this line, 廉 *lián* meant 利 *lì* (sharp),[14] while 刺 *cì* was defined as 傷 *shāng* (to wound).[15]

15 直而不肆 *zhí ér búsì* ([as] a straightness, but one that does not transgress): 肆 *sì* was defined in this context as 恣 *zì* (to transgress).[16]

16 The spirit of this line echoes that of chapter 52 (line 9).

CHAPTER 59

1 事天 *shìtiān* (cultivating the self): In this context, 事 *shì* meant 治 *zhì* (to cultivate), and 天 *tiān* referred to 身 *shēn* (one's body; the self).[1] (This term literally meant "to serve the heavens." However, the context of this chapter does not support such an interpretation. Moreover, according to Laozi's teachings, the heavens are subordinate to the Dao [chapter 25 (line 20)], so rendering this as "serving the heavens"[2] would not have been in concordance with Laozi's philosophy.)[3]

1 嗇 *sè* (husbandry): The definitions of the English word "husbandry" are oddly similar to that of the character 嗇 *sè*, for they include the concepts of resource conservation—愛 濇 *àisè* (parsimony)—as well as farming.[4] We follow the first definition here,[5] for it conveys the idea of restraining oneself from exerting effort[6] while conforming to self-realization (see chapter 25).

2 唯 *wéi* (because [of]): Here, this character meant 以 *yǐ* (because); see chapter 8 (second comment on line 11 and endnote 10).

2 服 *fú* (obtainment): In this context, 服 *fú* meant 得 *dé* (obtainment).[7] This character in line 3 should be read the same way.

4 則 *zé* (leads to): Because the text directly preceding this character contains the cause, and the succeeding text has the result, we have used "leads to" as its interpretation; see chapter 38 (endnote 14). This character in line 5 would have had the same reading.

4 無不克 *wúbúkè* (omnipotence): In this context, 克 *kè* meant 勝任 *shèngrèn* (to successfully achieve).[8] 無不克 *wúbúkè* therefore can literally be interpreted as "nothing cannot be successfully achieved," and so "omnipotence" is used. This term in line 5 should be read the same way.

6 有國 *yǒuguó* (to safeguard the country): In this context, 有 *yǒu* (lit., to have) meant 保 *bǎo* (to protect; to safeguard).[9]

7 有國之母 *yǒuguó zhī Mǔ* (safeguarding the country through retaining the **Mother**): 之 *zhī* was used here to mean 有 *yǒu* (to have; to retain).[10] Therefore, this phrase was another way of saying 保國有母 *bǎoguó yǒu Mǔ*, and we interpreted it accordingly.

8 柢 *dǐ* (established): This character literally referred to a "taproot"[11]—the part of a tree that allows it to stand firmly—or, in other words, that which allows a tree to be "established."

8 久視 *jiǔshì* (enduring): In this context, the character 視 *shì* meant 活 *huó* (to live; existence),[12] and so we have interpreted 久視 *jiǔshì* (lit., everlasting existence) as "enduring."

CHAPTER 60

1 鮮 *xiān* (fish): In this instance, the character 鮮 *xiān* (lit., fresh) was used to mean 魚 *yú* (fish). When cooking a fish, if we constantly toss it about (i.e., disturb it), the fish will fall apart. In the same vein, a ruler who constantly issues orders and interferes with the running of his country will cause splintering and disorder.[1]

2   立 *lì* (**overseen**): This character was read here as 涖 *lì*, which meant 臨視 *línshì* (to oversee).[2]

2   不神 *bùshén* (**[will] not arise**): 神 *shén* (lit., deity) would have been read in this context as 申 *shēn*, or, in other words, 伸 *shēn*, which meant "to arise."[3] When specters arose, they were believed to be harmful. However, no specters should arise when the world is governed by the Dao.[4] Even if they do manage to arise, they will not prove harmful, as described in line 4.

3–5 非 *fēi* (**not just**): 非 *fēi* (lit., not) would have been read in this context as 不唯 *bùwéi* (not just).[5] This character in line 5 should be read the same way.

6   弗 *fú* (**no one**): See chapter 2 (comment on lines 11–12).

8   交歸 *jiāo guī* (**both will thus be conferred unto**): 交 *jiāo* would have been read here as 俱 *jù* (both),[6] while 歸 *guī* (lit., to return) in ancient Chinese could be another way of saying 遺 *yí* (lit., to leave),[7] which was defined in this context as 贈 *zèng* (to confer).[8]

8   焉 *yān* (**them**): This character was used here to mean 之 *zhī* [mood word; a grammatical object],[9] which indicated "all men," and so it is interpreted here as "them."

CHAPTER 61

2   牝 *pìn* (**female**): This referred to all female animals.[1]

2   交 *jiāo* (**convergence**): The character 交 *jiāo* in this context would have been read as 歸會 *guīhuì* (convergence).[2]

3   牡 *mǔ* (**males**): This denoted all male animals.[3]

4   為 *wèi* (**due to**): In this instance, the first 為 *wèi* character was used to mean 因 *yīn* (because; due to).[4]

4   為下 *wéixià* (**to efface [themselves]**): The second 為 *wéi* in this sentence literally meant "to act," while 下 *xià* (lit., to be low) described a humble attitude. We thus interpreted this term as "to efface [oneself]."

5   取 *qǔ* (**to acquire**): In this instance, 取 *qǔ* meant 收 *shōu* (to receive; to obtain),[5] which we have modified as "to acquire."

6   取於 *qǔyú* (**to be acquired by**): 於 *yú* was used here to render 取 *qǔ* into the passive voice.[6]

7   以取 . . . 而取 *yǐqǔ . . . érqǔ* (**to acquire . . . to be acquired by**): If we compare this line with the patterns in lines 5–6, we know that 以取 *yǐqǔ* signaled the active voice and 而取 *érqǔ* the passive.

8   兼畜人 *jiānchùrén* (**inclusively unite with others**): In this context, 兼 *jiān* meant 盡 *jìn* (completely; inclusively).[7] 畜 *chù* meant 聚 *jù* (lit., to get together),[8] and so we have interpreted this term as "to unite" to better accommodate the description in this line. With regard to 人 *rén* (lit., man), this meaning is extended to indicate "others," which in this instance referred to "small states."

9   入事人 *rùshìrén* (**offer [its] services to others**): In this context, 入 *rù* meant 進 *jìn* (to go into),[9] which has been modified here as "to offer." Therefore, to "offer services" is employed here to clarify the concept of 入事 *rùshì*, while 人 *rén* (others; see the comment on line 8) in this context indicated a large state.

10   夫 *fú* (**they**): This was used here to mean 彼 *bǐ* [third person pronoun],[10] and is therefore interpreted in this context as "they," indicating both large and small states.

CHAPTER 62

1 注 *zhù* (**the Ruler**): From the context, this character (lit., to pour into) would have been read here as 主 *zhǔ* (the Ruler).[1] (The description of this line echoes the ideas imparted in chapter 4 [line 4].)

2 葆 *bǎo* (**treasure**): In ancient Chinese, this would have been read here as 寶 *bǎo* (treasure),[2] which has been modified as a verb to better fit the English reading.

3 葆 *bǎo* (**cultivates**): In this context, this character was read in ancient Chinese as 保 *bǎo* (mod. Ch., to protect),[3] and here meant 養 *yǎng* (to raise; to teach; to cultivate).[4]

4 市 *shì* (**transactions**): In ancient Chinese, this term was usually defined as "to buy," but here it referred to 交易 *jiāoyì* (to transact; transactions).[5]

5 賀人 *hèrén* (**exalt people**): In this context, 賀 *hè* would have been defined as 嘉 *jiā* (to honor; to exalt).[6]

6 之 *zhī* (**if**): In this context, 之 *zhī* would have been read as 若 *ruò* (if).[7]

7 何棄之有 *hé qìzhī yǒu* (**how could they be forsaken**): This phrasing turned 何有棄之 *hé yǒu qìzhī* into a rhetorical statement (using the passive voice here), where 有 *yǒu* (lit., to have) was used to mean 可 *kě* (can; could).[8]

6–7 These descriptions echo the teachings in chapter 49 (lines 3–6).

8 三卿 *sānqīng* (**three chief ministers**): In this context, 卿 *qīng* was the title of the highest official serving under the king (or 天子 *tiānzǐ*; lit., the son of the heavens). Semantically speaking, 卿 *qīng* had the meaning of "excelling at discerning fundamental truths."[9]

9 共之璧 *gòngzhībì* (**a large jade disc**): A 璧 *bì* was a carved jade disc with a small-diameter hole in its center.[10] In this context, 共 *gòng* would have been read as 拱 *gǒng*[11] (to extend one's arms level with the chest and cup the hands together, as if embracing something large). Thus, when a jade disc was described in this way, it must have been quite large.[12]

9 以先四馬 *yǐxiān sìmǎ* (**is presented before four horses**): 以 *yǐ* was literally defined as 用 *yòng* (to use),[13] and we have extended this as "to present" to fit the context. In ancient times, teams of four horses were used to pull vehicles, hence 四馬 *sìmǎ* (four horses).[14] (This also suggests how things were formally presented in pre-Qin times, for lighter objects were offered before heavier ones,[15] and so the lighter jade disc would have been proffered before the horses.)

10 坐 *zuò* (**to kneel**): In ancient times, chairs were not yet used. Instead, people knelt on mats with their buttocks resting on their heels (as can still be seen in Japan), and so this was the original meaning of the character 坐 *zuò*[16] (which today is usually translated as "to sit," a definition that cannot be applied here).

10 進此 *jìncǐ* (**proffer this**): 進 *jìn* in this context meant 薦 *jiàn* (to recommend; to proffer),[17] while 此 *cǐ* (this) referred to what the Dao meant to the king and the three ministers.

11 也 *yě* [**mood word indicating a question**]: This was used here as if it were 邪 *yé*,[18] which denoted a question.

12 以 *yǐ* (**then**): In both instances here, this character was used to mean 則 *zé* (then).[19]

12 與 *yú* [**mood word indicating a question**]: This character (commonly defined as "and" or "with") was read here as 歟 *yú*, which signified that this was a question.[20]

13 為 *wéi* [mood word] and 貴 *guì* (cherished): 為 *wéi* was to be read here as 被 *bèi* [passive voice],[21] while 貴 *guì* (lit., to esteem; to value) is rendered here as "cherished."

CHAPTER 63

2 事無事 *shì wúshì* (**manage [affairs] through no affairs**): The first 事 *shì* acted as a verb here and meant 治 *zhì* (to manage).[1] (無事 *wúshì* [no affairs] informs us that the object of "manage" was "affairs," and so the object of "manage" is added in the interpretation here for clarification.)

1–3 MN **Non-effort is the foundation for exerting effort:** This understanding of line 1 was inspired by chapters 47 (line 9) and 48 (line 5).

1–3 MN **No affairs is the foundation for managing affairs:** In chapter 2 (line 9), Laozi teaches that "sages administer affairs with non-effort," and so it is "with non-effort" that "leaders" (or even in modern terms, "we") will be able to achieve "no affairs," meaning that affairs will be managed through "self-realization"; see Wang Bi's note regarding 無 為 *wúwéi* (non-effort) in chapter 37 (comment on line 1).

4–5 大小 *dàxiǎo* (**the great [come from] the small**) and 多少 *duōshǎo* (**the many [come from] the few**): "The great" and "the small" concerned size, while "the many" and "the few" involved numbers.[2] It is obvious that there would be no great without the small and no many without the few.[3]

6 德 *dé* (**kindness**): This term conveyed a notion opposite to that of "spite" (怨 *yuàn*), and so its definition of 恩惠 *ēnhuì* (kindness)[4] is followed here.

7 圖 *tú* (**deliberate**): This would have been read here as 謀 *móu* (mod. Ch., to plot),[5] which meant 慮難 *lǜnán* (to weigh difficulties),[6] and is therefore interpreted as to "deliberate."

7 乎 *hū* (**when**): In this context, 乎 *hū* was used to mean 於 *yú* (at the time that),[7] and so is interpreted as "when." This character in line 8 had the same definition.

8 細 *xì* (**tiny**): 細 *xì* would have been read here as 微 *wēi* (tiny).[8] This line describes matters in the world differently from line 4.

9 作於 *zuòyú* (**arise out of**): 作 *zuò* would have been defined in this context as 起 *qǐ* (to arise).[9] This term in line 10 had the same reading.

15 猶 *yóu* (**ruminate**): In this instance, 猶 *yóu* would have been interpreted as 圖 *tú* (to deliberate; to ruminate).[10]

15 難之 *nánzhī* (**the difficult**): 之 *zhī* [which usually acted as the object of a verb] was used here to mean 者 *zhě* [the object of an adjective];[11] this character formed a noun phrase when it was conjoined with the adjective 難 *nán* (difficult), and this phrase is therefore translated as "the difficult."

CHAPTER 64

2 兆 *zhào* (**portended**): This denoted 事先見 [現] 者 *shìxiān xiànzhě* (that which appears before things occur),[1] and so we have interpreted it accordingly.

2 謀 *móu* (**planned**): This suggested the same idea as 圖 *tú*, which here meant 規劃 *guīhuà* (to plan).[2]

3 膬 *cuì* (**fragile**): 膬 *cuì* was the original, formal form of the character 脆 *cuì* (brittle; fragile).[3]

3   判 *pàn* (**divided**): This would have been understood to mean 分 *fēn* (to divide).[4]

4   幾 *jī* (**minute**): In this context, the character 幾 *jī* was defined as 微 *wēi* (tiny; minute).[5]

5   之 *zhī* [**object of a verb**]: 之 *zhī* was used to indicate an object of a verb, but what it referred to was uncertain, and so we cannot directly interpret it here.[6] This character in line 6 would have been read the same way.

5   於 *yú* (**where**): This literally meant "at," as indicated here in "at a certain stage of development," and so is rendered as "where." This character in line 6 had the same interpretation.

5   其 *qí* (**yet**): The character 其 *qí* was used in this context to mean 尚 *shàng* (still).[7] However, we rendered this as "yet" to provide a more fluid reading. 其 *qí* in line 6 should be read the same way.

7   毫末 *háomò* ([**like**] **the tip of a hair**): 毫 *háo* referred to a 長銳毛 *chángruìmáo* (long, pointed hair),[8] but here, it is simply interpreted as "hair." 末 *mò* indicated "the end" or "the tip" of something.

8   成 *chéng* (**stories**): In this context, 成 *chéng* meant 重 *chóng* (a level; a story [in a building]).[9]

8   蔂 *léi* (**baskets**): This character referred to a 盛土籠 *chéngtǔlóng* (baskets for carrying dirt).[10] In ancient China (generally in the north), buildings were constructed out of rammed earth (see chapter 11 [comment on line 7]).

9   百仞 *bǎirèn* (**several hundred lengths**): In pre-Qin times, a 仞 *rèn* was a unit for measuring height and was equal to the arms' breadth of an average-sized man,[11] so it was probably around six feet (1.8 meters). Because 百 *bǎi* meant "one hundred," the term 百仞 *bǎirèn* is roughly interpreted here as "several hundred lengths."

10   The first 之 *zhī* character here was used as a mood word and had no particular meaning.[12] The first 之 *zhī* character in line 11 would have been read the same way. The second 之 *zhī* character meant "it" and referred to the activity described in the first part of that line. The second 之 *zhī* character in line 11 would have had the same meaning.

14   之 *zhī* [**mood word**]: In this instance, 之 *zhī* turned this phrase (i.e., line 14) into a noun,[13] but this character itself is untranslatable here.

15   其 *qí* (**at hand**): This was used here to mean 將 *jiāng* (going to; near to),[14] and has been rendered as "at hand" to clarify the description.

16   This line only appears in the Guodian version. By including it, we are reminded that the descriptions in lines 17–18 are vital rules that all should obey.

16   臨 *lín* (**overseeing**): In this context, 臨 *lín* would have been defined as 監 *jiān* (to oversee).[15]

16   紀 *jì* (**canon**): Here, 紀 *jì* meant 法 *fǎ* (principle; canon).[16]

23   輔 *fǔ* (**to assist**): This character was another way of saying 助 *zhù* (to assist).[17]

24   弗敢 *fúgǎn* (**restrain from**): This term literally meant "to not have the audacity [to do something]," but because this was referring to the attitude one assumed, it is modified as "restrain from." The verb here was 敢 *gǎn* and the object was "them," which referred to "all things." (See chapter 3 [second comment on line 13] regarding 不敢 *bùgǎn*. For more on the use of 弗 *fú* to mean "不 + verb + object," see chapter 2 [comment on lines 11–12].)

CHAPTER 65

2   以 *yǐ* (**have ... [become]**): This was used here to mean 能 *néng* (to be capable of),[1] and we have modified this as "have ... [become]" to better fit the context. This character in line 3 should be read in a similar way; in other words, as "had ... [become]."

3   將 *jiāng* (**rather**): In this context, 將 *jiāng* meant 乃 *nǎi* (rather).[2]

4   之 *zhī* (**when**): This was used here to mean 若 *ruò* (if),[3] which has been modified as "when" to show that the case it was describing was definite.

4   以其知也 *yǐ qí zhī yě* (**this is owing to their shrewdness**): 以 *yǐ* was used here as if it were 由 *yóu* (to come from; to be owing to).[4] The character 知 *zhī* (mod. Chi., *zhī*) in this context meant the same thing as 智 *zhì* (shrewdness), for in ancient Chinese, 智 *zhì* was often written as 知 *zhī*.[5]

5   以知知邦 *yǐ zhī zhībāng* (**using shrewdness in the governing of a country**): 以 *yǐ* was used here as if it were 用 *yòng* (to use).[6] The first 知 *zhī* would have been read as 智 *zhì* (see chapter 10 [endnote 13]), while the second one (in the term 知邦 *zhībāng*) meant 為邦 *wéibāng* (to govern a country).[7]

6   賊 *zéi* (**detriment**): In this context, this character meant 害 *hài* (detriment).[8]

7   以不知知邦 *yǐ búzhī zhībāng* (**[and] using no shrewdness in the governing of a country**): See the comment on line 5 above.

8   德 *dé* (**a boon**): This character was used in contrast to 賊 *zéi* in line 6, and so is defined here as 恩惠 *ēnhuì* (a boon).[9]

9   恆 *héng* (**comprehensive**): In this context, the character 恆 *héng* meant 徧 *piàn* (fully),[10] and so this meaning is extended to "comprehensive" to enhance the reading of this line.

9   此兩者 *cǐliǎngzhě* (**these two**): This term referred to the descriptions in lines 5–8.

10   亦稽式也 *yì jī Shì yě* (**then be in conformity with the Standard**): 亦 *yì* was used here to mean 則 *zé* (then),[11] while 稽 *jī* was defined in this context as 合 *hé* (to concur with),[12] and so by extension meant "to be in conformity with." 式 *Shì* here denoted 模則 *Mózé* (the Standard).[13]

9–12 MN **According to Laozi's teaching ... "cleave to no shrewdness"**: Chapter 28 (lines 1, 7, and 13) imparts the principle of Laozi that when faced with a situation formed by two polarized factors, we need to be able to recognize the one that is active (such as "shrewdness") and cleave to the one that is inactive ("no shrewdness"). His crucial principle was not explicitly laid out in this passage, but it is nevertheless coherent.

14   與物反矣 *yǔ wù fǎn yǐ* (**[It] causes things to return**): 與 *yǔ* would have been read here as 使 *shǐ* (to make; to cause).[14]

CHAPTER 66

1–3 MN   This definition of king (王 *wáng*) comes from *Shuowen*.[1]

4   之 *zhī* [**mood word**]: This character was employed here to transform the text directly preceding it into a noun phrase[2] and cannot be rendered into English.

4   在 *zài* (**positioned**): In this context, 在 *zài* would have been defined as 居 *jū* (to situate; to position).[3] This character in lines 6, 8, and 10 should be interpreted the same way.

7   以 *yǐ* (**use**): The character 以 *yǐ* was used in this context to mean 用 *yòng* (to employ; to use).[4]

9   弗厚 *fúhòu* (**not be burdened**): For 弗 *fú* (not [with the object "by him" omitted]), see chapter 2 (comment on lines 11–12); this character in line 11 would have been read the same way, but in line 12 the understood object "by him" is added to the interpretation as a clarification. Here, 厚 *hòu* was defined as 重 *zhòng* (heavy; a burden).[5]

11 弗害 *fúhài* (**not feel antipathy**): In this context, 弗 *fú* meant "not . . . [toward him]." 害 *hài* denoted 惡 *wù* (dislike; antipathy).[6]

12 進 *jìn* (**following**): This character literally meant 前 *qián* (to advance; to go forward),[7] but is modified here as "following" to better clarify the context.

12 弗猒 *fúyàn* (**without being enervated [by them]**): In this context, 弗 *fú* meant "without . . . [by them]." 猒 *yàn* could be defined as 厭倦 *yànjuàn* (to be tired of; to be enervated by),[8] and that is what has been followed here.

13 以 *yǐ* (**because**): This was used here to mean 因 *yīn* (because).[9]

13–14 The same teaching can be found in chapter 23 (lines 13–14), as well as chapter 8 (line 11).

CHAPTER 67

1   我大 *wǒ dà* (**mine is great**): 大 *dà* was used here in contrast to 不肖 *búxiào* (as naught—see comment on line 2), showing us that 我 *wǒ* (lit., I; me) in this context ought to be read as "mine" (i.e., what Laozi knows), not Laozi himself.

2   不肖 *búxiào* (**as naught**): 不 *bú* was a negative word, while 肖 *xiào* would have been defined here as 類 *lèi* (comparable to; like [something]),[1] and so we used "as naught" as the interpretation of this concept.

3   夫 *fú* (**it**): This was employed here to mean 彼 *bǐ* [third person pronoun],[2] which referred to "mine" in line 1, and so "it" is used to interpret this.

3   唯 *wéi* (**because**): 唯 *wéi* was used in this context to mean 以 *yǐ* (due to; because).[3]

4   細 *xì* (**trivial**): 細 *xì* (lit., fine; small) was defined here as 微末 *wēimò* (trivial).[4] (This character was used to suggest the way in which 肖 *xiào* [as something] was used in line 2.)

5   有 *yǒu* (**keep to [me]**): 有 *yǒu* literally meant "to have," and so this translation is modified here as "to keep to [me]" in order to better fit the context of this line.

5   葆 *bǎo* (**treasures**): 葆 *bǎo* (lit., luxuriant growth) would have been read here as 寶 *bǎo* (treasures).[5]

6   而 *ér* (**then**): 而 *ér* would have been read here as 則 *zé* (then).[6]

6   葆之 *bǎo zhī* (**I am . . . secured**): 葆 *bǎo* (refer to the second comment on line 5) would have been read here as 保 *bǎo* (to secure),[7] while 之 *zhī* was a pronoun that represented "I" (i.e., Laozi, for he was the one speaking).

7   曰 *yuē* (**is**): This character was used here to mean 為 *wéi* (is).[8]

7   慈 *cí* (**profound love**): 慈 *cí* meant 愛之深 *àizhīshēn* (a love that is profound),[9] and so has been interpreted accordingly.

8   儉 *jiǎn* (**frugality**): This idea of frugality echoes the spirit of 嗇 *sè* (husbandry) in chapter 59.

9   不敢 *bùgǎn* (**restraint**): See chapter 3 (second comment on line 13) and chapter 64 (comment on line 24 regarding 弗敢 *fúgǎn*).

10 夫 . . . 故 *fú . . . gù* (**it is . . . that allows**): 夫 *fú* was used here to mean 以 *yǐ* (due to; because of).[10] This pattern therefore literally meant "because of . . . so," which is modi-

fied as "that allows" to render a more graceful reading in English. (夫 *fú* was omitted in lines 11–12 of the Chinese text because it was considered understood, but its interpretation is provided in lines 11 and 13.)

13 事 ***shì*** (**affairs**): Here, "affairs" was part of a continuing discussion in line 12, and therefore actually meant "the affairs of the world."[11]

13 長 ***zhǎng*** (**the sovereign**): This would have been defined here as 君 *jūn* (sovereign).[12]

14 今 ***jīn*** (**if**): In this context, the character 今 *jīn* was used to mean 若 *ruò* (if).[13]

14 其 ***qí*** [**mood word**]: 其 *qí* was used here to act as 乎 *hū*,[14] which was a mood word with no specific meaning in this context. 其 *qí* in lines 15–16 should be read the same way.

14 且 ***qiě*** (**in favor of**): 且 *qiě* here meant 取 *qǔ* (to take; to choose),[15] and that has been modified here as "in favor of." This character in lines 15–16 should be interpreted the same way.

18 夫 ***fú*** (**oh**): 夫 *fú* was used in this line as a mood word that signified the beginning of a discussion.[16]

18 則 ***zé*** (**lead to**): Refer to the usage of 則 *zé* in chapter 38 (endnote 14). This character in line 19 would have been read the same way.

20 將 ***jiāng*** (**when**): This was used here to mean 如 *rú* (if),[17] which has been modified as "when" to indicate a strong degree of certainty in this supposition.

21 如 ***rú*** (**thereby**): In this context, the character 如 *rú* would have been read as 則 *zé* (then; thereby).[18]

21 垣之 ***yuán zhī*** (**to fortify it**): 垣 *yuán* here suggested the notion of 援衛 *yuánwèi* (to fortify).[19]

CHAPTER 68

1 士 ***shì*** (**warriors**): In this instance, 士 *shì* indicated 戰士 *zhànshì* (a warrior; warriors).[1]

1 不武 ***bùwǔ*** (**surpass bravery**): 武 *wǔ* in this context would have been defined as 勇 *yǒng* (bravery),[2] and 不 *bù* meant "is not [through]." We modified this term as "to surpass" to better fit the description in this line. 不 *bù* in line 2 should be read the same way.

2 怒 ***nù*** (**high morale**): In ancient Chinese, the term used to refer to the courageous determination of warriors in battle was 怒 *nù*, which meant "high morale."[3] (The modern definition of 怒 *nù* is "anger" or "rage.")

3 弗與 ***fúyù*** (**do not engage them**): 弗 *fú* meant "does not . . . them,"[4] while 與 *yù* in this context denoted 對敵 *duìdí* (to engage the enemy).[5]

7 配天 ***pèi tiān*** (**concordance with the heavens**): 配 *pèi* here meant 匹 *pǐ* (to match),[6] which conveyed the notion of 合 *hé* (to be in concord with; concordance).[7]

CHAPTER 69

1 曰 ***yuē*** (**holds [that]**): This character literally meant "[which] says" here, but we modified it as "holds [that]" to better fit the context.

2 吾不敢 ***wǔ bùgǎn*** (**I restrain [myself]**): 吾 *wǔ* (I) referred to the one who first handed down this saying. For 不敢 *bùgǎn*, see chapter 3 (second comment on line 13); with regard to 弗敢 *fúgǎn*, see chapter 64 (comment on line 24). Because the English word "restrain" is a transitive verb that needs an object, "myself" has been added.

1–3 MN **The instigator in a conflict is referred to as "the host," while "the guest" is the responder:** This statement comes from China's ancient ritual theory, for it reversed the military terminology of the pre-Qin period, where "guest" referred to an invader, and a "host" was the defender or responder.[1] Even though this old teaching quoted by Laozi employed ritual theory to discuss military matters, its ingenious perspective nevertheless perfectly reflected a profound understanding of military affairs.

4　行無行 *xíng wúháng* **(arraying without formations):** The second 行 character was used as a noun, had the pronunciation of *háng*, and referred to an army's 陳次 *chénci* (formations).[2] The first 行 character was a verb pronounced as *xíng*, and defined as 為 *wéi* (lit., to do).[3] Because this described how a formation was being assembled, the English translation has been modified as "arraying."

5　攘 *rǎng* **(stretching):** See chapter 38 (first comment on line 9).

7　扔 *rēng* **(engaging):** This meant 就 *jiù* (to approach; to engage).[4]

9　吾葆 *wú bǎo* **(our security):** In this context during pre-Qin times, the character 葆 *bǎo* (lit., luxuriant growth) could be borrowed as 寶 *bǎo* (lit., treasure), which had the ancient usage of 保 *bǎo* (to protect; to secure).[5] This has been modified into a noun phrase— "our security"—to better fit the reading.

10　稱兵相若 *chēngbīng xiāngruò* **(when forces are raised of equal strength):** 稱 *chēng* would have been defined here as 舉 *jǔ* (to raise).[6] 相若 *xiāngruò* literally referred to the idea of "the same with each other," and so this is modified as "in equal strength" to clarify this line's meaning.

11　哀者 *āizhě* **(the side with love):** In this context, 哀 *āi* (lit., to grieve; sad) would have been read as 愛 *ài* (love).[7] 者 *zhě* was used to indicate "the one."[8] As this passage discusses two conflicting sides, its meaning has been extended to "the side [with]." (Quite often, people would read "哀者勝矣 *āizhě shèng yǐ*" as literally meaning "the grieving side will prevail." This misconception was even turned into a saying—哀兵必勝 *āibīng bìshèng* [grieving forces will definitely prevail]—that referred to the sort of implacable high morale necessary for a fight to the death, but this had no basis in Laozi's teachings.)

CHAPTER 70

1–4 MN **Because Laozi's words are in accord with the Dao . . . that is why they cannot fathom Laozi's words:** This understanding was inspired by Lü Jifu's note on these lines.[1]

3　而人莫之能知也 *ér rén mòzhī néngzhī yě* **(yet people cannot comprehend them):** This phrasing turned 而人莫能知之也 *ér rén mònéng zhīzhī yě* into a rhetorical statement and has been interpreted accordingly. 之 *zhī* [third person—in this instance, them] referred to the "words" in line 1. 之 *zhī* in line 4 was read the same way.

4　而莫之能行 *ér mòzhī néngxing* **(nor can they put them into practice):** Similar in format to line 3, this phrasing turned 而 [人] 莫能行之 *ér* [*rén*] *mònéng xíngzhī* into a rhetorical statement and has been interpreted accordingly. (In this line, the subject 人 *rén* [a person; men; people] was omitted in the Chinese text, for this was understood.)

5–6　君 *Jūn* **(Sovereign)** and 宗 *Zōng* **(Provenance):** These two terms could be used synonymously in ancient Chinese, for both intimated the notion of 主 *zhǔ* (ruler).[2] However, they are interpreted independently of each other here to show that these renderings were derived from two different characters.

5–6 MN "Sovereign" and the "Provenance" . . . two names for the Dao: This understanding was inspired by Su Che's note.[3]

7 夫 *fú* (they): This character was used in line 7 (but appears in line 8 of the English interpretation due to different grammatical rules) to mean 彼 *bǐ* [third person pronoun];[4] in line 3, it connoted the idea of 人 *rén* (people), and so has been interpreted here as "they."

7 唯 *wéi* (due to): In this context, the character 唯 *wéi* would have been read as 以 *yǐ* (because; due to).[5]

8 不我知 *bù wǒ zhī* ([they thus] do not comprehend [that which is] mine): This phrasing turned 不知我 *bùzhī wǒ* (do not comprehend [that which is] mine) into a rhetorical statement, and so is interpreted accordingly. What 我 *wǒ* (lit., I; we) represented here was clearly not a person, but rather what "my words" conveyed, and so has been interpreted as "[that which is] mine."

9 知者 *zhīzhě* (those who comprehend): 者 *zhě* [an auxiliary word] denotes those who have the ability to 知 *zhī* (comprehend).[6]

9 希 *xī* ([are] few): In this context, 希 *xī* would have been read as 稀 *xī*, which meant 罕 *hàn* (rare; few).[7]

10 聖人 *shèngrén* (sages): In this context, the term 聖人 *shèngrén* referred to perfectly cultivated people; see chapter 2 (first comment on line 9).

10 被褐 *bèihè* (clothe [themselves] in coarse garb): 被 *bèi* had the ancient meaning of 衣覆 *yīfù* (lit., to be covered with a garment),[8] which now would be interpreted as "to clothe." 褐 *hè* referred to the 粗衣 *cūyī* (coarse garb) worn by the people of the humble classes.[9]

10 懷 *huái* (underneath clasp): This character was defined as 包 *bāo* (to wrap in),[10] which has been modified to fit the context as to "underneath clasp."

10 玉 *yù* (jade): This has been a symbol of exemplary cultivation in China since very ancient times.[11]

CHAPTER 71

1–2 "Viewing . . . as" is added to the English interpretation of these two lines to clarify the meaning.[1]

2 病 *bìng* (is troublesome): This was defined as 難 *nán* (to trouble; troubles; troublesome).[2] Except for the first 病 *bìng* in line 4, this character in lines 3–5 should be read the same way.

3 之 *zhī* (the reason why): In this context, the character 之 *zhī* was used to mean 所以 *suǒyǐ* (that is why; the reason why).[3]

4 以 *yǐ* (because): 以 *yǐ* was used here to mean 因 *yīn* (because).[4]

4 病 *bìng* ([are] concerned with): Here, the first 病 *bìng* character was used to mean 憂 *yōu* (to worry; to be concerned [with]).[5]

CHAPTER 72

1 之 *zhī* (if): In this context, 之 *zhī* was used to mean 若 *ruò* (if).[1]

1 畏畏 *wèi wèi* (fear . . . fearsome): The first 畏 *wèi* character was a verb and meant 懼 *jù* (to fear).[2] The second one was a noun that acted as the object of this verb to mean "that which is feared," or "the fearsome."

2 將 *jiāng* (bound to): This was used here to mean 必 *bì* (must; bound to).[3]

3   毋 *wú* (not): 毋 *wú* literally meant "do not" and suggested that the action described was forbidden,[4] and so has been translated accordingly as "[verb +] not." This character in line 4 would have been read the same way.

3   狎 *xiá* (restrict): The character 狎 *xiá* would have been read here as 陕 *xiá* (i.e., 狭 *xiá*)[5] and meant 狭迫 *xiápò* (to compel; to restrict).[6]

4   猒 *yàn* (constrain): In this context, 猒 *yàn* would have been read as 厭 *yàn*,[7] which here meant 壓笮 *yāzhá* (to oppress; to constrain).[8] 猒 *yàn* in line 5 would have been read the same way.

5   夫 *fú* (they): This character was used in this line to mean 彼 *bǐ* [third person pronoun].[9]

5   唯 *wéi* ([it is only] when): In this context, it was used to mean 因為 *yīnwèi* (because; [it is only] when).[10]

5   弗猒 *fúyàn* (not constrained): 弗 *fú* was meant to convey "not . . . them [i.e., people]"[11] here. Because the passive voice was used, this is interpreted accordingly and therefore omits "them."

6   不猒 *búyàn* (be not resentful): 猒 *yàn* would have been read here as 厭 *yàn*[12] and meant 惡 *wù* (resentful).[13] (The reading of 猒 *yàn* [or 厭 *yàn*] here differs from that of lines 4–5.)

8   自見 *zìjiàn* (be self-regarding): See chapter 22 (comment on line 3).

CHAPTER 73

1   敢 *gǎn* (unrestrained): The term 不敢 *bùgǎn* ([with] restraint; see chapter 3 [second comment on line 13]) used the negative 不 *bù* to modify the same noun as in this line, so 敢 *gǎn* logically meant the opposite, which was "without restraint" or "unrestrained."

1   則 *zé* ([will] lead): The part following this term is the consequence of that which comes before it, and so is interpreted accordingly.[1] 則 *zé* in line 2 would have been read the same way.

2   不敢 *bùgǎn* (restrained): See the first comment on line 1.

4   天之所惡 *tiān zhī suǒwù* (what the heavens spurn): Chapter 25 says, "The heavens conform to the Dao." We may therefore logically infer that the heavens are a corporeal expression of the Dao. Thus, this phrase was actually another way of saying "what the Dao spurns."

6   The implication of this line echoes the spirit of chapter 23 (lines 13–14). See also chapter 66 (lines 13–14), as well as chapter 8 (lines 2 and 11) and chapter 68 (lines 1–5).

7   The meaning of this line is that the heavens always effectively respond to what the world needs, but they do so silently.[2]

8   弗召 *fúzhào* ([is] never summoned): This term would have been read in the passive voice, even though it was written in the form of an active statement; see chapter 20 (endnote 30). 弗 *fú* indicated 不 . . . 之 *bù . . . zhī* (not . . . It); see chapter 2 (comment on lines 11–12). "It" represented "the Dao of the heavens," which is omitted because of the passive voice.

8   To further understand this line, refer to the Qing Shizu emperor's note.[3]

9   墠 *shàn* (lax): 墠 *shàn* would have been defined here as 寬 *kuān* (lax).[4]

10 天網恢恢 *tiān Wǎng huīhuī* (the heavens' Net is so immense): 恢恢 *huīhuī* described a state that was 甚大 *shèndà* (immense).[5]

10–11 When Heshang Gong annotated these lines, he specifically pointed out that the heavens could "detect the good and the bad in man,"[6] which was not necessarily part of Laozi's philosophy, but is nevertheless a universal Daoist tenet.

CHAPTER 74

1 恆 . . . 不 *héng . . . bù* (are never): This phrase literally meant "always . . . not," and so is rendered here as "are never."

1 且 *qiě* (truly): In this context, 且 *qiě* was used to mean 必 *bì* (surely; truly).[1] 且 *qiě* in line 3 would have been read the same way.

4 而 *ér* ([and yet] there are): This would have been read here as 有 *yǒu* (to have),[2] but we have modified this as "there are" to provide a more fluid interpretation.

4 為奇者 *wéijīzhě* (transgressors): In this context, 奇 *jī* was defined as 邪 *xié* (wrong-doings; transgressions),[3] so 為奇者 *wéijīzhě* literally meant "those who commit transgressions," and is therefore interpreted as "transgressors."

5 得 *dé* (arrest): As used here, 得 *dé* meant 獲 *huò* (to attain),[4] which is then interpreted as "to arrest" to fit the idea in this context.

6 夫 *fú* (then): This character was used here to mean 則 *zé* (then).[5]

7 且必 *qiěbì* (truly): 且 *qiě* would have been defined here as 必 *bì* (truly—see the second comment on line 1 above), and so this compound term just meant "truly."

8 司殺者 *sīshāzhě* (executioner): This term literally referred to "one who is in charge of killing."

9 夫 *fú* (when): In this context, the character 夫 *fú* was used to mean 若 *ruò* (if; when).[6]

10 是 *shì* ([would be] like): This was meant as 猶 *yóu* (like) here.[7]

11 夫 *fú* (those): In this context, 夫 *fú* was used to mean 彼 *bǐ* [third person pronoun].[8]

12 希 *xī* (rarely): This character would have been read here as 稀 *xī*, which meant 罕 *hàn* (rare; rarely).[9]

CHAPTER 75

1 之 *zhī* (when): This character would have been read as 若 *ruò* (if); see chapter 72 (comment on line 1), and this has been modified here as "when" (as in a conditional statement) to better fit the context. 之 *zhī* in lines 4 and 7 would have been read the same way.

2 以 *yǐ* (because): This was used here to mean 因 *yīn* (because).[1] This character in lines 5, 8, and 10 should be read the same way.

2 其取食稅之多 *qí qǔ shíshuì zhīduō* (their taxes have been levied too heavily): With regard to 食稅 *shíshuì* (lit., the harvest tax), this was the sort of tax that was assessed on agricultural yields in ancient times,[2] a concept that has been abridged in our interpretation as simply "taxes." As for 之多 *zhīduō*, the character 之 *zhī* acted as a mood word here to emphasize the meaning of 多 *duō*,[3] and therefore "too" is used to express this; 多 *duō* meant "many" or "much," which has been adjusted as "heavily"[4] to fit the context. 取 *qǔ* (lit., to take) has been modified as "levied" for the same reason. Finally, 其 *qí* (lit., him; they; their) referred to the "people" in line 1, and this allows us to understand that 取食稅 *qǔ shíshuì* would have been read in the passive voice, even though it appears to be an active statement.[5]

4 百姓 *bǎixìng* (**subjects**): See chapter 5 (comment on line 4, as well as endnotes 5–6).

5 有以為 *yǒuyǐwéi* (**intentionally exerting effort**): 有以 *yǒuyǐ* was used as if to say 有所 *yǒusuǒ* (intentionally); see chapter 38 (second comment on line 5). 為 *wéi* (second tone) in this context meant "to exert effort," and so was read differently from the same character in chapter 38, which was pronounced *wèi* (fourth tone: lit., for [a purpose]).

8 厚 *hòu* (**inordinate**): This character literally meant "thick" or "abundant," but we have modified this as "inordinate" to better fit the context.

7–8 The teaching in these lines echoes that of chapter 50 (lines 4–7).

10 無以生為者 *wúyǐ shēng wéi zhě* (**[those who] do not exert effort in their lives**): This phrasing turned 無以為生者 *wú yǐwéi shēng zhě* into a rhetorical statement. 者 *zhě* acted as a mood word here to indicate a pause in this line.[6] 無以 *wúyǐ* would have been read as 無所 *wúsuǒ* ([to have] no intention),[7] and here we have modified this as "do not."

11 是 *shì* (**are able to**): This would have been defined here as 能 *néng* (can; to be able to).[8]

11 賢 *xián* (**perfectly**): 賢 *xián* was used here to mean 善 *shàn* (good; perfect; perfectly).[9]

10–11 MN   The understanding of these lines was inspired by Su Che's and Heshang Gong's notes.[10]

CHAPTER 76

1 柔 *róu* (**soft**): This character was a synonym for 弱 *ruò* (weak).[1]

2 柜信 *gèngshēn* (**lie stretched out**): 柜 *gèng* would have been read as 揯 *gèng*, which was defined as 橫亙 *hénggèng* (to lie across; to lie down),[2] and so we used "lie" to interpret this. 信 *shēn* here meant 伸 *shēn* (to stretch out).[3]

5 死之徒 *sǐzhītú* (**the dead**): In this phrase, 死 *sǐ* literally meant "dead" or "death," while 徒 *tú* (lit., a follower) was defined as 眾 *zhòng* (a mass [of people or things]),[4] so we used "the dead" in this interpretation. (In accordance with this understanding, 生之徒 *shēngzhītú* in line 6 is rendered as "the living.")

8 恆 *héng* (**fall down**): This would have been read as 亙 *gèng*[5] and meant "to lie across,"[6] so this connotation has been modified as "fall down."

CHAPTER 77

1 天之道 *tiān zhī dào* (**[is this] how the heavens behave**): 之 *zhī* was read here as 所 *suǒ* (what; how).[1] As for 道 *dào*, lines 2–7 describe the way in which the heavens perform, suggesting that this character as used here would have been read as 行 *xíng* (to act; to behave).[2] 道 *dào* in lines 6 and 8 should be read the same way. (The meanings of 天之道 *tiān zhī dào* and 人之道 *rén zhī dào* in this chapter actually differ from that of the identical phrases in chapter 81.)

1 猶 *yóu* (**like**): This was defined in this context as 若 *ruò* (like).[3]

1 者 *zhě* [**mood word**]: In this instance, 者 *zhě* served to indicate that the term in front of it was a given condition,[4] and so it had no translatable meaning.

1 也 *yě* [**mood word**]: Here this character was used like 邪 *yē*,[5] which acted as a question mark.

2 抑 *yì* (**pulled down**): The definition of this character was 按 *àn* (to press down),[6] which we then modified as "pulled down" to fit the context.

8 不然 *bùrán* (**is otherwise**): 然 *rán* meant 如是 *rúshì* (like this)[7] here. 不然 *bùrán* was another way of saying "not like this," and so has been interpreted as "is otherwise."

9 奉 *fèng* (**proffer**): In this context, 奉 *fèng* meant 獻 *xiàn* (to proffer).[8]

10 有以取 *yǒuyǐ qǔ* (**extract some**): Here, 以 *yǐ* was used to mean 所 *suǒ*,[9] which indicated "some" here,[10] while 取 *qǔ* meant "to take" or "to extract."

10 於 *yú* (**as**): This was used here to mean 如 *rú* (as).[11]

10 者 *zhě* (**do**): 者 *zhě* acted as a signifier[12] for that which the heavens do (as described in lines 6–7) and is interpreted accordingly.

10 乎 *hū* [**mood word**]: 乎 *hū* was employed in this context to indicate a question mood.[13]

11 有 *yǒu* (**with**): This character literally meant "to have," but this is modified here as "with" to create a more fluid reading.

11 乎 *hū* [**mood word**]: In this context, 乎 *hū* was used to indicate an exclamation.[14]

12 為 *wéi* (**exert effort**): The efforts of sages (or leaders) are conducted in accordance with the rules conveyed in chapter 64 (line 5), which says, "Exert effort where there is not yet materialization."

12 The description in this line echoes the spirit contained in chapter 51 (line 11).

12 弗 *fú* (**not**): Standard grammatical rules for ancient classical Chinese held that this ought to have been understood as "not . . . it," with the subject "it" always omitted (see chapter 2 [comment on lines 11–12]), and so has been interpreted accordingly. This character in line 13 should be read the same way.

13 居 *jū* (**possess**): In this context, this character had the meaning of 據 *jù* (to occupy; to grasp).[15] We modified this here as "to possess" (see chapter 2, comment on line 13).

13 The narrative of this line echoes the description in chapter 9 (lines 9–10).

14 見 *xiǎn* (**to reveal**): See chapter 3 (comment on lines 5–6).

14 賢 *xián* ([**what has been**] **achieved**): 賢 *xián* would have been defined in this context as 勞 *láo* (lit., diligence), which here meant 功 *gōng* (achievement; [what has been] achieved).[16]

CHAPTER 78

2 而攻 *ér gōng* (**and yet** [**when**] **struck**): Although this passage appears to be in the active voice, it is actually passive,[1] and so this term would have been understood to mean "struck" rather than "strikes." (As chapter 8 instructs, the nature of water "is magnanimous when competed with" and "competes not." So, water can only be the receiver of a blow—or the medium through which something else may be struck—but not the initiator.)

2 莫之能先 *mòzhī néngxiān* (**nothing . . . can surpass it**): This phrasing turned 莫能先之 *mònéng xiānzhī* into a rhetorical statement. 先 *xiān* meant 上 *shàng* (to surpass).[2]

3 無以易之 *wúyǐ yìzhī* (**that which cannot be changed**): In this context, 以 *yǐ* was used to mean 可 *kě* (can).[3] 易 *yì* meant 變 *biàn* (to change),[4] while 之 *zhī* [mood word] had no inherent meaning, but rather served to smooth the reading.[5] We rendered this phrase accordingly.

4 柔之 *róuzhī* (**softness**): 之 *zhī* was used here to transform 柔 *róu* (soft) into a noun,[6] and was used similarly in line 5 to change 弱 *ruò* into a noun meaning "weakness."

4–7 MN How water . . . can penetrate the hardest stone . . . wear away a mountain: Our understanding was inspired by Xi Tong's *jijie* note.[7]

6   弗 *fú* (**none . . . not of these**):[8] "These" represented the descriptions in lines 4–5.

7   而 *ér* (**[and] yet**): 而 *ér* was used in this context to mean 然 *rán* (but; yet).[9]

7   莫之能行 *mòzhī néngxíng* (**none are able to behave as these**): This phrasing turned 莫能行之 *mònéng xíngzhī* into a rhetorical statement, with 之 *zhī* representing the descriptions in lines 4–5.

8   云曰 *yúnyuē* (**hold that**): In this context, 云 *yún* was used to mean 有 *yǒu* (to have),[10] while 曰 *yuē* was another way of expressing 言 *yán* (saying).[11] So, this literally would have meant "to have a saying," but we have modified it as "to hold that" for a more graceful reading.

9   邦 *bāng* (**[their] states**): From the context of line 10, we know that 邦 *bāng* here referred to the individual states of these lords. This reading differs slightly from this character's usage in line 11 (see first comment on line 11).

9   垢 *gòu* (**disgrace**): This character (lit., filth) would have been read here as 恥 *chǐ* (disgrace).[12]

10 社稷 *shèjì* (**[their] domains**): 社 *Shè* was the Earth God[13] and 稷 *Jì* the Grain Deity.[14] Together, these represented the land and its food. In ancient times (particularly during the pre-Qin period), this term was used to designate the physical condition of a state or country, and so has been interpreted as their "domains."

11 邦 *bāng* (**the states**): By referring to line 12, we may understand that this 邦 *bāng* indicated all the states in the world.

11 不祥 *bùxiáng* (**misfortunes**): Our understanding of this term here differs slightly from the one in chapter 31 (second comment on line 1), since it represents things that have already occurred.

CHAPTER 79

1   和 *hé* (**[may] be appeased**): When used as a verb, 和 *hé* literally meant "to harmonize." This is modified here as "to be appeased" to fit the description.

1   怨 *yuàn* (**animosities**): This would have been understood here to mean 恨 *hèn* (hatred; animosities).[1]

1   必 *bì* (**[yet] in the end**): The character 必 *bì* was used in this context to mean 終 *zhōng* (finally; in the end),[2] with "yet" added to smooth the reading.

2   焉 *yān* (**how**): 焉 *yān* acted as 何 *hé* (how)[3] in this line.

2   為 *wéi* (**attained**): Here this character meant 成 *chéng* (to achieve; to attain).[4]

3   執左介 *zhí zuǒjiè* (**carry the left side of agreements**): In ancient China, when two sides agreed to an obligation, a wooden board (symbolizing the agreement) was split in half, with the left side retained by the borrower and the right side by the lender.[5] The holder of 左介 *zuǒjiè* (the left side of the agreement) was therefore beholden to the right side. In this term, the character 介 *jiè* would have been read as a 契 *qì* (contract; agreement).[6]

4   不以責於人 *bù yǐzé yú rén* (**make no demands of others**): 以 *yǐ* was used here to act as 用 *yòng* (to use; to make),[7] while 責 *zé* meant 迫迮而取 *pòzuó ér qǔ* (to compel and take; a demand),[8] and so this phrase is interpreted accordingly.

3–4 Wei Yuan's benyi note points out that the descriptions in these two lines suggest the spirit of "無我不爭之德 *wúwǒ bùzhēng zhī Dé*" (the De [i.e., cultivation] of transcending one's self and not competing).

5 司 *sī* (**[are] concerned with**): This was defined here as 察 *chá* (lit., to oversee),[9] which we have modified slightly as "to be concerned with." This character in line 6 would have been read the same way.

6 徹 *chè* (**clarifications**): In this context, 徹 *chè* meant 明 *míng* (to clarify; clarification),[10] which denoted stringent judgment.

5–6 We added "those who" to clarify these descriptions.

8 與 *yǔ* (**in accord with**): This was another way of saying 許 *xǔ* (to agree with; to be in accord with).[11]

CHAPTER 80

1 寡民 *guǎmín* (**few people**): When used as a modifier for 民 *mín* (people), 寡 *guǎ* meant 少 *shǎo* (a small number; few),[1] so this term referred to "few people."

2 十百人之器 *shíbǎirén zhī qì* (**instruments [that require] ten to one hundred men**): In this passage, 十 *shí* (ten) referred to the power of ten men, while 百 *bǎi* (hundred) stood for the power of a hundred. In this context, 器 *qì* (instruments)[2] would have been understood as a description of the equipment suitable for use by a large number of people. We have used "that require" here, rather than the literal interpretation of 之 *zhī* (i.e., of), to clarify the description.

3 重死 *zhòngsǐ* (**care about their dead**): 重 *zhòng* here meant 矜惜 *jīnxī* (to care about).[3]

3 遠徙 *yuǎnxī* (**not move away**): 遠 *yuǎn* was defined as 疏 *shū* (to keep a distance from),[4] so "not" is used here to simply express this. 徙 *xī* was defined as 遷移 *qiānyí* (to move away),[5] and this term has been interpreted accordingly.

4 無所 *wúsuǒ* (**[but] no place**): In this context, 所 *suǒ* was understood to mean 處 *chù* (place).[6] This character in line 5 would have been read the same way.

5 陳 *chén* (**to deploy**): In this context, 陳 *chén* would have been defined as 列 *liè* (to deploy [in a military sense]).[7]

4–5 The subjects of these two lines were omitted in the text. We have added "they" (referring to the people) as a clarification.

6 結繩 *jiēshéng* (**knotted cords**): Of special interest is the use of "knotted ropes" to communicate in lieu of teaching the common people the written language. This custom was actually quite conventional up through Laozi's time and was similar to the Inca culture's *quipu*. An example of this can be found in Eastern Han scholar Zheng Xuan's annotation (as quoted in Xi Tong's jijie note) on *Yijing* (*The Book of Changes*), indicating that "affairs that were great were recorded as great knots in their ropes, and affairs that were small were recorded as small knots in their ropes."[8]

CHAPTER 81

1 信 *xìn* (**truthful**): In this context, 信 *xìn* had the definition of 真實 *zhēnshí* (truthful).[1] This character in line 2 would have been read the same way.

3   知 *zhì* (**wisdom**): In this line, 知 *zhì* would have been read as 智 *zhì* (wisdom).[2] This character in line 4 would have been read the same way.

3   者 *zhě* (**then**): 者 *zhě* was used here to mean 則 *zé* (then).[3] This character in lines 4–6 would have been read the same way.

3   博 *bó* (**broad knowledge**): This was defined as 多聞 *duōwén* (lit., to have heard much),[4] and so has been interpreted here as "broad knowledge." This character in line 4 would have been read the same way.

8   既 *jì* (**unreservedly**): In this context, this character would have meant 盡 *jìn* (completely; unreservedly).[5] This character in line 9 would have been read the same way.

8   為 *wéi* (**devoting**): In this line, 為 *wéi* would have meant 施 *shī* (to devote).[6]

11   弗 *fú* (**without**): This character meant 不 . . . 之 *bù . . . zhī* (not . . . them),[7] and we modified it accordingly.

ENDNOTES

INTRODUCTION: UNDERSTANDING THE *DAO DE JING*

1. Durant, 653 and 657.

2. This understanding is per Sima Qian's *Shiji* (see endnote 8). The renowned scholar Guo Moruo has insightfully suggested that the content of the *Dao De Jing* was the 遺說 (bequeathed teachings) of Laozi, and they were edited into a book by later generations (Guo Dingtang, *Xian Qin tiandaoguan zhi jinzhan*, 41).

   Since ancient times, this book has been universally referred to in China as *Laozi* (spelled as *Lao-tzu* or *Lao Tzu*, among other renderings in various Western languages), for naming a book after its writer was a Chinese tradition during the pre-Qin period. Chinese references to what we now know as the *Dao De Jing* (a title that also has many variations, including the *Daodejing*, the *Daode jing*, and the *Tao Te Ching*) appeared only a little more than a thousand years ago. Regarding Laozi the person, see endnote 8.

3. This concept was first introduced by Karl Jaspers (*Vom Ursprung und Ziel der Geschichte*, 1949; English edition: *The Origin and Goal of History*, 1953), which centers around the years 500–300 BCE, for that was when key thinkers in China, India, Persia, Greece, Rome, the Levant, and Judea simultaneously—yet independently—arose, and in time their ideas became the foundations for most of the important philosophical and spiritual traditions of our times.

4. This refers to the copy of *Laozi* written on bamboo slips that was discovered in 1993 within a late Warring States period tomb in Guodian, near Jingmen, Hubei Province.

5. The foreword in *Guodian Chumu zhujian*, edited by Qiu Xigui, notes that the bamboo slats inscribed with the words of Laozi were estimated to be dated back to around 300 BCE, for the Guodian tombs were most likely sealed toward the end of the middle Warring States period.

   According to Prof. Gao Ming's preface to *Boshu Laozi jiaozhu*, both silk versions were estimated to be at least 2,200 years old. (Version A was written in 篆書, or seal script, and did not avoid the taboo character 邦 [the given name of the first Han emperor].

That means it would have been older than version B, which avoided the taboo character and was written in 隸書, or clerical script.)

6. See Zhu Qianzhi, *Laozi jiaoshi*, where an analysis of these ancient rhythms is included at the end of each chapter.

7. Jaspers, V2, 87–88.

8. *Shiji* ("*Laozi liezhuan*," V63, 2139–45). This biography of Laozi states that his family name was 李 (Li) and he had the familial given name of 耳 (Er), with another adult name of 聃 (Dan). Laozi was the 守藏室史, or administrator of books, for the Zhou court.

   According to this biography, when Confucius visited Zhou to ask Laozi about the rites, Laozi told him, "This that you have mentioned—these people and their bones decayed long ago, and only their words remain. When a gentleman's time has arrived, vehicles will serve him [for a person of rank will not walk in public]; if it does not, he will move about as a tumbleweed [i.e., will settle wherever he lands]. I have heard that 'a good merchant who hides in profundity will appear to possess nothing, and a gentleman who amply cultivates himself will give the impression of knowing nothing.' Leave behind your arrogance and endless desires, your haughtiness and excessive ambitions: these are of no good to you. This is all that I can tell you."

   Confucius left and told his disciples, "Birds, I know that they fly. Fish, I know that they swim. Animals, I know that they walk. The ones that walk can be caught with a net. The ones that swim can be caught with a fishing line. The ones that fly can be caught with a roped arrow. But as for a dragon, I know not whether it rides the winds and clouds, or if it ascends into the sky. And yet today I saw Laozi, and he is as a dragon!"

   This biography elaborates further that Laozi cultivated himself through the Dao and the De (see chapters 1 and 38), with his doctrine centered upon a withdrawal of the self and the surpassing of one's own reputation. This school of thought likely emerged while he was an official in the Zhou court. During his long tenure there, he grew weary of the deterioration in the Zhou state and finally left both his position and his homeland. Legend says that when he reached the border, the sentry known as Yinxi told him, "Since you are leaving, be sure to write a book for me." As the legend goes, Laozi then wrote this book. It has two parts that discuss, in about 5,000 characters, the significance of the Dao and the De. He subsequently departed, but to where, no one knows.

   The patrilineal descendants of Laozi's lineage were dutifully recorded and their deeds memorialized: His son Zong became a general of the Wu state, Zong's son was named Zhu, and Zhu's son was Gong; the great-grandson of Gong was Jia, and Jia officially served the Han Xiaowen emperor. Jia's son, Jie, served as the prime minister of the Prince of Jiaoxi (named Yang), and lived in the state of Qi. (The rest of these records discusses the conflict between Daoist and Confucian scholars, hence is omitted here.) This reading follows the views of contemporary scholar Xu Fuguan (485).

9. This famous historical event can be found in both citations in endnote 8, as well as *Shiji* ("*Kongzi shijia*," V17, 1909). Confucius is also noted in *Liji* ("*Zengzi wen*") as having received Laozi's advice on 禮 a total of four times (V19; 5b, 11b, and 12a–b). Moreover, *Kongzi jiayu* ("*Guan Zhou*") records that "[Confucius] went to Zhou and asked Lao Dan about the rites" (V3, 1a–2a). *Zhuangzi* includes many such records: once in "*Tiandi*"

(jijie, 104), once in "*Tian Dao*" (117–18), four times in "*Tianyun*" (126–31), once in "*Tianzifang*" (178–80), and once in "*Zhi beiyou*" (188–89).

10. See *Shiji* ("*Laozi liezhuan*") as edited by Pei Yin et al., which quotes Tang dynasty scholar Sima Zhen's suoyin note; in this, he pointed out that the 苦 (mod. Ch., *kǔ*) in 苦縣 was pronounced as 怙 *hù* (endnote 2, 2139).

11. See J. H. Huang (15–16 and endnote 6, 28).

12. In *Shiji* ("*Chen shijia*"), to the line "周武王克殷紂, 乃復求舜後," Sima Zhen noted: "遏父為周陶正" (V36, endnote 3, 1575).

13. Copies of the *Dao De Jing* that were handed down through generations, rather than discovered in archaeological sites, are referred to as the "received versions."

14. According to Wang Yousan, there were about 335 titles between the Han dynasty and the early Republic.

15. Quoted in Yu Wanli's preface to Fan Bocheng's *Laozi zhigui jiaojian* (cited on page 376 of the bibliography under Yan Zun).

16. "Pre-Qin" refers to Chinese history prior to 221 BCE, or the first year of the Qin dynasty.

17. Xiong Tieji (21).

18. Hsiu-chen Chang (146).

19. Goldin (119–20).

20. Jiang Xichang (foreword, 1).

21. The Chu tomb (archaeological site number 1) was discovered in 1993 near Jinmen, Hubei, and dated from before the Han dynasty. The Mawangdui tombs were discovered in 1972 near Changsha, Hunan, dating from the Western Han dynasty (206 BCE–9 CE).

22. *Beijing Daxue cang Xi Han zhushu* (2) notes: "We deduce that the time in which this bamboo version was written mainly lay within the late period of Han Wudi, or at the very least was no later than Han Xuandi" (foreword, 2). If we use Han Xuandi emperor's date of ascension to the throne (i.e., 73 BCE) to calculate this, then the Beida version ought to be 2,094 years old.

23. It appears that it was not until the eighth century—as seen in the Tang Xuanzong emperor's annotated version—that the familiar names of the Book of the Dao and the Book of the De were given to the two halves of this book. (The *Jing* at the end of this book title—as in other ancient works such as *Yijing* and *Shijing*—was used to convey the greatest level of respect because it was revered as an ultimate set of teachings.) Be that as it may, most scholars believed that, due to their interdependence, not much difference exists between the Book of the Dao and the Book of the De. The reason for this stance is that the De is mentioned in the Book of the Dao, and vice versa. Furthermore, it was assumed that the names for each book were derived from the subject of the first line of each half (i.e., chapters 1 and 38).

However, a careful comparison of the contents and manner of discussion in these two books suggests otherwise: Just as its title implies, the Book of the Dao revolves around a discussion of the Dao, with chapters 1, 4, 14, 25, and 32 specifically describing both the constitution and expression of the Dao. The remaining thirty-two chapters in this first half tend to be either discussions on how to achieve the type of cultivation that conforms to the Dao, or the types of behavior and governance that will be in accord with the Dao.

The Dao and the De can even be considered as a sort of mutually complementary cause and effect, for as Wang Bi's annotation in *Laozi Dao De Jing zhu jiaoshi* to chapter 38 pointed out: "何以得德? 由乎道也" (How can one obtain the De? Through the Dao). What this means, then, is that the Dao is the cause, and the De encompasses Its effects, which is why the De was occasionally mentioned in the Book of the Dao as needed.

　　Conversely, if we delve into the Book of the De, we will find that the different circumstances provided in each chapter allow us to observe the various connotations of the De. Every one of these discussions on cause refers naturally back to the Dao. Because of this, a clear delineation exists between the Book of the Dao and the Book of the De.

24. I surmise that the reason for this could have arisen out of an emphasis on the De, which relied upon the following theories:

- *Zhuangzi* ("*Tianxia*"), "以德為本, 以道為門" (jijie, 287), as well as ("*Shanxing*"), "夫德, 和也; 道, 理也. 德, 無不容, 仁也; 道, 無不理, 義也" (135).
- *Guanzi* ("*Xinshu shang*"), "德者, 道之舍" (jiaozheng, 220).
- *Zuo zhuan* ("*Xianggong ershisinian*"), "德, 國家之基也" (V35, 28b).
- *Kongzi jiayu* ("*Ruguan*"), "德者, 政之始也" (Song shu ben, V5, 17a).

(The first two books are considered Daoist—for *Guanzi* was involved with the Huang Lao School—and the last two books are Confucian.)

25. See endnote 23.

26. This becomes evident if we compare chapter 51, line 1 ("The Dao engenders all and the De fosters all") with line 7 ("The Dao engenders all, fosters all").

27. The Guodian version is not as complete as some of the other versions. While its chapter order is not the same as what we understand it to be, its original organization has been retained. This was not due to damage, but rather because this was the way it was discovered. Therefore, in the first section, the chapter order is: 19, 66, 46 (middle and end), 30 (beginning and middle), 15, 64 (end), 37, 63, 2, 32, 25, 5 (middle), 16 (beginning), 64 (beginning), 56, 57, 55, 44, 40, and 9. In the second section, the chapter order is: 59, 48, 20, 13, 41, 52 (middle), 45, and 54. Lastly, in the third section, the chapter order is: 17 and 18, 35, 31 (middle and end), and 64 (end).

28. The text of the Guodian version was written in the Chu style, while silk version A was written in the seal-style script and silk version B in the clerical style. These can be transcribed into the traditional Chinese font known as 隸定, which comprises the fundamental work provided by the editorial boards responsible for transcribing these versions.

29. Jiang Xichang (author's foreword, 1).

30. Gao Heng's preface to his *Laozi zhenggu* describes this perfectly: "*Laozi* is an ancient manuscript dating from the late Zhou dynasty that was written in archaic characters; these characters had ancient definitions. For example, 有 [lit., to have] meant 域 [lit., territory] . . . 則 [lit., then] meant 賊 [thief], and 隻 [orig., a short-tailed bird] meant 唯 [only], with 孩 [lit., child] meaning 閡 [obstructed] and 徒 [lit., follower] meaning 途 [path] . . . which is why it is so difficult to grasp the meaning of the book *Laozi*."

31. No book on ancient Chinese grammar existed until the end of the Qing dynasty, when *Mashi wentong* was published in 1898 (see entry under Ma Jianzhong [Qing]). Nevertheless, research on 虛字, or empty words (see page 7), existed over a century earlier, when Yuan Renlin's *Xuzi shuo* was released in 1746.

The ancient Chinese classics did not employ paragraphs or punctuation, so readers instead relied on their knowledge of each line's correct construction to comprehend the text. Even though a grasp of ancient grammar can prove useful, the chances of arriving at a correct understanding of the Chinese classics are often determined by a clear discernment of what each term refers to in that context, in that area of China, and in that period of time.

32. Different appellations can be applied to this term. In addition to 虛字, there are also 虛詞, 經詞 (or simply 詞, as in 釋詞 and 詞詮), and even 助詞. No matter the nomenclature, all are rendered "empty words" here.

33. Examples of such substitutions abound in this book, as in chapter 19 (comments on lines 1, 5, 7, and 8), as well as in endnote 30 above.

34. Many of the works I relied on to determine Laozi's meaning are listed in the bibliography beginning on page 372. Also, please refer to the acknowledgments (page 387) for a list of the professors who trained me in this field.

35. Four more self-styled "emperors" should also be mentioned: Liang Wudi, Liang Jianwendi, Liang Yuandi, and Zhou Wendi (see Wang Yousan, *Laozi kao*, table of contents, iv, v, and vi). Unfortunately, their annotations are no longer extant, in part because they ruled over individual territories, rather than all of China.

36. In the years stretching from the Warring States period to the beginning of the Han dynasty, Daoist (sometimes rendered as "Taoist") thought was referred to as "Huang Lao." (In fact, the term "Huang Lao" cannot be found in any records dating from before the early Western Han dynasty; see Ren Jiyu, *Zhongguo zhexue fazhanshi*, who wrote about "黃老連稱及黃老之學的起源" [V Qin Han, 95].)

The name "Huang" represented the doctrine of the 黃帝經 ("Yellow Emperor's canon," understood to have been fabricated some time prior to 221 BCE), which was developed from a school of thought that centered on the concepts of 天道 and 自然. "Lao," of course, referred to Laozi. For that reason, Huang Lao ostensibly held the spirit of Laozi as its fundament, but tended to lean more heavily toward teachings on the theories and application of 法 (law) and 治 (governing). This school of thought was used with great success in early Han politics up until the emperor Han Wudi accepted the suggestion of Dong Zhongshu to "獨尊儒術" (respect only Confucian methods). Huang Lao thought was silenced from then on until the two Jin (晉) dynasties.

37. Daoism as a folk religion was based on alterations of *Dao De Jing* thought through subjective annotations, or eisegesis. While "Dao" was used in its name, Laozi's true teachings were perverted in this religion. Written in the Han dynasty, its 想爾注 formed the foundation for Daoism's 天師道 sect, which was mainly concerned with superstition and attaining immortality. For more on this, see Rao Zongyi, *Laozi Xiang'er zhu jiaozheng*, as well as Gu Baotian and Zhang Zhongli, *Xinyi Laozi Xiang'er zhu*.

38. The idea that Laozi's thought had an influence on Confucianism has always been roundly opposed by Confucian scholars. However, in addition to the sources cited in notes 8 and 9 above that mentioned Confucius's visits to Laozi to discuss the rites, the following collections of Confucius's teachings should also be considered:

Lunyu ("*Weiling Gong*"), "子曰: 無為而治者, 其舜也?! . . . 恭己, 正南面而已矣" (zhushu, V14, 5b), as well as ("*Xian wen*"), "或問 '以德報怨' 何如?" (V14, 4a), which was a discussion on chapter 63 (line 6) of the *Dao De Jing*, and *Liji* ("*Zhongyong*"), "[至誠

無息] 如此者, 不見而章, 不動而變, 無為而成" (V53, 26a), as well as ("*Ai Gong wen*"): Confucius responded to Ai Gong's questions by saying, "無為而物成是天道也" (V50, 10a). Also in *Liji* ("*Daxue*"), "心正而後身脩; 身脩而後家齊而後國治; 國治而後天下平" (V60, 4b), which is very similar in meaning to that of chapter 54 (lines 4–8) in the *Dao De Jing*.

39. The famous scholar Tang Yongtong once pointed out: "Buddhism during the Han dynasty adhered to invocations [方術], [but] during the Wei and Jin [dynasties], monks admired Lao[zi] and Zhuang[zi]" (*Han Wei Liang Jin Nanbeichao Fojiaoshi*, 80; quoted in Xiong Tieji et al., *Zhongguo Laoxue shi*, section 3, 213). Wang Yousan's *Laozi kao* recorded the annotations of leading monks during the two Jin dynasties—such as Fotuzheng, Kumārajīva, Monk Zhao, Monk Yi, and Monk Huilin—in his table of contents (3–4), and these can be employed to prove Tang's view. Moreover, during the two Jin dynasties and the Northern and Southern dynasties, leading monastics such as Monk Huiyuan had "respect for Laozi and Zhuangzi," and often used Zhuangzi's thought to teach Buddhist adherents (Fung Yu-lan, *Sansongtang quanji, dierjuan*, 663–64). Of course, Monk Daozheng's (i.e., Shenggong's) theory on enlightenment (頓悟, also known as *satori* in Japanese) was key to transforming Indian Buddhism into Chinese Chan (and Japanese Zen); see Pan Ping and Ming Lizhi's *Hu Shi shuo Chan* (232–39) and chapter 5 of Tang Yongtong's *Lixue, Foxue, Xuanxue* ("*Zhu Dao sheng dunwuyi*," 232–39). However, as Hu Shi notes in *Hu Shi shuo Chan* (199), Monk Huijiao's *Gaozeng zhuan* describes Daozheng's theory as having been directly inspired by Zhuangzi. This proves that Laozi's philosophy formed the foundation for this transformation. It is also why Alan Watts had "The Philosophy of the Dao" as chapter one of his masterwork, *The Way of Zen*.

CHAPTER 1

1. See Heshang Gong's note in *Laozi Dao De Jing Heshang Gong zhangju*.
2. See Su Che's note in *Dao De Jing mingzhu xuanji* (er).
3. Wang Shumin, *Zhuangzi jiaoquan*, 565; endnote 6, 567–68. "道, 理也," in his comment on *Zhuangzi* ("*Shanxing*"). In modern Chinese, this is expressed as 道理 (as indicated by Jiang Xichang's note on this line of the *Dao De Jing*).
4. *Shijing* ("*Feifeng*"), "顧瞻周道"; Zheng Xuan's note (Mao Heng, *Mao Shi zhushu*, V7 zhi 2, 7b).
5. *Guangya* (V2 shang, 19b).
6. Wang Li, *Gu Hanyu tonglun* ("*Panduanju, ye zi*," V10, 90).
7. Liu Xi, *Shiming* ("*Shi yanyu*"), "名, 明也" (*Shuzhengbu*, V4, 5b).
8. Wang Xianqian's shuzhengbu note under the definition of 名 (see this chapter endnote 7) quotes *Xunzi* ("*Zheng ming*") as saying: "制名以指實" (V4, 5b). So, when 名 was used as a verb to indicate its object, it could be construed as meaning "to define."
9. 萬 has the literal meaning of "ten thousand," but for the ancient understanding of this character, refer to Zuo Qiuming, *Chunqiu Zuo zhuan zhushu ji buzheng* ("*Mingong yuannian*"), which notes, "萬、 盈數也," to which Kong Yingda's shu note indicates that "至萬則數滿也" (V11, 1b), so this is interpreted here as "all."
10. *Shijing* ("*Liao'e*"), "父兮生我, 母兮畜我" (V13 zhi 1, 1b–2a).
11. This character is usually interpreted into English as "desire," but that is not what Laozi meant here. Instead, it referred to "innate response." The proof for this lies in *Liji* ("*Yue-*

ji"), which tells us that "人生而靜—天 [i.e., 自然] 之性也. 感於物而動性之 [i.e., 有] 欲也]." Under this discussion is a very useful note from Zheng Xuan: "言, 性不見物 則無欲" (V37, 3a); Zheng Xuan's note informs us that our perceptive senses were also considered as part of the realm of our 性 (innate abilities) in ancient times. This allows us to understand that 欲 is how our "innate abilities" react to things. The theme of these two lines (7–8) concerns observation, and 欲 is the psychological condition in which we harbor our "innate responses." (性 can mean "nature," "characteristics," "disposition," or "innate abilities," with the meaning determined by context.)

12. See Wang Bi's note in *Laozi Dao De Jing zhu jiaoshi*.
13. *Yupian* (V10, "*Chi bu*," 119).
14. *Liezi* ("*Shuofu*"): "知言之謂者乎"; Zhang Zhan's note: "謂者, 所以發言之旨趣" (V8, 6b).
15. *Shuowen* (玄, V4 shang, 1b).
16. *Xunzi* ("*Zhengming*"), "名實玄紐"; Yang Jing's note (V16, 2b).
17. See chapter 10 (line 9). Concerning the location of this Gate, see chapter 6 (lines 1–3).

CHAPTER 2

1. Wu Changying, *Jingci yanshi* (其 17, 52).
2. Wang Shumin, *Guji xuzi guangyi* (之 28, 440). See also Xiao Xu, *Gushu xuci pangshi* (之 13, 334).
3. *Mozi* ("*Jinshang*," 66), Wu Yujiang's *jiaozhu*, 477.
4. Xu Hao, *Shuowen Xu jian* (聲) (see Ding Fubao, ed., *Shuowenjiezi gulin zheng, buhe bian*, 9–1093). This perception agrees with the description in chapter 12 (line 5): "五音使人 耳聾." (This understanding of 音 and 聲 might possibly be misconstrued as being the opposite of how they are described in the *Dao De Jing*; see *Shuowen* [聲, Duan Yucai's note, V12 shang, 5a], and J. H. Huang, *The Art of War* [footnote 14, 174].)
5. The ancient readings of these two characters were similar, and so most received versions used 處, which was defined as 制 (to administer) according to *Zuo zhuan* ("*Wengong shibanian*"), "德以處事"; Du Yu's note (V20, 35a).
6. The term 無為 can be found in *Shijing* ("*Chenfeng*," "*Zebei*"): " 寤寐無為." Kong Ying-da's *shu* note indicates that 無為 meant "更無所 [可] 為" (V7 zhi 1, 4b–5a). This poem came from a collection written in the Chen state, and as Laozi also was from there (see "Introduction: Understanding the *Dao De Jing*," page 1), that might be why he used this term to describe this philosophical theory of his.
7. For this definition of 自然 as "self-realization," see chapter 17 (comment on line 9), as well as chapter 24 (second comment on line 1).
8. Wang Bi's note (*Laozi Dao De Jing zhu jiaoshi*) on 無為 was "自然已足, 為則敗也," while in chapter 37 (line 1), his note on 無為 was "順自然也."
9. *Shuowen* (作, V8 shang, 5b).
10. Wang Li, ed., *Gu Hanyu tonglun* (弗, second explanation, 12–1, 111).
11. *Zhuangzi* ("*Xuwugui*"), "恃源而往者也" (jijie, 222). Under this line, Wang Xianqian's jijie note quotes Lu Deming, *Jingdian shiwen: Zhuangzi yinyi*, which indicates that 恃 was also written as 持. This proves that in ancient Chinese, 恃 and 持 could be used interchangeably. In this line of the *Dao De Jing*, we read 恃 as 持. *Shuowen* (持), "持, 握也" (V12 shang, 7b), so 持 literally meant "to hold."

12. *Guangya* ("*Shiyan*"), "居, 據也" (V5 xia, 1b). (The reading of 居 here differs from its reading in line 9, because the object in that line is "affairs," but here it is "all things.")

CHAPTER 3

1. This interpretation was inspired by the notes of Hanshan (Monk Deqing), *Dao De Jing mingzhu xuanji* (*wu*), and Zhang Wei and Zhang Wei, *Laozi zhujie*.
2. This interpretation was inspired by Su Che's note. See also chapter 5 (lines 1–4).
3. Zhu Junsheng, *Shuowen tongxun dingsheng* (上, V18, 32a–b, as well as 尚, V18, 17b–18a). Some received versions used 尚 here.
4. See Heshang Gong's note.
5. *Shuowen* (盜); Duan Yucai's note (V8 xia, 7b)—in other words, "theft."
6. See the notes on this line by Hanshan and Zhang Wei.
7. This interpretation was inspired by Su Che's note.
8. *Jiyun* ("*Qusheng*," 32 霰, V8, 2b).
9. See Wu Cheng's note, while Gao Heng's note (*Laozi zhenggu*) says, "使民無饑也."
10. See Zheng Huan's note.
11. See Fan Yingyuan's note.
12. Wang Yun, *Shuowen judou* (骨, V8, 11a–b).
13. See Gao Heng's note in *Laozi zhenggu*.
14. Wang Yinzhi, *Jingzhuan shici* (夫 3, 237–38).

CHAPTER 4

1. Heshang Gong's version used the character 冲, which was its informal form.
2. *Shuowen* (沖, V11 shang 2, 1b–2a).
3. See the "In-Depth Discussion on the Character 沖—An Appendix to the Comments on Chapter 4," page 265.
4. Wang Yinzhi, *Jingzhuan shici* (而 6, 144–45). (乃 could be used to mean 於是 [therefore], 却 [but; on the contrary], or 則 [then], but here we have employed the first definition to fit the context.)
5. Wang Yinzhi, *Jingyi shuwen* ("*Zhou Yi*" shang), the note under the line "乾、師、頤、坎、既濟, 言勿用" (*Huang Qing jingjie*, V1180, 1a–3a, or 13,631).
6. Yang Bojun, *Gu Hanyu xuci* (之 14, 352).
7. Zhu Junsheng, *Shuowen tongxun* (有, V5, 82a–b). Zhu gave as his proof *Guoyu* ("*Luyu*"), "共工氏之伯九有也"; Wei Zhao's note: "有, 域也" (which can be found in Dong Zengling, *Guoyu zhengyi* [V4, 15b]). In addition to this proof, *Xunzi* ("*Jiebi*") says, "成湯 . . . 受九有也"; Wang Tianhai's endnote 24 quotes Gao Heng's explanation: "'有借為域'; Wang then pointed out that "'有、域' 古通用, '或' 即古 '域' 字, 見《說文》" (*Xunzi jiaoshi*, 833, 838). During pre-Qin times, 有, 或, and 域 could be used interchangeably (see *Shuowen* [或]; Duan Yucai's note [V12 xia, 10b]), and their pronunciations were similar.
8. As inspired by Wang Bi's note in *Laozi Dao De Jing zhu jiaoshi*.
9. Lu Deming, *Jingdian shiwen: Laozi yinyi* indicated that 盈 was "或作滿" (1b), which means that 盈 and 滿 were interchangeable in ancient times.
10. *Shuowen* indicates that "滿, 盈溢也" (V11 shang 2, 3b), so 盈 could be used to imply the

idea of "overflow." (This character in chapter 9 [line 1] was interpreted as "overabundance" to fit the context there.)

11. *Shijing* ("*Yanyan*"), "其心塞 [i.e., 寒] 淵"; Kong Yingda's *shu* note (V2–1, 26b).

12. "夫道, 淵乎其居也" ("*Tiandi*," jijie, 100).

13. See *Shuowen* (佁); Duan Yucai's note (V8 shang, 6a). (In silk version A, this character was given as 始, and version B was 怡, but in ancient Chinese, both could be read as 似 [Wang Hui, *Gu wenzi tongjia shili*, under the line "始讀為似," 50].)

14. For instance, *Shangshu* ("*Gaozong youri*") has the line "王司敬民 [i.e., 啟]," as pointed out in Zang Kehe's jiaogu (note 15, 194–95). Qu Wanli indicated that 司 is used in *Shiji* as 嗣 (*Shangshu jinzhu jinyi*, 65). Also, *Xunzi* ("*Aigong*") has the line "若天之嗣," to which Wang Tianhai's endnote in his *Xunzi jiaoshi* quotes Wang Niansun's reading: "嗣讀為司" (1147, 1154). The ancient pronunciations of these two characters were similar.

15. Wang Shumin, *Guji xuzi guangyi* (之 4, 433–44). Also, Pei Xuehai, *Gushu xuzi jishi* (之 16a, 742–43).

16. *Guangya*, "宗, 本也" (Shigu, V3 xia, 7b).

17. *Guoyu* ("*Jinyu*" 3) quotes Guo Yan's remark: "光, 明之曜也" (V9, 2a).

18. Dai Zhen's note in *Fangyan shuzheng* (V13, 8a).

19. This follows both Heshang Gong and Wang Bi's (*Laozi Dao De Jing zhu jiaoshi*) notes.

20. See Wang Bi's note in *Laozi Dao De Jing zhu jiaoshi*. In the Zhou dynasty, 帝 could also be referred to as 上帝 (*Shijing* ["*Huangyi*," V16 zhi 4, 27b–31b]). 上 indicates that which is above us—in other words, the heavens, and therefore 天帝.

IN-DEPTH DISCUSSION ON THE CHARACTER 沖—
AN APPENDIX TO THE COMMENTS ON CHAPTER 4

21. V5 shang, 13b.

22. Unfortunately, this portion of silk version A is damaged and so cannot be used for comparison.

23. Fu Yi of the early Tang dynasty edited a copy of the *Dao De Jing* (referred to here as the Fu Yi version) that was said to have been unearthed from a very early Han tomb. The form of this character as used in the Fu Yi version is 盅. Although this version is certainly a valuable reference, no information exists on its condition, when it was found, or how Fu Yi reconstructed the damaged areas, and so it cannot be relied upon as offering the sort of authoritative proof that silk version B and the Beida version have provided.

24. See Han Zhongmin, *Wenwu*, 1974: 9, as well as Gao Heng and Chi Xizhao, *Wenwu*, 1974: 11.

25. See the Beida version (foreword).

26. Yu Yue additionally offered the line "大盈若沖" (chapter 45 [line 3]) as an opportunity to argue that because 沖 is used in contrast to 盈, 沖 should be considered a borrowed character for 盅 (quoted in Gao Heng, *Laozi zhenggu*, 10–11). Actually, Yu's argument is problematic, for in chapter 45, 沖 is confined by 盈, although in this chapter, it is not.

27. Wang Shumin, *Xian Qin Dao fa*, the line "道為實有" (38).

CHAPTER 5

1. *Shuowen* (仁, V8 shang, 1a).

2. Wang Yinzhi, *Jingzhuan shici* (以 2, 19). See also Wang Shumin, *Guji xuzi guangyi* (以 1, 8).

3. Wu Changying, *Jingci yanshi* (為 5, 19–20). See also Pei Xuehai, *Gushu xuzi jishi* (為 15c, 117–18).

4. Wang Xianqian (jijie, 125). This can also be found in *Huainanzi* ("*Qisuxun*"); He Ning's *Huainanzi jishi*, 792.

5. *Shangshu* ("*Yaodian*"), "平章百姓"; Qu Wanli's endnote: "百姓, 百官也. 義見 《詩》 「天保」毛傳, 及 《國語》 韋注" (*Shangshu jishi* [6, 8]). Also, *Shijing* ("*Tianbao*"), "群黎 百姓"; Mao Heng's note: "百姓, 百官族姓也" (V9 zhi 3, 11a). (Mao's explanation has inspired us to interpret 百姓 as "subjects" in other chapters of the *Dao De Jing*.)

6. *Guoyu* ("*Zhouyu*" zhong), "百姓兆民"; Wei Zhao's note: "百姓, 百官也. 官有世功 [i.e., 職], 受氏姓也" (V2, 3a).

7. Gao You's note can be found in "*Benjingxun*" under the line "鼓橐吹埴." Xi Tong (in *Laozi jijie*) indicates that 埵 and 橐 represented the same thing. According to the description in lines 5–6, the upper part of the bellows moves while the bottom is fixed, much as what is described in *Zhuangzi* ("*Tianyun*"): "天其 [i.e., 自] 運乎? 地其 [i.e., 自] 處乎?" (*Zhuangzi jijie*, 122). This metaphor is quite apt, as the Earth is of course fixed, while the heavens move above it.

8. This follows Xi Tong's note (in *Laozi jijie*).

9. Huang Huaixin's huijiao jishi to *Xiao Erya* ("*Guanggu*"), "愈, 益也" (58).

10. *Yijing* ("*Shuo gua*"), "萬物出乎震"; Yu Fan's note (in Li Dingzuo, *Zhou Yi jijie*, 409).

11. *Guangya*, "聞, 智也" (Shigu, V3 shang, 8a); Wang Niansun's shuzheng note quotes *Shiming*: "智, 知也. 無所不知也," where 無所不知 indicated "broad knowledge."

12. *Lülan* ("*Chaxian*"), "任其數而已"; Gao You's note (V21, 3b–4a). Moreover, Wang Shumin pointed out in his *Xian Qin Dao fa* (200) that "數與術古通" and 術 meant 方法 (measures).

13. *Yijing* ("*Jian gua*"), 得中; Lu Deming, *Jingdian shiwen: Yijing yinyi* quotes Zheng Xuan's note in defining this 中 as 和 (16a). See also *Lunyu* ("*Yongye*"), "中庸之為德也"; Huang Kan's yishu note also defined 中 here as 和 (V3, 61).

CHAPTER 6

1. This entire chapter can also be found in *Liezi* ("*Tianrui*," jijie, 3–4) and labeled as part of *Huangdi shu*. We suspect that this was adopted by the Huang Lao School during the Warring States period (see "Introduction: Understanding the *Dao De Jing*" [endnote 36]).

2. "神, 天神引出萬物者也" (V1 shang, 2a).

3. This follows Chen Qiyou's explanation of *Hanfeizi* ("*Jie Lao*") to chapter 59 (line 8): "所謂有國之母 . . . 樹木有曼根, 有直根 . . . 所謂柢也. 柢也者, 木之所以建生也; 曼根者, 木之所以持生也" (jishi, 353).

4. *Shijing* ("*Mian*"); Mao Heng's note under the line "緜緜瓜瓞" (V16 zhi 2, 20a). (In classical Chinese, a modifier could be formed by repeating a word, as in the example here, or by adding a mood word like 兮 or even 呵, etc., at the end, as in chapter 15 [lines 5–6]: "豫兮 . . . 猶兮.")

5. Yang Bojun, *Gu Hanyu xuci* (之 10, 348).

CHAPTER 7

1. This explanation was inspired by Wang Bi's note in *Laozi Dao De Jing zhu jiaoshi*.

CHAPTER 8

1. All the earliest extant copies of the *Dao De Jing*—both silk versions and the Beida version—read this term as 有爭, proving that 不爭 as it appears in the received versions was a subsequent alteration and therefore incorrect. (This term in silk version A was written as 有靜. The editorial board for the silk versions read 有靜 as 有爭, while the Beida version's editors followed Gao Ming's suggestion [*Boshu Laozi jiaozhu*, 253–56] to read 有爭 as 有靜, something that we do not necessarily agree with, because "有 [宥] 爭" better fits the context of this chapter.)

2. In ancient Chinese, 有 and 又 were always used interchangeably (*Shuowen* [有]; Duan Yucai's note: "古多假有為又字" [V7 shang, 7a].) *Zhengzi tong* ("*Ziji*" xia) has an explanation that says in ancient times "[又] 通作有" (又, 121a–b).

   In *Liji* ("*Wangzhi*") is the line "王三又," to which Zheng Xuan offered a note: "又當作宥. 宥, 寬也" (V13, 18a). Thus, based on our understanding that 又 and 有 were mutually interchangeable, we know that 有 could also be read here as 宥.

3. *Jiyun* (爭, rusheng, 44 諍, 21a).

4. *Liji* ("*Yueji*"), "知樂, 則幾於禮矣"; Zheng Xuan's note (V37, 2b).

5. This understanding was inspired by Fan Yingyuan's jizhu note, in which he explains that line 5 here means water is "中常湛靜," with 湛靜 referring to water's state in the depths.

6. *Shijing* ("*Yanyan*"), "其心塞淵"; Mao Heng's note (V2 zhi 1, 26b). Gu Menglin's *Shijing shuoyue* notes that 塞淵 denotes "德之蘊於內者" (V3, 10b); although 德 refers to people's cultivation, this character used here may be understood to describe the attributes of water.

7. *Zhuangzi* ("*Tiandao*"), "明大道者, 先明天"; Guo Xiang's note (Zhuang Zhou, *Zhuangzi* V5, 15a). The meaning here of the term 自然 differs from the way it was used in chapters 24 and 35, where it referred to "self-realization."

8. *Zhuangzi* ("*Tiandao*"), "[水] 平中準, 大匠取法焉"; Wang Xianqian's jijie (V4, 113). In addition, *Guanzi* ("*Shuidi*") says, "[是以] 水者, 萬物之準也"; Yin Zhizhang's note: "萬物取平焉, 故曰準也" (Yin Zhizhang, *Guanzi jiaozheng*, 236).

9. Wang Yinzhi, *Jingzhuan shici* (夫 3, 237–38).

10. Wang Yinzhi, *Jingzhuan shici* (唯 7, 68). Yang Bojun's *Xuci* defined this 唯 as 因為 (183–84). (Chapter 23 [lines 13–14] of the *Dao De Jing* says that "夫唯不爭, 故莫能與之爭," and chapter 66 [lines 13–14] says, "以其不爭也, 故天下莫能與之爭.")

11. *Lunyu* ("*Wei zheng*"), under the paragraph beginning with "子張學干祿," is the term 寡尤; He Yan's jijie note quotes Bao Xian's denotation of this as "尤, 過也" (V2, 4a).

CHAPTER 9

1. *Jiyun* (揰, "*Liu zhi*," V5, 13b).

2. Ma Rong, *Changdi fu*, "冬雪揣封乎其枝"; Li Shan's note on this line quotes Zheng Xuan's remarks that "揣 and 團 were used interchangeably in ancient readings" (*Zhaoming wenxuan*, V18, 234). Moreover, *Zhengzi tong* ("*Chouji*" shang) indicates that 團 and 摶 could also be interchangeable (106b).

3. The Guodian version used 羣 (silk version B and the Beida version both used 允 here;

silk version A was damaged in this area). 允 could be used interchangeably with 羣 in ancient Chinese (see Beida version [endnote 2]; however, that endnote follows Yang Xiong, *Fangyan shuzheng* [V2] to read this as 捃 [which means 拾 or 取], and that differs from our understanding).

4. *Shuowen* (羣); Duan Yucai's note (V4 shang, 9b).
5. *Zhuangzi* ("*Tianzifang*"), "緣而葆真" (*Jingdian shiwen: Zhuangzi yinyi*, zhong, 30a). See also chapter 62 (endnotes 2 and 3).
6. *Zhengzi tong* (保, which quotes *Zeng yun*, "*Ziji*" zhong, 39a).
7. Pei Xuehai, *Gushu xuzi jishi* (而 3-b, 523).
8. *Shuowen* (咎, V8 shang, 9b).
9. "天之道" also appears in *Zuo zhuan* as "盈而蕩, 天之道也" ("*Zhaogong sinian*") and as "盈必毀, 天之道也" ("*Aigong shiyinian*"). This term can be found in *Guoyu* as "天道皇皇, 日月以為常" and "天道盈而補溢, 盛而不驕" ("*Yueyu*"), as well as "天道無親, 唯德是授" ("*Jinyu*"). This last example is quite similar to the *Dao De Jing*'s "夫天道無親, 恆與善人" (chapter 79 [lines 7–8]) and *Guoyu*'s "天道賞善而罰淫" ("*Zhouyu*" zhong), quoted in Chen Guying and Bai Xi, *Laozi pingzhuan* (107). These all show that Laozi borrowed a term already in use during his time to convey his own philosophical meaning.

CHAPTER 10

1. *Shuowen* (戴); Duan Yucai's note (V3 shang, 10b).
2. See Heshang Gong's note.
3. *Shuowen* (魂 and 魄, V9 shang, 11a).
4. In addition to *Shuowen* (see endnote 3), a further explanation of this concept may be found in *Zuo zhuan* ("*Zhaogong qinian*"), "子產曰 . . . 人生始化曰 [i.e., 為] 魄. 既生魄, 陽曰 [i.e., 為] 魂" (V44, 26a). Du Yu's notes on this statement say, "魄, 形也" and "魂, 陽神氣也," which meant that 魂 indicated both 陽神 and 陽氣. (This discussion is quite extensive, so the rest has been omitted here, but it can be found in *Zuo zhuan* [V44, 26a], and in Ko Yosui's *Zuo zhuan jishi* [V19, 29b–30a].)
5. *Zhuangzi* ("*Zaiyou*"), "[慎守汝神 . . .] 我守其一以處其和"; the commentator Xuan Ying explains: "二氣 [i.e., 陰陽] 之和也" (jijie, 94). Moreover, Zhong Tai, in his *Zhuangzi fawei*, says that "言和, 即以見其一也" (530). The Tang Xuanzong emperor's note on chapter 39 (first paragraph) says: "一者, 道之和" (see entry under Xuanzong Emperor [Tang] on page 377).
6. *Guanzi* ("*Neiye*"), "搏氣如神"; Yin Zhizhang's note (*Guanzi jiaozheng*, 271).
7. *Shuowen* (悁); Duan Yucai's note (V11 shang 2, 9b).
8. *Liji* ("*Quli*" xia), "馳道不除"; Zheng Xuan's note (V4, 24a).
9. See *Shijing* ("*Bozhou*"), "[我心] 匪監"; Lu Deming, *Jingdian shiwen: Shijing yinyi* ("*Mao shi yinyi*" shang, 10b). (In the Beida version, this character was written as 鑑.)
10. *Huainanzi* ("*Xiuwu*"), "執「玄鑑」於心, 照物明白" (Gao You's jishi, 1, 362). Gao You defined 玄 as water. In ancient China, simple mirrors were made of shallow pans filled with water. So, Gao You's note was a metaphorical illustration of how one might "照物明白." For more information on this subject, refer to *Zhuangzi* ("*Tiandao*"), "聖人之心, 靜乎, 天地之鑑, 萬物之鏡也" (jijie, 113), in which 玄鑑 actually comes from this line

in the *Dao De Jing*, and is why this interpretation follows that of chapter 1 (comment on line 11) in this book here, and not Gao You's note.

11. *Yijing*, "悔吝者，言乎其小疵也" ("*Xici*" shang, V7, 2b). Lu Deming, *Jingdian shiwen: Yijing yinyi*, quotes Ma Rong's explanation that 疵 meant 瑕 (26a). For the definition of 瑕, see Gui Fu, *Shuowen jiezi yizheng* (瑕, V2, 27b–28a).

12. Wang Yinzhi, *Jingzhuan shici* (以 2, 6).

13. 知 and 智 were interchangeable in ancient Chinese; see *Shuowen* (智); Duan Yucai's note (V4 shang, 5a). Wang Li, in his *Tongyuan zidian*, points out that "知、智同源" (2 "Zhi bu," "Duan mu" [t], 109). Wang Bi's note on this line in *Laozi Dao De Jing zhu jiaoshi* reads 知 as 智.

14. *Zhuangzi* ("*Sanggengchu*"), "有乎生，有乎死. 有乎出，有乎入——入出而無見其形，是為天門" (jijie, 203). See also endnote 15.

15. *Shuowen*, "卯，冒也. [lunar calendar] 二月，萬物冒地而出——象開門之形. 故二月為天門"; Duan Yucai's note: "卯，為春門，萬物而出" (卯, V14 xia, 8b). The ancient form of 卯 was 夘, where the broken line on top showed that these doors were open. Also, *Shuowen*, "酉 . . . [lunar calendar] 八月 . . . 酉為秋門，萬物已入.「一」[i.e., the stroke at the top] 閉門之象也" (酉, V14 xia, 98); the ancient form of 酉 was 丣, which had a solid line on top to show that the doors were closed.

16. *Lunyu* ("*Xiangdang*"), "丘未達"; Huang Kan's yishu note (jijie, 103).

CHAPTER 11

1. 卅 is simply three 十 *shí* (ten) characters lined up in a row.

2. *Yili* ("*Yinli*"), "路先設"; Zheng Xuan's note: "凡君乘車曰路" (V27, 10b). See also Wang Pingzhen, *Da Dai Liji jiegu* ("*Baofu*"), "古之路車也 . . . 三十輻以象月" (V3, 10a).

3. Zhu Junsheng, *Shuowen tongxun* (挻 [i.e., 埏], V14, 103a).

4. *Shuowen*, "埴，黏土也" (V13 xia, 5b).

5. See Heshang Gong's note. (In ancient times, vessels were usually formed out of clay, while bronze vessels tended to be rare and precious.)

6. *Shijing* ("*Sigan*"), "約之閣閣，椓之橐橐"; Kong Yingda's shu note (V11 zhi 2, 6a).

7. Wu Changying, *Jingci yanshi* (之 18, 99).

8. Yang Bojun, *Gu Hanyu xuci* (則 5, 328–29).

CHAPTER 12

1. See Bo Yuchan's note. Also, J. H. Huang, *The Art of War* (chapter 5, comment 9, 174).

2. Zhu Junsheng, *Shuowen tongxun* (田, V16, 46b; and 畋, V16, 47a).

3. See Heshang Gong's note.

4. See endnote 1.

5. See Wang Bi's note in *Laozi Dao De Jing zhu jiaoshi*. Heshang Gong's note defined 爽 as 亡 *wáng* (lost; declined).

6. *Guanzi*, V19, "*Diyuan*," V19, jiaozheng version, 311.

7. *Liji* ("*Liyun*"), "聖人脩義之柄 . . . 以治人情" (V22, 31b); Zheng Xuan's note: "治者，去瑕穢，養菁華也." (The original copy of Zheng's note is erroneous in some places, and so Ruan Yuan's proofreading of the *Liji* is followed here [V22, 21a].) 治 is interpreted accordingly as "cultivation."

8. See chapter 2 (first comment on line 9).

CHAPTER 13

1. *Guoyu* (*"Chuyu"* shang), "其寵大矣"; Wei Zhao's note (V17, 2b).
2. Wang Yinzhi, *Jingzhuan shici* (若 9, third example, 156). See also Xiao Xu, *Gushu xuci pangshi* (若 3, 256–57); its first example uses lines 1–2 from this chapter of the *Dao De Jing*. (We agree that 若 as used in line 1 meant 至, as proven by the descriptions in lines 3–7. However, 若 in line 2 would have a different definition; see endnote 5.)
3. *Guangyun* (V2, Xiapingsheng, *"Shier geng,"* 驚, 28b).
4. *Liji* (*"Yueji"*), "論倫無患"; Zheng Xuan's note (V37, 4b).
5. Pei Xuehai, *Gushu xuzi jishi* (若 11, 560); its sixth example uses lines 1–12 in this chapter of the *Dao De Jing*. However, 若 as employed in lines 1, 3, and 5–7 cannot be defined as 以, for this does not easily fit the descriptions in lines 4–6. (As to where 若 must be read as 至, see endnote 2.)
6. *Laozi tongyi* (shang, 14a).
7. Yang Bojun, *Gu Hanyu xuci* (者 4c, 338–39).
8. Wang Shumin, *Guji xuzi guangyi* (為 4, 61).
9. Wang Yinzhi, *Jingzhuan shici* (及 2, sixth example, which cites lines 9–12 of this chapter, 113–14).
10. Pei Xuehai, *Gushu xuzi jishi* (以 20, 24–25). See also Xiao Xu, *Gushu xuci pangshi* (以 8, 7–8).
11. Pei Xuehai, *Gushu xuzi jishi* (為 15c, 117–18).
12. Wang Yinzhi, *Jingzhuan shici* (若 20, 158). The example it quotes is lines 13–16 from this chapter of the *Dao De Jing*.

CHAPTER 14

1. Wang Yinzhi, *Jingzhuan shici* (曰 2, 43).
2. Yang Bojun, *Gu Hanyu xuci* (之 10, 348).
3. *Liji* (*"Xueji"*), "其言也 . . . 微而臧"; Kong Yingda's shu note defined 微 as 幽 (V36, 22a–b). *Shuowen* (幽); Duan Yucai's note pointed out that 幽 was "微則隱" (V4 xia, 1b); he also described the two 幺 *yào* components inside 幽 as signifying that the character 微 meant "extremely tiny."
4. *Shuowen* (揗, V12 shang, 9b).
5. *Shuowen* (夷); Duan Yucai's note (V10 xia, 2b). Wu Cheng's note on this line of the *Dao De Jing* indicated that "夷謂平夷—夷則泯沒無迹," which echoed *Guangya*'s definition that "夷, 滅也" (Shigu, V4 xia, 5b). In this description by Laozi, the core meaning of 無迹 (no trace) was 夷. When we probe for something, it must express resistance to our touch for it to be felt. Without such resistance, it will not be felt, and that is what 夷 here refers to. (In both the Beida and received versions, 夷 was paired in line 1 with the verb 視. Logically speaking, though, a more suitable verb for 夷 would have been 揗, not 視.)
6. *Lülan* (*"Dangran"*), "理奚由至?"; Gao You's note (V2, 9b).
7. 計 and 稽 could be interchangeable in ancient times. See J. H. Huang, *The Art of War* (Comments, Book 6, footnote 6, 120), where 稽 was interpreted as "surveying" to fit the context of Sunzi's discussion.
8. Yang Bojun, *Gu Hanyu xuci* (故 8, 54). Wang Yinzhi, *Jingzhuan shici*, indicates: "故, 本然之詞也" (故 2, 124). Gao Heng's zhenggu note on this line of the *Dao De Jing* in *Laozi zhenggu* posits that 故 should be read as 固, which means that "言此三者合而成一也."

9. The Tang Xuanzong emperor's note on chapter 39, first paragraph, says: "一者, 道之和"; see also chapter 10 (endnote 5).

10. See the Beida version, endnote 4 of this chapter. See also Gao Ming, *Boshu Laozi* (285–86).

11. In *Shuowen*, 舀 is said to describe the dim light just before dawn. It was used interchangeably with 昧 (darkness), and this latter character was in fact substituted for 舀 in the received versions. Regarding 舀 and 昧, see Duan Yucai's note (舀, V7 shang, 1a).

12. As humans, we presume in our corporeal world that the top will always be bright and the bottom dark.

13. Gao Ming, *Boshu Laozi* (286).

14. See Heshang Gong's note.

15. Wang Yinzhi, *Jingzhuan shici* (謂 1, 63).

16. "若存若亡, 不可見之也."

17. Pei Xuehai, *Gushu xuzi jishi* (而 15b; 533 and 536).

18. *Zhengzi tong* (執, "*Chouji*" zhong, 22a).

19. This line in the Beida and received versions was altered by later generations to read "執古之道, 以御今之有" (cleave to the Dao of ancient times to have dominion over the beings that are of the now).

20. *Shijing* ("*Siqi*"), "以御家邦"; Zheng Xuan's note (V16 zhi 3, 26a).

CHAPTER 15

1. *Liji* ("*Wang zhi*," V11, 1a). Also *Mengzi* ("*Wanzhang*" shang), the paragraph beginning with "北宮錡問 (周室班, 爵, 祿)" (V10 shang, 13b).

2. *Liji* ("*Xueji*"), "士先志"; Zheng Xuan's note: "學士也" (V36, 20b).

3. *Shijing* ("*Beimen*"), under the line "刺士不得志"; Kong Yingda's shu note, which indicates that 士 meant "有德行之稱" (preface, V2 zhi 3, 36a). (In *Shijing*, 士 was originally written as 仕; Ruan Yuan's proofreading in *Shijing zhushu jiaokanji* points out that 仕 should be corrected to read 士; 10b.)

4. See chapter 14 (second comment on line 2).

5. 眇 and 妙 could be used interchangeably in ancient Chinese. *Yijing* ("*Shuo gua*"): "神也者, 妙萬物而為言者也" (V9, 16b). Ruan Yuan's jiaokanji indicates 妙 in the "王肅 [edition] 作眇" (25a). Moreover, in *Zhengzi tong* ("*Chouji*" xia): "妙, 精微也" (37a).

6. *Lunyu* ("*Xiangdang*"), "丘未達"; Huang Kan's yishu note (103).

7. *Shuowen* (志); Duan Yucai's note (V10 xia, 7a–b). (識 today has the reading of *shí* [to know].)

8. *Yupian* (頌, V4, "*Ye bu*" 36, 82). (頌 was the ancient form of 容 *róng*.)

9. Pei Xuehai, *Gushu xuzi jishi* (其, 11c, 394).

10. *Zhengzi tong* (猶), which tells us that "遲疑不決曰 '猶豫'" ("*Ziji*" xia, 29b). Also, *Chuci* ("*Jiuzhang, Xisong*"), "壹心而不豫兮"; Wang Yi's note: "豫, 猶豫也" (*Chuci zhangju*, 71).

11. *Yijing* ("*Huan gua*"); Zhu Xi's note, *Sishu zhangju jizhu* (benyi, V2, 24a).

12. *Zhengzi tong* (凌, "*Ziji*" xia, 35b).

13. *Shuowen*, "釋,解也" (V2 shang, 1b) and "解, 判也" (釋, V4 xia, 15b).

14. *Shijing* ("*Yeyou sijun*"), "白茅純束"; Zheng Xuan's jian note: "純讀如屯" (V1 zhi 5, 22a). We therefore know that 屯 could also be read as 純.

15. *Guangyun* notes that 沌 meant 混沌 ("*Shangsheng*," 21 混, 25b). Also, *Xunzi* ("*Fei shierzi*"), under the line "天下混然"; Yang Jing's note: "混然, 無分別貌" (V3, 7b–8a).

16. *Zhengzi tong* (濁, "*Siji*" shang, 86b).
17. Yang Bojun, *Gu Hanyu xuci* (者 5, 339). See also Yang Shuda, *Ciquan* (者 4, V5, 20).
18. Wang Yinzhi, *Jingzhuan shici* (將 4, 177).
19. *Yupian* (生, V29, "*Sheng bu*" 463, 402).
20. *Zhengzi tong*, which quotes *Zengyun* (保, "*Ziji*" zhong, 39a). Also, Wang Li, *Tongyuan zidian* ("6 *Youbu–bingmu*," 244). (The Beida version used 抱 here.)
21. In the Guodian version, this character appears as 浧, which can be understood to mean 逞.
22. *Zhengzi tong* (逞, "*Youji*" xia, 46b). (All other versions used 盈 instead of 逞. These two characters were interchangeable in ancient writings. However, 盈 had the basic definition of "fullness," and so using 盈 here instead of 逞 would not connote the correct meaning.)
23. *Zhengzi tong* (成, "*Mouji*" zhong, 3a).

CHAPTER 16

1. *Lülan* ("*Dangran*"), "所染不當, 理奚由至?"; Gao You's note (V2, 9b).
2. See chapter 5 (comment on line 10).
3. *Guangya*, "督、篤, 理也" (Shigu, 2 shang); Qian Dazhao's shuyi: "篤者, 古與督通" (quoted in Xu Fu, *Guangya gulin*, 149–50).
4. *Shuowen* (旁, V1 shang, 1b). 溥 meant 廣: see *Shijing* ("*Gongliu*"), "瞻彼溥原"; Zheng Xuan's jian note (V17 zhi 3, 13a).
5. See chapter 2 (first comment on line 11).
6. The term 天道 follows the Guodian version. This term appears as 天物 in both silk versions and in the Beida version. (In the received versions, 天物 was changed to 夫物, which is an obvious error.) What 天物 denotes is "天所生之物" (see the footnote to this chapter in the Beida version that quotes Kong Yingda's shu note on *Liji* ["*Wangzhi*"]: "田不以禮曰暴天物"). However, in the *Dao De Jing*, the only One that has the ability to 生 (engender) is the Dao (chapter 51), not 天. Therefore, we know that 天道 as it appears in the Guodian version is correct.
7. *Da Dai Liji* ("*Wenwang Guanren*"), "深道以利," wherein Huang Huaixin's jizhu quotes a certain Lu Bian's note (*Da Dai Liji huijiao jizhu*, 1,103).
8. In ancient times, 員 and 云 were interchangeable: *Shijing* ("*Chuqi dongmen*"), "聊樂我員" (V4 zhi 4, 29b). Lu Deming, *Jingdian shiwen: Shijing yinyi* ("*Maoshi yinyi*") points out that "[員] 本亦作 「云」" (V shang, 27b). For 云云, see *Shiming* (雲 [云], "*Shuzheng bu*," V1, 11a).
9. Pei Xuehai, *Gushu xuzi jishi* (曰 4, 135).
10. *Liezi* ("*Liming*"); Zhang Zhan's note: "命者, 必然之期 [i.e., 會], 素定之分 [i.e., 限]" (V6, 1a).
11. *Zhengzi tong* (妄, "*Chouji*" xia, 35a).
12. *Zhengzi tong* (容, "*Yingji*" shang, 27b). (This line from the *Dao De Jing* is cited as its example.)
13. Wang Yinzhi, *Jingzhuan shici* (乃 5, 128). For 則 used to mean "lead to be," see chapter 38 (endnote 14).
14. *Shiming* ("*Shiyanyu*"), "公, 廣也. 可廣施也" (Wang Xianqian, *Shuzhengbu*, V4, 15a).
15. *Shuowen* (王), "王, 天下所歸往也" (V1 shang, 5a).

CHAPTER 17

1. Lu Deming, *Jingdian shiwen: Laozi yinyi* (3a).
2. This follows the Qing Shizu emperor's note.
3. *Hanfeizi* ("*Nan san*") quotes this line from the *Dao De Jing* and then explains it as such (375).
4. *Zhengzi tong* (信, "*Ziji*" zhong, 39b).
5. Wang Yinzhi, *Jingzhuan shici* (安 3, 46–48).
6. See chapter 15 (comment on lines 5–6).
7. See *Guangya*, "然, 成也"; Wang Niansun's note (Shigu, V3 xia, 12b). Also, Jiang Xichang, *Laozi jiaogu* (113). (自然 as used here concerned the way those subjects accomplished their obligations, much like the self-realization of all things as overseen by the Dao, which is described in chapter 25 [line 21].)

CHAPTER 18

1. This appears as 古 in the Guodian version, while both silk versions record it as 故. The reason for this is that in ancient times the reading of 故 could follow that of 古 (*Shuowen*, 故, V3 xia, 9b).
2. Wang Shumin, *Guji xuzi guangyi* (故 4, 157).
3. *Shuowen* (廢); Duan Yucai's note (V8 shang, 1a).
4. Wang Yinzhi, *Jingzhuan shici* (安 3, 46–48).
5. See Wang Bi's note in *Laozi Dao De Jing zhu jiaoshi*.
6. J. H. Huang, *The Art of War* (chapter 2, comment 18c, 155–56).
7. *Zuo zhuan* ("*Xianggong qinian*"), "正直為直" (V30, 32b). (正 was used in the Guodian version. Both silk versions and the Beida version used the character 貞 here instead; nevertheless, 貞 meant 正 [*Guangya*, "貞, 正也" (Shigu, V1 shang, 9b)].)

CHAPTER 19

1. *Shuowen* (辯); Duan Yucai's note (V14 xia, 7a). See also *Zhengzi tong* ("*Youji*" xia), "辨, 別也" (30b).
2. *Guangya*, "偽, 為也" (Shigu, V3 xia, 17a).
3. *Xunzi* ("*Xing'e*"), "人之性惡, 其善者偽也"; Yang Jing's note: "偽, 為也 ... 凡非天性, 而人作為之者, 皆謂之偽" (V17, 1a).
4. *Shuowen Xu jian* (慮); Ding Fubao, ed., *Shuowen jiezi gulin zheng, buhe bian* (V10 xia, 8–1095).
5. Liao Mingchun, *Guodian Chujian Laozi jiaoshi*, the discussion on "民復季子" (12). (Instead of 季子, both silk versions and the Beida version used the term 孝慈. But this is problematic, for when we review chapter 18 [lines 5–6], we see that the term 孝慈 was used there to simply refer to man's moral attempts to save the world from its fall, rather than any accomplishment achieved through cleaving to the Dao.)
6. Pei Xuehai, *Gushu xuzi jishi* (以 25, 31). See also Xiao Xu, *Gushu xuci pangshi*, "惟也, 但也" (以 4, 6). (In modern Chinese, 但 is the equivalent of 只.)
7. Pei Xuehai, *Gushu xuzi jishi* (為 1, 110).
8. Qian Dazhao's explanation that 文 was "為采 [i.e., 彩] 之飾" (see Xu Fu, *Guangya gulin* [文, V2 shang, 136]). So, 飾 is only what is shown on the surface and is therefore interpreted here as "superficial expression."

9. *Shuowen* (命, V2 shang, 5a).

10. *Zhuangzi* ("*Pianmu*"), "且夫屬其性乎仁義者" (jijie, 80); Wang Xianqian's note quotes Lu Deming, *Jingdian shiwen: Zhuangzi yinyi*, "屬, 謂係 [i.e., 繫] 屬."

CHAPTER 20

1. *Shuowen* (絕); Duan Yucai's note, in which Duan points out that "[絕] 引申為 '極' . . . 是 '極至' 之義也" (V13 shang, 2a), with 絕 being used as an adjective in this line of the *Dao De Jing*. Moreover, Li Jiamou's explanation on this line says, "學不至於無所學, 非 絕學也" (*Laozi yi*). After considering both discussions, we read 絕 as "supreme."

2. The Tang Xuanzong emperor's note defined 絕學 as "絕 '有為俗學'." It should be pointed out that while he embellished his understanding of 學 by using this chapter's content, his explanation still more or less complemented what was being discussed.

3. This follows the silk versions; the Beida and all received versions categorized this as chapter 41.

4. *Guangya*, "畏, 敬也" (Shigu, V1 shang, 12b).

5. Wu Changying, *Jingci yanshi* (亦 2, 35). Yang Bojun also interpreted 又 as 也 (*Gu Hanyu xuci* [亦 1, 271]), and so they shared the same meaning.

6. *Shuowen* (宂); Duan Yucai's note (V11 xia, 1b). Gui Fu in *Shuowen jiezi yizheng* points out that "宂, 通作荒" (V36, 5b).

7. Pei Xuehai, *Gushu xuzi jishi* (未 4, 916).

8. *Guangya*, "央, 盡也" (Shigu, V1 xia, 21a).

9. *Xunzi* ("*Ruxiao*"), "熙熙兮, 其樂人之臧也"; Yang Jing's note (V4, 7a).

10. *Jiyun* ("*Shiyang*," "*Pingsheng*" 3, 31a). Wang Bi's version of the *Dao De Jing*, as reproduced in *Laozi Dao De Jing zhu jiaoshi*, substituted the character 享 here.

11. *Gongyang zhuan* ("*Huanggong banian*"), "冬曰烝"; He Xiu's note: "三牲曰太牢" (V5, 1a).

12. *Shuowen* (臺); Duan Yucai's note (V12 shang, 1b). See also chapter 64 (line 8).

13. Xi Tong's jijie note (in *Laozi jijie*) on this line points out that these two characters were "同聲相借." (In fact, the ancient reading of 怕 followed Fan Yingyuan's jizhu note.)

14. Monk Yuanying, *Yiqiejing yinyi* (憺怕, V7, 10a, as well as V25, 11a), although 怕 in modern Chinese has the sole definition of "fear." This could also be expressed as 澹泊 and still have the same definition (*Zhengzi tong* [under 泊 is the term 澹泊, "*Siji*" shang, 22b]); Wang Bi's note in *Laozi Dao De Jing zhu jiaoshi* defined 泊 as 廓, but his source is unknown.

15. *Zhengzi tong* (兆, "*Ziji*" xia, 5b–6a), and the example it cites is this line of the *Dao De Jing*.

16. *Shuowen* (咳, V2 shang). Heshang Gong's version substituted the character 孩 and defined this as 答偶人 (to respond to a person who is facing him); Monk Yuanying points out in his *Yiqiejing yinyi* that "咳, 古文孩" (V9, 1a).

17. *Liji* ("*Neize*," V28, 8b–9a). Gui Fu, *Shuowen yizheng* (咳, V5, 24a), quotes a note in *Shijing* ("*Juegong*," zhengyi): "謂指其有頤下, 令之笑而為之名"; this description varies slightly from that of *Liji*.

18. *Liji* ("*Yuzao*"), "凡祭 . . . 喪容纍纍"; Zheng Xuan's note (V30, 22a).

19. See Xi Tong's jijie note (in *Laozi jijie*).

20. Wang Yinzhi, *Jingzhuan shici* (也 7, 98).

21. *Xunzi* ("*Ruxiao*"), "不學問、無正義、以富利為隆, 是俗人者也" (V4, 9b).

22. *Liji* ("*Zhongyong*"), "亦孔之昭"; Zheng Xuan's note (V53, 28b).

23. *Erya*, "察, 審也" (Shigu xia, V2, 8a). See also Wang Bi's note on 察察, which says: "有所別析也" (*Laozi Wang Bi zhu jiaoshi*, Ishida Yoichiro, ed.).
24. *Jiyun* ("*Qusheng 27*," 悶, V7, 47a).
25. *Zhengzi tong* (惽, "*Mouji*" shang, 32b).
26. See Wang Bi's note in *Laozi Dao De Jing zhujiaoshi*.
27. *Shuowen* (頑), Duan Yucai's note (V9 shang, 2a–b).
28. Wang Yinzhi, *Jingzhuan shici* (以 8, 22).
29. *Zhengzi tong* (鄙, "*Youji*" xia, 89a). (The example cited by *Zhengzi tong* is none other than this line from the *Dao De Jing*.)
30. In the ancient Chinese classics, a passive voice could take the form of an active statement. For example, *Gongyang zhuan* ("*Zhuanggong ershibanian*"), "伐者為客, 伐者為主"; He Xiu notes, "伐人者為客, 見伐者為主" (V9, 20a). This means that 伐者為主 was actually in the passive voice despite the fact that it appears to be in the active voice. See Ma Jianzhong, *Mashi wentong* ("*Shoudongci*," 5.3, 274–75). See also Zhou Fagao, *Zhongguo gudai yufa* ("*Zaoju bian*" shang ["*wu, beidongshi*"; "*wu, bujia jihao*"], 96–98).

CHAPTER 21

1. *Erya* (Shiyan, 孔, V3, 13a). See also *Shijing* ("*Luming*"), "德音孔昭"; Zheng Xuan's jian note (V9 zhi 1, 5a). The Tang Xuanzong emperor's note on this line of the *Dao De Jing* interpreted 孔 as 甚. The Qing Shizu emperor's note follows Heshang Gong's definition in denoting 孔 as 大, but in his additional discussion at the end of this chapter, the emperor employed 甚德 to interpret 孔德. (Wang Bi's note in *Laozi Dao De Jing zhu jiaoshi* defined 孔 as 空, and explained it as "惟以空為德 [i.e., one's cultivation] 乃能動作從道." This explanation helps us to understand that 空 in fact means "to transcend one's own mind.")
2. See the Liang Jianwen emperor's note, as cited in Lu Deming, *Jingdian shiwen: Laozi yinyi* (3b). This was the same as the use of 容狀 in the Tang Xuanzong emperor's note.
3. "何以得德? 由乎道也" (in *Laozi Dao De Jing zhu jiaoshi*).
4. Yang Bojun, *Gu Hanyu xuci* (是 1, 147).
5. Shao Bowen's explanation—"物者, 道之形體也"—as quoted in the *Zhengzi tong* (物, "*Siji*" xia, 5b).
6. Xi Tong's jijie note (in *Laozi jijie*) explains, "怳忽, 猶仿佛, 謂見不審諦也." See also the comment on 惚恍 in chapter 14 (line 16).
7. 怳 can also be written as 恍, while 惚 may appear as 忽, with no difference in meaning or pronunciation. (As for 恍惚, see the Beida version, chapter 14 [footnote 6], as well as our chapter 14 [comment on line 16 with regard to 惚恍].)
8. See Heshang Gong's note.
9. Guo Pu, *Erya zhushu ji buzheng* (Shiyan, 幽, V3, 13a).
10. The silk version of *Yijing* has a chapter titled "要," and in it is a line that reads "男女購請" (see Deng Qiubo, *Boshu Zhou Yi jiaoshi*, chapter 2, 478). However, this same line in the received version of *Yijing zhushu* ("*Xici*" xia, V8, 12b) reads "男女媾精," which shows that 請 and 精 could be interchangeable in ancient Chinese.
11. *Shuowen* (順, V9 shang, 2b).
12. Gui Fu, *Shuowen yizheng* (父, V8, 47a).

13. *Erya* (Shigu shang, 矩, V1, 3b).

14. *Guangya* (Shigu, 然, V3 xia, 12). See chapter 17 (comment on line 9), as well as chapter 24 (endnote 2).

15. Wang Yinzhi, *Jingzhuan shici* (也 7, 98–100).

CHAPTER 22

1. This chapter numbering follows the structure of the silk versions. If we compare the discussion in this chapter with that of the next one (according to our reconstruction), we find that numbering the chapters this way creates a more logical arrangement than that of the received versions, which improperly assign this as chapter 24 (see chapter 23 [first endnote]).

2. Beida version (endnote 1 of this chapter)—this is denoted as chapter 24 in the received versions, but is considered in our reconstruction as chapter 22. (Our readings for both 炊 and 企 are provided here solely with their modern pronunciations to make things easier for our readers.)

3. *Shuowen* (企, V8 shang, 1a).

4. *Shiming* ("*Shizirong*," 視, *Shuzheng bu*, V3, 3a).

5. Yang Bojun, *Gu Hanyu xuci* (者 1, 335–36).

6. See Heshang Gong's note.

7. Heshang Gong's note comments on this phrase: "人自見其形容以為好, 自見其所行以為應道."

8. *Xiao Erya* ("*Guanggu*," 伐); Huang Huaixin, *Xiao Erya huijiao jishi* (36 and 38). See also He Yan, *Lunyu* ("*Gongyechang*"), "願無伐善"; Xing Bing's shu note: "誇功曰伐" (*Lunyu zhushu ji buzheng* [V5, 13a]); 誇 was another way of saying 美.

9. This phrase in the Beida version reads as "矜者" without the modifier 自.

10. *Liji* ("*Biaoji*"), "不矜而莊"; Zheng Xuan's note (V54, 1a).

11. *Guoyu* ("*Luyu*" shang), "魯之班長"; Wei Zhao's note (V4, 5b).

12. Zhu Junsheng, *Shuowen tongxun*, where Zhu indicated that 形 could be read as 行, and the example he cited was from *Liezi* ("*Tangwen*"), "太形王屋二山" (形, V17, 36a and b).

13. *Guangya*, "贅, 肬也" (Shiyan, V5 xia, 26a).

14. Xiao Xu, *Gushu xuci pangshi* (或 7, 70).

15. *Zuo zhuan* ("*Xianggong ershisannian*"), "國有人焉, 誰居其孟椒乎"; Du Yu's note: "居猶與也" (V35, 27a).

CHAPTER 23

1. This chapter numbering follows the structure of the silk versions, while the received versions make this chapter 22. However, if we compare lines 9–12 of this chapter with lines 2–5 in our chapter 22, it is obvious that these two chapters comprise a sequential discussion.

2. See chapter 2 (first comment on line 9).

3. See chapter 14 (second comment on line 19).

4. With regard to 一, see chapter 10 (endnote 5). 執一 in these two lines (7–8) was used to describe how one can be "a shepherd of the world," for someone who governs the world must cleave to the spirit of harmony.

5. Wang Shumin, *Guji xuzi guangyi* (幾 3, 197–98).

CHAPTER 24

1. This chapter numbering follows the structure of the silk versions, while the received versions make this chapter 23. The theme of this chapter concerns how the Dao accommodates the free choice of all things in the world.

2. Su Che's note, "言出於自然." Wang Bi's note in *Laozi Dao De Jing zhu jiaoshi* first quotes chapters 14 (lines 3–4) and 35 (lines 7 and 10), and then explains, "然則, 無味不足聽之言, 乃是自然之至言也."

3. See both Wang Bi (*Laozi Dao De Jing zhu jiaoshi*) and Su Che's notes.

4. *Guangya*, "然, 成也" (Shigu, V3 xia, 12b). Wang Niansun's shuzheng note quotes a line from *Huainanzi* ("*Taizuxun*")—"天地正其道而物自然"—and points out that "是然為成也." Under this line in the Shigu is also a buzheng note that quotes *Chuci* ("*Yuanyou*"): "無滑 [i.e., 亂] 而 [i.e., 汝] 魂兮, 彼將自然," and explains that 自然 meant 自成 (Xu Fu, *Guangya gulin*, 263).

5. See Jiao Hong's note in Li Jiamou, *Laozi yi*.

6. Pei Xuehai, *Gushu xuzi jishi* (而 4, 523–24). The received versions used the character 尚 here instead.

7. See chapter 2 (comment on lines 11–12).

8. Wang Shumin, *Guji xuzi guangyi* (而 12, 308). The example it gives is none other than line 7 of this chapter (24) in the silk versions of the *Dao De Jing*.

9. See chapter 38 (comment on line 1).

10. Wang Shumin, *Guji xuzi guangyi* (亦 11, 101–2).

CHAPTER 25

1. *Zhuangzi* ("*Dasheng*"), "凡有貌、象、聲、色者, 皆物也" (jijie, 157). See also *Zhanguo ce* ("*Qince* 4"), "物至而反, 冬夏是也" (132). Therefore, in those times, a "thing" did not necessarily have to refer to a tangible object.

2. See Heshang Gong's note. 空 was used to describe 無形 and not to indicate that this Entity is a void (see chapter 4 [appendix to the comments "An In-Depth Discussion on the Character 沖"] and chapter 14 [lines 1–16]).

3. Xiao Xu, *Gushu xuci pangshi* (可 1, 162); the example given is precisely line 5 of this chapter. See also Wang Yinzhi, *Jingzhuan shici*: "可, 所也" (可 1, 109–10).

4. *Xiao Erya* ("*Guanggu*"), "強, 益也" (V1, jishi, 58).

5. Wang Shumin, *Guji xuzi guangyi* (曰 10, 79–81), in which the cited example is none other than lines 6–11 here.

6. Wang Li, *Tongyuan zidian* ("*Bangmu*" [P], 581).

7. See Wang Bi's note in *Laozi Dao De Jing zhu jiaoshi*. (Wang's note on these [18–21] lines first says, "法, 謂法則也," and then he uses 不違 as his explanation.)

CHAPTER 26

1. *Liji* ("*Quli*" shang), "故君子式黃髮"; Kong Yingda's note (V3, 19b and 20a).

2. *Zuo zhuan* ("*Xuangong shiernian*"), "丙辰, 楚重至於邲"; Du Yu's note: "重, 輜重也," and Kong Yingda's shu note also points out: "輜重, 載器物糧食, 常在軍後" (V23, 15b). (This line from *Zuo zhuan* concerned war, so Kong's shu note emphasized that these carts were "常在軍後." However, because the example cited here by Laozi concerned

a lord's travels, we know that these carts were the type that followed his entourage to satisfy his needs while on the road.)

3. This character in both silk versions was read as 環, which could be used interchangeably with 寰. See Zhu Junsheng, *Shuowen tongxun*, under which is a quote from *Mengzi* ("*Gong-sunchou*" xia): "環而攻之"; Zhu points out that 環 could be read as 寰 ("環," V14, 117a). The definition of 寰 was "王者畿內也" (*Jiyun*, "*Qusheng*," 32 霰, V8, 3a). Because this was used here as an adjective, it is interpreted as "regional." (With regard to the term 環 [寰] 官, the Beida version reads this as 榮館 and the received versions used 縈觀, but neither of these phrases is a more precise fit to the discussion of this chapter.)

4. *Liji* ("*Yueji*"), "樂之官也"; Zheng Xuan's note (V37, 4b).

5. See Xi Tong's jijie note in *Laozi jijie*. (Although he followed the received versions here, the definition of this term fits the reading of the silk versions.)

6. *Shuowen* (昭); Duan Yucai's note (V7 shang, 2a).

7. Yang Bojun, *Gu Hanyu xuci* (若 13, 137–38).

8. Xiao Xu, *Gushu xuci pangshi* (而 1-b, 244).

9. Pei Xuehai, *Gushu xuzi jishi* (以 20, 24–25).

CHAPTER 27

1. *Yupian*, "轍, 車行迹也" (V18, "*Che bu*" 282, 267).

2. This understanding was derived from a passage in *Lunyu*: "顏淵死, [his father] 顏路請子 [Confucius] 之車以為槨 . . . 子曰: '吾從大夫 [i.e., a position similar to a Roman procurator] 之後, 不可徒行也'" ("*Xianjin*," V11, 12a; also Cheng Shude's jishi, 753).

3. *Zhengzi tong* (瑕, "*Wuji*" shang, 20a). See also chapter 10 (comment on line 6), where 疵 is defined as "blemish" to fit the context.

4. *Guangya*, "謫, 責也" (Shigu, V1 xia, 10a).

5. *Shuowen* (籌); Duan Yucai's note (V5 shang, 5b).

6. *Shuowen* (策); Duan Yucai's note (V5 shang, 4b).

7. Gui Fu, *Shuowen yizheng* (筭, V13, 45b).

8. Wang Yun, *Shuowen judou* (關 and 籥; however, the entry for 籥 in *Shuowen judou* used the ancient form with the 門 [gate] radical encompassing 龠, rather than with the 竹 [bamboo] radical on top).

9. *Shuowen* (繩, V13 shang, 8b). (All the received versions read this as 繩.)

10. *Shuowen* (約, V13 shang, 2b).

11. *Guangya*, "救, 助也" (Shigu, V2 shang, 11a–b).

12. *Jiyun* ("*Rusheng*," "8 勿," 物, V9, 21a). (Most scholars read 物 to literally mean "things," which does not fit the subject of this chapter.)

13. *Mengzi* ("*Jinxin*" shang), "有達財者"; Zhu Xi's note: "財與材同 . . . 達財 [材], 如孔子之於由、賜" (*Sishu zhangju jizhu* zhangzhu, 361). (We now use 才 to express this.)

14. See Zheng Huan's benyi note.

15. *Xunzi* ("*Xing'e*"), "不離其資而利之也"; Yang Jing's note (V17, 2a–b). (材 here differs in meaning from the one in the second comment on line 7.)

16. *Yijing* ("*Lü gua liusan*"), "眇能視"; its xiangci explains that 眇 is "不足以有明也" (V2, 14a).

17. *Xunzi* ("*Lilun*"), "以隆殺為要"; Yang Jing's note (V13, 5b).

CHAPTER 28

1. Wang Yinzhi, *Jingzhuan shici* (其 12, 119).
2. See Lü Jifu's note in *Laozi yi.*
3. Wang Yun, *Shuowen judou*, "谿, 山瀆 [i.e., 瀆] 無所通者" (V22, 7a).
4. Regarding the quality of an infant, see chapter 55.
5. For 白, see *Zhengzi tong* ("Wuji" zhong, 36b). For 辱, see *Guangya* (V3 shang, 12a–b).
6. *Shuowen* (谷), "谷, 泉水出, 通川, 為谷" (V11 xia, 2b).
7. *Zuo zhuan* ("Xianggong ershiwunian"), "言以足志, 文以足言"; Du Yu's note (V36, 41).
8. *Zhuangzi* ("Renjianshi"), "虛室生白." Lu Deming, *Jingdian shiwen: Zhuangzi yinyi* notes, "崔云, 白者, 日光所照也" (shang, 14a).
9. See Wang Bi's note in *Laozi Dao De Jing zhu jiaoshi.*
10. Pei Xuehai, *Gushu xuzi jishi* (則 7, examples 1 and 6, 593–94). See also Xiao Xu, *Gushu xuci pangshi* (則 2, 266).
11. *Liji* ("Liyun"), "禮義以為器"; Wang Fuzhi's note: "器, 成用者也" (*Liji zhangju* [V9, 565]). Even though 禮 and 義 were criticized by Laozi (chapter 38), they still have undeniable relevance to the Dao.
12. *Erya* (Shigu shang, 則); Guo Pu's note and Xing Bing's shu note in Zhu Zuyan, *Erya gulin* (151).
13. *Liji* ("Yueji"), "天地官矣"; Zheng Xuan's note: "官, 事也. 各得其事" (V37, 5b), so 官 meant 得事, and we therefore interpreted this as "duties."
14. Pei Xuehai, *Gushu xuzi jishi* (夫 12, 886–87).

CHAPTER 29

1. Pei Xuehai, *Gushu xuzi jishi* (將 14, 620–21).
2. Jiang Xichang's jiaogu note quotes Heshang Gong's note on chapter 48 (line 6): "取, 治也." Also, Heshang Gong's note on 取天下 in this line of chapter 29 says, "為天下主也." After referring to both of Heshang Gong's notes, we may conclude that the appropriate interpretation of 取 here is "to rule."
3. Wang Yinzhi, *Jingzhuan shici* (其 4, 115).
4. See chapter 2 (comment on lines 11–12).
5. Lü Shuxiang, *Zhongguo wenfa yaolue* (15.61–62, 矣、已, 275–76).
6. Wang Yinzhi, *Jingyi shuwen* (V1205, 14a–b), the debate on "從, 神、崇, 重也" in the discussion about *Erya* (Ruan Yuan, *Huang Qing jingjie* [19], 14,128). (With regard to the concept of ancestor worship, the Chinese have traditionally believed that their ancestors looked after their fates.)
7. *Yijing*, "形乃謂之器" ("Xici" shang, V7, 7b–8a).
8. 器 was usually understood to mean a "utilitarian object." However, 器 in this context describes something that transcends the world of man, and so we follow *Yijing*'s definition (see endnote 7 above) in interpreting it. (器 in ancient times could sometimes act as a synonym for 物, and so Heshang Gong points out in his note on line 3 here, "器, 物也." However, Laozi in chapters 21 and 25 used 物 to describe 道 [the Dao], and so Heshang Gong's note is not followed in this instance, for 道 cannot be considered 器.)
9. Pei Xuehai, *Gushu xuzi jishi* (之 8, 731).

10. See Heshang Gong's note.

11. Lu Deming, *Jingdian shiwen: Laozi yinyi*, "挫, 搦也" (4a). Also, in *Shuowen* (搦), Duan Yucai's note indicates that "古義, 搦同橈" (V12 shang, 12a). (橈 was defined as 曲: *Shuowen* [橈]; Duan's note [V6 shang, 7a].)

12. Fan Yingyuan's note quotes Fu Yi's explanations that he found in a source called *Zilin*: "(培) 益也" and "(墮) 落也."

13. *Shuowen* (奢); Duan Yucai's note (V10 xia, 4b).

CHAPTER 30

1. *Guangya*, "佐, 助也" (Shigu, V2 shang, 11a–b).

2. *Erya* (強); Guo Pu's note (Shiyan, V3, 11b).

3. This type of statement can be found in the ancient classics; for example, *Yili* ("*Xiang yinjiu li*"), "主人速 [召] 賓, 賓拜辱, 主人答拜, 還" (V8, 5b).

4. *Shijing* ("*Ziyi*"), "緇衣之好兮"; Mao Heng's note (V4 zhi 2, 21b).

5. Yang Bojun, *Gu Hanyu xuci* (以 11, 262–63). (Yang indicates that this usage is obsolete.)

6. Wu Changying, *Jingci yanshi* (而 5, 66).

7. Wang Yinzhi, *Jingzhuan shici* (而 7, 146).

8. *Zhanguo ce* ("*Qice* 1"), "早 [i.e., 蚤] 救孰與晚救之便?"; Gao You's note (169–70).

9. *Shijing* ("*Fengyu*"), "雞鳴不已"; Zheng Xuan's jian note: "已, 止也" (V4 zhi 4, 28b). See also *Mengzi* ("*Jinxin*" shang), "孟子曰, '於不可已而已者, 無所不已'"; Zhao Qi's note: "已, 棄也" (V13 xia, 19a).

CHAPTER 31

1. *Zhengzi tong* (祥, "*Wuji*" xia, 33a–b).

2. Pei Xuehai, *Gushu xuzi jishi* (或 8, 168).

3. Yang Bojun, *Gu Hanyu xuci* (則 5, examples 1 and 2, 328).

4. Wang Li, *Tongyuan zidian*, quotes *Shuowen*: "古, 故也" (3, "Yu bu," Jian mu "k," 127).

5. Pei Xuehai, *Gushu xuzi jishi* (故 13, 321). See also Wang Shumin, *Guji xuzi guangyi* (故 7, 158), as well as Xiao Xu, *Gushu xuci pangshi* (故 5, 118).

6. 銛龍 in all received versions was replaced with the term 恬淡 (with the second character sometimes written as 澹 or 憺), which is problematic for two reasons: 1) this term is not found in any of the earliest versions, including the Guodian and Beida versions, meaning that this was very possibly a later change; 2) *Zhuangzi* ("*Tiandao*") has the line, "虛靜恬淡, 寂漠無為者, 天地之平而道德之至, 故帝王聖人休焉" (jijie, 113). Therefore, 恬淡 could be understood as the cultivation of rulers. But because this chapter is discussing the correct attitude one should assume toward warfare, using 恬淡 here would have been incorrect. We have determined that 龍 is correct here, for even though this character appears in the Guodian and both silk versions in variant forms, they all included a 龍 as their phonetic component. In the Beida version, though, this was written as 儱, which could be read as 龍 per the editorial board's endnote 3; however, they suggest that this might have meant 鏴 (which was defined as 銛儱, or a sharp weapon), and that in our opinion is problematic, for the discussion in this chapter concerns armed forces and their conduction of warfare.

7. *Fangyan shuzheng*, "銛, 取也" (Shigu, V1 shang, 18a–19b). Dai Zhen's shuzheng note points out, "銛, 音忝," and that 取 meant "挑取" (V3, 9b).

8. *Shijing* ("*Zhousong*," "*Zhuo*"), "我龍受之"; Mao Heng's note: "龍, 和也"; Zheng Xuan's jian note pointed out that this ought to have meant 和同 (V19 zhi 4, 21b), and so we interpreted this as "peace."

9. This was a common practice in ancient Chinese, for all the received versions used 尚 here instead of 上. (This term can also be seen in lines 13–14.)

10. *Mengzi* ("*Jinxin*" shang), "孟子曰, 尚志"; Zhao Qi's note (V13 xia, 17b).

11. *Liji* ("*Tanggong*" shang), "孔子與門人立, 拱而尚右," which was then explained as: "我則有姊之喪, 故也" (V7, 9b). See also Wang Meng'ou, *Liji jinzhu jinyi* (84).

12. *Shuowen* (竦, V10 xia, 6a). (Duan Yucai's note indicates that in later times, the preferred form of this character became 茇.)

13. See chapter 2 (second comment on line 9).

CHAPTER 32

1. *Shuowen* (樸); Duan Yucai's note (V6 shang, 7b). See also *Zhengzi tong* (樸, "*Chenji*" zhong, 105b).

2. Pei Xuehai, *Gushu xuzi jishi* (敢 2, 331–32). See also Xiao Xu, *Gushu xuci pangshi* (敢 1, 131), which cites this line of the *Dao De Jing* as its example. (The received versions used 能 instead of 敢.)

3. *Erya*, "賓, 服也" (Shigu shang, V1, 3a).

4. *Shuowen* (輸); Duan Yucai's note (V14 shang, 14a).

5. *Baihutong* ("*Furui zhi ying*"), "甘露者, 美露也. 降, 則物無不盛也"; *Huang Qing jingjie xubian* (Book 9, "*Baihutong shuzheng*," V6, 23a, or 6,224).

6. *Shuowen* (制, V4 xia, 13a).

7. See chapter 1 (line 5) and chapter 52 (line 1).

8. This follows Wang Bi's note in *Laozi Dao De Jing zhu jiaoshi*. He used chapter 28 (lines 19–20) to explain the concept of 始制.

9. See chapter 28 (comment on line 19); this understanding was inspired by Wang Bi's note (*Laozi jiaoshi Dao De Jing zhu jiaoshi*).

10. Wang Yinzhi, *Jingzhuan shici* (亦 2, 82–83).

11. Wang Yinzhi, *Jingzhuan shici* (夫 3, 237–38).

12. Pei Xuehai, *Gushu xuzi jishi* (亦 5, 173–74).

13. Wang Shumin, *Guji xuzi guangyi* (將 4, 360).

14. *Shuowen* (止, 2 shang, 10b).

15. See the note by Monk Yuanying in his *Yiqiejing yinyi* that quotes *Guangya*, "[殆壞]: 殆, 敗也" (V15, 13a).

16. Qu Wanli, *Shangshu shiyi* ("*Junshi*"), "海隅出日, 罔不率俾" (163, 164); Qu's footnote 48 cites Wang Yinzhi's definition of 俾 as 從 in *Jingyi shuwen*. This character in the Guodian version and silk version B was read as 卑, which in ancient times was interchangeable with 俾. For example, *Shangshu* ("*Wuyi*") says, "文王卑服" (V16, 4a), while Lu Deming, *Jingdian shiwen: Shangshu yinyi* notes that 卑 in "馬本, 作俾" (V xia, 9a).

17. *Shuowen* (在); Duan Yucai's note (V13 xia, 7b).

18. Pei Xuehai, *Gushu xuzi jishi* (與 16, 11).

CHAPTER 33

1. See chapter 10 (endnote 13).
2. Pei Xuehai, *Gushu xuzi jishi* (有 17, 157–58).

CHAPTER 34

1. *Zhuangzi* ("*Dechongfu*"), "氾而若辭"; Guo Xiang's note (V2, jijie, 51); 氾 was a variant form of 汎. Also, in *Zhuangzi* ("*Lieyukou*"), there is the line, "汎若不繫之舟" (V8, jijie, 279), with 繫 used as 係. The Tang Xuanzong emperor's note on this line of the *Dao De Jing* points out that 汎兮 meant 無繫.
2. Su Che's note says, "汎兮, 無可無不可, 故左右上下週旋, 無不至也." Lü Jifu's note (in *Laozi yi*) also has this explanation: "可以左而不可以右, 可以右而不可以左 . . . 大道則無乎不在, 故汎兮其可左右也." Both notes therefore imply that the nature of the Dao must be neutral.
3. *Guangya*, "歸, 就也" (Shigu, V3 shang, 2b).
4. Liu Qi, *Zhuzi bianlue* (焉 5, 73). See also Pei Xuehai, *Gushu xuzi jishi* (焉 4, 96–101).
5. Wang Yinzhi, *Jingzhuan shici* (於 4, 34).
6. See also chapter 25 (lines 6–8).

CHAPTER 35

1. See chapter 14 (first comment on line 19).
2. Chapter 21 (lines 5–6) describes the Dao as, "So nebulous, so vague, within which lies the Form," while chapter 14 (line 15) indicates that the Dao is "the form of nothingness." Moreover, in chapter 25 (line 8), Laozi refers to the Dao as "Greatness."
3. Liu Xi, *Shiming* ("*Shiyanyu*," 往, *Shuzhengbu*, V4, 12b).
4. *Erya*, "安, 定也" (Shigu xia, V2, 9b).
5. *Shuowen* (平); Duan Yucai's note (V5 shang, 9a).
6. See *Zhengzi tong* (泰, "*Si*" shang, 27a). (This 安 had a meaning that differs from the 安 defined as 定 in endnote 4.)
7. Gu Yeyu, *Yupian lingjuan* (餌, 98, which cites *Cangjie pian*).
8. See Pei Xuehai, *Gushu xuzi jishi*, under the entry "故固顧姑" (故 5–b, 7; 309, 312, 314–15). Moreover, Wu Changying in *Jingci yanshi* defined 故 as 顧 (故 4, 55).
9. Pei Xuehai, *Gushu xuzi jishi*, "足, 能也" (足 3, 644). Heshang Gong's note defined 不足 as 不得, which had the same meaning as 不能.
10. Jiao Hong's note in *Laozi yi* says, "既, 盡也." Wang Bi's note in *Laozi Dao De Jing zhu jiaoshi* defined 不可既 as "不可窮極," which was the same idea.

CHAPTER 36

1. This reading follows Fan Yingyuan's jizhu note.
2. Pei Xuehai, *Gushu xuzi jishi* (必 7, 848). See also Wang Shumin, *Guji xuzi guangyi* (必 4, 518–19).
3. Yang Shuda, *Ciquan* (固 3, V3, 11–12). (The examples Yang cites are none other than lines 1–2 and 7–8 here, with 廢 used in place of 奪 in line 7.)
4. See the Beida version (endnote 2 of chapter 36).
5. See the Qing Shizu emperor's note.

6. *Erya*, "明, 成也" (Shigu xia, V2, 7a).

7. Our reading of this phrase follows all received versions, but in both silk versions this reads as "邦 [or 國] 利器" without the character 之, which is not as clear as the wording of the received versions.

8. *Mengzi* ("*Lianghuiwang*" shang), "有以利吾國乎"; Sun Shi's shu note (V1 shang, 1a–b).

9. *Zuo zhuan* ("*Chenggong shiliunian*"), "德、刑 . . . 戰之器也"; Du Yu's note (V28, 15a). He Yan's note in *Lunyu* under the line "君子不器" quotes Bao Xian's explanation: "器者, 各周其用" ("*Weizheng*," jijie, V2, 4a), which may aid in the comprehension of Du's note.

10. See Yang Bojun's note under the same line from *Zuo zhuan*, as cited in endnote 9 (*Chunqiu Zuo zhuan zhu* [880]).

11. Wang Li, *Tongyuan zidian*, "'視' 是看, '示' 是使看, 二字同源" (424).

CHAPTER 37

1. Wang Bi's note in *Laozi Dao De Jing zhu jiaoshi*: "順自然也." This note was obviously inspired by chapter 25 (line 21). However, Wang's guidance allows us to learn how to correctly perform with non-effort without being hampered by our own conjectures.

2. Wang Yinzhi, *Jingzhuan shici* (而 7, 146–47).

3. *Xunzi* ("*Bugou*"), "神則能化矣"; Yang Jing's note (V2, 4a).

4. Wang Shumin, *Guji xuzi guangyi* (而 11, 306–8). See also Pei Xuehai, *Gushu xuzi jishi* (而 12a, 529).

5. Wu Changying, *Jingci yanshi* (將 7, 85–86).

6. In his *Guodian Chujian Laozi jiaoshi*, Liao Mingchun cited a certain Guo Yi's opinion here, which happens to be the same as ours (chapter 7, 144).

7. *Guangya*, "鎮, 安也" (Shigu, V1 shang, 11b).

8. Wang Yinzhi, *Jingzhuan shici* (夫 3, 237–38).

9. Pei Xuehai, *Gushu xuzi jishi* (亦 5, 173–74).

10. Pei Xuehai, *Gushu xuzi jishi* (以 20, 114–15). See also Xiao Xu, *Gushu xuci pangshi* (以 8, 7–8).

CHAPTER 38

1. Wang Bi's note in *Laozi Dao De Jing zhu jiaoshi*, "何以得德, 由乎道也," which Lu Deming, *Jingdian shiwen: Laozi yinyi* explains: "德、道之用 [i.e., performance] 也" (1a). Moreover, *Guanzi* ("*Xinshu*") has this: "以 [i.e., 因] 無為之謂道, 舍之之謂德, 故道之與 德無間" (jiaoshi, 328; jiaozhu, 770).

2. *Liji* ("*Yueji*"), "德者, 得也" (V37, 26).

3. Based on the definition cited in the previous endnote, the meaning of 德 could be extended to the following categories:
   - *Shuowen* (德) notes that the original form of this character was 悳, which was further defined as "內得於己, 外得於人也" (V10 xia, 7b). This statement concerns one's own cultivation, as well as how to benefit others. (We follow Duan Yucai's reading and note on these lines.)
   - *Zhuangzi* ("*Tiandi*"), "物得以生謂之德" (jijie, 103). This 德 referred to the fostering of things, a concept that echoes chapter 51 (lines 1 and 7–10), as well as chapter 1 (lines 5–6).

- *Liji* ("*Yueji*"), "禮樂皆得, 謂之有德" (V37, 2b). Zheng Xuan's note suggests that according to Confucian theory, governance must entail the comprehension of music and ritual.
- *Guanzi* ("*Xinshu*" shang), "德者, 道之舍. 物得以生 . . . 故德者, 得也. 得也者, 其謂所得以然也 . . . 故道之與德無間" (jiaozhu, 770). This concerns how things obtain their existence, and through this we are able to see that 德 is the One realized by 道 in the corporeal world.
- *Hanfeizi* ("*Jie Lao*"), "德者, 得身也" (jishi, 326). This discusses how we may achieve our own cultivation.
- Liu Xi, *Shiming* ("*Shiyanyu*"), "德, 得也. 得事宜也" (*Shuzheng bu*, V4, 1a). This concerns "道術 [the means of the principle] 施行得理 [axiom]" as explained by *Jiazi* (i.e., Jia Yi, in his *Xinshu*), which is cited by Wang Qiyuan and included in Wang Xianqian's note.
- Wang Bi's note (*Laozi Dao De Jing zhu jiaoshi*): "德者, 得也. 常德而無喪, 利而無害, 故以德為名焉" (see the footnote on line 1).

4. 德 is often translated as "virtue," but that definition is solely concerned with moral principles. The actual meaning of 德 (as shown in endnotes 2 and 3) encompasses a much greater range than simply virtue. Because no English equivalent exists for 德, we are only able to render this august concept as "the De."

5. This reading was inspired by lines 5 and 10. (With regard to 無為 in line 5, see chapter 37 [line 1], which says, "道恆無為也.") The Dao is the ultimate Being that performs as the sole Source of all existence, which means that even the Earth and the heavens have to conform to It, and so with man, it could not be otherwise (chapter 25 [lines 18–20]). Moreover, chapter 21 (lines 1–2) says, "孔德之容, 唯道是從." See also Wang Bi's note (*Laozi Dao De Jing zhu jiaoshi*) on chapter 38: "何以得德? 由乎道也."

6. The structure of this term (i.e., 不 + noun) was particularly common in ancient classical Chinese. A clear explanation of this may be found in Huang Lupin's *Hanyu wenyan yufa gangyao*, where he points out that a noun in this structure "usually may also be converted into a verb" (8.14, 129).

7. See chapter 3 (endnote 3).

8. 所為 was used to define 以為 in Liang Qixiong, *Hanzi qianjie* ("*Jie Lao*," 140). Moreover, Chen Qitian indicates in *Hanfeizi jiaoshi* ("*Jie Lao*") that "以, 可訓所" (724). Both annotations can be found under the line "仁者 . . . 上仁為之而無以為也." This denotation may also be found in Pei Xuehai, *Gushu xuzi jishi*, as "[以] 猶所也" (以 24, 30).

9. Yang Shuda, *Ciquan* (而 14, V10, 11).

10. 之 in 莫之應也 was used to mean 能; see Wang Shumin, *Guji xuzi guangyi* (之 20, 441). Moreover, 應 would have been defined here as 當 (to be equaled), thus 當之 would have indicated "a proper response or "reciprocations" in this context—see *Shuowen* (應); Duan Yucai's note (V10 xia, 7b). 也 was used to mean 之 (it); see Pei Xuehai, *Gushu xuzi jishi* (也 9b, 237–40). We used the passive voice here to interpret this phrase.

11. *Shuowen* (攘, V12 shang, 6b).

12. Beida version (chapter 38, endnote 3).

13. Lu Deming, *Jingdian shiwen: Laozi yinyi* (V25, 5a). (In modern Chinese, 扔 is pronounced as *rēng* and means "to throw.")

14. "義其 [i.e., 則] 競 [i.e., 爭] 焉." (其 may be read as 則 [Pei Xuehai, *Gushu xuzi jishi*, 其 18, 402–5]. 則 is usually rendered as "then," but in this context, the passage immediately preceding this character forms the cause of what follows it [Yang Bojun, *Gu Hanyu xuci*, 則 4, 327–28], and so we have interpreted this as "to lead to.")

15. *Shuowen* (識); Duan Yucai's note (V3 shang, 4a).

16. Yang Bojun, *Gu Hanyu xuci* (者 4-a, 337–38).

17. See Heshang Gong's note: "謂得 [i.e., 知] 道之君也." In addition, *Wenzi* ("*Yuandao*") points out, "大丈夫 . . . 執道之要," while Xu Lingfu's note on this says that 大丈夫 meant "能體道者" (*Wenzi* [*Tongxuan zhenjing*], jiaoshi, 9, as well as 10, endnote 2), which did not confine this term to specifically describing a leader.

18. *Zhengzi tong* ("*Ziji*" xia) points out that 厚 was the opposite of 薄 (shallowness) (101a).

19. "去彼取此, 謂不為義、禮之類, 而為道也."

CHAPTER 39

1. The fundamental definition of 德 was 得 (see chapter 38 [comment on line 1], and endnotes 2 and 3). The character 一 in this term was understood to confine 德 (see endnote 2). Therefore, when 得 is confined by 一, we know that this 得 must be the means by which 德 is realized.

2. The Tang Xuanzong emperor's note reads: "一者, 道之和, 謂沖氣 [see chapter 42] 也, 以其妙用, 在 [i.e., 存] 物為一, 故謂之一爾." (In chapter 38, Wang Bi (*Laozi Dao De Jing zhu jiaoshi*) offered a very important note on this: "何以得德? 由乎道也." So, 德 is what is achieved through 道. *Zhuangzi* ["*Dechongfu*"] notes that "德者, 成和之修也" [jijie, 53], and that is why the "*Shanxin*" chapter in *Zhuangzi* further declares, "夫德, 和也" [jijie, 135].) The De is achieved in a state of absolute contentment, as indicated in chapter 38 (margin note on lines 1–4). When there is harmony, there is contentment. (See a related discussion on this in chapter 10 [endnote 5].)

3. *Guangya*, "靈, 善也" (Shigu, V1 shang, 6b).

4. *Guangya*, "正, 君也" (Shigu, V1 shang, 1b). Also, *Lülan* ("*Junshou*") has the line, "可以為天下正" with Gao You's note: "正, 主" (V17, 4a); 主 acted as a synonym here for 君.

5. Wu Changying, *Jingci yanshi* (其 6, 49–50). See also Wang Shumin, *Guji xuzi guangyi* (其 9a, 207).

6. *Zhuangzi* ("*Zhile*"), "天無為以清, 地無為以寧" (jijie, 150). These two lines are obviously variations of what Laozi wrote in lines 2–3. If we compare *Zhuangzi* and the *Dao De Jing* here, it becomes clear that to "have obtained the One" would have been achieved through the exertion of non-effort.

7. Wang Shumin, *Guji xuzi guangyi* (謂 6, 75). See also Xiao Xu, *Gushu xuci pangshi* (謂 5, 49).

8. *Shuowen* (毋); Duan Yucai's note (V12 xia, 8a).

9. Zhu Junsheng, *Shuowen tongxun* (已, V5, 25b). (In the ancient Chinese classics, 已 could be read as if it were 以.)

10. Pei Xuehai, *Gushu xuzi jishi* (以 18, 23–24).

11. Wu Changying, *Jingci yanshi* (將 8, 85–86). See also Pei Xuehai, *Gushu xuzi jishi* (將 3, 610–12).

12. *Han shu* ("*Tianwen zhi*"), "天開懸物," which annotator Meng Kang explains as "謂天裂

而見物 [i.e., 色; see the discussion below] 象" (Ban Gu, *Han shu*, V26, 1,298). (Because this line is followed by "地動坼絕," we know that 天裂 referred to calamities—see below.) See also *Zuo zhuan* ("*Xigong wunian*"), "凡分至啟閉, 必書雲物," where Du Yu's note explains that 雲物 meant "氣色災變也." Moreover, Kong Yingda's shu note on Du's explanation cites Zheng Xuan's annotation, which indicates that 氣 here represented 雲, and 色 signified 物 (V12, 9a). Du's note thus means that cloud color may portend calamities.

13. *Zhengzi tong* (發, "*Wuji*" zhong, 30a–b). See also *Shuowen* (發); Duan Yucai's note indicates that this meant 作起 (V12 xia, 16a), which conveyed the same meaning as 興.

14. This is just as described in *Han shu* ("*Tianwen zhi*"): "地動坼 [i.e., 裂] 絕, 山崩及阤 [i.e., 坡], 川塞谿垖 [i.e., (土) 堆集]" (1,298). Also, *Guoyu* ("*Zhouyu*"), "幽王二年, 西周三川皆震. 伯陽父曰, . . . 地震 . . . 川源必塞, 源塞國必亡" (V1, 10a–b).

15. *Shuowen* (歇); Duan Yucai's note defined this as 止歇 (V8 xia, 6a), which relayed a similar idea.

16. *Shuowen* (潠 [the original form of 渴]); Duan Yucai's note (V8 xia, 6b).

17. See Xi Tong's note (in *Laozi jijie*). Heshang Gong's note defined this character as 顛蹷, which meant the same thing.

18. Yang Shuda, *Ciquan* (以 9, V7, 11–12).

19. Wang Shumin, *Guji xuzi guangyi* (必 13, 522); the examples cited are none other than lines 13–14 in this chapter. See also Xiao Xu, *Gushu xuci pangshi* (必 11, 398).

20. Wang Shumin, *Guji xuzi guangyi* (而 24, 314). See also Xiao Xu, *Gushu xuci pangshi* (而 17, 250).

21. Pei Xuehai, *Gushu xuzi jishi* (夫 2, 881).

22. 孤, as indicated by *Shuowen* (孤), was defined as 無父; Duan Yucai's explanation says that "[孟子] 曰, '幼而無父曰孤.' 引申之, 凡單獨皆曰孤" (V14 xia, 7b). Moreover, *Guangya* notes that "孤, 獨也" (Shigu, V3 shang, 8b).

23. *Xiao Erya*, the line, "凡無妻、無夫, 通謂之寡" ("*Guangyi*," huijiao, 330–31). (This was just a delineation. Individually, though, a widow was called a 寡, while a widower was referred to as a 鰥.)

24. *Huainanzi* ("*Renjian xun*") "今日之戰, 不穀親傷"; Gao You's note, "不穀, 不祿也. 人君謙以自稱也" (V18, 3b; jishi, 1,249). Moreover, in ancient times, 祿 and 福 were often interchangeable (see Zhu Zuyan, *Erya gulin*, Shigu shang, "祿, 福也," as well as the shu notes by Xing Bing and the zhengyi notes by Shao Youhan [Shigu shang, 486–87]). So, 不祿 was another way of saying 不福 (i.e., 無福), and is interpreted accordingly.

25. Additional discussions can be found in chapter 42 (lines 3–4); regarding the spirit of this, see chapter 78 (lines 8–13).

26. Pei Xuehai, *Gushu xuzi jishi*, has this explanation: "其, 猶殆也, 是疑而有定之詞" (其 3, 377–78).

27. Wang Shumin, *Guji xuzi guangyi* (之 14, 433–34).

28. Yang Bojun, *Gu Hanyu xuci* (與、歟 5; 307–8).

29. Yang Bojun, *Gu Hanyu xuci* (也 7, 239).

30. *Shuowen* (致, V5 xia, 10a).

31. See chapter 20 (endnote 30).

32. See Fan Yingyuan's jizhu note on this line in chapter 39.

33. *Zhuangzi* ("*Xiaoyaoyou*"), "彼其於世, 未數數然也," regarding which Cheng Xuanying says: "數數, 猶汲汲" (Guo Qingfan, *Zhuangzi jishi*, 18–19). Moreover, *Zhengzi tong* notes, "汲汲, 不休息貌" ("*Siji*" shang, 8b), so this could be interpreted as "constant; many."

34. *Guangya*, "與, 譽也"; Wang Niansun's note quotes Zheng Xuan's note on *Liji* ("*She yi*," under the line "以燕 [i.e., 宴] 以射則譽"), in which he says, "譽, 或為與" (Shiyan, V4 xia, 9b).

35. Wang Yinzhi, *Jingzhuan shici* (無 1, 229). Also, *Zhengzi tong* ("*Ziji*" xia) points out that 勿 was a "禁止之辭" (78b).

36. *Guoyu* ("*Zhouyu*" xia), "為令聞嘉譽以聲 [i.e., 名] 之"; Wei Zhao's note: ". . . 以策命述其功美, 進爵加錫 [i.e., 賜] 以聲之也" (V1, 14a). The performance of "進爵加錫" can be seen in the *Dao De Jing*, chapter 62 (lines 8–9).

37. See Jiang Xichang's jiaogu note on this line in chapter 39. (In this, he quotes Li Shan's comment in *Hou Han shu* ["*Feng Yan zhuan*"], "馮子以夫人之德, 不碌碌如玉, 落落如石," where he says, "玉貌碌碌, 為人所貴; 石貌落落為人所賤," and goes on to add, "賤既失矣, 貴亦未得. 言當處才、不才之間." This remark was most likely derived from *Zhuangzi* ["*Shanmu*"], which says that "周 [i.e., Zhuangzi's given name] 將處乎材與不材之間" [jijie, 167]. Although Li's extended discussion here on the perceived value of jade and stone is accurate, it is not something that Laozi himself addressed in these lines; see the margin note on lines 17–19.)

38. See *Shuowen* (璓); Duan Yucai's note (V1 shang, 6a), as well as Jiang Sheng, *Shangshu jizhu yinshu* ("*Guming dijiushiyi*"), the note under the line "粤玉五重" (*Huang Qing jingjie*, V398, 13b, or 2,017).

CHAPTER 40

1. The Beida and all received versions assigned this chapter as 41, but we believe that following the structure of silk version B (this portion of silk version A was damaged) to consider this as chapter 40 makes much better sense, for it maintains the tone of chapter 39.

2. Beida version (chapter 41, endnote 3).

3. See Ma Xulun's jiaogu note.

4. *Shuowen* (夷), the line defining this obsolete character as "平行易也" (V2 xia, 4b).

5. *Zuo zhuan* ("*Zhaogong shiliunian*"), "行之頗類 [纇]"; Kong Yingda's shu note (V47, 10a).

6. *Zhengzi tong*'s ("*Ziji*" zhong) citation of *Shuowen* (57a). 苟 and 且 could be considered synonymous, and both were used to mean 假 (perfunctory; mod. Ch., false); see also *Yili* ("*Yanli*"), "賓為苟敬," Zheng Xuan's note: "苟, 且也、假也" (V15, 10a).

7. *Huainanzi* ("*Benjing xun*"), "質真而素樸"; Gao You's note (V8, 1a; jishi, 555).

8. *Erya* (渝, V3, 12b); Su Che's note on this line says that 渝 was "隨物變化," a definition that was adapted into this margin note.

9. *Guangya*, "曼, 無也" (Shiyan, V5 shang, 2b).

10. *Guangya*, "天, 大也" (Shigu, V1 shang, 1b); Wang Niansun's note quotes *Shangshu* ("*Duoshi*")—"天邑商"—and explains: "天邑, 猶大邑" (V1 shang, 1b). So, in other words, 天象 should be understood here to be the same thing as 大象 in chapter 35 (line 1).

11. See chapter 35 (line 1).

12. Zhu Junsheng, *Shuowen tongxun* (刑, V17, 6b); Zhu points out that this character could be borrowed to read as 形. See also *Xunzi* ("*Qiang guo*"), "形范正" (jiaoshi, V11, endnote

3, 648), where Wang Tianhai indicates that some other versions also substituted 刑 for 形. For a further discussion on 無形, see chapter 14 (lines 1–16).

13. Beida version (chapter 41, endnote 8). See also Gao Ming's note on this line, which quotes silk version B's editorial board (version A is damaged).

CHAPTER 41

1. The Beida and all received versions considered this to be chapter 40, but we follow the numbering of the silk versions instead. Using this arrangement, and according to our reconstruction, the subject under discussion in chapter 42 better complements that of this chapter.

 The actual meaning of chapter 41 was increasingly obfuscated over the centuries by many individuals who attempted to apply their own perspectives to its explication. Here, though, only Laozi's own words and logical processes have been followed to form our understanding.

2. A metaphorical description of the Dao's cyclical movement as reflected in the world can be found in chapter 15 (lines 12–13).

3. Wang Bi's note here in *Laozi Dao De Jing zhu jiaoshi* indicated that 無為 meant "順自然也."

4. *Guangya*, "柔, 弱也" (Shigu, V1 xia, 23a).

CHAPTER 42

1. "道 . . . 自無入有" (*Dao De zhenjing lun*, as cited in Lu Yusan, *Laozi shiyi*, 191). (Historically speaking, explanations of 道生一 have been varying and perplexing, with none of them fitting Laozi's theory better than Sima Guang's note.)

2. The interpretation of the yin and the yang as representing two breaths (氣 *qi*) was popular during the Han dynasty.

3. Zhu Junsheng, *Shuowen tongxun* (故 [假借為 "古"], V9, 46a).

4. Wang Shumin, *Guji xuzi guangyi* (亦 12, 102). Also, Xiao Xu, *Gushu xuci pangshi* (亦 14, 75).

5. *Zhengzi tong* (議, "Youji" shang, 83b).

6. Wang Yinzhi, *Jingzhuan shici* (而 8, 147–48).

7. *Guangya*, "學, 教也" (Shigu, V4 shang, 12a).

8. Wang Yun, *Shuowen judou* (父, V6, 12b); under this entry, Wang cites the definition in *Baihutong* that 矩 meant "以法度教子," so 法度 (rule) was the primary definition of 矩.

CHAPTER 44

1. This definition was inspired by Xi Tong's jijie note (*Laozi jijie*).

2. See Xi Tong's jijie note (*Laozi jijie*).

3. *Zhengzi tong* (愛, "Mouji" shang, 40b).

4. *Zhou Li* ("Kaogongji, gongren"), "厚其液"; Zheng Xuan's note (see *Zhou Li zhushu ji buzheng*, V42, 26a).

5. Wang Yinzhi, *Jingzhuan shici* (可 1, 109–10). See also Xiao Xu, *Gushu xuci pangshi* (可 1, 162).

CHAPTER 45

1. *Xunzi* ("Fuguo"), "以靡敝之"; Yang Jing's note (V6, jijie, 118).

2. *Shuowen* (蛊); Duan Yucai's note (V5 shang, 13b).

3. *Zuo zhuan* ("*Xuangong ernian*"), "盛服將朝"; Du Yu's note: "盛, 音成, 本亦或作成" (V21, 3a).

4. *Liji* ("*Pinyi*"), "其終詘然樂也"; Zheng Xuan's note: "詘, 絕止貌" (V63, 21b). (詘 was most likely used by Zheng as a simplified form of 詘然, with 然 indicating 貌, and so 詘 would have been defined here as 絕止.)

5. Guodian version (Qiu Xigui, *Guodian Chumu zhujian*, part B, endnote 23).

CHAPTER 46

1. Lu Deming, *Jingdian shiwen: Laozi yinyi* (卻, V25, 5b).

2. *Shiming* ("*Shizirou*"), "疾行曰趨" and "疾趨曰走" (*Shuzhengbu*, V3, 1b).

3. Chen Qitian, *Hanfeizi jiaoshi* ("*Jie Lao*"), the citation of Xu Shan's note on *Yantielun* (under "天下有道, 却走馬以糞也," endnote 2, 743–44). (This character in the Fu Yi version was given as 播. Liu Xiaogan points out that with regard to both 糞 and 播, "皆為治田義" [*Laozi gujin*, 466].)

4. The obsolete character 辠 *zuì* was considered so similar to that of 皇 *huáng* (emperor) that the Qin Shihuang emperor ordered the former to be altered to 罪 *zuì*. See *Shuowen* (辠); Duan Yucai's note (V14 xia, 6b).

5. *Lülan* ("*Zhenluan*"), "黔首利莫厚焉"; Gao You's note (V7, 5b).

6. Pei Xuehai, *Gushu xuzi jishi* (乎 1, 237).

7. This character had the ancient pronunciation of *dān*, but nowadays, it is pronounced as *shèn* and means "very; much; excessive."

8. *Shuowen Xu jian* (媅, V12 xia) in Ding Fubao, ed., *Gulin* (10–138).

9. Wang Yun, *Shuowen judou* (媅, V24, 14b).

10. *Shijing* ("*Jienanshan*," "*Shiyue zhi jiao*"), "胡憯莫懲," in Lu Deming, *Jingdian shiwen: Laozi yinyi*, under the term 胡憯 (zhong, 21a).

11. *Shuowen* (憯), "憯, 毒也"; Duan Yucai's note: "憯, 害也" (V10 xia, 12b).

CHAPTER 47

1. Xiao Xu, *Gushu xuci pangshi* (以 20, 11). See also Yang Bojun, *Gu Hanyu xuci*, whose explanation is, "表事情結果" (以 18, 265).

2. *Zhengzi tong* (闚, "*Xuji*" shang, 81b).

3. Wang Yun, *Shuowen judou* (窗, V20, 1a).

4. *Xiao Erya* ("*Guanggu*"), "彌, 益也" (V1, huijiao, 58).

5. *Liji* ("*Yueji*"), "使之行商容而復其位"; Zheng Xuan's note (V39, 14a).

CHAPTER 48

1. Pei Xuehai, *Gushu xuzi jishi* (者 12, 760–62).

2. Yang Bojun, *Gu Hanyu xuci* (則 4, 327–28).

3. Chen Zhu points out that these lines meant, "為學日益, 與夫為道日損, 雖似相反, 實則相成. 蓋為學不能日益, 則為道必不能日損. 損者, 損欲也" (*Laozi Hanshi shuo*, 84). Chen's comment was probably inspired by Li Xizai's note in *Laozi yi*.

4. Wang Yinzhi, *Jingzhuan shici* (而 7, 146).

5. *Guangya*, "為, 成也" (Shigu, V3 xia, 12b).

6. Wang Yinzhi, *Jingzhuan shici* (及 2, 113–14; the seventh example cited here is this line of the *Dao De Jing*).

7. Wu Changying, *Jingci yanshi* (又 2, 120). See also Wang Shumin, *Guji xuzi guangyi* (又 3, 93).

CHAPTER 49

1. Wang Yinzhi, *Jingzhuan shici* (以 2, 19). See also Wu Changying, *Jingci yanshi* (以 1, 3).
2. See chapter 38 (endnote 2).
3. Yang Bojun, *Gu Hanyu xuci* (之 12, first explanation, 349).
4. *Erya*, "在, 存也" (Shigu xia, V2, 9b).
5. Yang Bojun, *Gu Hanyu xuci* (也 2, 234).
6. *Zhengzi tong*, "歙, 合也, 與翕同" ("Chenji" xia, 11a).
7. *Lülan* ("*Guyue*"), "以比黃鍾之宮適合"; Gao You's note: "合, 和諧" (V5, 8b). Also, ("*Gushi*"), "夫物, 合而成"; Gao's note: "合, 和也" (V13, 1a).
8. Wang Yinzhi, *Jingzhuan shici* (焉 3, 49).
9. Beida version (endnote 5).
10. See Fan Yingyuan's jizhu note.
11. Wang Yinzhi, *Jingzhuan shici* (焉 1, 49).

CHAPTER 50

1. The logic evinced in all the past commentaries on lines 1–3 (including even the most authoritative ones) is extremely difficult to comprehend. We have therefore relied on the relationship between the "emergence" and "withdrawal" cycle of things, as well as the actual meaning that "the ten plus three" suggests, to obtain our interpretation as shown in the margin note on lines 2–3.
2. See Ma Xulun's jiaogu note.
3. Gui Fu, *Shuowen yizheng* (閏, V2, 3b–6a). Gui's discussion is quite extensive, but the point most relevant to our discussion here is his citation of an explanation by someone named Zhao Huanguang: "古之閏月, 隨於歲終, 謂之十三月."
4. Wang Shumin, *Guji xuzi guangyi* (而 23, 313–14). See also Xiao Xu, *Gushu xuci pangshi* (而 15, 249).
5. *Erya*, "之, 往也" (Shigu shang, V1, 3a).
6. "人莫不以其生生, 而不知其所以生生" ("*Chiyue*," V5, 4b). In addition, *Zhuangzi* ("*Dazongshi*"), "生生者不生." Guo Qingfan's note (*Zhuangzi jishi*) quotes Lu Deming, *Jingdian shiwen: Zhuangzi yinyi*: "李云, '矜生者不生也.' 崔云, '常營其生為生生'" (jishi, 253 and 255). Both are valuable references.
7. Xiao Xu, *Gushu xuci pangshi* (蓋 5, 143–44).
8. *Liji* ("*Quli*" shang), "坐必安, 執爾顏"; Zheng Xuan's note (V2, 9a).
9. *Erya* ("*Shidi*"), "高平曰陸, 大陸曰阜, 大阜曰陵, 大陵曰阿" (V9, 7a); Hao Yixing's note points out that "陸、阜、陵、阿, 皆土山也. 以高大而異名" (*Erya gulin*, 2,613).
10. *Shuowen* (兕); Duan Yucai's note (V9 xia, 12a). However, the form of this character suggests that it might have actually described a cape buffalo.
11. *Sunzi* ("*Junzheng*"), "合軍聚眾"; Cao Cao's note: "起營為軍陳 [i.e., 陣]" (V7, 105). 軍 literally indicated an armed force. In ancient times, as when these forces here were being used, they had to be deployed in battle arrays at all times, and this is what Cao Cao was describing in his annotation to *Sunzi*.

12. Wang Li, *Tongyuan zidian* ("19 *Ge bu–bin mu*," 446).
13. *Shuowen* (楄, V6 shang, 13a).
14. *Liji* ("*Zhengyong*"), "故時措之宜也"; Kong Yingda's shu note (V53, 26a).
15. *Shiming* ("*Shizirong*"), "容, 用也" (*Shuzhengbu*, V3, 1a). Gao Heng's note in *Laozi zhenggu* quotes Yu Yue's explanation (which also was based on this definition) that "兵無所容其刃, 言兵無所用刃."

CHAPTER 51

1. "All things" in line 3 echoes this.
2. Yang Shuda, *Ciquan* (之 12, V5, 7). See also Yang Bojun, *Gu Hanyu xuci*, "之字有時放在不及物動詞下 . . . 却不是賓語 . . . 只是多一音節罷了" (之 14, 352).
3. The Dao joins "being" and "void" together harmoniously to produce predictable functions (see chapter 11).
4. Wu Changying, *Jingci yanshi* (之 18, 102). See also Xiao Xu, *Gushu xuci pangshi* (之 25, 338).
5. Yang Shuda, *Ciquan* (也 2, V7, 39–40), as well as Yang Bojun, *Gu Hanyu xuci* (也 1, fourth example, 234).
6. Wang Yinzhi, *Jingzhuan shici* (夫 4, 238–39).
7. Wang Shumin, *Guji xuzi guangyi* (之 10, fifth example, 430; 以 3, first and second examples, 8–9).
8. *Zhou Li* ("*Taizai zhizhi*"), "一曰, 爵以馭其貴"; Zheng Xuan's note: "爵謂公、侯、伯、子、男、卿、大夫、士也" (*Zhou Li zhushu ji buzheng*, V2, 7b).
9. See chapter 24 (first comment on line 1).
10. *Liji* ("*Yueji*"), "氣衰則生物不遂"; Zheng Xuan's note (V38, 8b).
11. Xi Tong's note in *Laozi jijie* quotes the citation of *Cang jiepian* (regarding the note on Xie Lingyun's poem) that says, "亭, 定也."
12. Xi Tong's note in *Laozi jijie* quotes *Guangya*: "毒, 安也" (Shigu).
13. *Da Dai Liji* ("*Zengzi shifumu*"), "兄之行若不中道則養之"; Wang Pinzhen's note: "盧云, 養猶隱也" (V4, 12b).
14. *Yijing* ("*Qian gua*"), "反復其道"; Wang Bi's note in *Zhou Yi zhushu ji buzheng* explains this as 反覆 ("*Xiangci*," V1, 3b). Accordingly, 覆 and 復 could be used interchangeably in ancient times.
15. Yang Bojun, *Gu Hanyu xuci* (之 15, 352–53).

CHAPTER 52

1. Wu Changying, *Jingci yanshi* (既 4, 123). See also Xiao Xu, *Gushu xuci pangshi* (既 8, 139).
2. *Lülan* ("*Yishang*"), "武王得之矣"; Gao You's note (V14, 11b).
3. *Shuowen* (兌); Duan Yucai quotes this line of Laozi's and points out that 兌 was borrowed to mean 閱, which we read as being the same as 穴 in ancient Chinese (V8 xia, 3a).
4. *Huainanzi* ("*Daoyingxun*"), "王者欲久持之, 則塞民于兌"; Xu Shen's note (some editions ascribe this to Gao You; see Zhang Shuangdi [*jiaoshi*, 1326–27]) quotes "塞其兌" from line 5 here.
5. *Guanzi* ("*Xinshu*" shang), "潔其宮, 開其門, 去私毋言"; Yin Zhizhang's note indicates that "門, 謂口也" (jiaozheng, 219) and also points out that "下解中, 門, 謂耳目也" (jiaozhu, 764). (Although 門 had two connotations here, only its definition as "mouth"

best suits Laozi's description in this passage. A comparison of lines 5 and 6 shows that 塞其兌 and 啟其兌 are a pair of opposites, while 閉其門 and 濟其事 are another. Therefore, only the interpretation of 門 [whence words are issued, which may then shape affairs] as 口 [mouth] can be considered acceptable. An additional discussion can be found in the margin note on lines 5–6 in this chapter.)

6. *Guoyu* ("*Jinyu san*"), "光, 明之曜也" (V9, 2a). Our understanding of this line also relied on Wang Anshi's note (see entry under Wang Jiefu) on this line of Laozi's, "蓋光者, 明之用, 明者光之體," to which he added, "唯其能用其光, 復歸其根, 則終身不至於有咎, 而能密合常久之道" (collected in Meng Wentong's edition of the lost Wang annotations on the *Dao De Jing* in *Daoshu jijiao shizhong*, 700).

7. Yang Bojun, *Gu Hanyu xuci* (其 3, 11).

8. *Guoyu* ("*Zhouyu*" xia), "[德、夢、卦] 三襲焉"; Wei Zhao's note (V3, 4b).

CHAPTER 53

1. Regarding this character 挈, we may refer to *Zhuangzi* ("*Zaiyou*"), "絜 [i.e., 挈] 汝適復之撓撓" (jijie, 97) and Lu Deming, *Jingdian shiwen: Zhuangzi yinyi* (zhong), who quotes *Guangya* in defining 挈 as 持 (9b).

2. 知 was to be read as 智; see chapter 10 (endnote 13). Moreover, Yan Zun's note on line 1 here explains that 挈有知 meant 提聰挈明, and so defined 知 (i.e., 智) as 聰明.

3. *Erya* ("*Shigong*"), "一達謂之道路"; Xing Bing notes: "一達長道謂之道路" (V5, 20b).

4. In the received versions, 他 appears as 施. Wang Niansun's *Dushu zazhi* points out that "施讀謂迆," for 他, 施, and 迆 had similar readings in ancient times (as quoted in Gao Ming's discussion on this phrase in his *Boshu Laozi*, 80). *Shuowen* (迆) notes that "迆, 邪行也" (V2 xia, 2b), and so 他 (i.e., 迆) has been interpreted accordingly.

5. See chapter 27 (endnote 2).

6. *Erya*, "夷, 易也" (Shigu xia, V2, 7a).

7. Lü Jifu's note explains that the meaning of this line is "世人欲速, 由於 '捷徑'" (*Laozi yi*).

8. See Wang Bi's note in *Laozi Dao De Jing zhu jiaoshi*.

9. Ban Gu, *Han shu* ("*Huozhi liezhuan*"), "文采千匹"; Yan Shigu's note: "文, 文 [i.e., 紋] 繒也. 帛之有色者曰采" (3,687; endnote 15, 3,688).

10. *Yupian* (猒, V9, "*Gan bu*" 113, 156). *Yupian lingjuan* (see second entry under Gu Yeyu) has an additional explanation: "猒, 足而不欲復為也" ("*Ganbu, diyibaishisi*," 105).

11. This understanding follows Yan Zun's discussion on this line. (In Yan's version, this term was given as 財貨. The character 齎 could be read as 資, which was defined as 貨 [*Shuowen* (齎); Duan Yucai's note (V6 xia, 5a)], so 齎財 and 財貨 had the same meaning. Yan also indicates that 貨財 meant 金玉 and 珍寶.)

12. *Hanfeizi* ("*Jie Lao*"), "竽也者, 五聲之長也. 故竽先, 則鍾瑟皆隨 . . . 今大姦作 . . . 則小盜必和" (jishi, 380–81).

CHAPTER 54

1. Wang Yinzhi, *Jingzhuan shici* (以 2, 19). See also Wang Shumin, *Guji xuzi guangyi* (以 1, 8).

2. Wu Changying, *Jingci yanshi* (之 5, 98).

3. Wang Yinzhi, *Jingzhuan shici* (乃 1, 127). See also Wang Shumin, *Guji xuzi guangyi* (乃 1, 267).

4. *Shiming* ("*Shiyanyu*"), "貞, 定也" (*Shuzhengbu*, V4, 14b).

5. *Shuowen* (餘, V5 xia, 4a).

6. *Lülan* ("*Zhidu*"), "此神農之所以長"; Gao You's note (V17, 11b).

7. *Yijing* ("*Feng gua*"), "豐, 亨"; Kong Yingda's shu note (V5, 17b).

8. Monk Huiyuan, *Buding xinyi Dafangguang Fo, Huayan jing yinyi*, under the phrase, "溥蔭: '溥, 遍也. 今並作普'" (shang, 12b).

9. This is just as what Zhang An said in his note (under the Song Huizong emperor's note on this line): "天下之理 . . . 能盡之者, 不容私智."

10. *Liji* ("*Dazhuan*"), "周道然也"; Kong Yingda's shu note explains that "周道然也者, 言周道如此" (V34, 11a and 11b). Wang Yinzhi, *Jingzhuan shici* (然 4, 160); Wang Shumin, *Guji xuzi guangyi* (然 5, 332) defines this term as 如是, which conveys the same meaning.

CHAPTER 55

1. *Huainanzi* ("*Yuan Dao xun*"), "含德之所至也"; Gao You's note (V1, 2a; jishi 9). Heshang Gong's note indicates that 含 meant 含懷.

2. See the Qing Shizu emperor's note. Fan Yingyuan's jizhu note explains this phrase as having meant "其體 [i.e., 懷] 之 [a pronoun representing 德] 者, 至矣."

3. Ban Gu, *Han shu* ("*Jiayi zhuan*"), "故自為赤子, 而教固已行矣"; Yan Shigu's note: "赤子, 言其新生, 未有眉髮, 其色赤" (V48, 2,248–49).

4. *Shuowen* (螫, V13 shang, 14a).

5. In ancient times, many animals like the vipers and snakes mentioned in this passage were considered different forms of insects, so their names all shared the same 虫 radical.

6. *Shuowen* (朘), "朘, 赤子陰也" (V4 xia, 11a).

7. Heshang Gong's note describes this term as 作怒.

8. *Yupian* ("*Kou bu*," 嗄, 95); the example cited here is this line of Laozi's.

9. Pei Xuehai, *Gushu xuzi jishi* (曰 8, 137–38). See also Xiao Xu, *Gushu xuci pangshi* (曰 5, 51). For the definition of 則 as "to lead to," see chapter 38 (endnote 14).

10. See Xi Tong's jijie note (in *Laozi jijie*): "祥有眚誼." Xi also quotes *Zhuangzi* ("*Dechongfu*"): "常因自然而不益生," which he goes on to explain as, "生不可益, 益之則反乎自然而災害至矣."

11. See Wang Anshi's (a.k.a. Wang Jiefu's) notes: "氣者, 當專 [i.e., 摶] 氣至柔 [see chapter 10]. 今反為心所使, 不能專 [i.e., 摶] 守於內, 則為暴矣" and "此強者 . . . 乃強梁 [see chapter 42] 之強" (collected in Meng Wentong, *Daoshu jijiao*, 702).

12. Heshang Gong's note defined this character as 壯極, and thus 壯 here suggested the concept of 極.

CHAPTER 56

1. See chapter 10 (endnote 13).

2. See Wang Yinzhi, *Jingzhuan shici* (其 12, 119).

3. Pei Xuehai, *Gushu xuzi jishi* (得 2, 447). See also Wang Shumin, *Guji xuzi guangyi* (得 1, 240).

CHAPTER 57

1. Wang Shumin, *Guji xuzi guangyi* (以 1, 8).

2. This follows the reading of the Guodian and silk versions. (In his *Jingci yanshi*, Wu Changying indicates: "之猶為也" [之 16, 101]. 為 was often used in ancient China whenever

governance was being discussed, as in *Lunyu* ["*Weizheng*"], "為政以德" [V2, 2a], as well as ["*Zilu*"], "善人為邦百年"; Huang Kan's yishu note: "為者, 治也" [V7, jijie, 133].)

3. Wang Yinzhi, *Jingzhuan shici* (也 7, 48).

4. Pei Xuehai, *Gushu xuzi jishi* (夫 2, 881).

5. *Erya*, "天, 君也" (Shigu shang, V1, 2a). See also *Guanzi* ("*Shuyan*"), "帝王者, 審所先所後. 先民與地, 則得矣"; Yin Zhizhang's note: "君者, 民之天" (jiaozheng, 64).

6. Wang Yinzhi, *Jingzhuan shici* (而 7, 146).

7. *Xiao Erya* ("*Guangu*"), "彌, 益也" (huijiao, 58).

8. Zhu Junsheng, *Shuowen tongxun* (畔, V14, 87b).

9. *Zuo zhuan* ("*Xianggong sanshiyinian*"), "子皮曰, 愿吾愛之, 不吾叛也"; Kong Yingda's shu note cites an explanation by someone named Liu Xuan (V40, 28b).

10. This understanding follows the notes of the Tang Xuanzong emperor and Su Che, as well as the Qing Shizu emperor.

11. *Shuowen* (茲); Duan Yucai's note quotes Dai Zhen's explanation (V1 xia, 9b).

12. This follows Wang Bi's note in *Laozi Dao De Jing zhu jiaoshi*.

13. *Yijing*, "制而用之謂之法"; Kong Yingda's note: "法者, 言聖人裁制其物而施用之, 垂為模範, 故謂之法" ("*Xici*" shang, V7, 8a).

14. *Guanzi* ("*Qifa*"), "尺寸也、繩墨也、規矩也、衡石也、斗斛也、角量也, 謂之法"; Yin Zhizhang's note: "凡此十二事, 皆立政者所以為法也" (jiaozheng, 28; jiaozhu, 106).

15. *Shangshu* ("*Yaodian*"), "平章百姓"; Kong Anguo's note (V2, 6b).

16. *Shuowen* (盜); Duan Yucai's note quotes Zhou Gong's explanation: "竊賄為盜" (V8 xia, 7b).

17. *Xunzi* ("*Zhenglun*"), "故盜不竊, 賊不刺"; Yang Jing's note: "盜賊, 通名. 分而言之, 則私竊謂之盜, 動殺謂之賊" (V12, 10a).

18. Zhu Qianzhi's jiaoshi note on this line points out that "正, 定義通. 定從正聲, 形亦近同."

CHAPTER 58

1. Wang Yinzhi, *Jingzhuan shici* (其 7, 116). See also Yang Bojun, *Gu Hanyu xuci* (其 10, 114).

2. *Jiyun* ("*Pingsheng*" 2), "悶然, 不覺貌" ([23 Hun], 悶, 35b). (Both 悶然 and 悶悶 are adjectives connoting the same meaning.)

3. Wu Changying, *Jingci yanshi* (其 16, 52).

4. Regarding the reading of 屯, see chapter 15 (comment on line 9).

5. This follows Wang Bi's note (*Laozi Dao De Jing zhu jiaoshi*), which says, "立刑名, 明賞罰, 以檢姦偽, 故曰「其政察察也」." Moreover, 檢姦偽 was the core definition of 察察.

6. *Shuowen* (夬, V3 xia, 5a).

7. This follows Heshang Gong's note.

8. *Guangyun* ("*Rusheng*"), "伏, 匿藏也" (V5, 1 Wu, 4a).

9. *Lülan* ("*Zhiyue*"), "故禍兮福之所倚, 福兮禍之所伏. 聖人所獨見, 眾人焉知其極?"; Gao You's note (V6, 7a).

10. *Guangyun* ("*Qusheng*"), "正, 定也" (V4, 45 Jing, 46b).

11. *Erya*, "割, 裂也" (Shiyan, V3, 11a).

12. Wang Yinzhi, *Jingzhuan shici* (而 6, 144–47). See also Xiao Xu, *Gushu xuci pangshi*: "為 '却' '反' 字之義" (而 1b, 244).

13. Wang Bi's note (*Laozi Dao De Jing zhu jiaoshi*) under chapter 40 (line 14: "大方無隅"; received version, chapter 41) points out: "方而不割, 故無隅也."

14. *Lülan* ("*Mengqiu ji*"), "其器廉以深"; Gao You's note (V7, 1b).

15. *Jiyun* ("*Rusheng*," 22 Xi, 刺, 13b).

16. *Yupian* ("*Chang bu*"), "肆, 恣也" (V29, 399).

CHAPTER 59

1. Our understanding of these two terms follows Xi Tong's jijie note (in *Laozi jijie*), which quotes Gao You's explanations in *Lülan*: "事, 治也" ("*Xianji*," under "所事者末也") and "天, 身也" ("*Bensheng*," under "以全其天也"). Regarding the interpretation of 事 (which *Lülan* has pointed out as meaning 治, or "cultivating"), see *Liji* ("*Liyun*"), "以治人情"; Zheng Xuan's note: "治者, 去瑕穢, 養菁華" (V22, 31b); Ruan Yuan's proofreading of Zheng's note is followed here (22 jiaokanji, 21a).

2. This theory about 事天 can be found in *Mengzi* ("*Jinxin*" shang): "盡其心者, 知其性也. 知其性則知天矣—存其心, 養其性, 所以事天也" (V13 shang, 13b). (Fan Yingyuan's jizhu note quotes this passage from *Mengzi*, which is why previous annotators have used this line as proof that 天 is somehow related to 性, but of course that was a doctrine of the Confucian school and so is unacceptable in this context.)

3. Chapters 10 and 54 clearly show that a leader's personal cultivation forms the foundation for the governance of the country.

4. *Shuowen* (嗇); Duan Yucai's note (V5 xia, 9a). (In ancient times, a farmer was referred to as a 嗇夫, showing the direct relationship between 嗇 and farming. [嗇夫 in later times became 穡夫.] Wang Bi used that archaic notion of "farming" to compose his note.)

5. This was inspired by Yan Zun's note in his chapter 20 ("方而不割章," eighth paragraph, 129) on this line: "故治國之道 . . . 嗇為祖宗" and thereby be able to achieve "無為而無不成, 不爭而無不剋."

6. This determination was inspired by *Zhuangzi* ("*Tianxia*"), which contains an introduction to Laozi's philosophy, including "以約為紀" (jijie, 295), where the English concept of "parsimony" agrees with the Chinese concept of 約.

7. This follows Heshang Gong's note.

8. *Zhengzi tong* ("*Ziji*" xia), under 克, defines this as 勝也 and quotes an explanation by Zhou Boqi: "[The original figure of this character was delineated as] 象負荷形," and "凡能勝任者, 皆取此 [this, i.e., 克] 義" (7b–8a). (The spirit of 無不克 echoes that of 無為而無不為 [i.e., Yan Zun's 無為而無不成—see endnote 5] in our chapter 48 [line 5].)

9. *Liji* ("*Aigongwen*"), "古之為政 . . . 不能愛人, 不能有其身"; Zheng Xuan's note (V50, 9b).

10. Wu Changying, *Jingci yanshi* (之 12, 100–101) and Pei Xuehai, *Guji xuzi guangyi* (之 19, 746–47).

11. See chapter 6 (comment on line 4).

12. *Lülan* ("*Zhongji*"), "無賢不肖, 莫不欲長生久視"; Gao You's note (V1, 7b).

CHAPTER 60

1. This understanding was based on Heshang Gong's note, as well as *Hanfeizi*'s explanation of this line of Laozi's ("*Jie Lao*," jishi, 354–55).

2. Wang Yun, *Shuowen judou*, under the entry 隸, is a note that quotes *Zhou Li* ("*Diguan, Xiangshi*"): "以涖匠師, 注云: '故書, 涖作立.' 鄭司農云「立讀為涖, 謂臨視也」" (V20, 14a).

3. Gui Fu, *Shuowen yizheng*, which cites the definition for 神 in *Fengsutong* as "神者, 申也," and then quotes *Lunheng* ("*Lunsipian*"): "神者, 伸也" (神, V48, 28b).

4. This understanding was inspired by Heshang Gong's note: "以道德居位治天下, 則鬼不敢見 [i.e., 現] 其精神以犯人也."

5. Gao Heng's zhenggu note (*Laozi zhenggu*) indicates that "非者, 蓋 '不唯' 二字之合音." (A famous Qing dynasty scholar, Qian Daxin, discovered that labiodental pronunciation did not exist in ancient spoken Chinese [i.e., there was no "f" sound, which in Chinese phonology is referred to as a 輕唇音, or "light lip sound"; see Wang Li, *Zhongguo yuyanxue shi*, 154]. Hence, instead of "f's," bilabial sounds [such as "b's," which are referred to as 重唇音, or "heavy lip sounds"] took their place. Therefore, when read quickly, both 不 and 唯 would have sounded like *buī*, which was the ancient pronunciation of 非.)

6. *Xiao Erya* (交, Yizheng V2, 16b, or huijiao jishi, 234).

7. *Guangya* (Shigu, 歸, V3 shang, 14a). Also, *Lunyu* ("*Yanghuo*"), "陽貨 . . . 歸孔子豚"; Huang Kan's yishu note quotes Kong Anguo's explanation (175).

8. *Shuowen* (遺); Duan Yucai's note (V2 xia, 3a).

9. Pei Xuehai, *Gushu xuzi jishi* (焉 4, 96–101).

CHAPTER 61

1. *Shuowen* (牝), "牝, 畜母也" (V2 shang, 2a).

2. See Wang Bi's note in *Laozi Dao De Jing zhu jiaoshi*.

3. *Shuowen* (牡), "牡, 畜父也" (V2 shang, 2a).

4. Yang Shuda, *Ciquan* (為 10, V8, 19–20).

5. *Yupian*, "取, 收也" (V6, "*You bu*," 115).

6. Ma Jianzhong, *Mashi wentong* ("*Shoudongci*, 5.3.3," 277–79). See also Lü Shuxiang, *Zhongguo wenfa yaolue* ("3.83," 38–39).

7. *Xunzi* ("*Jiebi*"), "聖人縱其欲, 兼其情而制焉者理矣"; Yang Jing's note (V15, 8a–9b; jijie, 269).

8. *Yijing* ("*Xiaochu*"), "小畜, 亨"; Lu Deming, *Jingdian shiwen: Yijing yinyi*, "[畜] 積也, 聚也" (5a).

9. *Yupian* ("*Ru bu*" 211, 入, 233). ("To go into" means joining a large state to serve it.)

10. Wang Yinzhi, *Jingzhuan shici* (夫 3, 237–38); see also chapter 8 (first comment on line 11).

CHAPTER 62

1. This follows the reading determined by the silk versions' editorial board. In all the received versions, this character appears as 奧, which could also have meant 主 (as pointed out by Zheng Xuan's note in *Liji* ["*Liyun*"], under the line "故人以為奧也" [V22, 30a]; see also the Beida version, chapter 62 [endnote 1]).

2. This reading of 葆 follows Xu Kangsheng's opinion (*Boshu Laozi zhuyi yu yanjiu*, chapter 62, endnote 2, 44), in which he quotes a jijie note cited in *Shiji*: "徐廣曰, (史記) 珍寶字皆作葆." See also our endnote 5 in chapter 69.

3. See the Beida version, endnote 2 of this chapter, in which the editorial board notes: "葆、保、寶三字古常通用."

4. *Shuowen* (保, V8 shang, 1a). See also *Liji* ("*Wenwang shizi*"), "立太傅, 少傅以養之"; Zheng Xuan's note explains: "養猶教也. 言養者積浸成長之" (V20, 16a). So, in other words, 養 meant "to teach" or "to cultivate."

5. Heshang Gong's note says, "夫市者交易而退. 不相宜, 善言美語. 求者欲疾得, 賣者欲疾售也." This described the usual way in which dealings were conducted, which of course is still how transactions are done even to this day.

6. *Guangya*, "賀, 嘉也" (Shiyan, V5 shang, 6b–7a). (In the received versions, 加 was used in its place, which could be considered a borrowed character for 賀; see also the Beida version [endnote 3 of this chapter].)

7. Wang Yinzhi, *Jingzhuan shici* (之 3, 199–200).

8. Wang Shumin, *Guji xuzi guangyi* (有 16, 89–90).

9. *Shuowen* (卿), where Duan Yucai's note quotes *Baihutong*: "卿之為言章也. 章、善明理也" (V9 shang, 9b). (In the Beida and all received versions, the term 三公 was used instead of 三卿. However, 公 referred only to the highest official [as well as noble] rank under the king [*Yijing* ("Yi gua"), "六三 . . . 中行, 告公用圭"; Wang Bi's note in *Laozi Dao De Jing zhu jiaoshi*: "公者, 臣之極也. 凡事足以施天下, 則稱王. 次天下之大者, 則稱公" (V4, 8b), with 王 signifying 天子].)

10. *Shuowen* (璧); Duan Yucai's note (V1 shang, 6b).

11. 共 also happened to be the ancient form of 拱. See *Shuowen* (拱); Duan Yucai's note (V12 shang, 6b).

12. Jiang Xichang's jiaogu note on this line quotes *Zuo zhuan* ("Xianggong ershibanian"): "既崔氏之臣曰, '與我其拱璧,'" to which Du Yu notes: "崔氏大璧," and Kong Yingda's shu note also comments: ". . . 此璧兩手拱抱之, 故為大璧."

13. Yang Shuda, *Ciquan* (以 2, V7, 8). See also Wang Shumin, *Guji xuzi guangyi* (以 1, 8).

14. Gui Fu's *Shuowen yizheng* quotes *Shijing* ("Qingren"), "駟介旁旁"; Zheng Xuan's note: "駟, 四馬也" (駟, V30, 13b). Moreover, *Yupian* points out, "駟, 四馬一乘" (V23, "Ma bu" 357, 330).

15. *Zuo zhuan* ("Xianggong shijiunian"), "賄荀偃 . . . 乘馬先吳壽夢之鼎"; Kong Yingda's shu note quotes this line of Laozi's and explains: "以璧為馬先也 . . . 以輕物先重物 . . . 以輕先重, 非以賤先貴" (V34, 18a).

16. Zhu Junsheng, in his *Shuowen tongxun*, explains that "古席地而坐: 膝著席而下其臀曰坐" (坐, V10, 31a).

17. *Lülan* ("Lunren"), "貴則觀其所進"; Gao You's note (V3, 8b).

18. Wang Yinzhi, *Jingzhuan shici* (也 7, 98–100).

19. Wu Changying, *Jingci yanshi* (以 13, 7).

20. Wang Yinzhi, *Jingzhuan shici*, "[歟] 古通作與" (歟 1, 94).

21. Pei Xuehai, *Gushu xuzi jishi* (為 2, 111–12).

CHAPTER 63

1. *Lülan* ("Lunren"), "事心乎 [i.e., 於] 自然之塗"; Gao You's note (V3, 8a).

2. See the Song Huizong emperor's note.

3. *Hanfeizi* ("Yulao"), "有形之類, 大必起於小; 行 [i.e., 經歷] 久之物, 族 [i.e., 眾多] 必起於少" (jishi, 396).

4. *Lunyu* ("Xianwen"), "或曰 '以德報怨' 何如?'"; Zheng Xuan's note (V14, 4a).

5. *Erya*, "圖, 謀也" (Shigu shang, V1, 3a).

6. *Shuowen* (謀, V3 shang, 3b).

7. Yang Bojun, *Gu Hanyu xuci* (乎 2, 68). In ancient classical Chinese, the usage of 於 often varied depending upon the context.

8. *Guangya*, "細, 微也" (Shigu, V4 xia, 2b).
9. *Shuowen* (作, V8 shang, 5b).
10. *Shijing* ("*Ban*"), "猶之未遠"; Mao Heng's note (V17 zhi 4, 18b). The reading of 圖 here differs from the one discussed in the first comment on line 7 above (i.e., "deliberating" on obtaining an achievement), for here it concerns "ruminating" on the need to be careful.
11. Wu Changying, *Jingci yanshi* (之 19, 102). See also Pei Xuehai, *Gushu xuzi jishi* (之 9, 733–35).

CHAPTER 64

1. Monk Yuanying, *Yiqiejing yinyi* (形兆, V9, 11b). Note that the meaning of 兆 here differs from the 兆 in chapter 20 (line 9) due to the themes under discussion.
2. *Shuowen* (謀); Duan Yucai's note: "圖與謀同義" (V3 shang, 3b), and he points out under the entry for 圖 that this character meant "先規畫 [i.e., 劃] 其事之終始 . . . 出於萬全而後行之也" (V6 xia, 3b).
3. Wang Yun, *Shuowen shili*: "脃 [mod. Ch., 脆] 即膬之俗字," with *Shuowen* (脃) describing it as "小耎 [i.e., 軟] 易斷也" (V14, 11a; see also Ding Fubao, ed., *Shuowen gulin*, 4–793), and so this character is rendered here as "fragile."
4. *Shuowen* (判, V4 xia, 12a).
5. *Shuowen* (幾, V4 xia, 1b).
6. See Yang Bojun, *Gu Hanyu xuci* (之 14, 352).
7. Wu Changying, *Jingci yanshi* (其 4, 49). Wang Shumin, *Guji xuzi guangyi*, read this as 猶 (其 31, 216–17).
8. *Jiyun* (6 *Hao*, 毫, V3, 17a).
9. *Lülan* ("*Yinchu*"), "為之九成之臺"; Gao You's note (V6, 6a).
10. *Jiyun* (6 zhi, 虆, V1, 23a).
11. Wang Yun, *Shuowen judou* (仞, V15, 2a).
12. Yang Bojun, *Gu Hanyu xuci* (之 15, 352–53).
13. Yang Bojun, *Gu Hanyu xuci*: "[之] 把一個句子變成名詞子句" (之 12a, 349–50).
14. Wang Yinzhi, *Jingzhuan shici* (其 5, 115–16).
15. *Shuowen* (臨, V8 shang, 12b).
16. *Guoyu* ("*Yueyu*" xia), "四時以為紀"; Wei Zhao's note (V21, 5a).
17. *Guangya*, "輔, 助也" (Shigu, V2 shang, 11a).

CHAPTER 65

1. Pei Xuehai, *Gushu xuzi jishi* (以 18, 23–24).
2. Wu Changying, *Jingci yanshi* (將 4, 84–85). See also Xiao Xu, *Gushu xuci pangshi* (將 3, 273). In classical Chinese, 乃 could convey two notions: either "hence" and "then," or "but" and "rather," with its meaning determined by the context.
3. Wang Yinzhi, *Jingzhuan shici* (之 7, 199–200).
4. Wang Yinzhi, *Jingzhuan shici* (以 3, 19–20).
5. See chapter 10 (endnote 13).
6. Wang Shumin, *Guji xuzi guangyi* (以 1, 8).
7. *Lülan* ("*Changjian*"), "[申侯伯] 三年而知鄭國之政"; Gao You's note (V11, 8b). With regard to 為邦, see chapter 57 (endnote 2).

8. *Zhengzi tong* (賊, "*Youji*" zhong, 36a).

9. See chapter 63 (line 6), where 德 was contrasted with 怨. We therefore interpreted 恩惠 as "kindness." However, this character was used in this line in contrast to "detriment," so "boon" is used.

10. *Shijing* ("*Shengmin*"), "恆之 [i.e., 為 indicates 種] 秬秠"; Mao Heng's note (V17 zhi 1, 4b).

11. Pei Xuehai, *Gushu xuzi jishi* (亦 5, 73–74).

12. *Zhou Li* ("*Xiaozai*"), "二曰, 聽師田以簡稽"; Zheng Xuan's note (*Zhou Li zhushu ji bu-zheng*, V3, 13b).

13. See chapter 28 (line 14).

14. Pei Xuehai, *Gushu xuzi jishi* (與 14, 9–10).

CHAPTER 66

1. *Shuowen* (王), "王, 天下所歸往也" (V1 shang, 5a).

2. Yang Bojun, *Gu Hanyu xuci* (之 12, second explanation, 349–50).

3. *Guangya*, "在, 居也" (Shigu, V2 shang, 9b).

4. Wang Shumin, *Guji xuzi guangyi* (以 1, 8).

5. *Yupian* ("*Han bu*" 348, 厚, 318).

6. *Mozi* ("*Jingshang*"), "(27) 害, 所得而惡也" (jiaozhu, 471–72).

7. *Shijing* ("*Changwu*"), "進厥虎臣"; Zheng Xuan's note (V18 zhi 5, 40b). (進 was used in the Guodian version to describe how people follow their sovereign, and this echoes the notion in lines 1–3 of this chapter.) This character appears as 推 (to praise; to support) in the Beida and received versions. However, the context of chapter 17 describes how his people's praise should not be perceived as the paramount achievement of a sovereign. As *Yupian* points out, "推, 進也" (V2, 19b), and that is the definition we must follow here.

8. *Shuowen Xu jian* (猒, *Shuowen gulin* 4–1, 214). With regard to 弗, see chapter 2 (comment on lines 11–12).

9. Pei Xuehai, *Gushu xuzi jishi* (以 3, 13). See also Yang Shuda, *Ciquan* (以 9, V7, 11–12).

CHAPTER 67

1. *Guangya*, "肖, 類也" (Shigu, V3 shang, 10b–11a). See also *Xiao Erya* ("*Guangxun*"), "不肖, 不似也" (huijiao, 314–15); in this instance, 類 and 肖 had the same meaning.

2. Wang Yinzhi, *Jingzhuan shici* (夫 3, 237–38).

3. Wang Yinzhi, *Jingzhuan shici* (惟 [i.e., 唯] 7, 68).

4. *Zhengzi tong* (細, "*Weiji*" zhong, 11a).

5. See chapter 62 (comment on line 2).

6. Wang Yinzhi, *Jingzhuan shici* (而 7, 146).

7. We follow the Beida version's reading of these two lines.

8. Wang Shumin, *Guji xuzi guangyi* (曰 4, 78). (For this definition, Wang cites lines 5–9 from this chapter as his examples.)

9. *Zuo zhuan* ("*Zhuanggong ershiqinian*"), "夫禮樂慈愛, 戰所畜也"; Kong Yingda's shu note: "慈謂愛之深也" (V10, 29b).

10. Xiao Xu, *Gushu xuci pangshi* (夫 12, 412–13).

11. Silk version A is followed here, and this reading would appear to be substantiated by *Hanfeizi* ("*Jie Lao*"), which quotes lines 12–13 exactly as they appear in silk version A

(jijie, 152; jishi, 377–78). However, the character 事 appears as 器 in silk version B and all other versions. Be that as it may, as Zheng Xuan notes, "器, 謂所操以作事者也" (*Liji* ["*Jingjie*"], "有治民之意, 而無其器則不成" [V50, 7a]), and so we can roughly understand that 器 had something to do with 事, but its exact meaning remains unknown.

12. *Guangya*, "長, 君也" (Shigu, V1 shang, 1b).

13. Wang Yinzhi, *Jingzhuan shici* (今 3, 105–6).

14. Wu Changying, *Jingci yanshi* (其 17, 52–53). See also Wang Shumin, *Guji xuzi guangyi* (其 26, 215).

15. We follow Wang Bi's note in *Laozi Dao De Jing zhu jiaoshi* here. (Strictly speaking, this 且 should have been read as 怚 *qie*, and its annotation in *Guangya* says that "怚, 取也" [Shigu]; this was quoted by Gao Heng in his zhenggu note on this line in *Laozi zhenggu*.)

16. Yang Bojun, *Gu Hanyu xuci* (夫 3, 41).

17. Wu Changying, *Jingci yanshi* (將 5, 85). See also Pei Xuehai, *Gushu xuzi jishi* (將 14, 620–21).

18. Wang Yinzhi, *Jingzhuan shici* (如 7, 150). See also Pei Xuehai, *Gushu xuzi jishi* (如 4, 547–48).

19. *Shiming* ("*Shigongshi*"), "垣, 援也. 人所依阻以為援衛也" (*Shuzhengbu*, V5, 15b). (垣 in this line of Laozi's was used as a verb, therefore 援衛 is adapted to interpret 垣.)

CHAPTER 68

1. See the Qing Shizu emperor's note. Further discussion on 士 can be found in chapter 15 (comment on line 1); see also chapter 40 (comment on line 1).

2. *Guangya*, "武, 勇也" (Shigu, V2 xia, 18a).

3. In pre-Qin times, 怒 had no clear military definition, and so we refer to a line from *Sunzi* that says, "故殺 [i.e., 克] 敵者怒也" (which J. H. Huang translated in *The Art of War* as, "So, trounce the enemy by means of high morale" ["Mobilizing for Armed Conflict," 46]). (Regarding the conduct of battles, 氣 was also often used in ancient China to indicate "courage," and so was close in meaning to 怒, but not synonymous.)

4. See chapter 2 (comment on lines 11–12).

5. Zhu Qianzhi's discussion on this line in his jiaoshi note quotes Wang Yinzhi, *Jingyi shuwen*: "古謂對敵為與."

6. *Shuowen* (配); Duan Yucai's note (V14 xia, 10b).

7. *Erya*, "匹, 合也" (Shigu shang, V1, 3b).

CHAPTER 69

1. *Guoyu* ("*Yueyu*" xia), "天時不作, 弗為人客"; Wei Zhao's note: "攻者為客" (V21, 1a). See also *Gongyang zhuan* ("*Zhuanggong ershibanian*"), "春秋, 伐者為客, 伐者為主" [*sic*]; He Xiu's notes, respectively: "伐人者為客" and "見伐者為主" (V9, 20a).

2. *Zuo zhuan* ("*Xianggong sannian*"), "揚干亂行於曲梁"; Du Yu's note (V29, 26b).

3. *Mozi* ("*Jing*" shang [10]), "行, 為也" (jiaozhu, 469).

4. *Shuowen* (扔), "扔, 捆也" and (捆), "捆, 就也" (V12 shang, 12b).

5. With regard to reading 葆 as 寶, see Wang Hui, *Gu wenzi tongjia shili* ("*You bu*," 葆, 245–46). For a discussion on the use of 寶 as 保, refer to *Yijing* ("*Xici*" xia), "聖人之大寶曰位" (V8, 9b); Lu Deming, *Jingdian shiwen: Yijing yinyi*, points out that "'寶,' 孟 [僖本]

作 '保'" (28b), so in ancient Chinese these two characters could be used interchangeably. (Silk version B, Heshang Gong, and Wang Bi all used 寶 here, which had the more fitting reading of 保.) See also chapter 62 (endnotes 2 and 3).

6. *Guangya*, "稱, 舉也" (Shigu, V1 xia, 14b).

7. *Shiming* ("*Shiyanyu*"), "哀, 愛也" (*Shuzhengbu*, V4, 9a).

8. Yang Shuda, *Ciquan* (者 1, V5, 17–18).

CHAPTER 70

1. Lü's note: "道法自然, 其言亦希而自然. 自然則無為. 則知之行之也, 不乃甚易乎?" (collected in *Laozi yi*).

2. See Wang Bi's note in *Laozi Dao De Jing zhu jiaoshi*.

3. "言者道之荃, 事者道之迹."

4. Wang Yinzhi, *Jingzhuan shici* (夫 3, 237–38).

5. Wang Yinzhi, *Jingzhuan shici* (惟 [i.e., 唯] 7, 68).

6. Yang Bojun, *Gu Hanyu xuci* (者 1, 335–37). See also Yang Shuda, *Ciquan* (者 1, V5, 17–18).

7. Zhu Junsheng, *Shuowen tongxun*, "[希] 假借為稀, 《爾雅》「釋詁」: 希 [i.e., 稀] 罕也" (希, V13, 116a).

8. See Fan Yingyuan's jizhu note.

9. *Shuowen* (褐); Duan Yucai's note (V8 shang, 17a).

10. *Zhengzi tong* (懷, "*Mouji*" shang, 64a).

11. See Wang Yun, *Shuowen judou* (玉), "玉, 石之美者, 有五德" (V1, 13a–b). The text and Wang's note are extensive and so are not quoted here.

CHAPTER 71

1. This reading was inspired by these two lines of the *Dao De Jing* as quoted in *Huainanzi* ("*Dao yin xun*"): "知而不知, 尚矣. 不知而知, 病也" (see Zhang Shuangdi, *Huainanzi jiaoshi*, 1,284). In his endnote 8, Zhang quotes Ma Zonghuo's reading: "本文兩 '而' 字, 與 '如' 同義" (1,286), and so we have added "viewing . . . as" to express this.

2. *Guangya*, "病, 難也" (Shigu, V3 xia, 13a–b).

3. Wu Changying, *Jingci yanshi* (之 7, 102). See also Xiao Xu, *Gushu xuci pangshi* (之 25, 338).

4. Yang Shuda, *Ciquan* (以 9, 11–12).

5. *Guangyun*, "病, 憂也" (V4, "*Qusheng*," 43 ying, 46a). *Lunyu* ("*Yongye*"), under the line "堯舜猶病諸" is Huang Kan's shu note: "病猶患也" (61, 62). 患 and 憂 were synonymous.

CHAPTER 72

1. Wang Yinzhi, *Jingzhuan shici* (之 7, 199–200).

2. *Guangya*, "畏, 懼也" (Shigu, V2 xia, 5a).

3. Pei Xuehai, *Gushu xuzi jishi* (將 5, 612–14), and Wang Shumin, *Guji xuzi guangyi* (將 4, 360).

4. *Shuowen* (毋), "毋, 止之詞也" (V12 xia, 8a).

5. *Erya* ("*Shigong*"), "陿而修曲曰樓"; Guo Pu's note indicates that 陝 *xiá* was the same as 狹 (V5, 21a). See also Lu Deming, *Jingdian shiwen: Erya yinyi*, "陝, 或作狎" (Shang zhong, 20b). (The character 陝 *xiá* is written with two 人 *rén* components, while the character 陝 *shǎn* contains two 入 *rù* components; this latter character is the name of a Chinese province, 陝西.)

6. This follows Xi Tong's jijie note (in *Laozi jijie*).

7. *Zuo zhuan* ("*Zhaogong ershiliunian*"), "侵欲無厭"; Ruan Yuan's jiaokanji (in Zuo Qiuming, *Chunqiu Zuo zhuan zhushu ji buzheng*) on this line quotes Lu Deming, *Jingdian shiwen: Zuo zhuan yinyi*: "厭作猒" (V52, 9a).

8. *Zuo zhuan* ("*Xianggong sanshiyinian*"), "僑將厭焉" (V40, 28b); Lu Deming, *Jingdian shiwen: Zuo zhuan yinyi*, notes, "[猒] 本又作壓" (V4, 22b), so, in pre-Qin times, 厭 could be used interchangeably with 壓. Moreover, Duan Yucai's note in *Shuowen* quotes *Guangyun*'s definition that 壓 meant 笮 (壓, V13 xia, 9b), which is why Xi Tong's jijie note (in *Laozi jijie*) on this line of Laozi's explains this as 壓笮.

9. Wang Yinzhi, *Jingzhuan shici* (夫 3, 237–38).

10. Yang Bojun, *Gu Hanyu xuci* (惟 [i.e., 唯] 2, 183–84).

11. See chapter 2 (comment on lines 11–12).

12. See endnote 7 above.

13. This follows Zhu Qianzhi's discussion on this line in his jiaoshi note.

CHAPTER 73

1. See chapter 38 (endnote 14).

2. *Lunyu* ("*Yanghuo*") has a saying attributed to Confucius that may aid in the understanding of this line by Laozi: "天何言哉? 四時行焉, 百物生焉. 天何言哉!" (V17, 12a).

3. "陰盡陽生, 暑退寒來, 皆不召也."

4. This follows Heshang Gong's note. It should be pointed out that although the character 墠 normally appears as 繟 in Heshang Gong's notes, Wang Ka's dianjiao (endnote 14) indicates that according to Lu Deming, *Jingdian shiwen: Laozi yinyi*, 繟 was originally written as 墠.

5. This definition follows Heshang Gong's note.

6. "天所網羅 . . . 雖疎遠, 司察人之善惡, 無有所失."

CHAPTER 74

1. Pei Xuehai, *Gushu xuzi jishi* (且 18, 668–69). See also Xiao Xu, *Gushu xuci pangshi* (且 8, 287–88).

2. Wang Shumin, *Guji xuzi guangyi* (而 25, 314–15). See also Xiao Xu, *Gushu xuci pangshi* (而 13, 249).

3. See the Qing Shizu emperor's note.

4. *Yupian* (V10, "*Chi bu*," 119, 得, 157). (This term in all received versions appears as 得執. It seems that 執 must have been added after 得 at a later time as an explanation, for the definition of 執 [to grasp; to arrest] was close to that of 獲.)

5. Pei Xuehai, *Gushu xuzi jishi* (夫 10, 885–86).

6. Pei Xuehai, *Gushu xuzi jishi* (夫 14, 888–89). See also Xiao Xu, *Gushu xuci pangshi* (夫 2a, 410).

7. Wang Shumin, *Guji xuzi guangyi* (是 10, 492–93). See also Xiao Xu, *Gushu xuci pangshi* (是 10, 365).

8. Wang Yinzhi, *Jingzhuan shici* (夫 3, 237–38).

9. See chapter 70 (second comment on line 9).

CHAPTER 75

1. Wang Shumin, *Guji xuzi guangyi* (以 3, 8–9). See also Yang Bojun, *Gu Hanyu xuci* (以 5, 259–60).
2. See Xi Tong's jijie note in *Laozi jijie*.
3. Yang Bojun, *Gu Hanyu xuci* (之 15, 352–53).
4. The Qing Shizu emperor's note defined 多 as 太重.
5. See chapter 20 (endnote 30).
6. Yang Shuda, *Ciquan*, "語末助詞, 表提示" (者 3, V5, 19).
7. See chapter 38 (second comment on line 5).
8. Xiao Xu, *Gushu xuci pangshi* (是 9, 364–65).
9. *Jiyun* ("*Yi xian*," 賢, V3, 3b).
10. Su Che's note: "貴生之極, 必至於輕死. 惟無以生為, 而生自全矣," and Heshang Gong's note: "夫唯獨無以生為務者 . . . 則賢於貴生也."

CHAPTER 76

1. *Guangya* (Shigu 1 xia, 23a–b). In chapter 41 (i.e., chapter 40 in the received versions), Wang Bi's note in *Laozi Dao De Jing zhu jiaoshi* under the line "弱者, 道之用" indicates that 弱 meant 柔弱.
2. The pronunciation of these two characters was the same. In his *Shuowen xizhuan*, Xu Kai points out that 搄 was read as 亙 and meant "橫亙之也" (*Shuowen gulin*, V9, 1,299). As for the reading of the first character in this term, we follow the suggestion that 椢 be read as 搄, as posited by the editorial board of silk version A.
3. Zhu Junsheng, *Shuowen tongxun* (信, V16, 18b). (This character appears as 信 in both silk version B and the Beida version. In silk version A, though, it takes the form of 仞, which would still have been read as 信.)
4. *Jiyun*, "徒, 眾也" ("*Pingsheng*," "*Shiyi mo*," V2, 8b). The reading here of 徒 differs from those in chapter 50 (lines 2–3); see chapter 50 (comment on line 2).
5. Zhu Junsheng, *Shuowen tongxun*, points out that in ancient times, 恆 could be borrowed to mean 亙 (V2, 25a–b).
6. See endnote 2 above with regard to the meaning of 亙.

CHAPTER 77

1. Wu Changying, *Jingci yanshi* (之 16, 101–2). See also Wang Shumin, *Guji xuzi guangyi* (之 8, 429).
2. *Liji* ("*Wangzhi*"), "一道德以同俗"; Kong Yingda's shu note: "道, 履蹈而行" (V13, 16a–b). (This describes 道 as being related to 行.) See also *Xunzi* ("*Yibing*"), "必道吾所明, 無道吾所疑"; Yang Jing's note: "道, 言也; 行也" (V10, 7a).
3. *Shijing* ("*Xiaoxing*"), "寔命不猶"; Mao Heng's note (V1 zhi 5, 21a). 若 has two usual meanings—one is "[as] if" and the other is "like"—and the context here shows that the latter definition of 若 should be used to define Laozi's use of 猶.
4. Yang Bojun, *Gu Hanyu xuci* (者 4c, 338–39).
5. Wang Yinzhi, *Jingzhuan shici* (也 7, 98–100).
6. *Guangya*, "抑, 按也" (V3 xia, 12a).

7. Wang Yinzhi, *Jingzhuan shici* (然 4, 160). See also Pei Xuehai, *Gushu xuzi jishi* (然 10, 570–71).

8. *Guangya*, "奉, 獻也" (Shiyan, V5 shang, 1a).

9. Pei Xuehai, *Gushu xuzi jishi* (以 24, 30). See also Wang Shumin, *Guji xuzi guangyi* (以 21, 16).

10. This grammatical understanding came from the discussions on 有所 and 無所 in Ma Jianzhong, *Mashi wentong duben* ("Daizi" 2.3.2.4 and 2.3.2.5). See also Lü Shuxiang, *Zhongguo wenfa yaolue* (ch. 8, 8.3: 有所, 無所, 111–12).

11. Wang Yinzhi, *Jingzhuan shici* (於 6, 35).

12. Yang Shuda, *Ciquan* (者 1, V5, 17–18). Yang refers to this as "複牒代名詞," meaning that 者 was used to refer to an aforementioned subject to avoid repetition.

13. Yang Shuda, *Ciquan* (乎 3, V3, 45).

14. Yang Shuda, *Ciquan* (乎 5, V3, 46).

15. *Guangya*, "居, 據也" (Shiyan, V5 xia, 1b).

16. *Guangya*, "賢, 勞也" (Shigu, V1 xia, 9b–10a). See also *Zhou Li* ("*Xiaguan, sixun*"), "事功曰勞" (Zheng Xuan, *Zhou Li zhushu ji buzheng*, V30, 11a).

CHAPTER 78

1. Refer to chapter 20 (endnote 30).

2. *Lülan* ("*Quanxun*"), "故太上先勝"; Gao You's note (V15, 6b).

3. Pei Xuehai, *Gushu xuzi jishi* (以 19, 24).

4. *Shiming* ("*Shidianyi*"), "易 . . . 言變也" (*Shuzhengbu*, V6, 12b).

5. Yang Bojun, *Gu Hanyu xuci* (之 14, 352).

6. Yang Bojun, *Gu Hanyu xuci* (之 12, first discussion, 349).

7. "摧陷陵谷, 貫穿金石" was placed under line 2; Xi Tong in *Laozi jijie* believed that this meant water itself was doing the striking. While this appears questionable (see chapter 8 and our comment on line 2), his view on what the power of water could do is correct, but he ignored the fact that water's power is released in response to the environment. In other words, water never acts aggressively.

8. See chapter 2 (comment on lines 11–12).

9. Wu Changying, *Jingci yanshi* (而 4, 66). See also Pei Xuehai, *Gushu xuzi jishi* (而 7a, 524–25).

10. Wang Yinzhi, *Jingzhuan shici* (云 3, 69–70).

11. Wang Yinzhi, *Jingzhuan shici* (曰 1), which quotes *Guangya*, "曰, 言也" (42–43), and also points out (in 言 1) that "言, 語詞也" (107–8).

12. *Zuo zhuan* ("*Xuangong shiwunian*"), "國君含垢"; Du Yu's note defined 垢 as 恥 (V24, 19a).

13. *Shuowen* (社); Duan Yucai's note (V1 shang, 4b).

14. *Shuowen* (稷, V7 shang, 11a–b). (稷 usually referred to a type of grain [probably millet] that was an important staple for the ancient Chinese.)

CHAPTER 79

1. *Guangya*, "怨, 恨也" (Shigu, V4 shang, 14b).

2. Wang Shumin, *Guji xuzi guangyi* (必 7, 520). See also Xiao Xu, *Gushu xuci pangshi* (必 6, 397).

3. Wang Yinzhi, *Jingzhuan shici* (焉 2, 49). See also Wang Shumin, *Guji xuzi guangyi* (焉 10, 54).
4. *Guangya*, "為, 成也" (Shigu, V3 xia, 12b).
5. See Wei Yuan's benyi note on this line. (Some previous annotators hold that this term concerned matters of taxation in pre-Qin times, but that does not fit either the context of the discussion here [see lines 5–6] or the connotation conveyed in lines 1–2.)
6. This understanding was inspired by Wei Yuan's benyi note, which says, "券契有二, 我執其左. 但有執右以來責取者, 吾即以財務與之, 而未嘗有所責取於人." With regard to 芥, see Wang Hui, *Gu wenzi tongjia shili*, "芥 [i.e., 介] 讀為契" ("*Yue bu*," 729–30). See also *Shuowen* (契), "契, 大約 [i.e., formal contract] 也" (V10 xia, 2b).
7. Wang Yinzhi, *Jingzhuan shici* (以 2, 19). See also Wang Shumin, *Guji xuzi guangyi* (以 1, 8).
8. Xu Kai, *Shuowen xizhuan* (責, *Shuowen gulin*, 5–1, 198).
9. Zhu Junsheng, *Shuowen tongxun* (司), which quotes *Zhou Li* ("*Shishi*"); Zheng Xuan's note (V5, 16b).
10. *Guangyun* ("*Rusheng*," 17 Xue, 徹, 27a).
11. *Lunyu*, "吾與汝"; Huang Kan's shu note quotes the *Erya*'s definition of 與 ("*Gongyechang*," yishu, V3, 43–44).

CHAPTER 80

1. *Shuowen* (寡, V7 xia, 4a).
2. Chen Guying, *Laozi jinzhu jinyi*, quotes Hu Shi's explanation that 器 in lines 4–5 here meant 兵車 and 甲兵 (endnote 2, 323). Hu's opinion agrees with Wu Cheng's note. However, it is our view that 器 in this context should have consisted not only of those two things, but rather all equipment employed in large-scale work on behalf of the state.
3. Zhu Junsheng, *Shuowen tongxun* (重), which quotes *Guanzi* ("*Quanxiu*"): "必重盡其民力"; Fang Xuanling's (n.b., this originated with Yin Zhizhang) note (V1, 2a–3a).
4. *Guangya*, "遠, 疏也" (Shigu, V3 shang, 15b).
5. *Zhengzi tong* (徙, "*Yingji*" xia, 57b).
6. *Jiyun* ("*Shangsheng, ba yu*," 所, V5, 16b).
7. *Guangyun*, "陳, 列也" (Shigu, V1 shang, 12a–b).
8. "易, 繫辭下: 上古結繩而治, 後世聖人易之以書契. 正義 [i.e., Kong Yingda's shu note] 引鄭注云: 事大大結其繩, 事小小結其繩."

CHAPTER 81

1. See the Qing Shizu emperor's note.
2. In the Beida version, this character was written as 智. In ancient Chinese, 知 could be used as a borrowed character to mean 智; see Zhu Junsheng, *Shuowen tongxun* (知, V11, 4a–b). See also chapter 10 (endnote 13).
3. Pei Xuehai, *Gushu xuzi jishi* (者 12, 760–61). See also Wang Shumin, *Guji xuzi guangyi* (者 5, 444–45).
4. *Xunzi* ("*Xiushen*"), "多聞曰博" (V1, 8b).
5. *Guangya*, "既, 盡也" (Shigu, V1 xia, 21a).
6. *Guangya*, "為, 施也" (Shigu, V3 shang, 19a). In *Shuowen tongxun*, Zhu Junsheng quotes *Guangya*: "施, 予也" (施, V10, 11b and 12a).
7. See chapter 2 (comment on lines 11–12).

BIBLIOGRAPHY

The following is a list of all the works cited by the author, as well as the main sources consulted while researching and writing this book.

ARCHAEOLOGICAL FINDINGS

BEIDA VERSION

Beijing Daxue cang Xi Han zhushu (2) 北京
大學藏西漢竹書 (貳). Shanghai: Guji
chubanshe, 2012.

FU YI VERSION

Fu Yi (Tang), zhengli (唐) 傅奕, 整理.
Dao De Jing guben pian 道德經古本
篇. collected in Yan Lingfeng 嚴靈
峰. *Mawangdui boshu Laozi shitan* 馬王
堆帛書老子試探. Taipei: Heluo tushu
chubanshe, 1976.

GUODIAN VERSION (INCLUDING COMBINED STUDIES ON THE SILK VERSIONS)

Allan, Sarah; Crispin Williams
(Contemporary), eds. (近代、西方)
艾蘭, 魏克彬, 主編. *Guodian* Laozi:
Dongxifang xuezhe de duihua 郭店《老子》:
東西方學者的對話. (*The Guodian* Laozi:
*Proceedings of the International Conference,
Dartmouth College, May 1998*). Beijing:
Xueyuan chubanshe, 2002.

Asano Yuichi; Sato Masa (Contemporary),
trans. (近代、日本) 淺野裕一; 佐藤
將之, 監譯. *Zhanguo Chujian yanjiu*
戰國楚簡研究. Taipei: Wanjuanlou,
2004.

Chen Guying (Contemporary), zhubian
(近代) 陳鼓應, 主編. "*Guodian zhujian
zhuanhao*" "郭店竹簡專號." *Daojia
wenhua yanjiu* 道家文化研究. V17.
Beijing: Sanlian shudian, 1999.

Chen Xiyong (Contemporary) (近代) 陳
錫勇. *Guodian Chujian Laozi lunzheng* 郭
店楚簡老子論證. Taipei: Liren shuju,
2005.

Cheung Kwong-yue (a.k.a. Zhang
Guangyu) (Contemporary), zhubian
(近代) 張光裕, 主編. Guodian Chujian
yanjiu diyijuan (wenzi bian) xushuo 《郭
店楚簡研究》第一卷 (文字編) 續說.
Taipei: Yiwen yinshuguan, 1999.

Ding Yuanzhi (Contemporary) (近代) 丁原
植. *Guodian zhujian* Laozi *shixi yu yanjiu*
郭店竹簡《老子》釋析與研究. Taipei:
Wanjuanlou, 1998–99.

Foster, Christopher J. (Contemporary).
"Introduction to the Peking University

Han Bamboo Strips: On the Authentication and Study of Purchased Manuscripts." *Early China*, 40 (2017): 167–239.

Fukuda Tetuyuki (Contemporary); Sato Masa, Wang Xiuwen, trans. (近代、日本) 福田哲之; 佐藤將之, 王綉雯, 譯. *Zhongguo chutu guwenxian yu Zhanguo wenzi zhi yanjiu* 中國出土古文獻與戰國文字之研究. Taipei: Wanjuanlou, 2005.

Guo Yi (Contemporary) (近代) 郭沂. *Guodian zhujian yu xian Qin xueshu yanjiu* 郭店竹簡與先秦學術研究. Shanghai: Shanghai jiaoyu chubanshe, 2001.

Hendricks, Robert G. (Contemporary), trans. and comm.; Xing Wen, gaibian; Yu Jin, trans. (近代、西方) 韓祿伯; 邢文, 改編; 余瑾, 翻譯. *Jian bo Laozi yanjiu* 簡帛老子研究. Beijing: Xueyuan chubanshe, 2002.

———. *Lao-Tzu Te-Tao Ching: A New Translation Based on the Recently Discovered Ma-wang-tui Texts.* New York: Ballantine Books, 1989.

Ikeda Tomohisa (Contemporary); Cao Feng, trans. (近代、日本) 池田知久; 曹峰, 譯. *Jian bo yanjiu lunji* 簡帛研究論集. Beijing: Zhonghua shuju, 2006.

Jiang Guanghui (Contemporary), zhubian (近代) 姜廣輝, 主編. *Guodian Chujian yanjiu* 郭店楚簡研究. *Zhongguo zhexue* 中國哲學. V24. Shenyang: Liaoning jiaoyu chubanshe, 2000.

Li Ling (Contemporary) (近代) 李零. *Guodian Chujian jiaodu ji* 郭店楚簡校讀記. Beijing: Zhongguo renmin daxue chubanshe, 2007.

———. *Jian bo gushu yu xueshu yuanliu* 簡帛古書與學術源流. Beijing: Sanlian shudian, 2008.

Li Ruohui (Contemporary) (近代) 李若暉. *Guodian zhushu Laozi lunkao* 郭店竹書老子論考. Jinan: Qilu shushe, 2004.

Liao Mingchun (Contemporary) (近代) 廖名春. *Guodian Chujian Laozi jiaoshi* 郭店楚簡老子校釋. Beijing: Qinghua daxue chubanshe, 2002.

Liu Xinfang (Contemporary), zhuan (近代) 劉信芳, 撰. *Jingmen Guodian zhujian Laozi jiegu* 荊門郭店竹簡老子解詁. Taipei: Yiwen yinshuguan, 1999.

Liu Zhao (Contemporary) (近代) 劉釗. *Guodian Chujian jiaoshi* 郭店楚簡校釋. Fuzhou: Fujian renmin chubanshe, 2003.

Nie Zhongqing (Contemporary) (近代) 聶中慶. *Guodian Chujian Laozi yanjiu* 郭店楚簡《老子》研究. Beijing: Zhonghua shuju, 2004.

Peng Hao (Contemporary), jiaobian (近代) 彭浩, 校編. *Guodian Chujian Laozi jiaodu* 郭店楚簡《老子》校讀. Wuhan: Hubei renmin chubanshe, 2000.

Qiu Xigui (Contemporary), zhubian (近代) 裘錫圭, 主編. *Guodian Chumu zhujian* 郭店楚墓竹簡. Beijing: Wenwu chubanshe, 1998.

Wei Qipeng (Contemporary) (近代) 魏啟鵬. *Chujian Laozi jianshi* 楚簡《老子》柬釋. Taipei: Wanjuanlou, 1999.

Yin Zhenhuan (Contemporary) (近代) 尹振環. *Chujian Laozi bianxi* 楚簡老子辨析. Beijing: Zhonghua shuju, 2001.

SILK VERSIONS

Dai Wei (Contemporary) (近代) 戴維. *Boshu Laozi jiaoshi* 帛書老子校釋. Changsha: Yuelu shushe, 1998.

Gao Heng (Contemporary), Chi Xizhao (近代) 高亨, 池曦朝. *"Shitan Mawangdui Hanmu zhong de boshu Laozi"* "試探馬王堆漢墓中的帛書老子." *Wenwu*, 11 (1974): 1–7.

Gao Ming (Contemporary), zhuan (近代) 高明, 撰. *Boshu Laozi jiaozhu* 帛書老子校注. *Xinbian zhuzi jicheng* 新編諸子集成. V1. Beijing: Zhonghua shuju, 1996.

Han Zhongmin (a.k.a. Xiaohan) (Contemporary) (近代) 韓中民 (曉菡). "*Changsha Mawangdui Hanmu boshu gaishu*" "長沙馬王堆漢墓帛書概述." *Wenwu*, 9 (1974): 44–48.

Huang Zhao (Contemporary) (近代) 黃釗. *Boshu Laozi jiao zhu xi* 帛書老子校注析. Taipei: Taiwan xuesheng shuju, 1991.

Mawangdui Hanmu boshu zhenglixiaozu (Contemporary) (近代) 馬王堆漢墓帛書整理小組. *Mawangdui Hanmu chutu Laozi shiwen* 馬王堆漢墓出土《老子》釋文. *Wenwu*, 8 (1974): 8–20.

Xu Kangsheng 許抗生. *Boshu Laozi zhuyi yu yanjiu* 帛書老子注譯與研究. Hangzhou: Zhejiang renmin chubanshe, 1985.

Yan Lingfeng (Contemporary), zhuan (近代) 嚴靈峰, 撰. *Mawangdui boshu Laozi shitan* 馬王堆帛書老子試探. Taipei: Heluo tushu chubanshe, 1976.

Ye Chengyi (Contemporary) (近代) 葉程義. *Boshu Laozi jiao Liu Shipei Laozi jiaobu shuzheng* 帛書老子校劉師培《老子斠補》疏証. Taipei: Wenshizhe chubanshe, 1994.

Zhao Chao (Contemporary) (近代) 趙超. *Jiandu boshu faxian yu yanjiu* 簡牘帛書發現與研究. Fuzhou: Fujian renmin chubanshe, 2005.

GENERAL

Chen Fubin (Contemporary), zhubian (近代) 陳福賓, 主編. *Benshiji chutu sixiang wenxian yu Zhongguo gudian zhexue yanjiu lunwen ji* 本世紀出土思想文獻與中國古典哲學研究論文集. 2 vols. Xinzhuang, Taiwan: Fujen Catholic University, 1999.

WORKS ARRANGED BY HISTORICAL PERIOD

ZHOU DYNASTY 周代 (CA. 1046–256 BCE)

Guan Zhong (Zhou), zhuan; (Contemporary) Li Xiangfeng, jiaozhu (周) 管仲, 撰; (近代) 黎翔鳳, 校注. *Guanzi* 管子. Beijing: Zhonghua shuju, 2004.

Mo Di (Zhou: Spring and Autumn period) (周、春秋) 墨翟. *Mozi* 墨子; see (Contemporary) Wu Yujiang, *Mozi jiaozhu*.

Sun Wu (Zhou), zhuan; (Eastern Han) Cao Cao et al., zhu; (Contemporary) Yang Bing'an, jiaoli (周) 孫武, 撰; (東漢) 曹操等, 注; (近代) 楊丙安, 校理. *Shiyijia zhu, Sunzi jiaoli* 十一家注, 孫子校理. Beijing: Zhonghua shuju, 1999.

Zuo Qiuming (Zhou), zhuan; (Jin) Du Yu, zhu; (Tang) Kong Yingda, shu; (Qing) Ruan Yuan, jiaokanji (周) 左丘明, 撰; (晉) 杜預, 注; (唐) 孔穎達, 疏; (清) 阮元, 校勘記. *Chunqiu Zuo zhuan zhushu ji buzheng* 春秋左傳注疏及補正. Taipei: Shijie shuju, 1973.

———; (Three Kingdoms: Wu) Wei Zhao, zhu ———; (三國、吳) 韋昭, 注. *Guoyu* 國語. Taipei: Taiwan Zhonghua shuju, 1968.

WARRING STATES PERIOD 戰國時代 (475–221 BCE)

Han Fei (Warring States: Qin), zhuan; (Contemporary) Chen Qiyou, jishi (戰國、秦) 韓非, 撰; (近代) 陳奇猷, 集釋. *Hanfeizi (jishi)* 韓非子 (集釋). Taipei: Huazheng shuju, 1974.

———; (Qing) Wang Xianshen, jijie ———; (清) 王先慎, 集解. *Hanfeizi jijie* 韓非子集解. Taipei: Yiwen yinshuguan, 1974.

Xun Kuang (Warring States: Zhao), zhuan; (Tang) Yang Jing, zhu (戰國、趙) 荀況, 撰; (唐) 楊倞, 注. *Xunzi* 荀子. Taipei: Taiwan Zhonghua shuju, 1976.

Zhuang Zhou (Warring States: Song); (Qing) Xuan Ying, zhu; Wang Xianqian, jijie (戰國、宋) 莊周; (清) 宣穎, 注; 王先謙, 集解. *Zhuangzi* 莊子. Beijing: Zhonghua shuju, 1987.

QIN DYNASTY 秦代 (221–207 BCE)

Lü Buwei (Qin), zhuan; (Han) Gao You, xunjie (秦) 呂不韋, 撰; (漢) 高誘, 訓解. *Lüshi Chunqiu* 呂氏春秋. Taipei: Taiwan Zhonghua shuju, 1979.

Lülan 呂覽, see (Qin) Lü Buwei, zhuan: *Lüshi Chunqiu.*

HAN DYNASTY 漢代 (202 BCE–220 CE)

Ban Gu (Han), zhuan; (Three Kingdoms: Wei) Meng Kang, zhu; (Tang) Yan Shigu, zhu. (漢) 班固, 撰. (三國、魏) 孟康, 注; (唐) 顏師古, 注. *Han shu* 漢書. Taipei: Hongye shuju, 1984.

———; (Qing) Chen Li, zhushu ———; (清) 陳立, 注疏. *Baihutong* 白虎通. collected in (Qing) Ruan Yuan, bian

(清) 阮元, 編. *Huang Qing jingjie xubian* 皇清經解續編. Taipei: Hanjing wenhua, n.d.

Dai De (Han), zhuan; (Qing) Wang Pinzhen, jiegu (漢) 戴德, 傳; (清) 王聘珍, 解詁. *Da Dai Liji jiegu* 大戴禮記解詁. Taipei: Shijie shuju, 1974.

Gao You (Han), zhu (漢) 高誘, 注. *Zhanguo ce Gaoshi zhu* 戰國策高氏注. Taipei: Shijie shuju, 1975.

Gongyang Shou (Han), zhuan; (Han) He Xiu, jiegu; (Tang) Xu Yan, shu (漢) 公羊壽, 傳; (漢) 何休, 解詁; (唐) 徐彥, 疏. *Gongyang zhuan* 公羊傳. Taipei: Shijie shuju, 1970.

Heshang Gong (Han), zhangju; (Contemporary) Wang Ka, dianjiao (漢) 河上公, 章句; (近代) 王卡, 點校. *Laozi Dao De Jing Heshang Gong zhangju* 老子道德經河上公章句. Beijing: Zhonghua shudian, 1993.

Huainan, Lord of (Han) (a.k.a. Liu An), zhuan; (Han) Gao You, zhu (漢) 淮南王, 劉安, 撰; (漢) 高誘, 注. *Huainanzi* 淮南子. Taipei: Taiwan Zhonghua shuju, 1974.

Kong Anguo (Han), zhuan; (Tang) Kong Yingda, shu; (Qing) Ruan Yuan, jiaokan; (Qing) Jiao Xun, bushu (漢) 孔安國, 傳; (唐) 孔穎達, 疏; (清) 阮元, 校勘; (清) 焦循, 補疏. *Shangshu zhushu ji buzheng* 尚書注疏及補正. Taipei: Shijie shuju, 1973.

Liu Xi (Han), zhuan, see (Qing) Wang Xianqian, zhuan: *Shiming shuzheng bu.*

Ma Rong (Han); (Tang) Li Shan, zhu (漢) 馬融; (唐) 李善, 注. *Changdi fu* 長笛賦. collected in (Three Kingdoms) Xiao Tong (梁) 蕭統. *Zhaoming wenxuan* 昭明文選. Taipei: Qiming shuju, 1960.

Mao Heng (Han), zhuan; (Han) Zheng Xuan, jian; (Tang) Kong Yingda, shu (漢) 毛亨, 傳; (漢) 鄭玄, 箋; (唐) 孔應達, 疏. *Mao Shi zhushu* 毛詩注疏. Taipei: Shijie shuju, 1981.

Sima Qian (Han), zhuan; (Southern Dynasties) Pei Yin et al., zhu (漢) 司馬遷, 撰; (南朝) 裴駰等, 注. *Shiji* 史記. Taipei: Hongye shuju, 1980.

Wang Su, zhu 王肅, 注. *Kongzi jiayu* 孔子家語. Shu edition reproduction. Taipei, Zhonghua shuju, 1968.

Wang Yi (Han) (漢) 王逸. Chuci *zhangju* 《楚辭》章句. Taipei: Yiwen yinshuguan, 1974.

Xu Shen (Han); (Qing) Duan Yucai, zhu (漢) 許慎; (清) 段玉裁, 注. *Shuowen jiezi zhu* 說文解字注. Taipei: Shijie shuju, 1980.

Yan Zun (Han), zhuan; (Contemporary) Fan Bocheng, jiaojian (漢) 嚴遵, 撰; (近代) 樊波成, 校箋. *Laozi zhigui* 老子指歸. Shanghai: Guji tushushe, 2013.

Zhao Qi (Han), zhu; (Song) Sun Shi, shu; (Qing) Ruan Yuan, jiaokan (漢) 趙岐, 注; (宋) 孫奭, 疏; (清) 阮元, 校勘. *Mengzi zhushu ji buzheng* 孟子注疏及補正. Taipei: Shijie shuju, 1970.

Zheng Xuan (Han), zhu; (Tang) Jia Gongyan, shu (漢) 鄭玄, 注; (唐) 賈公彥, 疏. *Yili zhushu ji buzheng* 儀禮注疏及補正. Taipei: Shijie shuju, 1970.

———; ———; (Qing) Ruan Yuan, buzheng ———; ———; (清) 阮元, 補正. *Zhou Li zhushu ji buzheng* 周禮注疏及補正. Taipei: Shijie shuju, 1980.

———; ———. *Zhou Yi zhushu ji buzheng* 周易注疏及補正. Taipei: Shijie shuju, 1980.

———; (Tang) Kong Yingda, shu; (Qing) Ruan Yuan, jiaokan ———; (唐) 孔穎達, 疏; (清) 阮元, 校勘. *Liji zhushu ji buzheng* 禮記注疏及補正. Taipei: Shijie shuju, 1978.

THREE KINGDOMS 三國
(220–280)

He Yan (Three Kingdoms: Wei), jijie; (Southern Dynasties: Liang) Huang Kan, yishu (魏) 何晏, 集解; (梁) 皇侃, 義疏. *Lunyu jijie yishu* 論語集解義疏. Taipei: Shijie shuju, 1963.

———; (Song) Xing Bing, shu; (Qing) Ruan Yuan, jiaokan ———; (宋) 邢昺, 疏; (清) 阮元, 校勘. *Lunyu zhushu ji buzheng* 論語注疏及補正. Taipei: Shijie shuju, 1963.

Wang Bi (Three Kingdoms: Wei), zhuan; (Tang) Lu Deming, shiwen (魏) 王弼, 撰; (唐) 陸德明, 釋文. *Laozi Dao De Jing zhu* 老子道德經注. Taipei: Shijie shuju, 1966.

———; (Contemporary) Lou Yulie, jiaoshi ———; (近代) 樓宇烈, 校釋. *Laozi Dao De Jing zhu jiaoshi* 老子道德經注校釋. collected in *Wang Bi ji jiaoshi* 王弼集校釋. Beijing: Zhonghua shuju, 1980.

———; (Contemporary) Ishida Yoichiro, kanwu ———; (近代、日本) 石田羊一郎, 刊誤. *Laozi Wang Bi zhu* 老子王弼注. Taipei: Heluo tushu, 1974.

———; (Contemporary) Wang Zhiming, bian; Yan Lingfeng, jiaokan ———; (近代) 王志銘, 編; 嚴靈峰, 校勘. *Laozi weizhi lilue; Wang Bi zhu zongji* 老子微旨例略: 王弼注總輯. Taipei: Dongsheng chuban, 1980.

———; (Jin) Han Kangbo, zhu; (Tang) Kong Yingda, shu; (Qing) Ruan Yuan, jiaokan ———; (晉) 韓康伯, 注; (唐) 孔穎達, 疏; (清) 阮元, 校勘. *Zhou Yi zhushu ji buzheng* 周易注疏及補正. Taipei: Shijie shuju, 1978.

Xiao Tong (Three Kingdoms: Liang), bianxuan; (Tang) Li Shan, zhu (梁) 蕭統, 編選; (唐) 李善, 注. *Zhaoming wenxuan* 昭明文選. Taipei: Qiming shuju, 1960.

Zhang Yi (Three Kingdoms: Wei), zhuan; (Qing) Wang Niansun, shuzheng (魏) 張揖, 撰; (清) 王念孫, 疏證. *Guangya shuzheng* 廣雅疏證.

3 vols. Taipei: Taiwan Zhonghua shuju, 1970.

JIN DYNASTY 晉代
(266–420)

Guo Pu (Jin), zhu; (Song) Xing Bing, shu; (Qing) Ruan Yuan, jiaokan (晉) 郭璞, 注; (宋) 邢昺, 疏; (清) 阮元, 校勘. *Erya zhushu ji buzheng* 爾雅注疏及補正. Taipei: Shijie shuju, 1973.

Guo Xiang, zhu (晉) 郭象, 注. *Zhuangzi* 莊子. Taipei: Zhonghua shuju, 1969.

Zhang Zhan (Jin), zhu (晉) 張湛, 注. *Liezi* 列子. Taipei: Zhonghua shuju, 1979.

NORTHERN AND SOUTHERN DYNASTIES 南北朝
(420–589)

Gu Yeyu (Southern Dynasties: Chen), zhuan; Guoli zhongyang tushuguan, Guozi zhengli xiaozu, bian (南朝、陳) 顧野玉, 撰; 國立中央圖書館, 國字整理小組, 編. *Yupian* 玉篇. Taipei: Guoli zhongyang tushuguan, n.d.

——; ——. *Yupian lingjuan (Riben jiuchao juanziben)* 玉篇零卷 (日本舊鈔卷子本). Taipei: Guoli zhongyang tushuguan, n.d.

SUI DYNASTY 隋代
(581–618)

Lu Fayan (Sui), zhuan; (Song) Chen Pengnian et al., chongxiu (隋) 陸法言, 撰; (宋) 陳彭年等, 重修. *Jiaozheng Songben Guangyun* 校正宋本廣韻. Taipei: Yiwen yinshuguan, 1984.

TANG DYNASTY 唐代
(618–907)

Huiyuan, Monk (Tang), shu (唐) 沙門慧苑, 述. *Buding xinyi Dafangguang Fo Huayanjing yinyi* 補訂新譯大方廣佛華嚴經音義. Taipei: Xinwenfeng chubangongsi, 1973.

Li Dingzuo (Tang), zhuan (唐) 李鼎祚, 撰. *Zhou Yi jijie* 周易集解. 2nd ed. Taipei: Shijie shuju, 1978.

Lu Deming (Tang), zhuan; (Qing) Lu Wenshao, jiao (唐) 陸德明, 撰; (清) 盧文弨, 校. *Jingdian shiwen: Laozi yinyi* 經典釋文: 老子音義. Taipei: Hanjing wenhua, 1980.

——; ——. *Jingdian shiwen: Shijing yinyi* 經典釋文: 詩經音義. Taipei: Hanjing wenhua, 1980.

——; ——. *Jingdian shiwen: Yijing yinyi* 經典釋文: 易經音義. Taipei: Hanjing wenhua, 1980.

Xu Lingfu, zhu 徐靈府, 注. *Wenzi (Tong Xuan zhenjing)* 文子 (通玄真經). Taipei: Shijie shuju, 1966.

Xuanzong Emperor (Tang) (唐) 玄宗. *Yuzhu Dao De zhen Jing* 御注道德真經. Taipei: Ziyou chubanshe, 1979.

Yin Zhizhang (Tang), zhu; (Qing) Dai Wang, jiaozheng 尹知章, 注; (清) 戴望, 校正. *Guanzi jiaozheng* 管子校正. Taipei: Shijie shuju, 1985.

Yuanying, Monk (Tang) (a.k.a. Xuanying), zhuan (唐) 釋元應 (玄應), 撰. *Yiqiejing yinyi* 一切經音義. Taipei: Xinwenfeng chubangongsi, 1973.

SONG DYNASTY 宋代
(960–1279)

Bo Yuchan (Song) (宋) 白玉蟾. *Dao De Jing baozhang zhu* 道德經寶章註. Taipei: Ziyou chubanshe, 1979.

Ding Du (Song) et al., bian (宋) 丁度等, 編. *Jiyun* 集韻. 2 vols. Taipei: Xuehai chubanshe, 1986.

Fan Yingyuan (Song) (宋) 范應元. *Laozi Dao De Jing guben jizhu* 老子道德經古本集註. 2 vols. Taipei: Yiwen yinshuguan, n.d.

Huizong Emperor (Song) (宋) 徽宗. *Yuzhu Dao De zhen Jing jieyi* 御注道德真經解義. Taipei: Ziyou chubanshe, 1979.

Li Jiamou (Song), zhu (宋) 李嘉謀, 注. collected in (Ming) Jiao Hong (明) 焦竑. *Laozi yi* 老子翼.

Lin Xiyi (Song) (宋) 林希逸. *Dao De zhen Jing zhu* 道德真經註. Taipei: Ziyou chubanshe, 1979.

Lü Jifu (Song), zhu (宋) 呂吉甫, 註. collected in (Ming) Jiao Hong (明) 焦竑. *Laozi yi* 老子翼.

Su Che (Song), zhu (宋) 蘇轍, 注. collected in (Contemporary) Xiao Tianshi, zhubian (近代) 蕭天石, 主編. *Dao De Jing mingzhu xuanji* 道德經名注選集. V2.

Wang Jiefu (Song) (a.k.a. Wang Anshi) (宋) 王介甫 (王安石). *Laozi zhu, yiwen* 老子註, 佚文. collected in (Contemporary) Meng Wentong (近代) 蒙文通. *Daoshu jijiao shizhong* 道書輯校十種.

Xu Kai (Song) (宋) 徐鍇. *Shuowen xizhuan* 說文繫傳. collected in (Contemporary) Ding Fubao, zhubian (近代) 丁福保, 主編. *Shuowen jiezi gulin zhengbu hebian* 說文解字詁林正補合編.

Zhang An (Song), zhuanyi (宋) 章安, 撰義. collected in (Song) Huizong Emperor (宋) 徽宗. *Yuzhu Dao De zhen Jing jieyi* 御注道德真經解義.

Zhu Xi (Song), zhuan (宋) 朱熹, 撰. *Mengzi jizhu* 孟子集注. *Sishu zhangju jizhu* 四書章句集注. Beijing: Zhonghua shuju, 1983.

———. *Shijing jizhuan* 詩經集傳. Taipei: Shijie shuju, 1969.

YUAN DYNASTY 元代
(1271–1368)

Wu Cheng (Yuan), zhu (元) 吳澄, 注. *Dao De Jing zhu (Zhuzi huiyaoben)* 道德經注 (諸子薈要本). Taipei: Guangwen shuju, 1989.

MING DYNASTY 明代
(1368–1644)

Deqing, Monk (Ming) (a.k.a. Hanshan), zhu (明) 釋 德清 (憨山), 注. collected in (Contemporary) Xiao Tianshi, zhubian (近代) 蕭天石, 主編. *Dao De Jing mingzhu xuanji* 道德經名注選集. V5.

Gong Xiumo (Ming), zhu (明) 龔修默, 注. collected in (Contemporary) Xiao Tianshi, zhubian (近代) 蕭天石, 主編. *Dao De Jing mingzhu xuanji* 道德經名注選集. V4.

Gui Youguang (Ming), zhu (明) 歸有光, 注. collected in (Contemporary) Xiao Tianshi, zhubian (近代) 蕭天石, 主編. *Dao De Jing mingzhu xuanji* 道德經名注選集. V5.

Jiao Hong (Ming) (明) 焦竑. *Laozi yi* 老子翼. Taipei: Guangwen shuju, 1962.

Lu Xixing (Ming), zhu (明) 陸西星, 注. collected in (Contemporary) Xiao Tianshi, zhubian (近代) 蕭天石, 主編. *Dao De Jing mingzhu xuanji* 道德經名注選集. V6.

Taizu Emperor (Ming), zhu (明) 太祖, 注. in (Contemporary) Xiao Tianshi, zhubian (近代) 蕭天石, 主編. *Dao De Jing mingzhu xuanji* 道德經名注選集. V4.

Wang Fuzhi (Ming) (明) 王夫之. *Shuowen guangyi* 說文廣義. collected in Wang Fuzhi, *Chuanshan quanshu* 船山全書. V9. Changsha: Yuelu shuju, 1989, 1996.

———. *Laozi yan* 老子衍. in (Contemporary) Xiao Tianshi, zhubian (近代) 蕭天石, 主編. *Dao De Jing mingzhu xuanji* 道德經名注選集. V6.

———. *Liji zhangju* 禮記章句. Changsha: Yuelu shuju, 1991.

Xue Hui (Ming) (明) 薛蕙. collected in (Contemporary) Xiao Tianshi, zhubian (近代) 蕭天石, 主編. *Dao De Jing mingzhu xuanji* 道德經名注選集. V4.

Zhang Wei (Ming), zhuan (明) 張位, 撰. *Laozi zhujie* 老子註解. Taipei: Ziyou chubanshe, 1979.

Zhang Zilie (Ming), bian; (Qing) Liao Wenying, bu (明) 張自烈, 編; (清) 廖文英, 補. *Zhengzi tong* 正字通. Beijing: Guoji wenhua chubangongsi, 1996.

Zhu Dezhi (Ming) (明) 朱得之. *Laozi tongyi* 老子通義. collected in (Contemporary) Xiao Tianshi, zhubian (近代) 蕭天石, 主編. *Dao De Jing mingzhu xuanji* 道德經名注選集. V5.

QING DYNASTY 清代
(1644–1911)

Dai Zhen (Qing), shu (清) 戴震, 疏. *Fangyan shuzheng* 放言疏証. Taipei: Taiwan Zhonghua shuju, 1974.

Dong Zengling (Qing) (清) 董增齡. *Guoyu zhengyi* 國語正義. Kyoto: Chūbun shubbansha, 1980.

Gui Fu (Qing) (清) 桂馥. *Shuowen jiezi yizheng* 說文解字義證. Jinan: Qilu shushe, 1987.

Guo Qingfan (Qing), bianshi (清) 郭慶藩, 編釋. *Zhuangzi jishi* 莊子集釋. includes (Jin) Guo Xiang, zhu; (Tang) Cheng Xuanying, shu (晉) 郭象, 注; (唐) 成玄英, 疏. Taipei: Heluo tushu, 1974.

Hu Chenggong (Qing), zhuan (清) 胡承珙, 撰. *Xiao Erya yizheng* 小爾雅義證. Taipei: Taiwan Zhonghua shuju, 1979.

Jiang Sheng (Qing) (清) 江聲. *Shangshu jizhu yinshu* 尚書集注音疏. collected in (Qing) Ruan Yuan, bian (清) 阮元, 編. *Huang Qing jingjie xubian* 皇清經解續編.

Liu Qi (Qing) (清) 劉淇. *Zhuzi bianlue* 助字辨略. 7th ed. Taipei: Taiwan kaiming shudian, 1958, 1979.

Ma Jianzhong (Qing), zhuan; (Contemporary) Lü Shuxian, Wang Haifen, bian (清) 馬建忠, 撰; (近代) 呂叔湘, 王海棻, 編. *Mashi wentong duben* 馬氏文通讀本. Shanghai: Jiaoyu chubanshe, 2000.

Qian Yi (Qing), zhuan (清) 錢繹, 撰. *Fangyan jianshu* 方言箋疏. collected in *Han xiaoxue sizhong* 漢小學四種. 2 vols. Chengdu: Bashu shushe, 2001.

Ruan Yuan (Qing), bian (清) 阮元, 編. *Huang Qing jingjie xubian* 皇清經解續編. Taipei: Hanjing wenhua, n.d.

———. *Liji zhushu jiaokanji* 禮記注疏校勘記. collected in proofreading on (Han) Zheng Xuan, zhu 鄭玄, 注. *Liji zhushu ji buzheng* 禮記注疏及補正.

———. *Shijing zhushu jiaokanji* 詩經注疏校勘記. collected in proofreading on (Han) Mao Heng, zhuan 毛亨, 傳. *Shijing zhushu ji buzheng* 詩經注疏及補正.

———. *Yijing zhushu jiaokanji* 易經注疏校勘記. collected in proofreading on (Three Kingdoms) Wang Bi 王弼. *Zhou Yi zhushu ji buzheng* 周易注疏及補正.

Shizu Emperor (Qing), zhu (清) 世祖, 註. *Yuzhu Dao De Jing* 御註道德經. Taipei: Ziyou chubanshe, 1979.

Song Changxing (Qing), zhu (清) 宋常星, 注. collected in (Contemporary) Xiao Tianshi, zhubian. (近代) 蕭天石, 主編. *Dao De Jing mingzhu xuanji* 道德經名注選集. V7.

Wang Pinzhen (Qing), zhuan (清) 王聘珍, 撰. *Da Dai Liji jiegu* 大戴禮記解詁. Taipei: Shijie shuju, 1974.

Wang Xianqian (Qing), zhuan (清) 王先謙, 撰. *Shiming shuzheng bu* 釋名疏証補. annotations to (Han) Liu Xi, zhuan (漢) 劉熙, 撰. *Shiming* 釋名. Shanghai: Shanghai guji chubanshe, 1984.

———. *Zhuangzi jijie* 莊子集解. Beijing: Zhonghua shuju, 1987.

Wang Yinzhi (Qing) (清) 王引之. *Jingzhuan shici* 經傳釋詞. Hong Kong: Shijie tushu gongsi, 1975.

———. *Jingyi shuwen* 經義述聞. collected in (Qing) Ruan Yuan, bian (清) 阮元, 編. *Huang Qing jingjie* 皇清經解續編. No. 18, V19. Taipei: Hanjing wenhua, n.d.

Wang Yun (Qing) (清) 王筠. *Shuowen shili* 說文釋例. Taipei: Shijie shuju, 1969.

———. *Shuowen judou* 說文句讀. Beijing: Zhonghua shuju, 1988.

Wei Yuan (Qing) (清) 魏源. *Laozi benyi* 老子本義. Taipei: Shijie shuju, 1966.

Wu Changying (Qing) (清) 吳昌瑩. *Jingci yanshi* 經詞衍釋. Taipei: Chengwei chubanshe, 1975.

Xu Hao (Qing) (清) 徐灝. *Shuowen Xu jian* 說文徐箋. collected in (Contemporary) Ding Fubao, zhubian (近代) 丁福保, 主編. *Shuowenjiezi gulin zhengbu hebian* 說文解字詁林正補合編.

Yao Nai (Qing), zhu (清) 姚鼐, 注. collected in (Contemporary) Xiao Tianshi, zhubian. (近代) 蕭天石, 主編. *Dao De Jing mingzhu xuanji* 道德經名注選集. V7.

Zheng Huan (Qing), zhu (清) 鄭環, 注. *Laozi benyi* 老子本義. collected in (Contemporary) Xiao Tianshi, zhubian. (近代) 蕭天石, 主編. *Dao De Jing mingzhu xuanji* 道德經名注選集. V7.

Zhu Junsheng (Qing) (清) 朱駿聲. *Shuowen tongxun dingsheng* 說文通訓定聲. Taipei: Yiwen yinshuguan, 1975.

CONTEMPORARY 近代
(1911–PRESENT)

Ames, Roger T., and David L. Hall (Contemporary), trans. *Daodejing: "Making This Life Significant."* New York: Ballantine, 2003.

Cai Hong (Contemporary) (近代) 蔡宏. *Bore yu Lao Zhuang* 般若與老莊. Chengdu: Bashu shushe, 2001.

Chan, Wing-tsit, trans. and comp. *A Source Book in Chinese Philosophy*. Princeton: Princeton University Press, 1963, 1973.

Chang, Hsiu-chen (Contemporary). "On the Historicity of the *Tao Te Ching*," *Comparative Literature Studies*. Penn State University Press, 35, 2 (1998): 146–73.

Chen Guying (Contemporary), zhubian (近代) 陳鼓應, 主編. *Huangdi sijing jinzhu jinyi* 黃帝四經今注今譯. Beijing: Shangwu yinshuguan, 2007.

———, zhuyi 註譯. *Laozi jinzhu jinyi* 老子今註今譯. Taipei: Shangwu yinshuguan, 2001.

———, Bai Xi ———, 白奚. *Laozi pingzhuan* 老子評傳. Taipei: Wenshizhe chubanshe, 2002.

Chen Ligui (Contemporary) (近代) 陳麗桂. *Zhanguo shiqi de Huang Lao sixiang* 戰國時期的黃老思想. Taipei: Lianjing chuban shiye gongsi, 1991.

Chen Qitian (Contemporary), bian (近代) 陳啟天, 編. *Hanfeizi jiaoshi (xiuding)* 韓非子校釋 (修訂). Taipei: Shangwu yinshuguan, 1994.

Chen Qiyou (Contemporary) (近代) 陳奇猷. *Hanfeizi jishi* 韓非子集釋. Taipei: Huazheng shuju, 1974.

Chen Wenying (Contemporary) (近代) 陳文英. *Zhongguo gudai Han chuan Fojiao chuanbo shilun* 中國古代漢傳佛教傳播史論. Tianjin: Tianjin guji chubanshe, 2007.

Chen Zhu (Contemporary), zhuanzhu (近代) 陳柱, 撰註. *Laozi* 老子. Taipei: Taiwan shangwu yinshuguan, 1970, 1986.

———. *Laozi Hanshi shuo* 老子韓氏說. Taipei: Xinan shuju, 1979.

Cheng Man-jan (Contemporary) (a.k.a. Zheng Manran), zhu (近代) 鄭曼髯, 註. *Laozi yizhi jie* 老子易知解. Taipei: Taiwan zhonghua shuju, 1971.

———; Tam C. Gibbs, trans. *Lao-tzu: "My Words Are Very Easy to Understand."* Richmond, CA: North Atlantic Books, 1981.

Cheng Shude (Contemporary), zhuan (近代) 程樹德, 撰. *Lunyu jishi* 論語集釋. Beijing: Zhonghua shuju, 1990.

Deng Qiubo (Contemporary) (近代) 鄧柏. *Boshu Zhou Yi jiaoshi* 帛書周易校釋. Changsha: Hunan chubanshe, 1996.

Ding Fubao (Contemporary), zhubian (近代) 丁福保, 主編. *Shuowenjiezi gulin zhengbu hebian* 說文解字詁林正補合編. 12 vols. Taipei: Dingwen shuju, 1983.

Ding Yuanming (Contemporary) (近代) 丁原明. *Huang Lao xue lunwang* 黃老學論綱. Jinan: Shandong daxue chubanshe, 2000.

Dong Enlin (Contemporary) (近代) 董恩林. *Tangdai Laoxue: zhongxuan sibianzhong de lishen liguo zhi Dao* 唐代老學: 重玄思辨中的理身理國之道. doctoral dissertation. Beijing: Zhongguo shehuikexue chubanshe, 2002.

———. *Tangdai* Laozi *quanshi wenxian yanjiu* 唐代《老子》詮釋文獻研究. Jinan: Jilu shushe, 2003.

Du Shanmu (Contemporary) (近代) 杜善牧. *Lao Zhuang sixiang yu xifang zhexue* 老莊思想與西方哲學. Taipei: Sanmin shuju, 1968.

Durant, Will (Contemporary). *Our Oriental Heritage: The Story of Civilization, Volume I.* New York: Simon and Schuster, 1954.

Fan Shoukang (Contemporary) (近代) 范壽康. *Zhongguo zhexueshi gangyao* 中國哲學史綱要. Taipei: Taiwan kaiming shudian, 1964, 1982.

Feng Dafu (Contemporary), zhuan (近代) 馮達甫, 撰. *Laozi yizhu* 老子譯注. Shanghai: Shanghai guji chubanshe, 1991, 1996.

Fung Yu-lan (a.k.a. Feng Youlan) (Contemporary) (近代) 馮友蘭. *Sansongtang quanji, dierjuan* 三松堂全集, 第二卷. Zhengzhou: Henan renmin chubanshe, 2000.

———. *Zhongguo zhexueshi* 中國哲學史. 2 vols. Taiwan: n.p., n.d.

Gao Heng (Contemporary) (近代) 高亨. *Laozi zhenggu* 老子正詁. Taipei: Taiwan kaiming shudian, 1973.

Goldin, Paul R. (Contemporary). *After Confucius: Studies in Early Chinese Philosophy.* Honolulu: University of Hawai'i Press, 2005.

Gu Baotian (Contemporary), Zhang Zhongli (近代) 顧寶田, 張忠利. *Xinyi Laozi Xiang'er zhu* 新譯老子想爾註. Taipei: Sanmin chushu, 1997.

Gu Di (Contemporary), Zhou Ying (近代) 古棣, 周英. *Laozi tong* 老子通. 2 vols. Changchun: Jilin renmin chubanshe, 1991.

Guo Dingtang (Contemporary) (a.k.a. Guo Moruo) (近代) 郭鼎堂 (郭沫若). *Xian Qin tiandaoguan zhi jinzhan* 先秦天道觀之進展. Taipei: Shangwu yinshuguan, 1936.

Guo Xiliang (Contemporary) (近代) 郭錫良. *Hanzi guyin shouce* 漢字古音手冊. Beijing: Beijing daxue, 1986.

He Changqun (Contemporary) et al. (近代) 賀昌群等. *Wei Jin sixiang* 魏晉思想. Taipei: Liren shuju, 1984.

He Ning (Contemporary), jishi (近代) 何寧, 集釋. *Huainanzi jishi* 淮南子集釋. 3 vols. Beijing: Zhonghua shuju, 1998.

Hu Daojing (Contemporary), zhubian (近代) 胡道靜, 主編. *Shijia lun Lao* 十家論老. Shanghai: Shanghai renmin chubanshe, 2006.

Huang Huaixin (Contemporary), zhuan (近代) 黃懷信, 撰. *Xiao Erya huijiao jishi* 小爾雅匯校集釋. Xi'an: San Qin chubanshe, 2002.

———; Kong Deli, Zhou Haisheng, canzhuan. ———; 孔德立, 周海生, 參撰. *Da Dai Liji huijiao jizhu* 大戴禮記彙校集注. Xi'an: San Qin chubanshe, 2004.

Huang, J. H. (Contemporary) (a.k.a. Huang Zhuhua 黃柱華), trans., ed., and comm. *The Art of War (Sun-tzu).* HarperCollins Modern Perennial Classics. New York: HarperCollins, 2008.

Huang Kan (Contemporary), pijiao (近代) 黃侃, 批校. *Huang Kan shoupi Guangyun* 黃侃手批廣韻. Beijing: Zhonghua shuju, 2006.

Huang Luping (Contemporary) (近代) 黃魯平. *Hanyu wenyan yufa gangyao* 漢語文言語法綱要. Taipei: Huazheng shuju, 1974.

Jaspers, Karl (Contemporary); Hannah Arendt, ed.; Ralph Manheim, trans. *Anaximander, Heraclitus, Parmenides, Plotinus, Lao-Tzu, Nagarjuna. The Great Philosophers: The Original Thinkers, V2.* New York: Harcourt Brace Jovanovich, 1966.

Jiang Xichang (Contemporary) (近代) 蔣錫昌. *Laozi jiaogu* 老子校詁. Taipei: Dongsheng wenhua, 1980.

Kanaya Osamu (Contemporary) (近代、日本) 金谷治. *Rōshi* 老子. Tokyo: Kōdansha Ltd., 1997.

Kim Seong-Han (Contemporary) (近代、韓) 金晟煥. *Huang Lao Dao tanyuan* 黃老道探源. Beijing: Zhongguo shehuixue chubanshe, 2008.

Ko Yosui (Contemporary), zhuan (近代、日本) 安井衡, 撰. *Zuo zhuan jishi* 左傳輯釋. Taipei: Guangwen shuju, 1967.

Li Disheng (Contemporary) (近代) 李滌生. *Xunzi jishi* 荀子集釋. Taipei: Xuesheng shuju, 2000.

Li Dingshen (Contemporary), Xu Huijun, jiaoshi 李定生, 徐慧君 (近代), 校釋. *Wenzi jiaoshi* 文子校釋. includes annotations by (Tang) Xu Lingfu (唐) 徐靈府. Shanghai: Shanghai guji chubanshe, 2004.

Li Xueqin (Contemporary), Ge Zhaoguang, and Hachiya Kunio, zhubian (近代) 李學勤, 葛兆光, 蜂屋邦夫, 主編. *Daojia sixiang yu Fojiao* 道家思想與佛教. Shenyang: Liaoning jiaoyu chubanshe, 2000.

Li Zhenhua (Contemporary), Zhou Changji, bianzhuan (近代) 李珍華, 周長輯, 編撰. *Hanzi gujin yinbiao (xiudingben)* 漢字古今音表 (修訂本). Beijing: Zhonghua shuju, 1999.

Liang Qichao (Contemporary) (近代) 梁啟超. *Foxue yanjiu bashipian* 佛學研究八十篇. Taipei: Zhonghua shuju, 1936, 1966.

Liang Qixiong (Contemporary) (近代) 梁啟雄. *Hanzi qianjie* 韓子淺解. Taipei: Xuesheng shuju, 1984.

Liu Xiaogan (Contemporary) (近代) 劉笑敢. "'*Fanxiang geyi*' *yu Zhongguo zhexue yanjiu de kunjing—yi Laozi zhi Dao de quanshi wei li*" "'反向格義' 與中國哲學研究的困境—以老子之道的詮釋為例." *Journal of Nanjing University (Philosophy, Humanities and Social Sciences).* 2006: 76–90.

———. *Laozi gujin* 老子古今. Beijing: Zhongguo shehuikexue chubanshe, 2006.

Lü Shuxiang (Contemporary) (近代) 呂叔湘. *Zhongguo wenfa yaolue* 中國文法要略. Taipei: Wenshizhe chubanshe, 1974.

Lu Yusan (Contemporary) (近代) 盧育三. *Laozi shiyi* 老子釋義. Tianjin: Guji chubanshe, 1987.

Ma Xulun (Contemporary) (近代) 馬敘倫. *Laozi jiaogu* 老子校詁. Beijing: Zhonghua shuju, 1974.

Meng Wentong (Contemporary) (近代) 蒙文通. *Daoshu jijiao shizhong* 道書輯校十種. Chengdu: Bashu shushe, 2001.

Ōhama Akira (Contemporary); Li Junshi, trans. (近代、日本) 大濱皓; 李君奭, 譯. *Laozi de zhexue* 老子的哲學. Taipei: Zhuanxin qiye, 1974.

Pan Ping (Contemporary), Ming Lizhi, bian (近代) 潘平, 明立志, 編. *Hu Shi shuo Chan* 胡適說禪. Taipei: Jiuyi chuban, 1995.

Pei Xuehai (Contemporary) (近代) 裴學海. *Gushu xuzi jishi* 古書虛字集釋. Taipei: Chengwei chubanshe, 1975.

Qing Xitai (Contemporary), zhubian (近代) 卿希泰, 主編. *Zhongguo Daojiao (1)* 中國道教 (一). Shanghai: Dongfang chuban zhongxin, 1994, 1996.

Qu Wanli (Contemporary) (近代) 屈萬里. *Shangshu jishi* 尚書集釋. Taipei: Lianjing chuban shiye gongsi, 1983.

———. *Shangshu jinzhu jinyi* 尚書今註今譯. 8th ed. Taipei: Shangwu yinshuguan, 1979.

———. *Shangshu shiyi* 尚書釋義. Taipei: Zhongguo wenhua daxue chubanbu, 1980.

Rao Zongyi (Contemporary) (近代) 饒宗頤. *Laozi Xiang'er zhu jiaozheng* 老子想爾注校證. Shanghai: Guji chubanshe, 1991.

Ren Jiyu (Contemporary), zhubian (近代) 任繼愈, 主編. *Zhongguo zhexue fazhanshi* 中國哲學發展史. 3 vols. Beijing: Renmin chubanshe, 1998.

Rong Zhaozu (Contemporary) (近代) 容肇祖. *Wei Jin de ziranzhuyi* 魏晉的自然主義. Taipei: Taiwan yinshuguan, 1970, 1980.

Suzuki, Daisetz Teitaro (Contemporary). *Essays in Zen Buddhism (First Series)*. New York: Grove Weidenfeld, 1949, 1961.

Takeuchi Yoshio (Contemporary), zhuan; Jiang Xia'an, trans. (近代、日本) 武內義雄, 撰; 江俠菴, 譯. *Laozi yuanshi* 老子原始. Taipei: Yiwen yinshuguan, n.d.

Tang Junyi (Contemporary) (近代) 唐君毅. *Zhongguo zhexue yuanlun* 中國哲學原論. Taipei: Taiwan xuesheng shuju, 1986, 1993.

Tang Yijie (Contemporary) (近代) 湯一介. *Guo Xiang yu Wei Jin Xuanxue* 郭象與魏晉玄學. Beijing: Beijing daxue chubanshe, 2000.

———. *Wei Jin Nanbeichao shiqi de Daojiao* 魏晉南北朝時期的道教. Taipei: Dongda chuban, 1988, 1991.

Tang Yongtong (Contemporary) (近代) 湯用彤. *Lixue, Foxue, Xuanxue* 理學、佛學、玄學. Beijing: Beijing daxue, 1991.

Wang Hui (Contemporary) (近代) 王輝. *Gu wenzi tongjia shili* 古文字通假釋例. Taipei: Yiwen yinshuguan, 1993.

Wang Li (Contemporary), zhubian (近代) 王力, 主編. *Gudai Hanyu* 古代漢語. Hong Kong: Zhongwai chubanshe, 1976.

———. *Tongyuan zidian* 同源字典. Beijing: Shangwu yinshuguan, 1982.

———, zhubian 主編. *Zhongguo yuyanxue shi* 中國語言學史. Shanxi: Shanxi renmin chubanshe, 1981.

———, ———; Ma Hanlin, Guo Xiliang, Zhu Minche, zhuan ———; 馬漢麟、郭錫良、祝敏徹, 撰. *Gu Hanyu tonglun* 古漢語通論. Hong Kong: Zhongwai chubanshe, 1976.

Wang Liqi (Contemporary) (近代) 王利器. "*Dao cangben* Dao De zhenjing zhigui tiyao." "道藏本《道德真經指歸》提要." collected in *Wang Liqi lunxue zazhu* 王利器論學雜著. Taipei: Guanya wenhua, 1992.

Wang Meng'ou (Contemporary) (近代) 王夢鷗. *Liji jinzhu jinyi* 禮記今注今譯. Taipei: Shangwu yinshuguan, 1980.

Wang Pei (Contemporary) (近代) 王沛. *Huang Lao "fa" lilun yuanliu kao* 黃老"法"理論源流考. Shanghai: Shanghai renmin chubanshe, 2009.

Wang Shumin (Contemporary) (近代) 王叔岷. *Guji xuzi guangyi* 古籍虛字廣義. Taipei: Huazheng shuju, 1990.

———. *Xian Qin Dao fa sixiang jianggao* 先秦道法思想講稿. Taipei: Academia Sinica, 1992.

———. *Zhuangzi jiaoquan* 莊子校詮. 3 vols. Taipei: Academia Sinica, 1988, 1999.

Wang Tianhai (Contemporary), jiaoshi (近代) 王天海, 校釋. *Xunzi jiaoshi* 荀子校釋. Shanghai: Guji chubanshe, 2005.

Wang Xiaoyu (Contemporary), shuzheng (近代) 王孝魚, 疏証. *Laozi yan shuzheng* 老子衍疏証. Beijing: Zhonghua shuju, 2014.

Wang Yousan (Contemporary) (近代) 王有三. *Laozi kao* 老子考. Taipei: Dongsheng chuban shiye youxiangongsi, 1982.

Watts, Alan W. (Contemporary). *The Way of Zen.* New York: Pantheon, 1957–58.

Weber, Max (Contemporary); Wang Rongfen, trans. 馬克斯·韋伯; 王容芬, 譯. *Rujiao yu Daojiao* 儒教與道教. (*Konfuziamismus und Taoismus*). Beijing: Shangwu yinshuguan, 1995.

Woo Kang (Contemporary) (a.k.a. Wu Kang) (近代) 吳康. *Lao Zhuang zhexue* 老莊哲學. Taipei: Taiwan shangwu yinshuguan, 1951.

Wu Yi (Contemporary) (近代) 吳怡. *Chan yu Lao Zhuang* 禪與老莊. Taipei: Sanmin shuju, 1970.

Wu Yujiang (Contemporary), zhuan 吳毓江, 撰. *Mozi jiaozhu* 墨子校注. Beijing: Zhonghua shuju, 1993.

———; Sun Qizhi, dianjiao ———; 孫啟治, 點校. *Mozi jiaozhu* 墨子校注. Beijing: Zhonghua shuju, 1993.

Xi Tong (Contemporary) (近代) 奚侗. *Laozi jijie* 老子集解. Taipei: Yiwen yinshuguan, n.d.

Xiao Tianshi (Contemporary), zhubian 蕭天石, 主編. *Dao De Jing mingzhu xuanji* 道德經名注選集. 7 vols. Taipei: Ziyou chubanshe, 1979.

Xiao Xu (Contemporary) (近代) 蕭旭. *Gushu xuci pangshi* 古書虛詞旁釋. Yangzhou: Guangling shushe, 2007.

Xing Wen (Contemporary) (近代) 邢文. *Zhu hu zhu bo: Zhongguo gudai sixiang yu xuepai* 著乎竹帛: 中國古代思想與學派. (*Written on Bamboo and Silk: Thought and Schools in Early China*). Taipei: Laitai chubanshe, 2005.

Xiong Tieji (Contemporary) et al. (近代) 熊鐵基等. *Zhongguo Laoxue shi* 中國老學史. Fuzhou: Fujian renmin chubanshe, 1995, 1997.

Xu Fu (Contemporary), zhubian (近代) 徐復, 主編. *Guangya gulin* 廣雅詁林. Nanjing: Jiangsu guji chubanshe, 1998.

Xu Fuguan (Contemporary) (近代) 徐復觀. *Zhongguo renxinglun shi (xian Qin pian)* 中國人性論史 (先秦篇). Taipei: Taiwan shangwu yinshuguan, 1994.

Xu Weiyu (Contemporary), jishi 許維遹, 集釋. *Lüshi Chunqiu jishi* 呂氏春秋集釋. Taipei: Shijie shuju, 1958.

Yan Fu (Contemporary), pingdian (近代) 嚴復, 評點. *Pingdian Laozi Dao De Jing* 評點老子道德經. Taipei: Guangwen shuju, 1970.

Yan Lingfeng (Contemporary), jijiao (近代) 嚴靈峰, 輯校. *Laozi Song zhu congcan* 老子宋注叢殘. Taipei: Taiwan xuesheng shuju, 1979.

———. *Laozi chongning wuzhu* 老子崇寧五注. Taipei: Chengwen chubanshe, 1979.

Yanagita Seizan (Contemporary); Wu Rujun, trans. (近代、日本) 柳田聖山; 吳汝鈞, 譯. *Zhongguo Chan sixiang shi* 中國禪思想史. Taipei: Shangwu yinshuguan, 1980.

Yang Bojun (Contemporary) (近代) 楊伯峻. *Chunqiu Zuo zhuan zhu (xiudingben)* 春秋左傳注 (修訂本). Beijing: Xin Hua shudian, 1990.

———. *Gu Hanyu xuci* 古漢語虛詞. Beijing: Zhonghua shuju, 1981.

Yang Shuda (Contemporary) (近代) 楊樹達. *Ciquan* 詞詮. Taipei: Shangwu yinshuguan, 1929, 1977.

Yang Wei (Contemporary), zhubian (近代) 楊薇, 主編. *Erya gulin jingwen ciyu suoyin* 爾雅詁林經文詞語索引. Wuhan: Hubei jiaoyu chubanshe, 1999.

Yang Zongyi (Contemporary), bian (近代) 楊宗義, 編. *Bei Song* Laozi *zhu yanjiu* 北宋《老子》注研究. Chengdu: Sichuan chuban jituan, 2004.

Yin Shun, Dharma Master (Contemporary) (近代) 印順 導師. *Zhongguo Chanzong shi* 中國禪宗史. Taichung: Dharma Master Yin Shun, 1971.

Yu Mingguang (Contemporary) (近代) 余明光. *Huangdi sijing yu Huang Lao sixiang* 黃帝四經與黃老思想. Harbin: Heilongjiang renmin chubanshe, 1989.

Zang Kehe (Contemporary) (近代) 臧克和. *Shangshu wenzi jiaogu* 尚書文字校詁. Shanghai: Jiaoyu chubanshe, 1999.

Zhan Jianfeng (Contemporary) (近代) 詹劍峰. *Laozi qi ren qi shu ji qi Daolun* 老子其人其書及其道論. Wuhan: Huazhong shifan daxue chubanshe, 2006.

Zhang Chunyi (Contemporary), zhuanzhu (近代) 張純一, 撰註. *Zhuzi Qinghualu shibazhong* 諸子菁華錄十八種. Taipei: Hongye shuju, 1970.

Zhang Jiliang (Contemporary) (近代) 張吉良. *Lao Dan* Laozi *taishidan* Dao De Jing 老聃《老子》太史儋《道德經》. Jinan: Jilu Shuju, 2001.

Zhang Shuangdi (Contemporary), zhuan (近代) 張雙棣, 撰. *Huainanzi jiaoshi* 淮南子校釋. Beiing: Beijing daxue chubanshe, 1997.

Zhang Songru (Contemporary) (近代) 張松如. *Laozi shuojie* 老子說解. Jinan: Jilu shushe, 1998.

Zhang Yangming (Contemporary) (近代) 張楊明. *Laozi kaozheng* 老子考證. Taipei: Liming wenhua, 1985, 1995.

Zhang Zaiyun (Contemporary) et al., jiaoyi (近代) 張在雲等, 校議. *Ciquan jiaoyi* 詞詮校議. Kunming: Yunnan jiaoyu chubanshe, 1998.

Zhong Tai (Contemporary) (近代) 鍾泰. *Zhuangzi fawei* 莊子發微. Shanghai: Guji chubanshe, 2002.

Zhou Fagao (Contemporary) (a.k.a. Chou Fa-kao), zhubian (近代) 周法高, 主編. *Hanzi gujin yinhui* 漢字古今音彙. Hong Kong: The Chinese University Press, 1974, 1979.

———. *Zhongguo gudai yufa, zaoju bian* (V1) 中國古代語法、造句編 (上). Taipei: Tailian guofeng chubanshe, 1972.

Zhou Zumo (Contemporary), zhuan (近代) 周祖謨, 撰. *Erya jiaojian* 爾雅校箋. Kunming: Yunnan renmin chubanshe, 2004.

———, jiaojian 校箋. *Fangyan jiaojian* 方言校箋. Beijing: Zhonghua shuju, 1993, 2004.

Zhu Qianzhi (Contemporary) (近代) 朱謙之. *Laozi jiaoshi* 老子校釋. Taipei: Huazheng shuju, 1986.

Zhu Zugeng (Contemporary), zhuan (近代) 諸祖耿, 撰. *Zhanguo ce jizhu huikao* 戰國策集注彙考. 3 vols. N.c.: Jiangsu guji chubanshe, 1985.

Zhu Zuyan (Contemporary) (近代) 朱祖延. *Erya gulin* 爾雅詁林. Wuhan: Hubei jiaoyu chubanshe, 1996.

LIST OF CHINESE CLASSICS
REFERRED TO BY TITLE ONLY

Baihutong see Ban Gu (Han), *Baihutong*, 375

Da Dai Liji see Dai De (Han), *Da Dai Liji jiegu*, 376

Erya see Guo Pu (Jin), *Erya zhushu ji buzheng*, 377

Gongyang zhuan see Gongyang Shou (Han), *Gongyang zhuan*, 375

Guangya see Zhang Yi (Three Kingdoms: Wei), *Guangya shuzheng*, 376

Guangyun see Lu Fayan (Sui), *Jiaozheng Song-ben Guangyun*, 377

Guanzi see Guan Zhong (Zhou), *Guanzi*, 374

Guoyu see Zuo Qiuming (Zhou), *Guoyu*, 375

Hanfeizi see Han Fei (Warring States: Qin), *Hanfeizi (jishi)*, 375

Han shu see Ban Gu (Han), *Han shu*, 375

Huainanzi see Huainan, Lord of (Han), *Huainanzi*, 375

Jiyun see Ding Du (Song), *Jiyun*, 377

Liezi see Zhang Zhan (Jin), *Liezi*, 377

Liji see Zheng Xuan (Han), *Liji zhushu ji buzheng*, 376

Lülan see Lü Buwei (Qin), *Lüshi Chunqiu*, 375

Lunyu see He Yan (Three Kingdoms: Wei), *Lunyu jijie yishu*, 376

Kongzi jiayu see Wang Su (Han), *Kongzi jiayu*, 376

Mengzi see Zhao Qi (Han), *Mengzi zhushu ji buzheng*, 376

Mozi see Wu Yujiang (Contemporary), *Mozi jiaozhu*, 384

Shangshu see Kong Anguo (Han), *Shangshu zhushu ji buzheng*, 375

Shiji see Sima Qian (Han), *Shiji*, 376

Shijing see Mao Heng (Han), *Mao Shi zhushu*, 375

Shiming see Liu Xi (Han), *Shiming*, 375

Shuowen see Xu Shen (Han), *Shuowen jiezi zhu*, 376

Sunzi see Sun Wu (Zhou), *Shiyijia zhu, Sunzi jiaoli*, 374

Wenzi see Li Dingsheng and Xu Huijun (Contemporary), *Wenzi jiaoshi*, 382

Xiao Erya see Hu Chenggong (Qing), *Xiao Erya*, 379

Xunzi see Xun Kuang (Warring States: Zhao), *Xunzi*, 375

Yijing see Zheng Xuan (Han), *Zhou Yi zhushu ji buzheng*, 376

Yili see Zheng Xuan (Han), *Yili zhushu ji buzheng*, 375

Yupian see Gu Yeyu (Southern Dynasties: Chen), *Yupian*, 377

Zhanguo Ce see Gao You (Han), *Zhanguo ce Gaoshi zhu*, 375

Zhengzi tong see Zhang Zilie (Ming), *Zhengzi tong*, 379

Zhou Li see Zheng Xuan (Han), *Zhouli zhushu ji buzheng*, 378

Zhuangzi see Zhuang Zhou (Warring States: Song), *Zhuangzi*, 375

Zuo zhuan see Zuo Qiuming (Zhou), *Chunqiu Zuo zhuan zhushu ji buzheng*, 374

ACKNOWLEDGMENTS

T he creation of a book is rarely the work of a single person. And so, I would first like to thank my editor, Peter Hubbard of Mariner Books (a HarperCollins imprint), for his unqualified support and patience, as well as his remarkable knowledge and editing skills. This book owes much to associate editor Molly Gendell, assistant editor Jessica Vestuto, production editor Laura Brady, copyeditor Sinnie Lee, interior designer Alison Bloomer, and art director Mark Robinson. I would also like to express my sincere gratitude to my literary agents, Laurie Liss and Mary Krienke of Sterling Lord Literistic, Inc., for championing my work and always being there for me.

My wife, Carolyn, brought her experience of editing Chinese academic works in Taiwan to this book. She devoted considerable time and effort in helping me locate reference materials and typing endless drafts for both the English and Chinese parts of *The Dao De Jing: Laozi's Book of Life*. Because she is an accomplished artist as well as an author in her own right, she also assisted in the design of this book.

I first encountered *Laozi*, or the *Dao De Jing*, very early in life. Just as how my late father, Col. Lung-chin Huang 黃龍金, presented me with a copy of Sunzi's *Art of War* on the day I set off for middle school, my late mother slipped me a copy of *Laozi* when I began high school. My mother, Yueh-ming Chou 周月明, said to me, "You should take a look at this book" (which should come as no surprise, because she had majored in Chinese classical literature at National Southwestern Associated University). Of course, I could not make heads or tails of it at the time. It was not until I began to study the ancient language of the pre-Qin period as a college student that this book began to

reveal its secrets. My major—like my mother's—was Chinese classical literature. What made my education at Taipei's National Chengchi University so
unique, though, was that in addition to studying every variety of archaic Chinese, all our reports and essays had a strict requirement: they had to be written
in classical Chinese.

An old Chinese saying tells us that "when you drink water, you should not
forget its source." The fact that I now have the ability to study ancient works
from the pre-Qin period is entirely thanks to the instruction I received from
my exemplary professors in both undergraduate and graduate schools: From
Prof. Lu Yuanjun 盧元駿, I learned to become fluent in both reading and
writing ancient Chinese; with Prof. Xie Yunfei 謝雲飛, I studied Chinese etymology; Prof. Ying Yukang 應裕康 taught me phonology; Prof. Lai Yanyuan
賴炎元 gave me a firm grounding in ancient semantics; Prof. Xiong Gongzhe
熊公哲 instilled a good familiarity with traditional annotations on the classics in me; and Prof. Chen Daqi 陳大齊 (who was an authority on Buddhist
logico-epistemology) showed me how to apply logic to achieve an understanding of the classics. Also, Prof. Wang Meng'ou 王夢鷗 taught me literary criti-
cism, and it was under the tutelage of Prof. Wang Wenjun 王文俊 (who had
completed a degree in philosophy in Germany) that I first became interested
in Western philosophy.

I would be remiss if I did not mention the warm support that I have received over the years from respected elders and good friends. The talks I had
with Master Cheng Man-ran 鄭曼髯 about ancient Chinese thought and the
meaning of existence bestowed in me the confidence to undertake what was
to become my life's work. And I have been incredibly fortunate to have had a
number of renowned scholars share their research and ideas with me about
Laozi: One of them was Prof. Ren Jiyu 任繼愈, who was an expert on Chinese
philosophy, as well as a professor at Peking University and an honorary director of the National Library of China. Another was Prof. Qiu Xigui 裘錫圭,
who specialized in the study of paleography at Fudan University. Prof. Zhu
Bokun 朱伯崑, a maven on *Yijing*, or *The Book of Changes*, spoke to me about
his studies on *Yijing*, and thereby thoroughly inspired me in my understanding
of *Laozi*. In addition, Prof. Chen Guying 陳鼓應 and Prof. Liu Xiaogan 劉笑敢

are both well-known scholars of *Laozi*, and they have provided me with many invaluable materials over the course of my research, along with their continued support.

I have been exceptionally lucky when it comes to good friends, even though some only live in my memory now. Whenever I spoke with Prof. Yi Junbo 易君伯 of National Chengchi University, our chats would ultimately return to the topic of Western philosophy. I still fondly remember Tam Gibbs and how our talks would always circle back to *Laozi* whenever we got together. Another friend who had passed on, but is far from being forgotten, was my literary rights attorney, Jack McGannon of Townsend & Townsend. He provided much-needed advice at a time when I was at a crossroads. His generosity was as great as his love for ice cream.

Finally, I want to thank my parents—not only for always giving me their love, but also for taking every opportunity they could to find materials that they thought would prove helpful to my research for me. Back when my *Art of War* was first published in 1994, they were still very much alive and healthy. Now that this study of the *Dao De Jing* is finally completed, I only wish that they could still be with me so I could tell them how much I love and miss them.

INDEX

abundance, 28–29, 266, 287, 347n5

acceptance of all, 34–35, 60–61, 96–97, 144–45, 156–57

accommodation, 34–35, 100–101, 142–43

accumulation, 36–37, 268, 333n9n3

achievement
  shrouded, 122–23, 290
  through non-effort, 102–3, 130–33, 152–53, 160–63, 208–9, 299

active *vs.* inactive, 311

active *vs.* passive voice, 307Ch61n7, 317Ch75n2, 319Ch78n2, 341Ch20n30

adages, 46–47, 80–81, 271, 280

affairs, terms for, 282, 283, 284, 285, 299, 309, 313, 344Ch26n3, 344n12, 365Ch67n11. *See also* effort; non-effort

ancestors, 252–53, 285, 345Ch29n6

anxiety, 46–47, 70–71, 271

appearances, 230–31

archaic Chinese language, 6–7, 326n30
  empty words in, 7, 8, 326n31, 327n32
  "f" sounds in, 362Ch60n5
  grammar, 326n31
  homonyms in, 8, 327n33
  interchangeable characters in, 7, 8, 333Ch8n2, 335n13, 347n16, 357Ch51n14
  modifiers in, 332Ch6n4
  nouns converted to verbs in, 350n6
  the passive voice in, 319, 341n30, 350n10

assent *vs.* rebuke, 70–71, 277

assumptions, 232–33

Axial Age, 1, 323n3

Baihutong, 347n5, 354n8, 363n9

Ban Gu, 358n9, 359n3

Bao Xian, 333n11, 349Ch36n9

beauty and ugliness, 18–19, 70–71, 277

Beida version, 4, 5, 261, 298, 303, 333Ch9n3, 338n6, 338n20, 346Ch31n6
  alterations in, 337n19
  discovery and age of, 4, 325n22
  editorial decisions of, 333Ch8n1, 346Ch31n6, 362Ch62n3
  ingenuousness in, 339Ch19n5

magnanimity in, 333Ch8n1

"the mirror" in, 334Ch10n9

vs. received versions, 4, 265, 291, 333Ch8n1, 338Ch16n6, 342Ch22n1, 344Ch26n3, 346Ch31n6

"self-regard" in, 342n9

"the void" in, 265, 331n23

being and void, 42–43, 146–47, 261–62

bellows, 28–29, 266, 332n7

bì Dào (obeyance to the Dao), 288, 347n16

blemishes, 38–39, 269, 283, 335n11

bloodlust, 106–7

bones, 22–23, 263

Book of the Dao and Book of the De, 4, 5, 325n23

bow metaphor, 244–45

breath
  mind's domination over, 184–85
  Pulsing, 148–49, 296
  yang, 38–39, 269, 334Ch10n4
  yin and yang as types of, 296, 354Ch42n2

brightness, 50–51, 196–97, 264, 272, 301, 331n17, 337Ch14n12
  terms for, 272, 278, 301–2, 340n22

brutality and brutal people, 150–51, 184–85, 303

Buddhism, 10, 328n39

bù Dé (free of the De), 291, 350n6

the calendar, 166–67, 299, 335n15

Canjiepian, 357Ch51n11

Cao Cao, 356Ch50n11

capital punishment, 238–39

cause and effect, 298, 326n23

the Celestial Generating Spirit
  perfection attained by, 136–37
  perishing, 136–37, 293, 352n15
  of the Valley, 30–31, 266–67

centering, 267, 333n5

Chen Guying, 371Ch80n2

Cheng Yuanying, 353n33

Chen Qitian, 350n8

Chen Qiyou, 332Ch6n3

Chen state, 2–3, 329n6

Chen Zhu, 355Ch48n3
Chinese language. *See* archaic Chinese language
chōng (to pulse), 264, 265–66, 330Ch4n1,
331n23, 331n26
Chuci, 337Ch15n10, 343Ch24n4
Chu tomb discovery, 4, 325n21
circumspection, 54–55, 178–79, 214–15, 274,
276, 337Ch15n10
clarity, 136–37, 196–97
clean *vs.* unclean, 96–97, 284, 345Ch28n8
cleaving to the Dao, 262, 273, 280–81, 284,
337n19
definition of, 96–97
dominion through, 52–53
effects of, 110–11, 120–21, 126–27, 134–35
as the Essential, 98–99, 284
through non-effort, 84–85, 102–3, 126–27,
281, 287
shepherding the world through, 80–81,
342Ch23n4
as true knowledge, 256–57
cleverness, 68–69, 276
clothing, 230–31, 252–53, 315
coercion, 102–3, 285–86, 292
communication
through silence, 20–21, 152–53, 262
via knotted ropes, 252–53, 321
the community, 180–81, 303
competition, resisting, 32–33, 82–83, 114–15,
220–21, 256–57, 267, 333n10
encouraging others in, 22–23, 263
non-effort linked to, 297
by the soft and weak, 22–23, 122–23, 267
in warfare, 226–27
water metaphor for, 34–35, 267, 297, 319
completeness, 80–83, 156–57
comprehension, 38–39, 269, 273, 337n7
the concealed or hidden, 50–51, 124–25, 261,
272, 273, 290, 305, 336Ch14n3
conflict, 130–33
Confucianism, 327n36, 327n38, 361Ch59n2
Confucius, 2, 287, 324n8, 324n9, 347Ch31n11,
368Ch73n2
confusion, 94–95
constancy, 60–61, 184–85, 275
the law of, 98–99, 284
constraints, 134–35, 196–97
contentment, 154–55, 291
of a country, 200–201, 252–53
the De as, 131n, 180–81, 351n2
vs. effort, 68–69, 277

of infants, 184–85
as self-perpetuating, 158–59
sensory pleasures *vs.*, 120–21
stillness and, 126–27
as wealth, 114–15
countries
advantages for, 124–25, 290, 349Ch36n7,
349Ch36n9
capital punishment and, 238–39
harmony of, 148–49, 180–81
husbandry of, 198–99
ideal, 252–55
ingenuousness of, 214–17
large, 200–205, 307
power of, 202–3
regulations of, 190–91, 194–97
small, 202–5, 307
courageousness, 222–25, 236–37
courtesy, 22–23, 70–71, 263
creation, 14–15, 40–41, 146–47
endless, 30–31
mathematical description of, 148–49, 296
cultivated people. *See also* leaders
abiding by the De, 279
agreements entered into by, 250–51
appearance of, 54–55, 72–75, 230–31, 273,
274
contentment of, 154–55
the cycle embraced by, 56–61
and the difficult, 210–11
self-transcendence of, 82–83, 220–21,
246–47, 256–57, 321
shèngrén as, 262, 266, 315
as "shepherds" to the world, 80–81,
342Ch23n4
shì as, 273, 337n2, 337n3
as untroubled, 232–33
cultivation, terms for
bǎo, 308, 362Ch62n4
huà, 291, 349Ch37n3
shì, 273, 294, 306
shìtiān, 306, 361Ch59n1
zhì, 271, 306, 309, 335Ch12n7
cycles of life, 28–29, 80–83
acceleration of, 122–23
accommodating, 142–43
conforming to the Dao, 58–59, 156–57
cultivated people embracing, 56–61
the De guiding, 218–19
emergence and withdrawal, 166–67,
356Ch50n1

cycles of life (*cont.*)
  gain and loss, 154–55
  harmony within, 150–51
  life and death, 166–67
  between polarized factors, 18–19, 80–81, 261–62, 280
  seasonal, 170–71, 301
  stillness dominating, 60–61, 146–47

dà (great, greatly, big, Greatness), 271, 275, 282, 289, 295, 312
Dadai Liji, 338n7, 357Ch51n13
Dadai Liji jiegu, 335Ch11n2
Dai Zhen, 346Ch31n7, 360Ch57n11
danger, recognizing, 234–35
the Dao. *See also* cleaving to the Dao
  absurd appearance of, 140–41
  adapting to limitations, 24–25
  blandness of, 120–21, 290
  as boundless, 116–17, 266
  choices governed by, 84–85, 88–89
  conforming to, non-effort and, 78–79, 84–85, 142–43, 162–63
  corporeal form of, 76–77, 279, 341n5
  cycles of life conforming to, 58–59, 156–57
  cycling motion of, 28–29, 52–53, 86–87, 146–47, 272–73, 282, 295–96
  the De coming from, 5, 279, 325n23, 326n26
  the De obeying, 76–77
  disregard of, 66–67, 276
  dominion of, 24–25, 52–53, 116–17, 264, 273, 289
  as eternal, 14–15, 52–53, 62–63, 76–77, 110–11
  existing in harmony, 50–51, 272, 337Ch14n9
  front and back of, 52–53, 272–73
  generation by, 28–29, 146–49, 170–73, 261, 264, 267, 269, 300, 326n26, 338n6, 350n5
  as Greatness, 86–87, 116–17, 120–21, 144–45, 289, 295
  of the heavens, 36–37, 160–61, 236–37, 250–51, 256–57, 268, 316, 318, 334Ch9n9
  heavens conforming to, 88–89, 236–37, 244–45, 268, 316, 350n5
  heavens in harmony with, 58–59, 62–63
  infringements on, 104–5, 186–87
  language transcended by, 14–15
  Law of, 104–5, 144–45
  learning, 140–41, 162–63, 298
  of man, 256–57, 268
  as nameless, 14–15, 110–11, 126–27, 144–45, 260, 287, 291

names given to, 14–15, 76–77, 86–87, 230–31, 265, 279, 282, 315
as the Nebulous, 50–51, 76–77, 272
as neutral or impartial, 116–17, 250–51, 288
obeying, 76–77, 106–7, 112–13, 170–71, 291, 300, 347n16
as the One, 50–53, 272, 273, 337Ch14n9
the One brought about by, 148–49, 296, 354Ch42n1
as profound, 24–25, 76–77, 260, 261, 264
pulsing of, 24–25, 264
as Reality, 16–17, 261
as safeguard, 56–57, 62–63, 112–13, 198–99, 250–51, 306
self-realization and, 84–85, 88–91, 126–27, 170–73, 198–99, 212–15, 262, 281–82, 290, 333n7
tangible existence of, 265–66
as thoroughfare, 178–79, 302
tininess of, 110–11, 116–19, 261, 265–66, 287, 289
as undefinable, 76–77, 260
as void, 146–47, 264
water similar to, 34–35, 112–13
weakness and, 146–47, 296, 354Ch41n3
dào
  "to act, behave," 318, 369Ch77n2
  "long road," 302, 358Ch53n3
  translating, 260, 275, 328n3
Dao De Jing. See also specific versions
  eisegesis of, 327n37
  historical significance of, 10
  holistic approach to, 7–8, 9
  methodology for translating, 6–9, 327n31, 327n34
  modern significance of, 10–11
  organization of, 5, 325n23, 326n24, 342Ch22n1, 342Ch22n2, 342Ch23n1, 343Ch24n1, 353n1, 354Ch41n1
  origins of, 1, 6, 323n2
  purpose of, 2
  rhythm of, 2, 324n6
  translations of, 3–4
  versions of, 1, 3–5, 323n5
Daoism, 10, 317, 326n24
  vs. Confucianism, 327n36
  as folk religion, 327n37
  Huang Lao School of, 326n24, 327n36
Dào shēng Yī (the Dao brought about the One), 296, 354Ch42n1
Dào shēng zhī (the Dao engenders all), 300
Daozheng, 328n39

knowledge, supreme
    as infinite, 70–71
    perception of those with, 72–75
    vs. secular knowledge, 70–75, 222–23,
        256–57
Kong Anguo, 362Ch60n7
Kong Yingda, 359Ch54n10
    on "acting, behaving," 369Ch77n2
    on "all," 328n9
    on "the concealed," 336Ch14n3
    on cultivated people, 337n3
    on disobedience, 360Ch57n9
    on gift-giving, 363n15
    on the heavens cracking, 352n12
    on jade discs, 363n12
    on military supply carts, 343Ch26n2
    on non-effort, 329n6
    on profound love, 365Ch67n9
    on rules and standards, 304, 360Ch57n13
Kongzi jiayu, 324n9, 326n24

language, transcending, 14–15, 260
Laozi, 1
    in accord with the Dao, 314, 324n8
    background of, 2, 324n8
    Buddhist respect for, 328n39
    Confucius consulting, 2, 324n8, 324n9
    descendants of, 324n8
    as *táozhèng,* 2–3, 325n12
law of constancy, 98–99, 284
laws, 190–91, 238–39
laziness, 210–11
leaders. *See also* the king
    abiding by reality, 20–21, 100–103,
        134–35
    adhering to the Essential, 38–39, 98–99,
        110–13, 126–27
    artless *vs.* surveillant, 194–95, 305
    becoming like water, 248–49
    danger recognized by, 234–35
    failure of, 110–11, 138–39, 214–15, 288,
        347n15
    gifts to, 206–7, 308, 363n15
    greatness of, 118–19
    in harmony with people, 138–39, 164–65
    humility of, 138–39, 148–49, 220–21, 294,
        353n37
    husbandry of, 198–99, 222–23
    impartiality of, 26–27, 68–69
    insignia of, 138–39, 206–7, 294
    morality and, 194–95

non-effort and, 102–3, 126–27, 162–63,
        192–95, 198–201, 208–9, 212–13,
        240–41, 276, 309
    obliviousness of, 194–95, 305
    obtaining the One, 136–37
    people accepting, 64–65, 164–65, 192–93,
        220–21
    people appreciated by, 92–95, 148–49, 206–7
    people reflecting qualities of, 8, 22–23,
        64–65, 92–93, 110–11, 214–15, 276
    people's treatment of, 64–65
    perfect governance of, 64–65, 80–81,
        192–93, 198–99, 222–23, 236–37, 306,
        361Ch59n3
    pursuing fortune, 194–95
    selflessness of, 32–33
    self-realization encouraged by, 126–27,
        190–95, 198–99, 212–17, 222–23,
        246–47
    self-sufficiency of, 90–91, 343Ch26n2
    shrewdness eschewed by, 8, 38–39, 66–69,
        190–93, 216–17, 290, 311
    stillness of, 90–91
    terms for, 275, 292, 293, 302, 304, 313, 314,
        351n4
    traveling, 90–93, 344n1, 344n2
    valuing practical needs, 20–23, 44–45,
        244–45
    wealth of, as theft, 178–79, 302
leap months, 166–67, 299, 356Ch50n3
learning. *See also* knowledge, supreme
    the Dao, 140–43, 162–63
    rejection of, 278, 340n21
    supreme, 70–71, 277, 340n1
    translation of, 277, 297, 340n2
left and right, 106–9, 116–17, 266, 286,
        347Ch31n11
the left side of agreements, 250–51, 320,
        371Ch79n4
lǐ (rites, rituals, etiquette, social rules), 2, 284,
        292, 324n8, 324n9, 345n11
Liang Jian-wendi, 327n35
Liang Qixiong, 350n8
Liang Wudi, 327n35
Liang Yuandi, 327n35
Liao Mingchun, 349Ch37n6
Liezi
    "*Liming,*" 338n10
    "*Shuofu,*" 329n14
    "*Tangwen,*" 342n12
    "*Tianrui,*" 332Ch6n1

supply carts, 90–91, 282, 343Ch26n2
supreme achievement, 92–93
supreme learning. *See* learning
surplus and deficiency, 244–45

Tang Xuanzong, 10, 263, 296, 305, 325n23,
    334Ch10n5, 337Ch14n9, 340n2, 341n1,
    348Ch34n1, 351n2, 360Ch57n10
Tang Yongtong, 328n39
táozhèng, 2–3, 325n12
taste, 44–45, 208–9, 270
taxes, 240–41, 317
teaching, wordless, 20–21, 152–53, 262
thieves, 22–23, 68–69, 190–91, 263
"thoroughfare" metaphor, 178–79, 302
the Three, 148–49, 296
Tiān (Nature, the heavens), 268, 293
Tiāndì (Heavenly Providence), 265, 331n20
tigers, 166–69
time and the now, 52–53, 76–77, 273, 337n19
tininess of the Dao, 110–11, 116–19, 261,
    265–66, 287, 289. *See also* the small
tiptoeing, 78–79, 280
transcendence. *See also* the self, surpassing
    of the De, 40–41, 172–73, 216–19, 269
    of one's mind, 341n1
    of secular concepts, 114–15, 288
    translation of, 261, 269, 329n16
Transcendental Sameness, 188–89, 264
the Transcendent Feminine, 30–31
the transcendent mirror, 38–39, 269, 334n10
translation, methodology of, 6–9, 327n31,
    327n34
tree metaphor, 242–43
trust, 64–65, 164–65, 275
truth, 256–57
tumors, 78–79, 280
turbulence, 24–25, 188–89, 264
the Two, 148–49

uprightness, 190–91
utilitarian objects, 144–45, 170–71, 276, 300
    armed forces as, 106–7, 286
    being and void in, 42–43, 270
    the Essential becoming, 98–99, 287
    terms for, 284, 285, 286, 300, 345Ch29n8,
        345n11
utopia, 252–55

vagueness, 30–31, 74–77, 267, 279,
    348Ch35n2

valleys
    drying up of, 136–37, 293
    metaphor of, 54–55, 96–97, 136–37, 142–43,
        274, 284, 293
    terms for, 266, 274, 284, 293, 295,
        345Ch28n6
valuables, 302, 358n11
    dangers of treasuring, 22–23, 44–45, 178–79,
        263
    vs. the self, 154–55
vehicles, 270, 283, 302, 324
    four horses drawing, 308
    function of, 42–43
"Venerated Object," 100–101, 285,
    345Ch29n6, 345Ch29n7, 345Ch29n8
vessels, 42–43, 270, 335Ch11n5
void
    being and, 42–43, 146–47, 261–62
    the Dao as, 146–47, 264
    the Dao coming from, 296
    function inhering in, 42–43, 270
    translating, 265–66, 270
    Zenith of, 98–99, 284

wáng (to follow, being followed by the world, the
    king), 275, 289, 311, 365Ch66n1
Wang Anshi, 358Ch52n6, 359n11
Wang Bi, 4, 131n, 261, 281, 289, 331n19,
    333Ch7n1, 340n14, 357Ch51n14
    on "conforming," 343Ch25n7
    on the De, 349Ch38n1, 350n3, 350n5
    on discernment, 341n23
    on enjoyment, 340Ch20n10
    on the Essential, 347n5
    on fruition, 285
    on justice, 292
    on non-effort, 262, 267, 290, 329n8,
        349Ch37n1, 354Ch41n3
    on obtaining the De, 295
    on the One, 351n2
    on self-realization, 343Ch24n2
    on shrewdness, 263, 335n13
    on softness, 369Ch76n1
    square metaphor in, 360Ch58n13
    on surveillant rulers, 360Ch58n5
    terms for rulers in, 363n9
    on the unconstrainable, 348n10
    on vagueness, 267
Wang Fuzhi, 345n11
Wang Ka, 368Ch73n4
Wang Li, 335n13, 346Ch31n4, 349n11